MAKING THE MOST OF IT

Also by Bryan Magee

MAKING THE MOST OF IT

Bryan Magee

Studio 28

A CIP catalogue record for this book is available from the British
Library

Independently published by Studio 28

ISBN 9781980636137

Please visit
www.curtisbrown.co.uk/bryan-magee
for further information

Contents

Book Three:
My Second Go at Life

Book One

My Oxford

to
Robin Burke, Robin Schur
and Robin Hallsmith
with love
to you all

1

Overview

The Oxford I went up to in 1949 was different from its normal self. During the Second World War, 1939-45, young men of university age were nearly all in the armed services; and most of those were not released immediately when the war ended. British forces continued to occupy Germany and Austria for several years, and were committed in other parts of the world too, so compulsory call-up at eighteen continued well into the 1950s. Meanwhile the post-war Labour Government, having made full employment its priority, was careful not to flood the labour market by demobilizing too many servicemen at any one time. So the release of those who had fought in the war was phased out over a couple of years. The first to be let go were older men with families, and those who had jobs waiting for them, or skills that were in demand. Younger men without any of these, having also served less time than the older ones, were made to wait.

So for some years after the war, Oxford was taking in ex-servicemen who could be any age up to about twenty-four when they arrived. This meant that undergraduates in their third or fourth years could be twenty-seven or twenty-eight. The President of the Union in my first summer term, Robin Day, was twenty-six, and had been in the army in Africa during the war. This was typical. Most students had served overseas, and many had seen actual fighting. So they were exceptionally mature to be students. The whole atmosphere of the university was transformed by them. Many of the time-honoured rules and regulations, such as students not being allowed to go into pubs, collapsed for ever. Their relationships with their tutors were close to being on an equal footing – one or two of the third-year men were older than their tutors. Everything became more open and free, and it was a strangely optimistic time. The war, after years of struggle, and millions of dead on both sides, had been won. The undergraduates felt they were survivors, and wanted to build a new life for themselves in a world which they hoped to make a better one. There was a grown-up idealism among them, not the callow idealism of youth but one edged with practicality, and charged by experience of war.

Because the university needed to find places for students of so many different ages it was not able to offer them to boys straight out of school. Girls were in a different situation. There being no call-up for them, they went straight from school to university. Boys, however, even though the war was over, had to join the armed forces at eighteen and do up to two years of military service. Only in special circumstances would colleges take them otherwise. And this was the position I found myself in, typical of my student generation: I had won an open scholarship from school to Oxford, but my college would not accept me until after I had completed military service.

I have told elsewhere (in *Growing Up In A War*) how, when I joined the army, I was sent unexpectedly into the Intelligence Corps. They trained me at the School of Military Intelligence, and sent me to Austria's frontier with Slovenia, which was then part of Yugoslavia. My job was to interrogate illegal frontier-crossers, some of whom were Yugoslav secret agents. For an eighteen-year-old it was heady stuff. In my late twenties I wrote a novel set in that world, called *To Live In Danger*. Its background is entirely authentic, though its plot and characters are fictitious. When I was nineteen I was shifted to my local headquarters in Graz (the second city in Austria after Vienna) to interrogate newly returned Austrian prisoners of war from Soviet Russia. A huge number of Germans and Austrians were still being held there, more than four years after the war had ended. I found the work fascinating – and my out-of-hours life was almost as colourful and interesting. I had a girlfriend to whom I was devoted. My social life with colleagues of my own age was more uninhibited than it would have been in England. We were under the command of older men, but they allowed us an amazing degree of latitude, socially as well as professionally. So long as we did our jobs well, and did not cause them embarrassment otherwise, they did not care what we did. So we lived with great personal freedom. And then, of course, there were the attractions of Graz itself. Of particular interest to me was its opera house, which I went to frequently. (I saw my first *Tannhäuser* there, and my second *Tristan*). I spent my leaves in Vienna, whose opera company was then going through a golden age which remains a legend even today, and which I visited almost every night regardless of what they were performing.

It was from this life that I went up to Oxford as an undergraduate. There was something known as a Class B Release that soldiers with places earmarked for them at universities applied for: if you got one, it meant you left the army early to catch the beginning of an academic year instead of having to be demobilized in mid-year and then hang around for several months. I got one of these, as did most of my colleagues, and that meant that from my first day at Oxford I had friends in several colleges. (The University of Oxford is a federation of many self-governing colleges – more than two dozen then, more than three dozen now.) One acquaintance, a music-lover working with the Intelligence Corps in Vienna, enjoyed his life there so much, gorging on opera at a level of performance not to be found anywhere else at that time, that he deliberately did not apply for a Class B Release, and spent a whole extra year there before joining us in Oxford. None of the rest of us – to my surprise, now that I look back on it – thought of doing that.

For many of us, Oxford was a let-down at first. It was so much less exciting than the life we had left in order to go there. No doubt our expectations were unrealistic. Mine certainly were. I had imagined Oxford to be full of people who were passionately interested in ideas, perhaps especially political ideas; and also in the arts, especially literature. I had expected to find myself surrounded by such people, either arguing formidably or chattering amusingly into the small hours night after night, floating down rivers of wonderful talk. I had, in other words, imbibed the romantic image of Oxford peddled in novels, plays and films, and perhaps been encouraged in it by one or two personal acquaintances. The reality was otherwise. Most people at Oxford were not particularly interested in ideas, nor in politics; nor did they have any particular interest in the arts. This was as true of the dons as it was of the undergraduates. There were plenty of parties, though, and for a freshman these were the most enjoyable thing that Oxford had to offer. But I cannot say that the conversations at them were special: drink and girls were what parties were chiefly about. I took as much advantage as I could of both, and derived a lot of enjoyment from them. But my life as a whole was not what I had expected Oxford to be.

My home town was London, and I had grown up accustomed not only to the scale, diversity and vivacity of a capital city but also to its standards. I loved Vienna – and Paris, which I had got to know when I was a boarder at the Lycée Hôche in Versailles in 1947. In all these cities I had feasted on music. Of course, and inevitably, there was no counterpart to them in Oxford. How could there be? I hankered for London, and kept on going there, and also carried on nostalgic correspondences with now-distant friends in Austria and France, half wishing I were still in those places. It was a year or more before Oxford drew me into itself. During that time my ties elsewhere were almost as strong. I would go up to London to take part in events of which Oxford remained oblivious. For example, in my first year I went to the world premiere of Richard Strauss's *Four Last Songs* at the Albert Hall (sung by Kirsten Flagstad and conducted by Furtwängler). Even afterwards I knew of no one in Oxford who had been there – some were, no doubt, but I never heard it mentioned. That was typical of Oxford as I perceived it when I first went there: provincial, out of the mainstream of life, and uncaring that this was so.

One or two undergraduates I knew decided for reasons such as these that Oxford was not for them, and chose to leave at the end of their first year. I never contemplated doing that – I would not have known where to go, or what to do with myself. But I did make a conscious decision at that point that in the hope of getting more out of Oxford I would put more in to it. In my second year I threw myself into Oxford life in a new way, with an active desire to get everything out of it that I could.

A contributory reason for my alienation had been that my college had not allowed me to study the subject of my choice. I had come up on a history scholarship, but wanted to change to music, and the college would not let me. So by my third term I found myself deep in the study of medieval English constitutional documents, and not getting enough out of them to stave off boredom. I made a milestone decision. I would study only things I found rewarding. Those parts of the history syllabus that interested me I would tuck into with relish, but the rest I would deliberately let go, and would read instead whatever else interested me. This would, I thought, maximize (given my circumstances) the educational value to me of the work I did, and would keep me interested in what I was doing. Inevitably, it would mean that when my final exams came I would not do well in those papers for which I had skipped the work; but I had no intention of becoming an academic, and thought that the class of degree I would get could make no difference to my life. There was a good deal of history that I found richly nourishing. For my special subject I chose the Italian Renaissance, and for my special period of international history the years 1871-1939, and my studies in those were to become a valued and lifelong possession. But I let a lot of the rest just go.

Once I had made these decisions I felt liberated, and was able to enjoy Oxford. There were some things, of course, that I had enjoyed from the beginning – party life for one, which I slipped into as a duck into water. Oxford's best hotel, the Randolph, had a huge bar in those days, and if I met a man at a party whom I found *simpatico* I would arrange to meet him at the Randolph. It was in every way the best drinking hole for undergraduates. A world of its own had developed there that was like a perpetually on-going party in itself. Most of the regulars knew one another, and I remained in touch with them throughout my years at Oxford, alongside other and very different activities, and the other worlds I moved in. Among its various delights it was a magnet for attractive women who were otherwise alone in Oxford. There were families in British colonies, and other English enclaves abroad where 'acceptable' husbands were thin on the ground, who sent their grown-up daughters to Oxford for a couple of years, ostensibly to study at one of the private language schools, or to train as secretaries or nurses, but in fact in the hope of finding a young man with good prospects. We thought of these girls as camp followers. They came from all over the world, and included some of the most likeable and interesting people I knew at Oxford. They tended to latch on to the more outstanding of the undergraduates, who would introduce them around, so they would often pass from one to another: typically they would be hanging from the arm of a young man who was himself a person admired by the rest of us. They were an invaluable part of the Oxford scene, and one or two remained my friends for ever after.

Undergraduates in those days were especially in need of mature girlfriends. As ex-soldiers we were used to having sex lives, but not many of the female undergraduates straight from school were ready to join us in that, at least not immediately. In any case there were far fewer women than men: the colleges were all monosexual, and only five of them out of twenty-something were for women. So we had to find our partners elsewhere, at least to begin with. Our biggest source of supply was the hospitals. In addition to its teaching hospital, Oxford had several others, so the nurse population was helpfully large; and nurses, being used to coping with people's bodies and bodily functions, tended to make good sexual partners in those inhibited days. Then there were the language and secretarial schools, the former full of enterprising foreign girls who were alone, far from home. Together, they equalled our needs – though inevitably this had the effect of leaving out most of the female undergraduates from that side of our lives, until such time as they chose to join us – which, during the course of their three or four years at the university, large numbers did, including, I think, most of the most interesting ones. The outcome of all this was that first and second year men usually had extra-mural girlfriends, whereas third and fourth year men were often involved with female undergraduates.

Another thing that I enjoyed from the beginning at Oxford was the opportunity to see and hear, in the flesh, public figures in whose work I was already interested, especially writers and politicians. Undergraduate life was teeming with clubs and societies, organized by the students themselves around every imaginable one of their interests and pursuits, many of them not at all intellectual, some arcane; and these societies would hold meetings which they invited well-known figures from outside to come and address. During term there would be several such meetings every evening in different parts of the university. Most would be of little interest to me, but there were some that interested me very much. I could be one of a group listening to, say, a well-known poet or novelist talking about his work, and I could then question him. There was always a coffee break at these meetings, and if I had a question I wanted to pursue I could talk to the speaker over coffee, or after the meeting. Before, I had always thought of such people as inhabiting a different world from me. Once, when I was younger, my sister Joan had seen T. S. Eliot sitting in the back of a taxi stuck in traffic in Soho; and I had been awe-stricken at the very thought. How incredible, how unimaginably marvellous, to *see* T. S. Eliot. It bordered on the impossible, I imagined, because such people lived in a different dimension from the rest of us. Their real habitation was not 'here' at all, but on some other plane. Well, in Oxford, we were all on the same plane. And I found it fascinating to meet them and talk to them, above all about their work.

Like quite a few students, I joined all the main political clubs so that I could see and hear the country's leading politicians in all parties, and put questions to them. For the first time I became used to thinking of them as fellow human-beings, people I could meet and talk with. I know now from long experience that most people never think of them in that way. But what began for me at Oxford was later to become everyday experience. After leaving university I earned my living chiefly in television, and then became a Member of Parliament, and in both capacities I was meeting well-known people all the time. So, inevitably, I came to take it for granted. However, at Oxford I did not as yet take it for granted, and found it new and exciting. By the end of my fourth year I had had one-to-one conversations with a considerable number of poets, novelists, Cabinet Ministers and the rest, and was familiar with the experience. Cumulatively, it made up part of my education that I would never have got anywhere other than in Oxford. (Not even in Cambridge: Oxford is so much easier to visit from London that visitors are more willing to go there; and its Union operates on a higher level.)

All this was organized by the undergraduates themselves, not by the university. At student parties, too, I met surprisingly interesting people. In my first year I found myself in an engrossing conversation alone, outside the party, with Oscar Wilde's son, Vyvyan Holland. He told me how, during the scandal that engulfed and destroyed his father, no one, literally no one, would explain to him and his brother what had happened, nor did anyone explain it for years to come. The two boys were surrounded on all sides by shock and horror, and their lives were shattered; they were made to go into purdah and change their surname; yet they could never find out what it was all about. He talked with moving objectivity, without self-pity, about the effect all this had on him while he was growing up. It was one of the most emotionally memorable conversations I have ever had. But again, it had nothing to do with the university; we were there because a friend of mine had invited us both to the same party.

This, I began to see, was the point about being a student at Oxford. All around me the great big university, with its unconsidered and uncaring requirements, lumbered along like a juggernaut, prepared to crush you under its wheels if you ingested its values. Out of its thousands of students it was impossible to know more than a few; and among the hundreds of organized activities it was also not possible to engage in more than a handful. So I had to piece together my own Oxford. There were enough fellow-spirits, and enough congenial activities, to keep me happy. I woke up to the fact that my disappointment with Oxford had been caused by mistaken attitudes on my part. If I embraced it for what it was, instead of wanting it to be something else, I could enjoy it and get a lot out of it. There were all these congenial people of my own age, with all this self-created social life, all these clubs, societies and magazines, all these attractive women, in a setting of astounding beauty. What more could anyone ask? Precisely because an individual could participate in only a fraction of what was going on, each individual's Oxford was bound to be different – an anthology selected by him from the mass of available possibilities, leaving most of them out.

I made my own anthology. In so far as there was a pattern to it, it was something like this. I went to at least one party, or to the Randolph, most days. Over four years I went to every single weekly meeting of the English Club, and all but one of the weekly debates at the Oxford Union, and became President of both. I had a volume of poems published in London by the Fortune Press, wrote for several magazines in Oxford, and edited a college magazine. I became engulfed in what was, up to that time, the most passionate love affair of my life. I accepted the fact that there were huge regions of the university that I had nothing to do with. Sport was the biggest as far as other undergraduates' interests were concerned: it contained many worlds within its one big world. Religion was another. There were innumerable clubs and societies whose meetings I never attended; and there were colleges I rarely entered, because I had no friends in them. The only aspect of this that I regret now is that I did not take more interest in undergraduate music and theatre. These – music and theatre – were my greatest loves of all, but I had become so conditioned by metropolitan standards of performance that I regarded student performances as not really worth going to. Unconsciously, I was the victim of a sort of London-snobbery. I took little interest in that side of undergraduate life, though actually it was rich. I realize now that the writing and public speaking that I did go in for were no nearer to professional standards than the acting and instrument-playing that my friends were going in for. But where I was an active practitioner it came naturally to get involved, whereas I was a passive consumer otherwise, and therefore unconcerned with anything except how good something was. When I did go to an OUDS (Oxford University Dramatic Society) production of Shakespeare's *Richard III*, simply because the play itself meant so much to me, I was astonished at how good John Wood was in the title role – it remains, I think, the best piece of amateur acting I have seen. For the first time I got an inkling of what I might be missing. Since then I have heard about other performances that I wish I had seen. In particular, contemporaries whom I did not know at that time, because they were wholly immersed in those worlds, have since become friends, and I wish intensely that I had seen their earliest performances, some of which are still reliably reported to have been good. I could so easily have done so, but felt I couldn't be bothered. That attitude now seems to me ignorant and snooty, and I am embarrassed by the thought that it may have seemed so to others at the time.

Some of the limitations this might have inflicted on me were countered by a tendency for the people at or near the top of the various undergraduate worlds to be brought together by circumstances (chiefly parties) and get to know one another. There were seven thousand seven hundred undergraduates, and these were said to divide into the seven thousand and the seven hundred. The seven thousand were oriented to their colleges. They made their friendships in them, and carried out their other activities – dining and drinking, sport, acting, debating, writing for magazines, attending society meetings, and so on – in college organizations. The seven hundred had these relationships with the university as a whole: they represented it in sport (and sometimes went beyond – an undergraduate at my college, Alan Dick, was a gold medallist in the Olympic Games) and organized the university-wide clubs and societies, produced or starred in the

OUDS productions, edited or wrote *Isis* and *Cherwell* magazines, were Presidents of the Union, and so on. Because they did things on a university-wide scale they were involved with other undergraduates without regard to their colleges, and their friendships reflected that. Then, through that most worthwhile of all undergraduate institutions, the drinks party (there were, fortunately for the rest of us, people who were interested in being successful hosts), they were continually meeting their opposite numbers in other fields. Socially these constituted the top layer of the undergraduate world, lords of the little universe that was undergraduate Oxford, the figures the gossip columnists in the student magazines (and sometimes the national press) wrote about. They were the young men who were expected to become stars in the outside world – and in a way it was surprising how many did. To pick examples from my own largest cabbage patch, the Union: when later, though still only in their thirties, Jeremy Thorpe became leader of the Liberal Party, William Rees-Mogg editor of *The Times*, Robin Day a household face on television, and Dick Taverne the youngest QC in the country, it was no more than the rest of us had assumed would happen. For such figures there was something heady and unrepeatable about that first fame in Oxford, the first fame of adult life; and its possessors knew that. Years later, Robert Robinson wrote in his memoirs: 'Robin Day was President of the Union the term I was editor of the *Isis* – 'We'll never be as famous again', he told me, and of course he was right – being well-known isn't the same.'

Also many years later, but this time to me, Robert Robinson said: 'When we were at Oxford it never entered my head to think of academic study as the purpose of our being there. I thought of it as the collateral we had to put up.' With the precision of language characteristic of him, this expresses what was also my attitude. What the majority of students at Oxford got most out of, and learnt most from, was not their relationship to the University but their relationship to one another, and to the world they created for themselves. None of the ablest ones I knew were focused primarily on academic work. Those who wanted to be writers were more concerned with writing for the student magazines, perhaps editing them, and also with learning from established writers at meetings of the English Club and the Poetry Society – and in discussing all these things with like-minded friends. Those who wanted to go into politics were focused on the Union, and perhaps the political clubs. Those who aspired to a life in the theatre were wrapped up in one student production after another, each of which they would spend most of a term rehearsing. The whole experience of being at Oxford, the totality of it, was a preparation for life in the world outside, and students who devoted themselves primarily to academic work seemed to me to be missing the point of being there. I saw them as blinkered creatures who were preparing themselves for nothing more than a continuance of life in Oxford while missing out on most of its fun. As far as my own academic work was concerned I studied what fed my spirit, and tried to keep out of trouble. I did not apply myself to it in a sustained way until my fourth year, when I had already taken my first degree and had drunk undergraduate life to the full – and was at last taking a degree in something I was emotionally committed to: Philosophy, Politics and Economics.

The prevailing attitude to academic work was different in those days from what it is today. Many undergraduates came up explicitly to have a good time – to take part in sports, go to parties, make friends, meet girls, and generally have fun for three or four years before having to buckle down to earning a living and bringing up a family. They were more than happy with a third class honours degree, which was known as 'a gentleman's degree': for the rest of their lives they would have the cachet of being Oxford men, with honours degrees. In those days something like a third of the undergraduates got thirds. A standard saying among them about their results was: 'If you get a first you're a friend of the examiners. If you get a second, you're a filthy swot. If you get a third you're a proper chap. If you get a fourth you're a friend of the examiners.' Such people made an invaluable contribution to the character and life of the place, and plenty of my friends were in that category. They would have no chance of getting in nowadays: the university would not dream of accepting them. Yet they nourished a wonderful atmosphere that we all shared and fed on. Nearly all of us, including most of those who might be called intellectuals, saw our aims as being to have fun while preparing ourselves for life across a very broad front. Today, however, Oxford undergraduates are given no alternative but to work hard at their academic studies; and for most of them this is a loss. There has been a transformation in student life: the number of third class degrees in any year is negligible, because anyone who looks like getting one is not admitted in the first place.

It might seem to the reader as if I myself came into the category of people who lived like that, and I nearly did – but not quite, because I did have strong and serious intellectual interests. When all is said and done I did do *some* academic work during my first three years; and it was to have a lifelong influence on me, though the effect was cumulative, and slow to establish itself. Lectures were not compulsory, and only a small proportion of undergraduates went to them; but individual tuition, which the whole system was based on, was compulsory, and consisted of having to read for, and write, weekly essays under the personal supervision of a tutor. I would spend an hour alone with my tutor once or twice a week; and these tutorials constituted above all else a training in analytic thinking. To almost any assertion I made he would come back with a response like one of the following: What exactly do you mean by that? Yes, but what do you mean by the key term there? What is your evidence for this? Aren't the implications of what you're saying now incompatible with those of what you said about so-and-so last week? How in that case do you explain such-and-such? Have you considered the following counter-example? Ought you not to draw a distinction between so-and-so and such-and-such?

At every step I found myself being challenged and forced to defend my use of words, my use of evidence, my arguments, my logic, my conclusions, their implications, my omissions. In particular, the paramount need to base opinions on evidence, and not just on emotion, was dinned into me; and alongside that the need to be critical of the evidence itself. I was taught to take a responsible attitude to meaning, and to pay attention to even small distinctions of meaning, for they could turn out to have important consequences. I learnt that before committing myself to any argument I needed to ask myself what objections could be brought against it, and how I would answer those objections. I needed also to ask myself what side-implications it held, and whether I was willing to go along with all of them.

The more intelligent you were, the more difficult these challenges were to meet, and the more good they did you. To develop a person's mind there is nothing like it. Quite apart from anything to do with the subject of history, it was a marvellous training in analytic thinking as such, and was intellectually the most valuable thing I got out of being at Oxford. That, in fact, *was* the university education. That it changed me, and made a difference to my whole life, is without question. But this was a slow process. When I came up I was a teenager, and there was still something of the teenager about the way my mind worked. For instance, I was a passionate socialist, given to making sweeping and deeply felt assertions. I was also used to arguing with contemporaries who were as immature as I was. Except for one master at school I had never encountered anything like this dispassionate analysis of my views, and my schoolmaster had done it with nothing like the same relentless determination. At first I found it disorienting. It was contrary to my natural way of thinking. What seemed to me right and natural was to base your position on true, spontaneous feeling and then think up the best arguments you could to support it. To base your opinions on evidence seemed too detached, too cerebral, too cold and calculating, too unfeeling – all right, perhaps, for those who were not engaged, but not for those who were. I saw it as the attitude of a bystander. But I had already in me enough potential for rational thinking to feel I was being successfully got at by this formidable critique of my approach, and to feel a need to produce an effective answer to it – and to be embarrassed when I knew I had failed. Slowly, against powerful emotional resistance from inside myself, I began to learn to think. But I was to find that learning to think was not a neat process that ran its course and came to a natural conclusion. It was a never-ending process that has been going on, with some difficulty, ever since.

The Oxford approach is not without its limitations. The most serious of these is that it stops short with analysis. We were not encouraged to have ideas of our own but to criticize other people's. If anything, we were made to feel that if we stuck our necks out and said anything positive we would be shot down in flames and deserve to be. All generalizations were distrusted. Nothing could be said to be like anything else, because there were always differences. Theory itself was distrusted, because theory involved generalization. We were trained to be effective critics, but at the same time we were given inhibitions about being creative, imaginative, or original. When misused, as it so often is, this approach encouraged second-rate people to take a critical and superior attitude to everything without committing themselves to anything. Properly used, though, it constituted a wonderful training for someone who was going to think positively for himself, and be willing to commit himself, because it equipped him with invaluable means of self-criticism and self-correction, and gave him a permanent antidote to self-indulgence. But it was dangerously limiting for the others. It made them frightened to say anything positive of an intellectually serious kind. It was a first-class training for senior civil servants, for it made them brilliant at seeing the flaws in everything that was proposed while making them, partly for that reason, unwilling to propose much themselves. And of course this is not a coincidence, because much of the character of Oxford education was consciously developed during the last two hundred years as a way of training individuals to run the administration of the country.

I ought not to leave this subject without saying something about the one respect in which I think the process may have done me harm. It did not, I think, materially diminish my independence of mind, or my underlying urge for synthesis, or my willingness to commit myself, and it did give me powers of analytic thinking and self-criticism that are indispensable accompaniments to these. As far as those things go, it was gain. But the aesthetic side of my nature did not pass through a corresponding development – and I am by nature a predominantly aesthetic person. I arrived at Oxford as someone whose greatest loves in life were for music, theatre and poetry: I was a greedy consumer of all three, and a writer of poetry that would later be published. My approach to life, including its intellectual dimension, was primarily one of feeling. However, there took place a huge development not of my involvement with any of those things but of my capacity for conceptual thinking, which is not central to the arts or to feeling, and can be at odds with them. This altered the balance of my personality. The imbalance remained, I think, for a number of years. I was never corrupted by intellectualization – that lethal curse of academe – in my approach to the arts, but I developed a hypertrophy of the analytic intellect without a counterbalancing development in emotional or aesthetic awareness. It took me quite a long time after I had left Oxford to rediscover and recover the equilibrium that had been natural to me before; and I may never quite have recovered it. As a result of going through Oxford I am on balance more 'intellectual' than I would have been otherwise. And I do not think this is an improvement.

One unquestionably good thing about it, though, is the full realization that if you are going to think rationally and realistically, and to some purpose, you need facts and logic as well as feelings. Thought, and above all analytic thought, needs a subject-matter, something to think *about*. However, that subject is the vehicle for your education, not the education itself. I happened to be cutting my teeth on history, but I could have acquired a similar training through the study of another subject. As things were, in the study of history my adolescent attitudes were able very much to make themselves felt. Not only was I sceptical of authority of every kind, which is in itself a good thing: I automatically assumed the worst about governments and their motives, which is foolish, because divorced from reality. Here again my tutor would challenge me. 'All right,' he would say: 'Suppose you yourself had been the King in those circumstances, what would you have done? What were the alternatives confronting you? You could have done x, or you could have done y, or you could have done z – or you could have done nothing, which is always an option, and sometimes the best one. There were serious drawbacks to each of these policies, and a cost to be paid for each; but can you think of any others? If not, think these through carefully, and tell me next week what you would have chosen to do, and why.' And again, slowly, I learnt that to govern is to choose, and that all choices have drawbacks and costs; there is always opposition, always resistance, resources are always finite and therefore limited, and the range of options is also limited. Not even the most powerful dictator can do whatever he likes. I came to see political situations from the point of view of whoever has to take the decisions. This is not to say that I necessarily liked the people or approved their decisions, but I began to realize what it was like to be in their shoes, and this made me better at understanding them and what they did. In fact, the more I read about them the more evident it was that in essentials they were human beings like me. I think this fundamental insight had already been instilled in me by Shakespeare, but the study of history clothed that skeleton with a great many real-life examples of flesh and blood. When I arrived in Oxford I looked at government from the outside, always with a measure of hostility, but by the time I left it I looked at political problems in terms of what needed to be done about them, and therefore from the point of view of those who are, or others who want to be, in power. This was a part of growing up, of course, part of becoming mature, and might partially have happened at that stage of my life anyway, but it was also a part of my education.

The upshot of all this was that during my time as an undergraduate I shifted to the right politically, though remaining left of centre. It has always been a well-known fact that people who have extreme left-wing views when young tend to move in a rightward direction as they grow older, and I realize now that this is, essentially, a learning process. When I went up to Oxford I was almost as far to the left as a democrat can be. I had never been a communist – first and foremost because of my unshakable commitment to personal freedom, but also because of the knowledge I had gained in Austria about the realities of communist Yugoslavia and the Soviet Union. When I arrived in Oxford direct from counter-intelligence work in Austria I was taken aback by the wrong-headedness of many left-wing attitudes to communism, their ignorance or denial of the murderousness of it. Like George Orwell, whose journalism I had started to read in my late teens, I was an anti-communist socialist, and thought other socialists should be so too. But I was opposition minded, hostile to compromise – and therefore hostile to the Labour Government, which was at that time in power. All this changed while I was a student, and my rightward shift eventually brought me within the spectrum of opinion covered by the Labour Party. I joined it eighteen months after I graduated. But I was never a member of it while I was an undergraduate.

My wrestlings with these questions went on through embattled arguments with friends who held political opinions of other kinds, ranging from one who was a member of the Communist Party to some who were supporters of the Conservative Party. There were undergraduates who preferred to live unchallenged – who were members of, let us say, the Labour Club, and formed all their close friendships within that club and with like-minded people, with the result that they were always being reinforced in their existing attitudes, and never radically opposed. Luckily for me, not many of my friends were like that. In fact, the three closest consisted of a Communist, a Conservative, and one who was contemptuously dismissive of party politics. We were all the time arguing in a youthful, head-on way. The result was educative for all of us. I knew quite a lot of other undergraduates who took a disparaging view of party politics but had an intelligent interest in social problems, and it was especially refreshing to discuss such problems with them. One often hears people say that at university they learnt more from their fellow students than they did from their teachers, and I think this is an important truth for many university graduates who do not have strongly rooted intellectual interests. In my case, I cannot quite bring myself to go so far, but I did get a huge amount of sheer instruction from my contemporaries.

The process took time, but gradually I made the transition from being disappointed with Oxford for not being something else to falling in love with it for being as it was. I was living cheek by jowl with some of the most interesting people of my generation. Not all, or even most, undergraduates were very clever, but many were, and many were outstanding in other ways that made indispensable contributions to the life we shared. The result was a life-giving richness and range of friendships. The two most worthwhile things a university can be to an undergraduate are a training ground for thinking and a breeding ground for friendship: for me Oxford was both. We were adults, yet we did not have adult responsibilities, and were almost completely masters of our own time. We could get up and go to bed when we chose, and work, or not work, when we wanted to. Except for tutorials, which we had to attend, the whole of each day was our own. The contrast with our lives up to that point – in the armed forces, and before that at school – was total. It was our first experience of freedom, and was intoxicating. Never again would we have such liberty, and among so many fellow spirits close to us in age, and for so long. The friendships formed in these circumstances dug deep. Many have lasted throughout life – at each stage of mine I could say truthfully that half my closest friends were from Oxford. They come from every variety of social background, and are of many different characters, in a variety of professions. The fortunes of life have treated them differently, and taken them to widely varying places. Sometimes they and I go for long periods without seeing one another. But the bond is always there.

Often, especially in my second year, I would spend a whole day simply at leisure with friends. After getting up late (as I have all my life) I would go in mid-morning to my favourite coffee house, the Kemp, on the corner of Broad Street and the Cornmarket, and meet friends. Then I would drift over to the Randolph and meet more friends. I would return to my college for lunch, then go to another college and see another friend. After a while the two of us would go off to a third college to see someone we both knew. And so it would go on. At some point I might play a couple of games of billiards in the Union, or go with one or two companions to a cinema, or to one of Oxford's theatres, or a pub, or one of the college bars, or the Union bar. Most days there was a party somewhere. The days drifted by as beautifully as the banks of a river that one floats down on a summer afternoon. On the surface it may have looked to an outsider like pure self-indulgence, a waste of time, but I was beginning to find myself, and forming deeply harmonious relationships that have lasted a lifetime. What learning processes can be more worthwhile? There was depth to those days, and they are unforgettable.

One important difference between students then and now is that we were more accepting of radical differences of opinion among ourselves. That may or may not have been so in the circles everyone moved in, but it was true in mine. Today, at the time in which I write, no such circles exist. Not all that many years ago it would have killed any Oxford dinner party stone dead if a guest had expressed enthusiastic agreement with President George W. Bush, and approval of his invasion of Iraq. The other guests would have been appalled, embarrassed, or violently angry, and someone might well have walked out. Few hosts today would welcome such a spectre at their feast. But that is only an example. There is a whole range of politically incorrect views that it is now considered 'unacceptable' for an individual to hold, and people who do hold them tend to keep quiet about them. Half a century ago the intellectual atmosphere in the Oxford I inhabited was totally different from that. Round the same table would sit confident reactionaries and revolutionary communists, feminists and male chauvinists, militant Catholics and militant atheists, liberals and illiberals on every subject; and they would argue nineteen to the dozen, and be friends and lovers at the same time. Defending George W. Bush is as nothing compared with defending Stalin, which some of my contemporaries did (Stalin was alive and in power). That whole world came to me as a liberation. The institutions I had belonged to since the age of eleven – a boarding school and the army – had been hierarchical, conformist, and profoundly conservative, not to mention their male chauvinism and their institutionalized religion. At school I had aroused serious disapproval by being left-wing at all, and had shocked some of the masters so much by being openly anti-religious that they wanted to have me removed from the school. Now, for the first time, I found myself in a world whose ethos was truly liberal, a world in which it was taken for granted that authority had no place in matters of opinion, because every individual had a right to his own opinion, and differences of opinion could not be settled by authority but only by rational discussion. It was considered natural that individuals should differ and disagree, argue, dissent, object; and it would have been thought absurd to be shocked by another person's being different. All assumptions, all opinions, were open to attack; and the only defence was reason. I believed then that such a world would always exist in Oxford; but alas, it has turned out not to be so.

2

Caroline

The outstanding personality among the women of my year was Caroline Carter, who was studying Philosophy, Politics and Economics at Lady Margaret Hall. Like nearly all the female undergraduates, she was eighteen when she came up – a year and a day younger than me, in fact. But even to much older ex-army men she seemed disconcertingly confident, intelligent, and beautiful. The combination was alarming. Although she was generally admired there were some people, women as well as men, who were scared of her. Tall and strongly built, with a big head and a lot of face on which the features were also big – a broad, sensual-looking mouth, and a nose that spread slightly, as it does sometimes on Russian faces – she was aptly described as a Slav beauty. Her brow was wide, with pale, perceptive eyes, and her hair a particular shade of chestnut which ran in her family, who had invented the word 'losmue' for it.

In her first term she joined the Communist Party. From then on this fact dominated other people's perceptions of her – she was that formidable woman who was a Communist. There was a female populist leader still famous from the Spanish Civil War (then only ten years in the past), a woman nicknamed La Passionaria; and Caroline was sometimes dubbed La Passionaria.

But of course, all this took time to establish itself, so it took that time for Caroline to become known. The fact that Oxford's girls were younger than the men meant that it took them longer as individuals to make a mark. Because of the college system student life was disparate and dispersed; and the women – less numerous than the men anyway – lived in separate colleges on the edge of town. I was so bound up in my own friendships and pursuits that it was not until our second year that I became aware of Caroline. The two centres on which my own life focused were the Union and the Randolph, and at that time she never came to either. The Union did not allow women members. I was studying history then, not yet PPE, so we were not in the same academic field. I went to meetings of the Labour, Liberal and Conservative clubs, but as a card-carrying member of the Communist Party Caroline made no attempt to go to any of their meetings. For a long time our paths did not cross. I heard about her before I met her. People began to mention this striking woman to me, and to ask me if I knew her.

The political club she went to was the Socialist Club. This had been formed because the Labour Club, being affiliated to the Labour Party, was strict about not allowing known Communists in. The Socialist Club had come into existence to provide an association of the broad left, a Popular Front club, a club to which all the different sorts of people who called themselves Socialists could belong. In practice it straddled the left of the Labour Party and all the various Marxist revolutionary groups. At one time or other all the national notables of the far left came to Oxford to address it; and it was to see one of those in action that I first went to one of the club's meetings. There was Caroline.

My attraction to her was immediate. I was instantly aware of a desire to go to bed with her. I embarked on a course of action with this as its aim. To attend that meeting I had had to join the Socialist Club: now I became its college representative, and also joined its Committee, both of which gave me regular dealings with the club's Secretary, who was Caroline. I started inviting her to things that had nothing to do with the club, and she accepted. We became friends – whereupon I discovered that she had a boyfriend. This had not been evident: he was a scientific research student who took little notice of undergraduate life. However, this had the beneficent consequence that he was rarely with her when I was, or at the kind of meetings and parties that she and I both attended. The result was that we became ever closer as friends, and did more and more things together, without this creating any awkwardness with him. Of course she knew that I found her attractive, but so did most men, and she was used to that – used to being just good friends with people who she knew wanted to go to bed with her. As matters turned out, the fact that we developed such a close friendship before anything else happened transformed the attitude with which I began my pursuit of her, so that when eventually we did become lovers our relationship had real substance and depth to it and was far from being just a matter of sex. We were a thoroughgoing friendship as well as partnership.

From the beginning this changing relationship was a relationship between equals, and this was a new and thrilling experience for me – to have as a friend, companion and lover a woman who was in every way my equal. That was still an age when the man was expected to have a certain predominance, and I had never experienced anything else. Women seemed to take this as much for granted as men did – and there was a sense in which even Caroline did. She and I discussed this once, and she said she did not want a 50-50 relationship with me, she wanted a 51-49 one. Then, on reflection, she withdrew that and said 52-48. But then, she added, this was what we already had. I was sceptical. To me it felt like 50-50. But I realize, looking back, that I was still making unconscious assumptions about male superiority, and was seeing equality when in fact I had slight advantages. Be that as it may, we were both exceedingly happy with the balance of our relationship as it was, and we found it exciting.

Even from the beginning it contained a high level of conflict, which we were always trying to resolve. Things between us were always in a dramatic state. It sometimes felt as if the very mode of our relationship was conflict-management. Long before the reality of sex reared its head, there was politics. This was a subject on which our opinions were passionately opposed. Like all but the most morally corrupt Communists in the West, Caroline had a deluded conception of the social reality of Communism. It needs to be remembered that Stalin was still very much alive and in power in Russia. His regime was horrific on a colossal scale: it had murdered at least twenty million of its own citizens, and maintained a vast network of slave-labour camps that contained, at its height, about a tenth of the national labour force. From the top of society to the bottom, terrorization and lawless violence were everyday; and this was carrying on in a country that covered a sixth of the earth's surface. There was no way of keeping such happenings a secret, and after the Second World War they became widely known. In fact a substantial literature about them had grown up well before that time. But Communists believed that all true descriptions, and all true such references, were lies: they were anti-Communist propaganda. The truth, they believed, was that the Soviet Union was a good state and not a bad one, a well-meaning attempt to establish socialism in a vast and backward country. Okay, they would say, harsh methods were sometimes used – but so they had to be in what was still a revolutionary situation. They were given to quoting Robespierre's remark that you cannot make an omelette without breaking eggs. The rulers of Russia were, they believed, tough-minded idealists who were forcing the country along a path of industrialization and modernization towards freedom, democracy and equality within a socialist economy. The populace was being driven hard, certainly, but the people themselves approved of this, and supported the regime. So rulers and people alike were determined to reach their socialist goal; and what is more they were succeeding.

This view of the matter bore scarcely any relation to truth. It was the propaganda picture put out by the dictatorship itself, and swallowed whole by Communists in non-Communist countries. In Communist countries it was not possible even for the Communists themselves to believe it, and none of them did. In fact they despised Western Communists – Lenin described them as 'useful fools'. But there were large numbers of such fools, probably millions of them during the period between the two world wars, and then for quite a few years afterwards. During the Second World War the propaganda of the democracies presented the Soviet Union as a great ally against Hitler, and it was only when that fight finished that their inhibitions about telling the truth dissolved. More and more books appeared about the unbelievable heartlessness of the Russian system, especially its labour camps. But an astonishing number of socialists clung to their old illusions. In spite of their gullibility, many of them were intelligent, some highly so. It is hard nowadays to get young people to understand how this is possible – how anyone who was either intelligent or idealistic could have been a torch-carrier for Stalin and the Soviet Union – but it was so. *Why?* is a fascinating question, but a complex one, and not one I want to go into here. The point I want to stress is that Caroline was not alone among intelligent people in holding such views. She had been born into a family that held them, and she had been indoctrinated from birth. She believed there were sinister forces in Britain that were preventing the truth about Russia from becoming known to the general public because that would threaten the position of the ruling class here. The deception was being carried out daily through the media, and more insidiously through the brainwashing to which the cultural superstructure of our society subjected us. She was experienced in arguing for these views, as part and parcel of what she thought of as her socialist outlook, and she had become effective at doing this. But I presented her with a problem for which she was unprepared.

My recent year of counter-intelligence work in Austria had given me a kind of knowledge of what Communist societies were actually like that she had not met with before. I had spent most of the year living on the frontier of Communist Yugoslavia and carrying out long, detailed interrogations of individual Yugoslav frontier-crossers, plus an occasional Hungarian or Czech, about the social and economic conditions under which they were living. I had then spent three months carrying out even longer and more detailed interrogations of individual Austrians newly returned from the Soviet Union after living there for several years as prisoners of war, and often, once the war was over, working under supervision alongside Russians – on railways, in shipyards, in steelworks, and so on. I had specific and often detailed knowledge of actual conditions, knowledge that I had not got from the media, or from books. On top of that I was myself a Socialist: so, far from having any prejudices against socialism, I believed in it and wanted it to work. I agreed with some of Caroline's more principled arguments for it, and also with many of her arguments against the alternatives; but, unlike her, I had reliable knowledge of the fact that Communism bore no significant relation to any of this. One might have thought this would leave her with no ground on which to stand, and indeed she had none, but it took her more than a year to realize and come to terms with that fact. Throughout that period she attacked me in argument like a tiger. She was fighting fiercely, even savagely, not just for what she believed in but for her family background and relationships, her social world, a whole way of looking at things, her whole life. In total, the experience was traumatic for her, disorienting. And I understood that.

Our arguments were the longest and most impassioned I have ever had. They went on for hours. On my side, from the beginning, and on hers increasingly, other passions became involved. We would blaze away at one another with our whole selves. And it goes without saying that as an arguer, even though I had the better case, I was not perfect: sometimes I would get my facts wrong, or make unjustified connections, or contradict myself; and then she would pounce on what I had said and beat me about the head with it joyfully, getting her own back. I did, in the end, win the match, but I lost quite a few points along the way, so I was always stretched. In fact we stretched one another to our limits. I particularly remember what turned out to be the decisive argument of all, the one that marked the turning point in her adherence to Communism. In boxing it can happen that two equally matched opponents fight one another to a standstill, reaching a stage when each has given and received so much punishment, and become so exhausted, that he is only just managing to stay on his feet: at that point a single blow from either side, not even a hard one, can end the fight in a knockout; and the victory can go either way. This particular argument felt to me like that. We had been battling for hours, and had reached a state of exhaustion. Every time I put an argument to her which I thought would be the knock-out blow she came back with some ingenious and not-impossible get-out. She was infuriatingly good at ducking out of corners, and I kept on chasing her round the ring, only to be foiled again and again. I felt myself running out of steam, becoming desperate. But so was she. Simultaneously, we reached the point where, unrealized by me, she had no resistance left – and I could think of only one more shot in my locker. I landed my punch, but I knew in that moment that this was the end of the argument as far as I was concerned. I was now finished, spent. But, to my amazement, down she went on the canvas, out for the count. I was still on my feet, though only just.

During those blazing months I learnt my way around the inside of a left-wing outlook that I was to find myself battling against for the rest of my life. It is so devoted to the notion of a rational and humane social order to be arrived at through public planning that it is hostile in practice to individual freedom and choice, because these are at odds with, and get in the way of, centralized planning. Holders of this attitude will exonerate dictatorships anywhere in the world so long as they are left-wing. And they are full of emotional antagonism towards free societies, an antagonism that sees those societies in terms of their faults rather than their virtues.

My closeness to Caroline brought me up against the double-think that had become notorious among Communists – George Orwell had recently drawn attention to it by coining that term. Early on in our friendship I bumped into her one afternoon with her boyfriend (who was also a Communist) in George Street, and they asked me if they could use my name to hire a hall for a public meeting. I said I was not free on the date they mentioned; but they said I did not need to be there, they just wanted my name on the posters. I asked why – why could they not do it themselves? They said that if they did, people would think it was just another meeting organized by the Communists, whereas they wanted left-of-centre people more generally to attend it – so they wanted a well-known figure on the non-Communist left to front the publicity. I questioned them further, and it emerged that the meeting was indeed being organized by the Communist Party, not just by these two but at the behest of the national party in London, who had advised them to front it with a non-Communist. I declined to accept the role of stooge. Then by chance I bumped into the two of them the same evening at one of the cheap student eating places we all frequented, and sat having dinner with them and others. Someone started teasing them about the way Communists worked underhand, through fronted activities – and the two became hotly indignant in their denials, protesting that this was part of the way Communists were routinely slandered, and was grossly untrue. At first I could scarcely believe my ears. I sat there incredulous, watching them getting angrier. Their anger was real. I looked to see if either of them was betraying any sign of embarrassment at what they were saying in my presence, when they had been asking me that very afternoon to provide a misleadingly respectable front for a Communist-Party-organized public meeting. And I realized, watching their eyes closely, that they believed what they were saying.

In addition to this, Caroline gave me my first detailed familiarity with an attitude to the arts that I was to encounter ever after. There was quite a lot of Modernist art that I was intimate with and loved, above all the poetry of T. S. Eliot, but Modernism as a theory, a general approach, struck me as absurd. It advocated sweeping away the art of the past and making a fresh start. People who thought like this felt that the only art that really mattered was the art being created now. New novels, new plays, new poetry thrilled them in a way the rest did not. They were avid for avant-garde painting, and for first performances of contemporary music. They were absorbed excitedly in whatever was currently going on, and impatient to know what was coming up next. But to have the same feelings for the art of the past seemed to them a form of necrophilia. Past art, they thought, belonged in museums. They even derided opera-houses as 'museums'. And they saw people whose loves in art were mainly of works of the past as belonging to yesterday and not to the modern world. A great deal of self-congratulation accompanied these attitudes. Such people tended to think of themselves as being on the cutting edge of taste, in the vanguard of artistic development, while everyone else was wandering about in the past, unwilling to let go of the familiar.

Historically there had been strong links between Modernism, which came to full flower in the 1920s, and Communism. Both were self-consciously revolutionary, and advocated the sweeping away of the past; and therefore, not surprisingly, both practised an extreme devaluation of the past. Both sets of attitudes tended to be militantly intolerant, dictatorial, ruling out of consideration any approach that differed from their own. Part of Marxism was a theory of art that saw the value of art as lying in what it had to say about contemporary society. All art was thought a product of the socio-economic forces surrounding it, though it might well be, and usually should be, a critique of them. Art of the past can therefore have significance for us now only if it is relevant to the political/social/economic conditions that we ourselves are living in – 'relevant' being the key word. If it is not, it does not speak to us. This Marxist view of art was taken over by Modernists, and provided them with a philosophical explanation of why past art is of secondary importance. It also provided a positive rationale for the Modernists' celebration of the new. The new was 'relevant' in a way nothing else could be. In general it was the same intellectuals who embraced both sets of ideas – not creative artists themselves (who are seldom intellectuals) but such people as arts administrators, teachers, critics, authors, journalists and their audiences, the chattering classes generally. The phrase 'left-wing intellectual' was common in those days, and usually meant someone who in politics was a fellow-traveller with the Communists and in the arts an enthusiast for Modernism. Not only Caroline's family but, as I came to discover, the world they inhabited was so saturated with these attitudes that they had become assumptions, taken for granted. Everything was seen in the light of them. Getting to know Caroline's family was an education in the small and closed, as well as deluded, mental world that even intelligent Communists lived in.

Caroline's approach to the arts was so profoundly misconceived that sometimes I was unable to see what she was getting at. I once remarked that I wished I could see a particular production at Glyndebourne that was being highly praised. She said one should not go to Glyndebourne. What could that mean, I wondered? I asked, and she explained that one ought not to *want* to go to Glyndebourne. The more she tried to explain this the more confused I became. Refusing to go to wonderful performances of great works of art because one feels a class prejudice against other members of the audience is so mind-bogglingly moronic (and nasty with it – and talk about irrelevant!) that it did not occur to me that Caroline could be saying this. I thought she must be saying something else that I was failing to get. But slowly, with almost complete incredulity, I realized that she *was* saying that. And so deep did these crazy attitudes go that she was having as much difficulty in understanding my inability to understand them as I was having in understanding her.

I was to encounter the same attitudes quite often in later life, and it was Caroline who had familiarized me with them, and given me as much understanding of them as is possible. In multiple ways, over a long period of time, she gave me a detailed education in the values of the far left. It proved invaluable in later years when I became an active member of the Labour Party, especially when I was a Labour MP, because these attitudes – impossible to hold, one might have thought, for anybody with a sense of proportion, let alone a love of the arts – were found not only among Marxists but also, more generally, among socialist intellectuals who came from middle-class family backgrounds of the sort that imbued them with class-consciousness about everything.

For Caroline, the emotional process of breaking with the beliefs of a lifetime was all mixed up psychologically with a parallel process of detaching herself from her Communist boyfriend and attaching herself to me. This was so gradual, and so fraught, that while it was going on I myself had little idea how it was progressing. Meanwhile I was trying to bring her into my other worlds as much as I could. We had met in the Socialist Club, and because of her I had become active in it. As a socialist I was far from being out of place there, though the Communists in it perceived me, correctly, as a mortal enemy. But the club was afflicted with the pokiness and parochialism that characterize organizations at both extremes of the political spectrum, with more than its fair share of oddities and misfits. Caroline became its Chairman, and I had no choice but to accept that, but it was not a world I wanted to spend much of my time in, and I never did, except to be with her. It was in that environment that I coined a nickname for her, 'the Body Politic', which not only caught on but leaked into the university at large.

I introduced Caroline to my non-political, or other-political, friends. One of the closest, a Conservative called Andrew Cuninghame, thought she was glorious. He told me that she gave him and others a way of broadening their relationship with me. I was seen by some, he told me, as dauntingly intellectual, but when they met me with Caroline they could feel the zing of emotion in the air, and saw me in a different light. Actually, she caused me to see them in a different light too. Their reactions to her separated the men from the boys. The high calibre ones – for instance the leading figures in the Union, though not only they – took to her appreciatively, and were delighted by her. But some of the others felt intimidated by her, and avoided her. It embarrassed me to see this happen, and I found myself viewing those individuals as lesser people than I had imagined. Even so, it has to be said that, by the age of twenty, Caroline had a startlingly powerful personality. It is hard to pin down what it consisted in, and even harder to put that into words. Several decades later, when the youngest of her four children, Zoë Heller, was a professional writer, Zoë published a pen portrait of Caroline as Zoë had perceived her while growing up. It contains sentences like: 'Even without her beauty, though, my mother would have made people sit up and look. She had an intense, intimidating presence' … and: 'I saw her as a super-woman, swooping through life, and slaying all-comers with her charisma.' This is offered to us as a child's-eye view; and the Caroline being described was by then in her late thirties; but a lot of it was already true of her at twenty. Many would have felt that those two adjectives 'intense' and 'intimidating' were especially apt. When I reached the point of spending most of my time with her I found myself having, of necessity, to shed friends who were not strong enough to take it.

In the last term of each academic year the President of the Oxford Union would invite whoever was thought to be the outstanding woman undergraduate to make a speech in one of the debates. Caroline was invited in the term in which I was Secretary of the Union. I had nothing to do with the invitation: she was the obvious choice, and was invited by an American President called Howard Shuman. She was by this time familiar with Union debates – she would sit watching them from the Visitors' Gallery when I spoke – and she was also an experienced public speaker in the Socialist Club and elsewhere. So it was with consternation that I discovered, in private, how frightened she was at the prospect of speaking at the Union. It was not only that she started wanting obsessively to discuss preparation with me in each detail: she was irresolute about making the decisions that have to be made in preparing any speech. She kept seeking reassurance about a particular wording, or line of argument, and then, when I had given it, changing her mind. She became jittery. I did everything I could to calm her down, and everything I could to help her with the speech, but she started going round in circles. It was my first perception of a hidden, deep-lying, irrational self-doubt in Caroline, a fear that she was not going to live up to the high expectations that others had of her, or the demands she made on herself. She was abundantly supplied with all the abilities the situation required; but buried deep inside her was an insecurity about it, a terror. I shall want to come back to this much later, because I suspect it was the decisive factor in the way her life eventually turned out.

We had agreed that, a couple of days before the debate and while there was still plenty of time for her to change things, she would come to me with her speech complete, and I would tell her with total honesty what I thought of it. When that day came, the speech was formless: there were plenty of good things in it, but it was a mass of unconnected points, some at odds with others. She knew it was not good, and was in a panic about it. She said she could not deliver it. She would feign illness, she said, and withdraw from the debate. I gave her the most rousing pep-talk I have ever given anyone, to the effect that she had both the time and the ability to make a good speech. She said she was now in such a state that she was incapable of producing a new speech. I offered to recast the one she had prepared, re-ordering her points, grouping them into structured arguments and connecting these with one another while getting rid of the apparent self-contradictions, and adding some of her own best jokes – but all the time using only *her* opinions, and *her* ways of putting things, with both of which I was intimately familiar. She doubtfully agreed, and we got down to the task together. We spent a whole day on it. When the debate came she delivered the speech superbly. Because of the prolonged, intense concentration with which we had prepared it she knew it by heart, and had scarcely any need to look at the notes she was holding in her hands. So she seemed to be communicating directly with her audience, and to be riding effortlessly on top of the whole occasion.

It was part of the role of the Secretary of the Union, in his white-tie and tails, to sit in an armchair at a big table with two despatch boxes on either side from which the opposing speakers made their speeches. So the speakers stood at one or other of his elbows, and he, seated, had to crane his neck sideways to look up at their faces as they spoke. I always found this awkward, and was self-conscious while doing it; but it was especially so when Caroline spoke. However, she herself looked a picture of poise and elegance. I was proud of her. To match the men's formal clothes she had had a classic suit of slate grey made for the occasion, and she looked simply beautiful. The debating chamber was full, so there were about 600 people there. It was a triumph for her, unquestionably the high point of her Oxford career.

With Caroline at her apogee like this, and me about to be elected President of the Union, we were probably the best known student couple of our generation. We were invited everywhere together. By this time we were a couple in every sense. Our private relationship came close to being all-consuming, but at the same time we were also, separately, public figures in our own little worlds. We enjoyed together a many-sided life across the whole range of our two worlds combined. I began to think of us as going through life like this, confronting a multiplicity of private and public worlds side by side.

We were now spending several hours of every day together. But to our bitter frustration it was not possible for us literally to *sleep* together. Caroline lived in her college, and had to be there every night, or her absence would be reported and she would risk being sent down. I lived in what were reputed to be the best digs in Oxford, and had the best landlady imaginable; but she would have risked losing her licence if she had allowed Caroline to stay in her house overnight, or had failed to report an overnight absence on my part. Our sex life was confined to the afternoons, in my single bed. We were intense personalities, both of us, and our sex was intense too. It made us happy, but there was none of the ease, depth or amplitude that some of my relationships later in life were to have. However, as yet I had no such comparative knowledge, and I was actively content. One thing that was revealed to me was that although Caroline had such a sensual face she was not as sensual as she looked, by which I mean that she was not proactively sensual. In spite of having already had a boyfriend, she was not fully aroused sexually until her relationship with me; and then it seemed specifically in response to me. There was little common-or- garden lust on her part, though a great deal of it on mine. She told me that she had not begun to feel any active longings for sex with me until after we had started having it – and then, she said, it was the me-ness of it she wanted, not the just-sex. (I wanted both.) She became more and more responsive, though, and sex was a deep satisfaction for both of us.

Considering how seriously forbidden all this was in the Oxford of those days we were lucky to get away with it. The age of majority at that time was twenty-one, and for undergraduates below that age (as Caroline was then, and as most of the girls always were) the university exercised the legal responsibility of parents. Undergraduates who were known by anyone in authority to be having sexual relations were sent back to their real parents. And there was one occasion, though only one, when Caroline and I were caught, and thought we would be sent down.

All undergraduates were supposed to be in their rooms by midnight, so by one o'clock in the morning colleges and digs would be wrapped in darkness and, usually, silence. One night, in the early hours of the morning, I slipped away from my digs with the intention of climbing into Caroline's room, which had a window that gave on the street. (That whole wall of rooms has since been enclosed within the college.) I woke her by tapping on the glass, and she got out of bed and let me in. I was, cumbersomely, clambering in when to my horror I heard the big street door of the college open and close behind me. Caroline, who could see past me out of the window, gestured to me to freeze, so I did, with my head in the room and my bottom sticking out into the street. I held that ridiculous posture for what seemed like a lifetime. Then I heard the big door open and close again, and Caroline helped me scramble into the room. What she had seen was the college Bursar, a tough, streetwise female don, step outside and stand on the front steps smoking a cigarette. She had, apparently, looked up at the moon, and then let her gaze drift along the outside wall until it rested on a man's bottom sticking out of one of the windows. Caroline watched her count the windows to identify the room, and then turn and go back into the college.

We bolted the door, kept the light off, and quickly decided to do and say absolutely nothing when, as we knew she would, she arrived to challenge us. We waited. So much time went by that we began to think she must be intending to wait until next morning to take action – but then footsteps came along the corridor. These made a fiercely commanding sound in spite of the hour: *Bang! Bang! Bang! Bang!* They halted outside the door. Then, again imperious, a set of knuckles went *Rat! Tat! Tat!* on the door. We remained motionless in the dark and held our breaths. Then another aggressive *Rat! Tat! Tat!* Another silence. Then the Bursar tried to open the door but found it bolted. She rattled it noisily. At last she spoke: 'Miss Carter, open the door.' We did nothing. She rattled it again. Then she said, 'It's no good, Miss Carter: I know he's in there. I saw him.' There was then a very long silence indeed, during which we both got the impression that she was baffled. Then the footsteps bang-bang-banged away down the corridor.

At that moment we saw expulsion from Oxford staring us both in the face. Obviously the Bursar had seen me, and had identified the room correctly, and knew it was Caroline's. For Caroline not to be in it at that hour would itself have been a capital offence. However, if she had been there and innocent, why would she not have opened the door when ordered to? Whichever way we looked at it, we could find no credible defence for ourselves, not even by lying. But to our amazement, Caroline was not summoned to see the Bursar – or the Principal – the next day, or any other day. We never heard a word about it. Raking it over in conversation, we came to the conclusion that either the Bursar or someone else at Lady Margaret Hall must have realized that if they carpeted Caroline and she denied all knowledge of the charge, and insisted that there must have been some mistake, there would be no further action they could take. In everyone's mind except that of the Bursar the possibility would exist that the Bursar had mis-identified the room. If Caroline claimed she had slept through the knocking there would be no way of proving that she had not. Given this element of doubt, Caroline was not the kind of student that the college would want to lose in such circumstances. She had too high a profile in the university at large to be sent down unnoticed, as happened with some girls.

We decided that as soon as term was over we would go somewhere where we were unknown and could simply sleep together, at least for two or three weeks, before Caroline went back to her family. We chose Cambridge. No one there would recognize us; and separately, as individuals (neither of us told anyone we were going together), we could produce plausible reasons for going there. Like Oxford, it was a town full of cheap student accommodation that would mostly be empty during vacations, so we knew we could easily find somewhere to stay. I made a day trip to Cambridge to pin down the arrangements. The landlady was insistent that she would let double rooms only to married couples, so I said we were married. Back in Oxford I bought a curtain ring at Woolworth's and, when the time came, Caroline wore it as a wedding ring. I do not believe for one moment that it fooled the landlady. But that did not matter to us – nor, I suspect, to the landlady.

It was the first time Caroline and I slept together. We luxuriated in it, and felt liberated. But I also received my introduction to real-life feminism. We had a bed-sitting room with our own cooking facilities, not because we intended to do any cooking (we did not: we ate all our meals out except for breakfast) but to be independent. When we woke up on our first morning I took it for granted that, at some point, after some love-making, Caroline would get up and make coffee, perhaps breakfast. I assumed this not because I had given it any thought but because it was what women did. When, in answer to an innocent question from me, she said: 'Why should it be me who gets up first? Why don't you get up and make some coffee?' I was disoriented. It was against Nature. This feeling had nothing to do with the power-balance in a relationship – there were always plenty of women who did all the chores in their homes and at the same time dominated their husbands. It was simply a fact about women: they were the carers, the ones who did such things. We lay side by side arguing about it. And of course I got the worst of the argument. In fact, I did not have any real arguments: what I had was a mental blockage. But I did have it: it was psychologically impossible for me to get up and make that coffee, still less to prepare breakfast. Nothing Caroline could possibly have said would have induced me to do it. When she realized this she got up grumbling and protesting. This scene was re-enacted each morning for the rest of our stay in Cambridge. She never accepted it, and tried to broker a 50-50 deal, but I was not having that either. She had been wont to say that I had abnormally few prejudices, but on this question she saw me as antediluvian. It was one of the most significant turning points in outlook that I have ever been through. Her arguments were impeccably rational, and I was painfully aware that I had no such arguments to come back with. She made me question assumptions I had taken for granted all my life. I found it excruciatingly difficult, and it was to be a very slow process.

Apart from that, when I look back on our time in Cambridge what I remember is mostly bed, which, I think, is what it mostly consisted of – a highly fulfilling relief after so much frustration. When we were out of doors our base in the middle of town was the Cambridge Union, which was open but empty during vacations, and very useful to us. From there I remember a moment of trivial but pink-making embarrassment. We were walking along one of the corridors and, as we passed a ladies' lavatory, Caroline said: 'I think I'll just drop in here for a moment.'

I said: 'I've never been in a ladies' lavatory. I'd rather like to see one.'

'Well come in and have a look,' she said. 'There's no one around.'

'You go first,' I said, 'in case there's someone in there already.'

She went in, and the door closed behind her. I stood immediately outside, under an overhanging sign saying LADIES. At that moment a distinguished-looking older man turned the corner beside me. Just as he was between me and the door, Caroline's voice trilled out from inside: 'Come on in, darling, there's nobody here.'

We saw a film together in Cambridge that had a disturbing effect on me. In it, a talented young man full of high, heady ambitions for himself has a girlfriend who is severely crippled in an accident. The question then is: will he sacrifice all his other hopes in life to stay with her, whom he genuinely loves, and look after her – or will he try to live his own life to the full at the expense of his relationship with her? Afterwards Caroline spoke straight to my thoughts. 'What would you do, if that happened to me?' she said. 'Would you give up your future to stay with me? I don't think you would.'

I murmured, in troubled tones: 'I think I would.'

She smiled with relaxed confidence. 'No you wouldn't,' she said.

The appalling thing is, I knew she was right. I would not have volunteered to sacrifice the rest of my life for another person – not even for Caroline, my first great love. It was a dismaying thing for me to realize. I was dominated by a deeply felt need to go out into the world, venture, explore, discover, face challenges, do things, stretch myself, travel along the road of life at full throttle on all cylinders. If I had been denied that my spirit would have died. I had begun to believe that Caroline and I would live a life like this together, as partners in the adventure of it all. But I saw all this in terms of her joining her life to mine, not of me joining mine to hers. It was my first intimation that my commitment to her was less than fully reciprocal. I was seriously unnerved by it.

Caroline left Oxford a year before I did. We both took degrees in the summer of 1952, and then she went down while I remained in Oxford in order to take a degree in philosophy and be President of the Union. We both knew that my first finals term would be our last opportunity, for another year, to be together every day. As a result, being together was what mattered. We did absurdly little academic work, even though our degree exams were upon us. We were in thrall to one another – 'living in one another's pockets', as my landlady disapprovingly put it. We kept agreeing on plans to spend more time away from each other in order to work for our exams, but we kept not keeping to our arrangements. We were besotted with each other, that was all there was to it. It was like being drugged, or drunk.

Academically, Caroline came to feel in her last year that she had wasted her opportunities at Oxford. She had arrived at the university a committed Marxist, and this had meant that in all three of her subjects – Philosophy, Politics and Economics – there was an approach which she believed to be the right one, and all others wrong. So she had not been open to what her tutors were trying to teach her. She had dismissed in advance what they were saying as bourgeois special pleading; and she felt superior to it, because she knew better. Only by her last year did she come to understand how mistaken Marxism was, and how deeply in need she had been all along of alternative ways of thinking. But by now it was too late, at least as far as the university was concerned. The examiners gave her an alpha in only one of her final papers, the history of economics, and – like me – she got a second class degree. With both of us, separately, our careers at Oxford seemed starry to others, but we left the university more dissatisfied than they would have guessed. Far too late – having decided so confidently that it would make no difference to me what class of degree I got, I found I minded having the label Second Class attached to me, predictable though it was as a consequence of the choices I made.

During my own last year I went to London many times to stay with Caroline in her flat in Kent Terrace, alongside Regent's Park. And she often came to Oxford to be with me. Like all other students, I did not have a telephone; but we wrote letters. The Central Post Office in Oxford guaranteed that any letter posted there before midnight would be delivered in London by first post the following morning, so night after night I would be in my digs by eleven so that I could write a letter and post it before twelve.

The bond between us remained powerful. And there is a sense in which it was to be so for the rest of our lives. But the time of its utmost intensity had passed. Now that we were no longer in the same town, or spending much time together, it was as if our honeymoon was over, and we were having to cope with a difficult normality. We were now in different worlds, and becoming more and more preoccupied with different things, with different people. There was even an aspect of this that I welcomed. I had become bound up with Caroline to such an extent that other sides of my life, and other friendships, had been sacrificed, and I was losing touch with certain aspects of myself. She felt the same, if anything more than I did. In her letters, in amongst the declarations of love, she complained that I was devouring her, swallowing her up – that her separate self was disappearing in our relationship. We were both obstinate people, strong-willed and strong-minded, bent on doing our own thing, going our own way. Our relationship had all along been charged with tensions and conflicts: we had always found it difficult to make the compromises and accommodations necessary to a relationship. We had each fought all the time against giving up as much as we had to, so when our separation lifted a part of the burden of this I found it a relief as well as a loss. When I pondered this in earnest it caused me to realize that I did not, as yet, want to marry Caroline. I did want to eventually, but not yet. With my new-found elbow-room I felt it was still too early to pin myself down to a life in which everything had to be accommodated to her. There was still too much unexplored possibility. I needed to give the unknown future a chance. I had absolutely no desire to end our relationship – that thought did not even occur to me – but I felt I needed to continue this period of greater freedom and more many-sided life. I needed, in a sense, to recover more of my independent, pre-Caroline self.

A poem I wrote at that time, dated January 1953, embodies this frame of mind. Without making claims for it as poetry, I reproduce it here to reveal what my inmost thoughts were – thoughts which I would not then have voiced to anyone.

> The journey back, the light in the crystal ball
> The losmue stranger, exciting, familiar dis-ease
> Of the eve of travel: the trains if they run will resume
> A service dead too long to be normal now.
>
> No marriage yet, to be met instead by a tall
> Dark future. Thanks are due, and also the blame
> To a sense of loss, but the loss is of loneliness
> Which must be found, to reverse the personal fall.

There was another factor which, under the surface, was tending not so much to pull us apart as to impede our coming more closely together. It was that when Caroline left Oxford she returned to the background from which she had come. This was inevitable – the world she returned to was the only one she had apart from Oxford, and consisted of all the people she had known the longest. By contrast, the friendships she had made at university, however close, were with people she had known for three years at most, and was now seeing only occasionally. Her break with

Communism was real, and it lasted; but, having been brought up with Communists, and having been one herself, she found it the easiest thing in the world to live among them on intimate terms while not sharing their views – just as, if it comes to that, I had loved her and been intimate with her when she had been a Communist. For the remainder of her life she was in rebellion against that mental world, but in fact she never broke entirely free of it. Its pull on her was subterranean, and its effects insidious.

A lot of this had to do with the fact that – like most of the remarkable women I have known – she had a strong and complex relationship with her father. He, Julian Carter, known as Bobby, had long been the Librarian of the Architects Association, and was now working for UNESCO. In the former capacity he had become well known before the war in the world of professional architecture as a key figure in the dissemination of revolutionary ideas, in particular ideas that related Modernism to Marxism. He had been one of the leading organizers of the Left Book Club, which by the outbreak of war had acquired 57,000 members in 1,200 organized groups, one in nearly every town in Britain. Largely forgotten now, the Left Book Club was more militant than its name suggests: it organized rallies, protests and marches, as well as group discussions, lectures and cultural activities. It started out as an independent organization to promote the ideas of the broad left, but is now known to have been taken over behind the scenes by the Communist Party and turned into a 'front' organization that was consciously manipulative and fraudulent. It was a shameful operation: Philip Toynbee, who was a member of the Communist Party at that time, was later to write that the Left Book Club 'came to represent for many people much that they wanted to forget in their lives.'

Bobby made each of his homes a meeting place for Marxists of every kind, mostly those in the arts and the media; and what with his five children, and his other relations, there was always a lively crowd. In his house life seemed a perpetually on-going party of talented and stimulating people. But they were very much an in-group, because all held the same outlook and opinions. Their euphemism for these was 'progressive', a word which was constantly on their lips. The first question to be asked about any stranger was 'Is he progressive?' Bobby and his wife Deborah were intelligent, generous, imaginative hosts, and were helped in this by the fact that they both came from well-to-do backgrounds: they had a country house as well as their house in London, and retained both when they made a new home in Paris, and Bobby joined UNESCO.

The first time I visited them was at their house in London. They had recently moved to St John's Wood from Hampstead, where Caroline had grown up, and they were close to being a caricature family of Hampstead socialists. They lived their politics as if it were a fundamentalist religion, complete with earnest jokes and communal singing. George Orwell had lampooned such people memorably. Angus Wilson had just made his name by publishing a book of short stores, *Such Darling Dodos*, in which they were portrayed as fish out of water in the post-war world. Caroline had already remarked to me that most of her family's friends were like characters in Wilson's book. She also commented on the curiosity of the fact that every time there was a spy scandal the spy turned out to be someone Bobby knew – not only the Cambridge spies that he had been with at university, Guy Burgess and Donald Maclean, but less likely figures such as Klaus Fuchs and Alan Nunn May. When I got to know him better – I stayed with the family in Paris, and saw a little of what went on behind the scenes of his job as one of the top few people in UNESCO – I came to suspect that his never having joined the Communist Party was planned, and that he might have been an agent of influence for the Soviet Union since his Cambridge days. Certainly he would not have behaved differently if he had been, most notably in his choice of organizations to channel resources to, but also in the chess-like way in which he advanced the careers of particular individuals (I met some of them in his home). The Communist Party way of thinking had been ingested by him into his personal outlook, and he would believe whatever the party told him to believe. He once assured me in all seriousness – not knowing that I had special knowledge in the matter – that he knew for a fact, from unimpeachable personal contacts, that Tito's Yugoslavia had become a Fascist state, and that Tito had turned himself into a Fascist dictator. There was something inexpressibly servile, abject, self-abasing, about his attitude to 'the party', as he always referred to it. If it had ordered him to pour the contents of a rubbish bin over himself he would have done so. He did the equivalent of that in some of the beliefs he held. I became not just suspicious of him, I formed a contempt for him. As I have said before, it needs to be remembered that the Russia in whose interests he was behaving like such a lackey was Stalin's.

Bobby referred constantly to working-class people and values, but did not have the remotest idea what these were. He had only foolish notions of how working-class people did in fact live and think, feel, and see things. He did not actually *know* any working-class people, had never met any on equal terms. His ideas about them were the stereotypes and clichés of middle-class thinking. He viewed the workers with dissociated benevolence, as one might look on one's friends' children. His attitudes were – unconsciously, of course – patronizing and authoritarian. He saw working class people as children who needed to be educated, brought on, given a lead by people like himself. They did not understand what was good for them, but Bobby and his friends knew, and were dedicated to leading them in the right direction. He embraced Lenin's notion of a vanguard party, an enlightened elite which, though not elected, had every moral justification for leading and behaving without constraints. He realized perfectly well that the people in whose name all this was being done did not want it and disapproved of it; but he did not care what they thought or wanted. He knew what was good for them. Being children, they would understand and appreciate it when they grew up, and be grateful for it.

His whole mental (and real) world is now, thank God, an almost vanished one. But it existed with great self-confidence, and made itself felt internationally, throughout the first half of my adult life, and I developed a hatred for it not unlike the hatred I felt for Nazism. In many ways the two were, behind their rhetoric, similar. During those early post-war and post-Nazi years Bobby's mind-set was an international phenomenon, and it did immeasurable harm. Whole societies were devastated by it, and many millions of people were murdered because of it.

I never criticized Bobby to Caroline, except when she asked me direct questions. Even then I chose my words carefully. From the incandescent arguments that she and I had been through she knew not only my thoughts about these issues but also my feelings. She shared more and more of my thoughts, but never so many of my feelings. I understood her situation. Bobby was, when all is said and done, her father, and she was devoted to him. There could never have been any question of my turning her against him – I would never have dreamt of trying, and would certainly not have succeeded. But at that time he and I were far and away the two most important men in her life, and she was being pulled between us. It complicated the difficulties that our separation was causing, and did so for me as well as her.

For the rest of my time at Oxford she and I were still in love. As lovers we never finally fell out, never 'broke up'. What happened was that we drifted apart over a longer and indefinite period, in a way that was unforeseen by either of us, and somehow left the friendship between us still in existence.

3

The Oxford Union

On my first day at Oxford I took the cheque for my first term's grant to a bank in the centre of town and opened my first bank account. When they gave me a cheque book they told me I could draw on the money immediately, so I walked a couple of hundred yards to the Oxford Union and wrote my first cheque. It was for life membership of the Union, the best money's-worth I ever got during my four years as an undergraduate. Like most people who got a lot out of Oxford I moved in a number of very different circles; and I was always more interested in people than in institutions; but of the institutions to which I was attached the one that mattered to me most was the Union. I made more friends there than anywhere else, and it became the most important single centre of my social life.

In the facilities the Union offered it was like a traditional London club. Owned and run by its members, it employed a large staff, and contained a generously proportioned bar, restaurant, billiard room, two libraries (one of them the largest lending library in Oxford University) and several rooms for private meetings. When Michael Heseltine became its President in 1955 he turned the extensive cellars into a night club. It was founded in 1825, and acquired most of its buildings in the mid-nineteenth century. They look their age, being of red Victorian brick. Built on the scale of a small college, they enclose three sides of a garden in the very heart of Oxford. Whether an undergraduate belongs to it or not is up to him (and her nowadays) but he has to pay a subscription. In my day only male undergraduates could belong, and about a third of them did: today it is for both sexes, and the proportion of members is higher. Most belong for the bar, and the lending library, and for the cheerful social life that bustles all the time. In the outside world the Union has always been known for its weekly debates – which often get national publicity – and it is true that this is how reputations there are made. But the regular attenders at those debates number only some hundreds out of the membership of thousands.

I was one of the regulars at the debates. In four years I missed only one. They took place every Thursday evening in the high-roofed, purpose-built debating hall that occupied one side of the garden. When packed it held about 600 people. Every week there would be at least two guest speakers who debated against one another, while the remaining speeches came from undergraduates. The guests were usually national figures of some sort; if politicians they would be leading parliamentarians or Cabinet Ministers. Chairing the proceedings from a raised throne at one end of the hall sat the President. Below him, but above everyone else, were the Librarian and the Treasurer; and below them the Secretary, who sat at a table keeping the minutes. These four, elected anew each term, wore white tie and tails. They were the individuals who ran the Union, together with an elected Committee. The half dozen leading speakers – called paper speakers, because their names appeared on the order-paper that was distributed throughout the university – would wear dinner jackets. Everyone else was dressed informally. The procedure for debates was adapted from the House of Commons. As there, the atmosphere was at the same time tense and jocular. The audience had a reputation for being merciless, but was a thrilling one to talk to if you had it with you.

There were two chief motives behind all this. The first was enjoyment of the debates. At their best they were, by student standards, high-class entertainment, which is why so many people went to them who never spoke. The fact that my student generation consisted mostly of ex-servicemen, many of them war veterans, meant that they were more mature in discussion than students usually are, more worldly-wise, more self-confident, more adultly witty; and all this raised the level of the debates. The other motive was to be trained in public speaking. The first time I stood up to make a speech there my whole body burst into a sweat. I felt my underclothes sticking to me all the way down. The notes in my hand shook so much that I laid them on the Secretary's table so that people would be less likely to notice my shaking hands. Three years later I stood on the same spot as a confident speaker, in control of myself and of the audience, having learnt – slowly, through three years – the basic requirements of public speaking, including what mistakes to avoid. I had learnt not only how to construct a speech but also the pitfalls of preparation; and I learnt how to vary a speech in response to the unexpected, how to deal with interruptions and hecklers, how to exploit the rules of procedure, how to hold my own against nationally famous speakers. It was an invaluable part of my education; and only something on the scale of the Oxford Union could have provided it. It was also an excellent training for the House of Commons, and did indeed function as such. When I became an MP, a quarter of a century later, I found myself bumping into people I had known years before at the Oxford Union and not seen since. My first days in the House of Commons were like an Oxford Union reunion.

The best speech I heard an undergraduate make came in the first week of my second term. Forty years later it was described by its maker in his published memoirs as 'a tour de force, a speech packed with wit and anecdote ... It made a big impression, particularly among the freshmen of that year. A few weeks later I was elected President by an enormous majority.' As one of the freshmen referred to I can vouch for the truth of that description. I had never heard anything like it. And my vote was part of Robin Day's enormous majority. There is a new President each term, but for the rest of my time at Oxford I thought of Robin as *the* President, the President of Presidents. He was twenty-six at the time, six feet tall, and more than seventeen stone in weight – a larger-than-life figure in every sense, utterly dominating. He had been in the army in Africa during the war. We all thought he was bound to become a national leader, probably Prime Minister or Foreign Secretary. No one in those days had any thought of television. But he turned out to be the begetter of modern television interviewing. And to the end of his days he was the best of all speech-makers for occasions such as public dinners, anniversaries, openings, weddings, memorial services and the like. There was no one to touch him.

Since I followed in his presidential footsteps, it is worth quoting the description in his memoirs of what it was like to be President of the Union:

> For the eight weeks of his, or her, term of office and for the preceding vacation, the President of the Oxford Union Society enjoys a position of prestige and patronage unique in the University. Indeed he will probably not enjoy such a position again for many a year after he goes down. Like an impresario or business executive, he has a large book-lined office, a vast desk, a private telephone, headed stationery and a hospitality allowance. The President's favours are continually sought by ambitious undergraduates. He decides which undergraduates are called to speak in debates. He chooses the motions for debate and invites the distinguished visitors …

As Robin says at one point in these not-exactly diffident memoirs, scores of undergraduates in each year get first-class honours degrees, and scores get sporting blues, but only three become President of the Union.

It was Robin who invited me to make my first speech, and launched me on my Union career. During the subsequent year, which was his last, he and I became friends, and remained so for the rest of his life. Psychologically, he was one of the most complicated people I have known. Although an exceptionally powerful personality he was never a fulfilled one. His dominant interest all his life was parliament, yet he never became an MP, though with his gifts and personality he could certainly have done so had he persevered. He wanted to, yet he never did. As a natural Tory he should have stood as a Conservative candidate; and he would have risen to Cabinet office, perhaps as one of the nation's law officers (he was a trained barrister). During the years when we knew each other as young men in London, and co-professionals in television, I used to urge this course on him, but he would never take it. His wife got angry with me once for attempting to persuade him – she thought he was earning too much money in television to switch jobs, what with their mortgage and two sons. But he was eventually overtaken, as I warned him he would be, by a feeling that he had wasted his talents and his life. Towards the end he became addled with self-contempt and a sense of failure. That he was nationally famous and financially secure was of no consolation to him then. He grasped pathetically at his knighthood, hoping it would show him to be somebody. But the level of the title did not satisfy him – he thought he ought to be a peer. I have never known anyone more dissatisfied with himself, yet it was his own fault.

After Robin, the best student speaker at the Union was Jeremy Thorpe. Unlike Robin, Jeremy performed like an actor, with theatrical self-projection, dramatic gestures, and a rare gift of mimicry. He and Robin were rivals in the Liberal Club, as well as in the Union (they both became President of both), and could not abide one another. Robin had several aversions: another was Norman St John Stevas. Norman had already been through Cambridge, where he had been President of the Union, and had come to Oxford with the aim of being the first person ever to be President of both Unions. Robin thought that as a graduate of Cambridge Norman had an unfair advantage over Oxford's undergraduates, and set out, successfully, to put a spanner in the works. He did so by a sustained campaign of ridicule and interruption in the debating chamber. Robin was a uniquely accomplished interrupter. When another speaker complained about this during a speech, Robin declared, from his sitting position, 'Some people's speeches are *improved* by interruption.'

Student enmities played a role in later life. When Robin had become the best known television interviewer in the country, and Jeremy was leader of the Liberal Party, and also when Norman was Leader of the House of Commons and a Cabinet Minister, these lifelong antagonisms played a part in their public encounters.

Altogether, the Union was an extraordinary breeding-ground of what is conventionally thought of as worldly success. Of its officers during my four years, five became lords, four of the others knights (some of the lords having also passed through being knights), another a national party leader. Several were Members of Parliament, and one was editor of *The Times*. People's views about what constitutes success have changed since those days, and rightly so; but the fact remains that these were also an exceptionally interesting bunch of characters to be young with. They came together in the Union from all the colleges of the university. No single college could have come anywhere near to matching the Union as a seed-bed of talent or, much more importantly, of friendship. Those who used it every day, or most days, came to know one another well, and lifelong friendships resulted. Some of my closest friendships in life began there – with

Andrew Cuninghame, Oleg Kerensky, Tyrrell Burgess – and other good, warm, lasting friendships too: with Dick Taverne, Robin Day, Ivan Yates, Howard Shuman, John Gilbert, Patrick Mayhew. Paddy Mayhew, who was President the term before me, became my pair for the period of nearly ten years that I spent in the House of Commons.

We vied against one another in elections each term for promotion up the Union ladder. First we tried to get voted on to the committee that decided what books to buy for the library, on which large sums were spent. If successful, we served on that committee for two terms, after which we could not stand for re-election to it. So from there we tried to get ourselves elected to the committee that ran the Union, the Standing Committee. Once on that we could either go straight for the high-jump to one of the four offices of Secretary, Treasurer, Librarian or President, or bide our time by standing for re-election to the Standing Committee. As in a Grand National race, most of the runners failed to complete the course: they fell at one of the fences. These included many who became well known in later life: George Carman and Gerald Kaufman spring to mind; and others had successful careers as MPs and journalists.

In those days canvassing in any form was forbidden in our elections, a prohibition that I do not believe was often broken: quite apart from the disqualification which it invited, it would have been regarded as infra dig. What decided the way votes were cast was the reputation won by individuals in the debating hall. Even so, some outstanding personalities were pipped for the Presidency. This happened interestingly to Dick Taverne, who held all three of the other offices. If he had stood for the Presidency one more time he would have got it, and he knew this, but he decided not to stand. He had hopes of getting a first-class degree, and did not think he had time to do both, because being President was too time-consuming. He got a first in Greats: but I remember finding it unintelligible that someone could prefer doing that to being President of the Union.

Looking back, it seems almost quaint that we valued these baubles so highly, but we did. So had people before us. Roy Jenkins, who was ten years older than me, had an experience like Dick's, though he felt about it as I would have done. He got a first, but missed the Presidency of the Union twice, once by only five votes; and when he was eighty years old he told me that, subjectively, this had been the most crushing disappointment of his whole life, more even than not becoming Prime Minister. He would not, he said, have felt anything like as bad about not getting a first.

I carry with me still the liveliest memories of individual debates and speeches – an indication of how much it all meant to me at the time. Naturally, the best of the visiting speakers were far better than the students. The most dazzling debater in the country was Dick Crossman, a former philosophy don at New College who was now a Labour MP: he could take an opponent's speech and immediately, without preparation, rip it to pieces in brilliant style, with scintillating logic and cruel wit. It was an amazing thing to watch. A practical problem for us was that so many of the best speakers came, as Crossman did, from the Labour left – figures such as Michael Foot, Ian Mikardo, Donald Soper and Barbara Castle (as pretty as paint with her red hair) – that it was difficult to maintain a balance on the other side. The Union's favourite Conservative speaker was Robert Boothby, a heavyweight out of office, and a delinquent character (unknown to us he was the long-term lover of Harold Macmillan's wife, and the real father of one of their children). An uproarious rogue, he was always deliciously indiscreet in private, after the debate, about what was going on in national politics. Also good value was Quintin Hogg, Lord Hailsham to be, who was a former President himself.

There were innumerable people in public life who were former officers of the Union, so much so that those of us who were there felt ourselves to belong to an ongoing tradition. In the debating hall were busts of officers who had become Prime Minister – Gladstone, Salisbury, Asquith. Other politicians were about to continue this tradition: Macmillan and Heath. We who were still there took it for granted that we were part of all this – that the next generation in public life would be us, and then another new generation of Oxford Union people would follow us.

Before each week's debate there would be drinks and dinner with the visiting speakers, and afterwards more drinks in the President's office. In all of this the four officers of the Union were always present, so they became acquainted with many of the most colourful notables of their day – and in doing so would feel themselves to be in touch with their own future. When I took my finals in History a question on the examination paper was why King George V had called on Baldwin, not Curzon, to form a government in 1923. It was not one of the questions I had chosen to answer, but a week after seeing it I met Leo Amery at a Union party, and knew that he had been one of the two people who had advised the king about this. I told him about the degree question, and asked him what the answer was. He told me at fascinating length. A few weeks later, when I was called for my viva (the oral examination), I was asked precisely this question, and was able to provide the history examiners with an authoritative answer straight from the mouth of the primary source. Being active in the Union had plugged me in to living history. Not even our examiners or tutors were in this position; and those of us who ran the Union could not help knowing this, with our weekly off-the-record drinking sessions with Cabinet Ministers and the like.

The social life we enjoyed among ourselves had its fulcrum in the Union's dining room, where we had our own table, the so-called Committee Table. This could seat nine at a pinch, was elliptical in shape, and fitted neatly into the bay window. Most of us would take our lunch there most days. It became the site of an experience that had a lot of significance for me inwardly. When I first joined it, as a newly elected member of the Standing Committee, the other people sitting round the table seemed to me dauntingly, almost intimidatingly clever. They knew so much about politics and current affairs, their conversation moved so quickly, they were so confident, and they were often witty. In particular, they were constantly expressing good insights that I would not have been able to think of for myself. I'm not up to this, I thought, and was chary of joining in the conversation at first. But I got used to it, and slowly lost my inhibitions – and then, after this had been going for a while, was made aware by remarks uttered round the table that *they* thought that *I* was clever. And then I realized that we were all in the same boat. All of us were quite bright, but we were bright in different ways, and each one of us was capable of seeing things, and saying things, that the others were not. So each of us confronted the same situation. It was the exact counterpart of an experience that I had had in my first year, to do with a more purely social kind of self-confidence. When I started going to Oxford parties as a freshman it had seemed to me that everyone in the room was self-confident except me. But then, in one-to-one conversations, the others (especially the girls, but not only they) would confide their shyness to me, and say how they envied me my self-confidence – and I realized that we all felt the same way. Now I was having the same experience again. The fact that each of the others understood things that I did not, and said things that I could not have said, did not mean that they were more intelligent than I was. It meant we were all on a level. The realization made a permanent difference to the way I felt in the company of people whose abilities I did not share.

Some of them were semi-professional already in their relationship to politics: well informed about public policy, cognizant of the law in relation to it, and keeping themselves abreast by studying the daily press, which they discussed enthusiastically. These were people who, it turned out, were going to be politicians or lawyers, or Treasury mandarins, or ambassadors, or political journalists; and already it was as if they had one foot on the first step of their chosen careers. Linking the Union's entrance hall to its main library was a wide corridor which contained all the newspapers and was referred to as the Newspaper Lobby: these people could be found in it at all times of day, absorbed in the broadsheets. They would often greet you by asking you what you thought about the previous day's goings-on in the House of Commons. Some were quite capable of asking what you thought of events in Nigeria, in the same sort of way as they might ask about the cricket scores (which I was less well informed about). This was never my style, and I was never one of them. If I lingered in the Newspaper Lobby it would be to read the music and theatre reviews. In that library I received quite an education, for it was where I habitually browsed outside my own subjects. In its comfortable armchairs I did several years of voracious reading at an age when everything I read made an impression on me and stayed in my mind.

Another part of the Union I frequented on an almost daily basis during my first couple of years was the billiard room (now the bar), with its two full-sized tables. I adored billiards, in a way I have never loved any other game, and I had friends in the billiard room whom I never met elsewhere. Once upon a time the university had awarded a half-blue in billiards, and I seriously thought of trying to get it re-instated, but other preoccupations took me away from the game before I got round to it.

Members of the Union with every kind of interest would congregate in its capacious bar before meals, and then again afterwards. One could spend a full, varied day in the Union, from after breakfast until midnight, with no feeling of monotony or confinement.

Whenever one arrives at a place like Oxford there are recently departed stars who are constantly being referred to but are no longer there, so the newcomer hears them talked about but does not see them. For me at Oxford this was true in particular of three people, two of whom had been President of the Union – Tony Benn and Edward Boyle – and the third its Secretary, Kenneth Tynan. I got to know the first two later, but only after hearing them talked about for years. Of Boyle it was said that, as an undeniably brilliant man who had been given a third-class degree, he had made a third respectable, as against another well-known Union figure of the time who had drained a first of all its kudos. Eventually Boyle was to become Minister of Education. He once confided to me that when he was a Conservative Cabinet Minister there had been a general election in which he had indeed voted but not Conservative, because he had looked round the Cabinet table and thought: 'These people ought not to be running the country.' He and Benn became MPs in the first term of my second year, only a couple of weeks apart; so, one after another, each was 'baby of the House'. This confirmed an assumption widespread in the Union that if you became President you could expect to be in the Commons not long after going down from Oxford. That may have been an illusion I shared.

4

Friends

The closest among the friends I made in the Intelligence Corps who went up to Oxford with me was Richard Sarson. He was at Brasenose College, reading Modern Languages. Before going into the army he had been to school at Wellington, and soon he started introducing me to his old school friends who were now at Oxford. One of these was Christopher Elrington, reading History at University College. Chris became one of the two or three closest friends I made at Oxford: towards him, together with Andrew Cuninghame, and of course Caroline, I felt a kind of love, which I did not towards any of the others. My own closest friend from schooldays, Richard Cavendish, was still doing military service in Hong Kong, and did not arrive in Oxford until the following year. By a double coincidence he went to Brasenose and found that the best friends he made there were Wellingtonians, so before long I was plugged in to two overlapping networks of Wellingtonians and Brasenose men. None of these, so far as I remember, were active members of the Union.

The first friend I made at any of the women's colleges was Marie Naughton, at Lady Margaret Hall. She was never my girlfriend in a physical sense but was a very good friend in every other sense, and has remained so ever since. She and her husband are today the closest friends I have in the United States. Her upbringing had been unusual. Her father, Bill Naughton, had started life as a coal-bagger and lorry driver, with almost no education, and had turned himself into a full-time writer successful enough to give two children a good education and get them to Oxford: Marie and her brother Larry. As a writer, Bill was later to hit the jackpot with *Alfie*, which he wrote successively as a radio play, a stage play, a film, and a novel. The film was one of the two that made Michael Caine a star. The novel sold more than a million copies. Bill ended his days as a tax-exile in the Isle of Man. He was far from being a one-success writer: he wrote two other plays that ran in the West End, and both were turned into films with well-known actors; and he produced hundreds of short stories, some of them first-rate. His two volumes of autobiography were published by Oxford University Press. I came to know him quite well, and found him exhilaratingly different from other people. He was self-absorbed and yet enjoyable to talk to – disconcertingly pungent. His commitment to writing was total, but he felt no great sense of responsibility for anything else, or indeed anybody else. In a way he was a monster, but a monster one enjoyed. Marie was devoted to him. One always had to be careful how one criticized him to her.

Starting with Marie in my first term, Lady Margaret Hall was to provide me with the closest and most lasting women friends I made at the university: Caroline, Robin Burke (to whom this book is dedicated), Paddy Fullerton, and Philippa Copley-Smith. For my first two years I lived in Keble College, and the two colleges were at diagonally opposite corners of the university's park. The walk across the park from one to the other is a walk I have done scores of times. If I were an eccentric millionaire I would leave LMH money, for I am lastingly grateful to it for its enrichment of my life.

Paddy Fullerton, who was at LMH studying to be a doctor, was Richard Sarson's girlfriend for a long time, and that meant I saw quite a lot of her. The two of them were committed enough to announce their engagement in *The Times*, but I do not believe they ever published a retraction. Several years later – after all of us had gone down from the university, and she and Richard had broken up – she became my girlfriend; and after that we remained good friends for the rest of her life. It was uncommon then for women to have senior careers, but she made one as a hospital consultant, first at the country's leading hospital for neurological diseases, then at the Middlesex Hospital. Partly because of this she married late, and in her forties had two sons. I made a speech at her wedding. One of the things nearly all her friends remember her for is that she gave parties that lasted through a long weekend during which a complete recording of Wagner's *Ring* would be played, with long, comfortable gaps for meals, drinks, and walks on Hampstead Heath. Guests would drop in and out at their leisure, perhaps for only one of the operas, even for just a single act. As a combination of several of life's most enjoyable and worthwhile pleasures they were unforgettable.

Another woman I got to know at Oxford who, unsuspected by me at the time, was to become my girlfriend in later years was Philippa Copley-Smith. She was short, blonde, curvaceous, luscious, and the girlfriend of a man called Freddy Noad. He was a charming man, witty and sensitive. He was later to spend his life playing and teaching the guitar in California, where he acquired his own television programmes for that purpose, and edited a lot of published music for the instrument. He and Richard Cavendish, together with two other Brasenose friends, had moved out of their college into a house in North Oxford, and it was there that I met Philippa. It seems strange to me now that I did not really like her at that time. I saw her as tantrummy, spoiled. She was probably the university's best-known sexpot, and seemed to me too used to having her own way, with men falling over themselves to get at her. She treated them, I thought, in a capricious, self-indulgent way. Perhaps that was all true and she grew out of it. She and I were not to come together until a long time afterwards, in our middle thirties, and by that time she was more mature altogether – still very attractive, but with an innocent heart and a surprisingly unselfish nature. Our relationship then was enriched by the fact that we had known one another all those years, and shared many friends.

It is a tragic fact that, of the women I have written about so far, three were to die prematurely of cancer: Philippa at thirty-nine, Caroline at fifty-nine, and Paddy at sixty-eight. I suspect that nearly all of us, when young, assume that we and our friends are going to live to be old; but this is not what happens. At least half the people I got to know well at Oxford died before reaching old age, some while still young. But of course, since none of us knew this was going to happen, it could play no part in the way we then saw one another.

Even while I was still at Oxford my friendships tended to be weeded out by time. Perhaps this was inevitable. During my first year a lot of them were superficial, either party-based or Randolph-based. Some of these I became attached to, and retained for several years. People can be interesting for all kinds of reasons. But quite a lot of friendships are exhaustible, in the way some works of art are: you go on being interested in them up to a certain point in time, and then you realize, perhaps suddenly and with surprise, that you have reached the end of what is there for you – whereupon your interest fades, involuntarily. In the case of friends this can be accompanied by guilt; but the reaction is an honest one, and cannot be wished away.

If the lightweight but entertaining world of the Randolph had a pre-eminent personality it was Stanley Parker. He was thirty-five, Australian, and unconnected with the university. Podgy but handsome, he earned his living, if he did, as a freelance writer and artist, mostly to do with the theatre. What drove his life was that he was star-struck, and he used his skills as a portraitist to meet star actors and actresses, whom he then cultivated. He had come to live in Oxford in 1942 with his mother and his brother Leslie, a photographer – I think it was to get away from the bombing of London. He could never bear to be alone, and was always in search of a party. Rampantly homosexual, outrageously camp, effortlessly funny, an endless stream of hilarious talk gushed from him with inexhaustible energy. The year before I came up, Ken Tynan – a close friend of his, and one whose life was also dominated by being star-struck – published a profile of him in an undergraduate magazine which he reprinted in at least two subsequent books. He knew Stanley so much better than I did that I can leave the rest of the description to him. 'Stanley is the Vulgar One, the Big Imp, a laughing Buddha sculpted in lava; a Savoy Grill Falstaff; a sophisticated Billy Bunter ... in Oxford he has the loony unexpectedness of a giant panda at the Algonquin ... Observe the quick fastidious step, hips held high, shoulders almost in flight ... his finest gift is talk. He is the funniest talker I have ever heard ... as a boulevardier he is unique in Oxford, perhaps in England ... he can make the Randolph bar at midday seem as innocent and sunlit and sensual as Hieronymus Bosch's Garden of Delights.'

Stanley must have been at half the parties I went to, but I was never one of his special friends. To be that you had to be high camp, and at least bisexual. But he could dominate a room, and often dominated rooms I was in.

The Randolph friend I saw most of, away from the hotel and parties, was David Ramkeesoon, who was reading PPE at St Peter's Hall. An Indian but not from India, he came from the Indian minority in Trinidad. This was a small community in which everybody knew everybody else, so when Vidia Naipaul arrived from it in Oxford the following year I got to know him too. It could never have entered my head then that Vidia would one day win the Nobel Prize for Literature. Although he was highly intelligent he was also highly strung, to the point of near-breakdown, and I feared that a damaged life was lying in wait for

73

him. The strength of mind and character with which he fought against his demons, and overcame them, is not unconnected with his development as a writer of international stature.

David was a good-looking, naturally elegant young man with a carefree attitude to life. He had a beautiful English girlfriend who was known to us all as V, and for reasons I cannot recall he asked me to organize a twenty-first birthday party for her in London. I did, and during my years at Oxford it was the biggest private party I ever organized – apart, that is, from more formal and grand affairs at the Union. The party was in Chelsea, and went on for three days and nights. Forever associated with it in my mind is a memory of waking up on the floor one morning to the sound of *I'm In The Mood For Love* played on the saxophone by Freddy Gardner. To this day that record almost paralyses me with nostalgia for that whole dimension of my young life.

V had a sister who was hopelessly in love with a young man who treated her badly while exploiting her affection for him. He lived perpetually in Oxford while striving unsuccessfully to get into the university. His Russian family lived in Paris, and there he was heir to a fortune. He was trilingual in Russian, French and English, but could never pass Oxford's entrance examination to study these languages. While we were still at Oxford his father died, and he had to return to Paris. There he lived in luxury. Attractive Parisian women hurled themselves at him in the hope of becoming his wife, and he exploited them too. Finally he decided he wanted to marry and have children. But in Paris he knew not a single woman who, he could be sure, was interested in him for himself rather than his money. After much thought, he made the trip to Oxford and asked – begged – V's sister to marry him. She refused. She said he did not want her for herself.

A source of enduring friendships was the house, 3 St John Street, where I lived when I moved out of college. Being there at all was a stroke of luck. I had arranged to move in to digs in the

High Street at the end of my second year; but at the last moment the existing occupant decided to stay on, and the arrangement fell through. By that stage desirable digs, for which there was always great competition, had all been taken up. Only with great difficulty did I find somewhere else. I booked it for the following term, and left a deposit. However, when I returned to Oxford next term I found I had been gazumped. A student had arrived two months before from South Africa and offered to take the room at a higher rent provided he could move in straight away and stay in it throughout all vacations. The landlady let him have it. Red with embarrassment, she thrust my deposit back into my hand on her doorstep. And there I was in Oxford, the term having begun, and I had no roof over my head even for that night. In desperation I accepted a room in St John Street in the house of a sinister couple that no one wanted to live with. Having reached an agreement with them I was coming away from their house in the deepest of depressions, about to begin the process of moving in, when I bumped into a casual friend, Guy Barnett, emerging from the door of number 3. I poured my woes out to him – whereupon he told me that his landlady was currently in a distressed state because she had received a telegram that morning telling her that one of her students would not be coming back. He was Michael Levey, who had just been offered his first job at the National Gallery, of which he was to become head. He had decided to take the job rather than continue at Oxford. After a quick discussion, Guy and I went back into the house together, found the landlady, and within minutes I had agreed to take Michael's room.

There then followed one of the most humiliating scenes of my student life. Mistakenly, I felt too embarrassed to do what I ought to have done and go straight back to the sinister couple, just up the road, and withdraw the agreement I had entered into with them. Instead (shamefully) I thought I would simply not show up there again. I went to Keble, piled all my worldly goods on to a large trolley belonging to the college, and trundled it across St Giles towards my new digs. As I wheeled it round the corner of Wellington Square into St John Street there – to my horror – stood the sinister man in his open doorway between me and number 3. When he saw me coming he naturally assumed I was bringing my things to his house. Instead, I pushed the trolley straight past him, looking fixedly ahead, overwhelmed with embarrassment, simply not knowing what to say. It is a moment I shall never forget. I then felt I had no alternative but to go back and explain. I tried to talk as if this was my first opportunity to tell him, because what had occurred had been so unexpected and so sudden. But he saw perfectly well what the truth was, and he was very nasty to me about it.

However, living at 3 St John Street turned out to be one of the best things that happened to me in all the time I was at Oxford. The digs were so good they were famous, and I spent three years in them. The house was attractive Georgian, only a hundred yards from the Randolph – fewer from the Playhouse Theatre. The landlady, Mrs Slay, was a characterful woman who took pride in her house, not least in her cooking. She furnished the rooms with an eye to colour and style as well as comfort, and served excellent meals. We had a cooked breakfast, which five of us ate together while still in our pyjamas and dressing gowns. Separate teas were set out on trays in the afternoons for whoever asked for them, and for their guests too. And we ate Sunday lunch together. Mrs Slay's roast potatoes are to this day the best I have tasted (she peeled the potatoes the day before and left them soaking in water overnight). For all this, plus the servicing of our rooms, she charged us three and a half pounds a week. (She was at the top end of the market.) Her husband, Wilfred, was a travelling salesman for one of the most popular marmalades of the day, Chunky, and its name had become his nickname. Their only child Ashley was named after the character Ashley Wilkes in *Gone With The Wind*, played in the film by Leslie Howard, with whom Mrs Slay had fallen in love.

Several of the people I met in that house became enduring friends. Before I moved in, Guy Barnett and I had been little more than friendly acquaintances, but living together brought us close. Years later, when he married, I was his best man; and we were in the House of Commons together as Labour MPs. Another lasting friend was Alan Stewart: years later I became godfather to his son Alexander, while Alan himself became air-pilot to the King of Morocco. Yet another friend was Michael Donelan, an austere Catholic intellectual of right-wing views – different from me in every way, and therefore especially rewarding to argue with. He was to have a career in International Relations at the London School of Economics. But most important of all was a young woman from Lady Margaret Hall whose parents lived overseas, and who came to lodge with us during vacations (when there was always at least one empty room): Robin Burke. She was to be a lifelong and intimate friend. All these people came into my life through 3 St John Street. When I went down from Oxford I passed my digs on to Tyrrell Burgess, who was to become President of the Union a year after me, and he too became a lifelong friend.

My memories of Oxford have 3 St John Street as the reference point from which movement begins: *out of the front door and turn right for Keble or Lady Margaret Hall, but turn left, and then left again, for the Randolph and the Union – or left and then right for Worcester College.* Worcester was the college of the man who, along with Chris Elrington, was my closest man-friend, and was only a couple of hundred yards away. He was Andrew Cuninghame, the President of the Union two terms after me. The fundamental thing he and I had in common was that we were enjoyers rather than moralists. We were more concerned to live life to the full than to make the world a better place, and shared an overflowing love of music, women and social life as well as a passionate interest in politics. We expanded each other's perceptions of all these things: it was from Andrew that I first heard of Vivaldi, and in his room that I first heard *The Four Seasons*. His sense of humour was different from mine, but it appealed to me enormously: predominantly visual, with an understated yet semi-clowning use of body language. Some of his visual jokes still have a dreamlike vividness in my mind's eye. He was studying Philosophy, Politics and Economics, and wanted us to go for long walks together in which we discussed problems in those subjects. This was not so much a way of learning anything as a way of clearing our minds, but we also learnt a lot from each other. He moved in to digs in St John Street. But I continued the habit I had formed of going to Worcester whenever I suffered from writer's (or reader's) block. I would get up from my desk, walk the short distance to Worcester, walk round the lake and the playing fields inside the college, and then return to my desk. I do it still, occasionally, from an address in Oxford that is much farther away. I must have done that walk over a hundred times.

When Andrew was still at school his father had died and left him a baronetcy, though not much else. His mother married again, a Swedish diplomat called Jan Killander, but she went on calling herself Lady Cuninghame. She was to become an important figure in my life a few years later. The first time I met her was when she visited Oxford to see Andrew: when she took him out to lunch she took me too. We clicked. She was not at all conventional for a middle-aged woman of her class and period. She had a lewd, raunchy interest in sex which she did not dissemble. She was like Lady Bracknell talking the dialogue of a sex comedy. Andrew and she had a wonderful relationship, a real closeness. I had never met anyone like her and was immensely entertained. Soon after that lunch, when Andrew and I were invited as a two-man debating team to speak at University College London, she asked us to stay with her in London for a couple of nights. From then on she invited me to things with or without Andrew. When I went down from Oxford my first job was in Sweden, and there I was a house guest of hers near Stockholm. Soon after that, appallingly, Andrew contracted Hodgkin's Disease, and died while still in his twenties. From then onwards Nancy, his mother, tried to treat me as a surrogate son, and for many years I was a semi-detached member of the family. But it goes without saying that when Andrew and I were close friends at Oxford all this lay in an unknowable future.

His early death was a horrific blow. I loved him, and his memory remains a presence for me. After Oxford he went into the Foreign Office, and hoped eventually to become a Conservative MP. This caused me to miss him especially when I entered the House of Commons myself. It seems absurdly self-centred to complain on one's own behalf about the death of friends, but I was unlucky when young to experience the premature death of some of my closest.

The other male friend I had at Oxford about whom I felt as strongly as I did about Andrew was Chris Elrington, but there was little about that relationship that can be described. It was a sitting-around-and-talking relationship. We had no great special interest in common: not music, not theatre, not philosophical ideas, which Chris distrusted – and certainly not politics, which he referred to with indifference or disdain. We were both reading History, and he loved that. We would argue with strident intensity about it – and every other subject under the sun – to the annoyance of others.

Unusually, Chris got married while still an undergraduate. For this he needed his college's permission – not permission to marry, of course, but to stay on as an undergraduate. I did not know any other example of this, though I heard of some among the ex-service men. Chris and his new wife Jean moved in to a flat to which I was a frequent visitor. Given that they were poor themselves, I was impressed by how generously they fed their friends. Chris left Oxford a year earlier than I did, and became a professional historian, his specialism being local history. He devoted most of his career to the Victoria County History, a detailed local history down to the level of every hamlet and significant old building in Britain. He started on it as a legman in Gloucestershire and rose to become Editor of the whole, and a Professor in the University of London. However, our friendship was to come adrift when we were still young. But that did not happen until after Oxford.

There was an unmistakably private-life character to my friendship with the Elringtons, and with people like Richard Sarson, Richard Cavendish and their friends, in that there was no public dimension to it at all. Our relationships were entirely a matter for us personally, and had nothing to do with anyone else, or with any organization. This was in contrast to my friendships with Caroline and Andrew, and with other people at the Union, or in the political clubs, and in the magazines. Although my one-to-one relationships with those went every bit as deep, and sometimes deeper, there was also a public-life dimension. Both could be contrasted with the purely social-chat-over-a-drink character of the friendships I formed at parties, or in the Randolph. Each of the three groups was viewed disparagingly by the others. The public-life people were seen by the others as over-earnest, playing at being grown-up, taking themselves too seriously, and sometimes being boring as a result. The Randolph or party people were seen by the others as lightweights, irresponsibles, barflies. The private-life people were seen as well-intentioned but not sufficiently interesting – the sort of people we all had as relations. I found a part of my happiness and fulfilment with each of them, and lived with each on its own terms. Each gave me something I needed. And they too accepted me on their own terms, though I found that their incomprehension of one another would extend to me whenever I crossed a borderline. For instance, the Randolph people were dumbstruck when I became President of the Union: it was incomprehensible to them that one of *them* could do that. They took it for granted that I must in some way have bamboozled the people at the Union.

For a long time I made a conscious effort to integrate the friendships from my different worlds. My attempts to do this went on for many years after I left university. They never succeeded. The different sorts of people had simply not enough interest in one another – and, in the end, not enough time for one another. So I have always lived simultaneously in different worlds, not from choice but with the deepest regret, because those worlds themselves resisted all attempts to integrate them. One consequence of this has been that wherever my feet have led me since leaving university I have met people I knew at Oxford – or at least people I remember from Oxford, who remember me. This is true not only of the worlds in which I have been professionally active, such as literature, politics, the media, academic life, and criticism of the arts, but also those in which I have been a mere guest or visitor, such as the countryside, industry, the City, diplomacy, and foreign countries. To people who did not go to Oxford this sort of thing sometimes looks as if there is some sort of freemasonry, a network that promotes its own, but this is not so. As far as personal ability is concerned, institutions like Oxford can turn out only what they take in. At least a third of the ablest students in every generation used to go to Oxford (and a third to Cambridge, and the remaining third to other universities), so inevitably Oxford graduates were common in the upper reaches of the professions. It was not nepotism, it was pre-selection. And my being subsequently in the same professions and institutions encouraged friendships that had already had beginnings at Oxford.

Some of the longest and closest friendships of my life had only the scrappiest beginnings at Oxford. For instance, my friendship with Oleg Kerensky. He was a year ahead of me, someone I saw around in the Union and heard speak in debates, but met only in groups. The first time we exchanged words directly he was rude to me. Having been asked by the student magazine *Isis* to report a lunch meeting of the Labour Club which was to be addressed by G. D. H. Cole I arrived with my lunch ticket and press accreditation, and introduced myself to the Chairman of the meeting, who was Oleg. He told me I could not report the meeting. He wanted Cole to talk as indiscreetly as possible, and had already encouraged him to that effect. I said that if Cole uttered anything indiscreet it would be impossible to keep it a secret with so many people present, so I refused to accept the embargo. Oleg swore at me fiercely and tried to prevent my getting a seat at any of the tables. But I managed to nab one and, short of having me physically thrown out, there was nothing he could do about it. He was exceedingly angry. That was the only one-to-one exchange that passed between us as undergraduates. So I cannot say we were friends at Oxford, yet we had met there. This meant that when we met again in the outside world we knew one another, and greeted each other, and talked. And in London, in our late twenties, we became good friends. It was a friendship that never stopped growing for the rest of our lives. By the time he died in his sixties I was warmly attached to him.

Oleg was the closest friend I have ever had who was a homosexual. It was he who opened my eyes to the realities of that whole world and educated me about its ways. Eventually I wrote a book on the subject, *One In Twenty*, which was a plea for tolerance; and it was dedicated to him – though not by name, for his sexual activities were still illegal. He was also the only person I have ever known who had a greater passion than I have for attending the performing arts. This was really the bond between us. Both of us went most nights to a theatre, concert, opera or live performance of some kind – he even more than I. He knew more than I did about the performers and the gossip. I was always interested to hear all this but never went to any effort to find it out. We would often go to performances together; and when we went separately to anything special we would ring each other up afterwards for an exchange of views. His speciality was my blind spot, ballet. He wrote books about it, and was ballet critic of the *Daily Mail*, the *New Statesman* and the *International Herald Tribune*. He was gargantuanly promiscuous. To a greater extent than with anyone else I have known, his life was organized round his sex life. This led him eventually to leave England and make his home in New York, in Greenwich Village. I visited him there whenever I was in that part of America; and when the New York theatre started having matinees on Sundays as well as Saturdays we would sometimes go to four plays together in a weekend. He became HIV-positive, but it was cancer that killed him – though most of his friends kept saying he had died of AIDS. After he knew he was HIV-positive he hoarded a lethal dose of morphine. When, unexpectedly, cancer brought him to the point where he judged he wanted to use it, he telephoned me to tell me so and say goodbye. It was among the most harrowing conversations I have ever had.

Someone I saw even less of at Oxford but later became almost as long-lasting a friend – and who, again, would probably not have done so but for the Oxford connection – was Bernard Williams. He was two years ahead of me at Oxford, and by the time I arrived had gained a reputation for being hypernaturally brilliant. Not only were other students in awe of him, his tutors were too. They thought he might become the next great philosopher – the next Wittgenstein, so to speak. Although not a member of the Union he was invited to make a speech there in my first year, as if he were a distinguished visitor from outside the university. He married the outstanding woman of his year, Shirley Catlin, whereupon she became Shirley Williams. He and I were not to be brought together until later in our twenties, in London, by people we knew in common. We shared involvements in philosophy, Labour Party politics and opera. As with Oleg, the friendship became stronger as the years passed, and reached a high point in middle age. Also like Oleg, Bernard was to die of cancer after an unusually full life. He had one of the highest IQs I have ever known, and did indeed become a professional philosopher; but his achievement in that role was not up to the level of his promise or his intelligence. It was my opinion that his approach to philosophy was flawed – though in fairness I should say he thought the same about me. Although I regarded him as the embodiment of what was wrong with academic philosophy, and he regarded me as uncomprehending of the work produced by himself and those of his colleagues he most admired, our friendship was a genuine one, and we hugely enjoyed one another's company. Separately from that, we were in Isaiah Berlin's inner circle, and that itself was a powerful magnetic field (and yet again, incidentally, an Oxford-centred pattern of friendships, though of a different character).

There is a magic about those friendships that started at university which it is rare for other friendships to equal. Individuals are choosing one another freely for the first time in their lives. They are in their earliest adult years, and before that their closest relationships have been with members of their own families, and their neighbours, and unchosen individuals forced on them at school (and also, in my generation, in the army). Now, at long last, they are grown up and independent, living away from those things, and free to choose for themselves whom they associate with. A university provides them with a large pool of people to choose from, people of their own age, already pre-selected for intelligence or other interesting characteristics. Most importantly, none of them have the responsibilities of job or family, so they have endless time to devote to one another. For most of them, all these factors will never come together again. And all this happens at the most impressionable time of their adult lives.

It is common for people to feel that the most valuable and important thing about being at a place like Oxford is the making of friendships that have these qualities. This is itself an invaluable contribution to their personal development, and as such it should be seen as part of their education. The life I have lived since Oxford would not have been possible if I had not been there, not only because of other considerations but because it would have been fundamentally different in this crucial matter of my closest personal relationships. This being so, if I consider also the intellectual development I went through there, I am tempted to say that going to Oxford was the most significant happening of my life.

5

Writers

All the larger clubs and societies in the university had a member in each college who acted as the club's representative. During the first few days of each term he would visit his fellow students in their rooms and try to get them to join, for a small subscription. He had with him folded membership cards that contained the printed programme of the club's activities for the forthcoming term, and showing this was his sales pitch. Thus even freshmen were immediately made aware of the full range of what was on offer, and could make their choices. At the beginning of my first term I was attracted by the English Club, with its programme of talks by well-known writers, and also by the political clubs, with their roster of national politicians; and in my first week I started going to their meetings. I also went in my first week to the Union debate.

Soon I was meeting some of the leading novelists of the day: Elizabeth Bowen, Joyce Cary, Pamela Hansford Johnson. I remember having feelings of 'Gosh, can this really be me?' when I found myself in a three-way conversation with Elizabeth Bowen and Lord David Cecil about Jane Austen, on whom Cecil had published a book. Joyce Cary lived a few doors away from my college, and I would bump into him in the street. A thing he said that I have never forgotten was: 'People often ask me who I'm writing for. The only person a writer can possibly write for is himself. All you can do is work at something till you think you've got it as good as you can get it. When you can't see any more ways of making it better it's finished. But you've got only your own judgement to go on. All you can do is get it so that it seems right to *you*.' Something he said that surprised me was that he did not write his novels sequentially: he might start work on a book by writing a scene that occurs in the middle, and then write a passage that comes near the end. He worked, he said, over the whole surface of a book simultaneously, in the way a painter works on a picture. Even in the course of a single day he might work on widely separated parts of a book.

Writers I heard speak in the flesh were continually saying things that surprised me. At a panel discussion at the Poetry Society, C. Day Lewis remarked that he seldom thought about his own past work. While he was writing something he was totally absorbed by it, and usually regarded it as the best thing he had ever done; but as soon as he finished it he moved on to the next thing, and became equally absorbed in that. So he almost never thought back to his earlier work. I was astounded by this. How can it be, I thought, that a famous poet does not think about his own *oeuvre*? Now, as a writer myself, I find that what he said is true of me; and I suspect it is true of many if not most full-time writers.

I did, it must be confessed, have a disillusioning experience as regards C. Day Lewis's involvement with his own work. A new volume of his appeared, and I, full of enthusiasm, bought it on publication day and devoured it immediately. The next Sunday a rave review by Harold Nicolson appeared in *The Observer*, containing quotations from the poems, and I happened to notice that one of the quotations was incorrect. I checked with my copy, and indeed it was. I put the newspaper aside to go to a pre-lunch drinks party at Wadham College – and there at the party was C. Day Lewis. I congratulated him on his book, and on the rave review, which he had just read. I remarked what a pity it was that the review had misquoted him. He denied that it had. I reminded him of his own line, and then of the reviewer's misquotation. He insisted *No*, what the reviewer said was what he had written. It was I, he said, who was misremembering. I was taken aback by this, because I had checked, so I knew I was right. As an undergraduate I did not have the self-confidence to persist in contradicting a distinguished writer about his own work, especially in front of other people (I might have done so had we been alone together), so I said no more. In case I was suffering from a mental aberration I re-checked as soon as I got home, and I had been right. So C. Day Lewis did not know his own newly-published poetry. This gave me serious doubts about the authenticity of the work he was publishing then, his later work. But I still think that the earlier work includes outstandingly beautiful poems, and is underrated.

A well-known writer who surprised me in a different way was the novelist C. P. Snow (who became Pamela Hansford Johnson's husband) when he said that a writer did not need a first-class mind to be a great novelist, and, what is more, scarcely any of the great novelists did have first-class minds. Only one of the great English novelists of the nineteenth century, he said, possessed the level of intellectual ability required to be an Oxford don, and that was George Eliot: not Dickens, not Trollope, not Thackeray, not Jane Austen, none of the Brontës. There was nothing defensive or self-justificatory about his opinion because he had been a Cambridge don, and had the kind of mind that he said was not required. Today, now that I have a better understanding of the fact that intelligence is multi-track, I am sure he was right, but at that time it came to me as a revelation, difficult to accept.

Another thing I remember Snow saying was that the claim made for writers like Henry James and Virginia Woolf – and, in a different way, James Joyce – that they render human experience with unprecedented exactitude and subtlety is false, and false in a crass way, because we experience things in nothing like the way they represent us as doing. Their writing is untrue to reality of any kind, he said.

As a would-be writer I was fascinated to hear what the leading practitioners of the day had to say about their craft. Even in that respect, I discovered, I was part of a living tradition. A best-selling popular novelist called Norman Collins told me that when he was my age he had met Arnold Bennett and asked his advice. Bennett told him: 'Write something every day. However little it is, write something every day. After a year, or whatever, you'll find you've got a book-length manuscript. Now you've got something you can really work on. You can then get down to the serious business of turning it into a book.' Collins said he had followed this advice with great profit ever since, and strongly urged it on me.

At the meetings of the English Club there were lively discussions in which the brighter students talked as if the leading current writers were people I had not read, such as Ernest Hemingway and Graham Greene. At school I had read several novels by D. H. Lawrence and Aldous Huxley, and all those of E. M. Forster, and I was still thinking of these as the most 'modern' of the classics. Huxley and Forster were still alive then, and were to remain so for some years. But now I realized I was a generation behind: Graham Greene was already in his mid-forties, while Hemingway had entered his fifties. It was time I caught up. I started reading their novels, and those of their contemporaries, not least the novelists I was meeting and talking to. My engagement with contemporary fiction took a long leap in a short time.

Among my undergraduate contemporaries, many were to write and publish novels after leaving university, but I can think of none who did so while I was there, except for one cheap-thriller-writer. Poetry was a different matter. The university teemed with poets, publishing in little magazines on every side. Surprisingly many of them were subsequently to achieve wider reputations. In my own college there was Geoffrey Hill, who is now regarded by some leading critics (for instance Christopher Ricks) as the best living English poet. Al Alvarez, Edward Lucie-Smith, Anthony Thwaite and Alan Brownjohn all became well known. Jenny Joseph and Martin Seymour-Smith acquired reputations within, if not outside, literary circles. The focal organization of these and other Oxford poets was not the English Club but the Poetry Society, whose meetings I attended. These could be riotous, unlike the decorous meetings of the English Club. The role model for many of the young poets was Dylan Thomas, a genius who was currently drinking himself to death in public while still in his thirties. That, they thought, was how to be a poet. They came to meetings staggering and shouting. The Chairman, too, could well be drunk, especially if he was Martin Seymour-Smith. Semi-uproar was a common state for a meeting of the Poetry Society. And a good time was had by all.

The first reporting assignment I ever had was of a meeting of the Poetry Society. Robert Robinson, Editor of *Isis* in my first summer term, had advertised for freshmen who wanted to try their hand at reporting. He interviewed me and asked me to cover a meeting to be addressed by George Barker. This poet, still in his thirties, had a reputation with the young that was second only to that of Dylan Thomas. He arrived drunk, and gave a marvellously drunken performance. The problem for me as a reporter was how to convey this without giving grounds for a libel suit. My report had to be brief, too. Bob Robinson liked it, and the story it told attracted attention, so it launched me as a writer for undergraduate magazines.

In the same year, 1950, an anthology of poems by undergraduates was published in London by The Fortune Press under the title *Poetry from Oxford*. It contained a one-page extract from a longer poem of mine, and the comment this received was favourable. Several people asked me: 'Why didn't you publish the whole poem?' In fact I had sent the whole poem to the editor, but he said it was too long (four pages) for the book. It was he who had decided on the extract, which I did not care for. But the poem would have been too long for any magazine. My only chance of getting it published, I thought, was as part of a volume of my own. This gave me the idea of sending a couple of dozen poems to The Fortune Press to be published as a book. I knew I was aiming high – it was they who had published the first volumes of Dylan Thomas and Philip Larkin – but now they had published a piece by me I thought they were worth a try.

To my surprise my book was accepted. The publisher said he would make a loss on it, so his conditions were that there was to be no royalty, and that I must undertake to purchase £25 worth of copies. I agreed. I cannot remember what the book sold for, but *Poetry from Oxford* had been priced at six shillings, so my guess is that I bought 100 copies of my own book at trade rates. It came out in 1951 with the title *Crucifixion and other poems*. All the poems had been written during my teens, before I came to Oxford, and they contained a lot more promise than achievement. I was still getting better, though, publishing better poems in Oxford magazines. But after leaving the university I published no poems at all (with one exception). However, I continued to write poetry – until, to quote Philip Larkin, 'I did not give poetry up, poetry gave me up.' My unpublished poems are certainly better than my published ones, and may be published one day.

Crucifixion came out halfway through my time as an undergraduate. What made the strongest impression on my fellow-students was not anything to do with the quality of the poems but the fact that the book had been published at all – and by the publishers who had made Dylan Thomas famous. Even would-be poets were impressed. I was more like Dylan Thomas than their getting drunk was. The book was prominently displayed in Blackwell's. Even non-poetry people in Oxford got to hear of it. I believe I was the only undergraduate of my generation to have a book of poems published. The upshot was that I came to be thought of as a poet, even in circles outside the literary ones. For instance Shirley Williams has told me that the first time she heard of me was as a poet, and that she went on thinking of me as a poet for years. But the truth is, I thought of myself as a poet. I wanted to write books as well, and go into politics, but the three aims seemed to me compatible. And I certainly thought the most worthwhile of them was to be a good poet.

Although this was my situation, I did not think of myself as an *Oxford* poet, any more than I subsequently thought of myself as an Oxford philosopher. I looked on the Oxford poets as a gang. They were competitive with one another, responding all the time to one another's doings, measuring themselves against one another, so that what each was doing could be understood only with reference to what the others were doing. I have never had this sort of mentality. I tend to go my own way and do my own thing without (usually) feeling myself to be part of a group or in competition with anyone. I have encountered such gangs, or packs, in every one of the worlds in which I have moved, not only poetry and philosophy but also politics, broadcasting, the world of books, academic life, music criticism – they are everywhere. Even some good people go along with them. I never have. People who do often say they have to if they are to get anywhere, but I have never found this. On the contrary, not doing so makes it easier to do what you want to do.

When a man called Anthony Lejeune became President of the English Club he invited me to be its Secretary. The two of us would meet visiting speakers off the train and take them to the Golden Cross Hotel in an old coaching yard in the centre of Oxford. Having made them comfortably installed, we would give them dinner there, then take them to the meeting, which was usually at Lady Margaret Hall. Anthony would chair the meeting, after which he would accompany the speaker back to the hotel, invite him to have a drink before going to bed, and sit up with him for as long as he wanted. I was to do the same the following term. Since Anthony's mother, C. A. Lejeune, was famous as the film critic of *The Observer*, she was one of the speakers he invited, to discuss writing about films. I did not care for her – at the meeting she put Anthony down in front of the audience as if he were a child. In any case, I thought her not a good film critic like Dilys Powell of *The Sunday Times*. For more than a generation, those two women dominated English film criticism, in the same sort of way as their contemporaries Agatha Christie and Dorothy L. Sayers dominated English crime fiction.

The leading book reviewer on *The Observer* was Philip Toynbee, so we had him too, discussing book reviewing. He spent his entire talk trying, and failing, to light the same cigarette while he was talking. His audience became hypnotised by this process. He would put the unlit cigarette into his mouth, talk round it for a bit, take it out and wave it about, put it back, take it out, put it down, take out a box of matches, put the box down, pick it up again, take out a match … He lit several matches and held them away from his face while the words flowed, until the flames burned down to his fingernails and he had to shake them out, still talking and still not lighting the cigarette. His voice, and the content of what he was saying, were decisive and to the point, unlike his behaviour. This spectacle went on for three quarters of an hour. Only after he had finished his talk did he light his cigarette, and the audience doubled its applause. I watched the whole thing with such intensity and incredulity that my visual memory of it is still vivid. Of what he said I remember only the scorn with which he dismissed Somerset Maugham, whom I enjoyed reading and whom he regarded as so bad as to be beneath discussion. In one of Maugham's novels, said Toynbee (I think it was *The Razor's Edge*), he writes of a character that 'she was exquisitely gowned.' 'I *ask* you,' he said, shrivelling his face up as if he had bitten into a lemon and then had its acid juices trickling into his voice; '*exquisitely gowned.*' He shuddered and squirmed. I was so struck by this – my admiration for Maugham as a literary craftsman was, if anything, greater than my enjoyment of his books – that I looked up the passage afterwards, and found that Toynbee had misrepresented it. The phrase describes one character as seen through the eyes of another, and its use by the author is distanced and ironic. But Toynbee's treatment of Maugham was in keeping with that of the literary establishment of his time.

I succeeded Anthony Lejeune as President of the Oxford University English Club, and so became the one who chose the speakers, telephoned them at their homes to invite them, and then sat up drinking with them in the Golden Cross. Compton Mackenzie was the embodiment of charm. His conversation was easy, amusing and delightful, while being almost wholly without substance. This came to be my opinion of his writings also. I saw quite a lot of him in subsequent years, but never felt I knew him any better. The charm was immense and unforced; but if there was anything behind it I never got much inkling of what it was.

Another speaker I invited was C. E. M. Joad, who was the best known popularizer of philosophy at that time, and also a household name as a broadcaster. I asked him to speak on the art of popularization. I was a consumer of serious popularization in several subjects, and could see that this was on the verge of becoming a literary genre in its own right. He asked me about my way of taking notes on the books I was reading, and I said I was ceasing to be a note-taker, because I always seemed to lose the notes – or else they would be in some place separate from both me and the book when I needed them. He gave me a bit of advice. Nearly every published book, he said, has a few blank pages at the end, so use them for your notes. Then, as long as you have the book, you have the notes, and the two can never be separated. This advice was so simple and so brilliant that I have followed it to this day. As soon as I could afford it I started buying all the books I read, if only in dog-eared second-hand paperback editions, and until that time I bought all those I knew I was going to make the most use of. It meant that the walls of my home became covered with bookshelves, after which I needed to have a clear-out of books every few years to make space for more.

Joad asked me what I intended to do after leaving Oxford, and I said my ambitions were spread between writing and politics. His advice was to plump wholeheartedly for politics. What everybody really wants, he said, is power. It's the only satisfying thing. Look at me, he said: I'm a successful writer, and through broadcasting I'm one of the most famous people in the country, so I've got money and fame. But I have no power at all. And it's almost intolerably frustrating to see contemporaries of mine, who I've known for years, and who I know to be less able than I am, running everything. I made the wrong choice. I ought to have done what they're doing. Don't make that mistake. Even if you're successful as a writer it won't satisfy you. You'll want to run things. Go into politics. Give it all you've got.

As an idealistic young socialist I was shocked by this, and contemptuous of what it revealed about Joad. Even so, it was instructive, not about how things are but about how some people see them – and think others should too.

I had never felt much respect for academic approaches to Shakespeare's plays. The atmosphere in Oxford was clogged by them, so I thought it might clear the air a bit to bring in the viewpoint of a great actor. I invited Donald Wolfit, the supreme King Lear, to speak. His thesis was that only someone who acts in, or directs, Shakespeare's plays can appreciate to the full the subtlety and depth of their practical stagecraft. They are so extraordinarily insightful and understanding about the possibilities of theatre itself that only a man of the theatre could have written them. Not only did their author know to a nicety how everything would work in actual performance, he kept bringing off things that most people would never have expected to work at all. Wolfit illustrated this with some good examples, and his talk was exceptional. No one could have thought of him as an intellectual, yet it was the most enlightening thing I heard about Shakespeare during all my years as a student.

After the meeting Wolfit said he did not want to sit in the hotel lounge, where he might be recognized, so he asked if we could go to my digs. There he started questioning me about girls' schools. He had two daughters, he said, to whom he wanted to give the best possible education. Where should he send them? I told him I knew nothing about girls' schools. Except for Cheltenham, Roedean and the North London Collegiate, I did not even know their names. He became exasperated with me, out of frustration. Look here, he said: here you are at Oxford, and students come here from all the best schools in the country. You obviously know a lot of people, including girls. Which are the best of the schools they come from? … I told him I didn't know which schools most of my female friends had been at – it wasn't a subject that came up. He insisted that I help him, because none of the people he knew in the theatre could, and he was desperate. His attitude was naïve in the extreme (and he had just delivered one of the most sophisticated talks I had ever heard, on the refined significance of practicalities). There was nothing I could say to help him. He visibly came to the conclusion that I was useless. When he got home he wrote me a letter on Garrick Club writing paper asking for a trivial sum to cover his expenses. No other speaker had ever done this, and the club had no procedure for dealing with it. After his wonderful performance I did not want to expose him to the disdain of others, so – indigent student though I was – I sent him a cheque drawn on my own account.

To open the term I arranged a talk on Bernard Shaw by someone who had known him well, Kingsley Martin, Editor of the

New Statesman. Over dinner Martin asked how many people would be at the meeting. Before I could answer, the Secretary – whose application for the job I had mistakenly accepted – jumped in and said: 'It could be anything between twenty and fifty'. In fact twenty was the smallest audience we had ever had, and fifty was no better than average. Martin's face collapsed. He clearly thought he had been mistaken in accepting the invitation, and was annoyed. I myself was annoyed with the Secretary, and also sure he was wrong. Not wishing to contradict him too bluntly I said: 'The truth is we don't know, because this is the first meeting of the term, and it's only at this meeting that we'll find out how many members we've got. I'm confident it'll be more than fifty. It could be a lot more.' When we arrived at Lady Margaret Hall the room was packed: there were well over a hundred. In addition to all the chairs being occupied, people were sitting on window sills and every square inch of floor, even under the grand piano; and more were standing round the walls. As Martin and I picked our way across those sitting on the floor to reach the table from which we were going to speak I murmured into his ear what were meant to be propitiatory words: 'I said we'd get more than fifty.' He half turned, smiled at me condescendingly, put a reassuring hand on my arm, and said: 'I know, I know. It's always like this when I speak.'

He gave a good talk, in which he claimed that Shaw was a better writer of English prose (quite apart from dialogue) than any of the currently famous novelists – a verdict with which I agree, except for Evelyn Waugh. Over drinks at the Golden Cross afterwards he revealed himself as one of the vainest people I have ever met. He told me how, when he had been awarded a starred first at Cambridge, only he and Keynes had ever been given that honour: 'Keynes and I were the only people for whom it was considered that a first wasn't good enough.' He said a number of things of that kind, and I began to feel that such vanity was in itself a form of silliness – he must, I thought, be at some deep level an unintelligent man. I met him quite often during the following years, and grew to regard silliness as his salient characteristic.

But he was a good editor, as well as being a good speaker. He made one observation to me in particular which was simple and excellent, and which affected my writing from then on. Most writers of comment and criticism, he said, keep starting sentences with 'In my opinion … In my judgement … I think … It is my view that …', and so on. They think modesty requires it. But it's unnecessary. 'Of course it's their opinion. No one would dream of taking it for anything else. What else could it be? Cut all that out. Just say what you think.'

All the speakers during my term were good, and were well received. Compton Mackenzie made up in actor-like handsomeness, flair and charm for what he lacked in content. Although he had been a famous writer for forty years the classic film comedy *Whisky Galore* (based on his novel of the same name, with him in it) was still recent, and students were fascinated to see him because of it. One way and another, I learnt more from those meetings of the English Club than I did from the university's lectures, and I have remembered them individually, decades after the event. It is true that some professors in the English faculty had impressive reputations – J. R. Tolkien, C. S. Lewis, Lord David Cecil – but because they were in Oxford all the time we used them as fall-backs, inviting them to our meetings only as last-minute stand-ins when outside speakers cancelled. As it happened, all three were at the height of their powers, and it was during those years that they were writing the books that came later to be considered their best. But we were not to know that. And we wanted fresh voices as our speakers, not the people we could hear any time we liked. We were more welcoming to professors from Cambridge, and we invited F. R. Leavis. I found him exceedingly unpleasant, and was not at all persuaded by his judgements, which seemed to me not just puritan and philistine but wrong.

My interest in the English Club was intense, and in four years I did not miss a single weekly meeting. The fact that I was not studying English increased its value to me: it gave me a different sort of education alongside the one I was receiving. In fact, during my teaching years after leaving the university I found that having been President of the Oxford University English Club was looked on as some sort of quasi-academic qualification in support of my degrees in PPE and History.

Apart from poetry, my published writings as an undergraduate were confined to university magazines. Most of my pieces were anonymous, as was generally the case, especially with reporting. Some of my outlets were surprising. For a period I reviewed the Union debates in a magazine called *Oxford Tory*. As a left-wing poet writing in those pages I felt like Orpheus in the Underworld, so I signed my contributions Orpheus. I doubt whether anyone guessed it was me. I also, for a different period, reviewed debates for *The Oxford Magazine*. The queen of the magazines, *Isis*, carried weekly a full-page pen-portrait of a student chosen by the Editor, anonymously written – I wrote those of Caroline and Andrew (and Caroline wrote the one of me). It was all studenty stuff, and there is no point in pretending otherwise. But some distinguished journalists came out of the Oxford of those days, and they took their student apprenticeship seriously. I myself never expected to be a print journalist (and have never earned my living as one) so I looked on it as a more general introduction to writing for publication. As such it was instructive. And it was fun. I even acquired some experience of editing, with an expensively produced Keble College magazine called *The Clock Tower*. I had to write some of it myself, and I included a poem by Geoffrey Hill. I like to think I might have been the first editor to publish his work.

6

Colleges

The University of Oxford is a federation of self-governing colleges, each with its own endowment, head, and governing body. Each hires its own staff and selects its own students. Some of the colleges are very old, some new; some are big and some small; some are rich (these are not necessarily the old or the big ones) and some poor. The oldest were founded in the thirteenth century. Each century since then has seen the creation of new ones, so the university has been perpetually changing and growing. Today there are thirty-eight colleges, but when I was a student there were only twenty-something. Keble became a fully-fledged college while I was there. At that time there were only two all-graduate colleges, now there are seven or more.

During my adult lifetime there have been at least four fundamental changes in the university each of which is revolutionary for an institution nearly 800 years old. First, it has doubled in size. Second, all its colleges, which were one-sex in my day (and had been for 700 years) are now co-educational. Third, postgraduate students, who when I was a student were a handful of people on the fringe of things, now constitute a third of the student body. Fourth, both the student body and the faculty have become internationalized: half a century ago there was the merest scattering of foreigners at all levels, but now Oxford is truly cosmopolitan.

It was after the Second World War that these momentous changes got under way and spread to all the colleges. Before then these had differed from one another significantly in the profile of their students. One or two had been scholarly, one or two sporty, one or two aristocratic, one or two for the un-well-off, one high-church, one low-church, one associated with north-country grammar school boys, one with clever Welsh boys, and so on. None of these characterizations was exclusive, and exceptions tended to include the most interesting undergraduates, but even so they gave a college its public image. When I arrived, the reality behind most of the brand images was seriously decaying. The majority of the students were from state schools, and 84% of the total were on public grants, which were freely available to anyone with a place and not enough money to pay for himself. No one needed to worry any longer about having to get a scholarship: people simply got in to whatever college they could, and a grant automatically followed. Religion was no longer relevant as an entry requirement. The central mass of students in all the colleges was becoming much of a muchness. But the process has gone even farther since. Colleges still contained then, as minorities, the sort of people who had given them their public character. More of the titled undergraduates, or heirs to titles, were at Christ Church than at any other college. The less intelligent members of the upper classes (the braying ex-guards officer types) tended to cluster in Trinity. Balliol was still the self-consciously clever college. People still thought of Corpus Christi as a quiet corner of classical scholarship, while associating Jesus College with Wales, and Queens' with north country grammar schools. The branding and its misleadingness were both well illustrated by Brasenose. It was seen as being far and away the most sporty of the colleges, manically so, yet I had more friends there than in any other men's college, and not a single one of them was sporty – quite the contrary. For reasons like this it was already an indication of crassness in an undergraduate to assume that a fellow-student must be like the stereotype of his college.

I say this feelingly because my college, Keble, had the worst image of all. There were two components in it. First, it was said to have the lowest standards of entry in the university and therefore to consist of students who were not good enough to get into Oxford otherwise. Second, it was seen as risibly churchy – all these dim people were going to be vicars. As with other colleges, there still remained an element of truth in the stereotype. A higher-than-average proportion of Keble undergraduates went into the church. And nearly two thirds of the students in my year got third-class degrees, or worse – eight got fourths, and several got no degree at all. At a time when one third of the entire undergraduate body of the University got thirds this was not as dreadful as it now looks, but it was pretty bad. Of course, as always, there were first-class people who got thirds: it has never been possible to judge the calibre of an individual by the class of his degree. But the fact is that too many of the Keble students were place-fillers, taken by the college to make up the numbers; and this lowered the vitality of the college. It also provided a touch of substance for the university's caricature-conception of a Keble man as an inadequate vicar-in-the-making struggling to achieve a third in Theology.

Actually, there were as many outstanding individuals in Keble during my time as one would probably have come across in most colleges. I have mentioned the poet Geoffrey Hill and the Olympic gold medallist Alan Dick: other names might include Michael Elliott, who became Artistic Director of the Old Vic while still in his thirties and was co-founder of the Royal Exchange Theatre in Manchester; John Hayes, who was head of the National Portrait Gallery for twenty years, and the leading authority on Gainsborough; David Wilson, who became Governor of Hong Kong and then Master of Peterhouse; Roderick MacFarquhar, the doyen of China experts in his generation, a Member of Parliament and a Harvard professor. I suppose the truth is that the Keble student body was like a cricket team with excellent early batsmen but a long weak tail. The solid middle was missing. It is that fault that has since been rectified.

The college had been founded in the nineteenth century by the high-church Oxford Movement. After I got there in 1949 I found that attendance at chapel for at least one service on Sunday was mandatory. I was full of goodwill to start with, and on my first Sunday I went to chapel. 'I can manage this,' I told myself: 'I can happily listen to the music, or just let my mind wander agreeably.' But I got bored. And the realization crept over me that I could not face doing this every Sunday. Apart from anything else, I could not face having to give up all the other things I might be doing instead, just to do this. I had tried, with the best of intentions, but contact with the reality forced me to realize that it was not going to work. I never went to the chapel again.

This was a breach of the college's regulations. I discussed my attitudes with my fellow students, and they were on tenterhooks to see how the college authorities would react. Halfway through my first term I was summoned by the Warden. He was Harry Carpenter, the only man I have ever known with four firsts. My demeanour during our meeting was not defiant or belligerent. In response to his questions I told him courteously that, although I did not believe in God, let alone in Christianity, I had started out with the intention of complying with the rules, but once in chapel I had felt the prospect of carrying on with it intolerable. He started to argue with me, but I could see him begin to feel that he was getting the worse of the argument. It dawned on me, with a strange feeling of certitude – and to my surprise – that there was nothing he could do. He could not, in that day and age, expel me from Oxford for not going to chapel, as he most certainly could have done before the war. It would be a national scandal now, taken up by all the newspapers, a cause célèbre which would damage the college. And any punishment short of that would achieve nothing at all, because I would accept the punishment while refusing to go to chapel. We were both, I think, surprised at the unspoken conclusions that we found ourselves coming to. I could see him realizing he had no options, because no effective sanctions. He became embarrassed, and brought the conversation to an end by saying, as authoritatively as he could make it sound, that he hoped I would reconsider.

When I emerged from his lodgings into the quad I found several of my friends hanging around chatting – they were in fact waiting for me. I gave them a detailed report outside the Warden's door. The following Sunday a significant number of the students did not go to chapel. And that was the end of compulsory chapel in Keble.

Harry Carpenter, who ended his career as Bishop of Oxford, was an eloquent example of how little a person's degrees may tell you about his abilities. He was well meaning but did nothing with distinction, and was in some ways a rather silly man. He had an only child, Humphrey, who lived with him and his wife in the Warden's lodgings. Humphrey was the college mascot. He was three and a half years old when I arrived, and had free run of the college provided he did not go outside it. He was all the time wandering around by himself, in quads, up staircases, chattering with whoever he bumped into. He was everybody's favourite: everyone petted him and had conversations with him. I remember seeing him once, when he was five, chatting in a quad with a group of workmen and using polysyllabic words that they did not understand, while they thought it a wonderful joke that this little fellow should be talking to them in this way, with so unselfconscious an air. They made a huge fuss of him. He grew up with an enviable and un-vain feeling that everybody loved him. He was to become nationally known as a broadcaster, writer and musician. In particular he wrote excellent biographies. Although he had only one degree, and that was second-class, he was more intelligent than his father, more talented and more creative. Whenever I saw him in the days of his maturity and public success I would at the same time see in my mind's eye the tiny little fellow, eager yet thoughtful, happily pottering around Keble by himself and being fussed over by everyone.

I took only a small part in college life. My closest friends were in other colleges, and my main interests were elsewhere – the Union, parties, the Randolph, the Socialist Club, the English Club. I did not think of things in college terms: both I and most of my friends looked on the whole university as our domain. However, for my first two years I lived in Keble, and tended rather to treat it as a hotel.

In those days male undergraduates throughout the university had two rooms, a living room and a bedroom, with no running water or central heating. The stately primitiveness of those conditions has been described a thousand times. To get a bath I had to cross two quadrangles in my pyjamas and dressing gown, and climb several flights of unheated stone stairs. In my bedroom I had a wooden washstand on which stood an enormous bowl, and each morning my middle-aged scout, Tredwell, would wake me with a correspondingly huge pitcher of hot water. His words were always a weather report, usually delivered in a lugubrious tone: 'Morning, Mr Magee, sir. Frost and fog.' Before waking me he would clean my shoes and wash up the dirty glasses, and perhaps tea and supper things, from the previous day; and while I was at breakfast he would make my bed and tidy both rooms. I took all this for granted, both the personal service and the primitiveness. Having had domestic servants in the Intelligence Corps in rural Austria, and before that fags at a spartan English boarding school, it was what I was used to.

Food rationing was still in force, and the food in college was neither plentiful nor good. To obviate disputes we were each given our own little ration of breakfast marmalade and butter, or margarine, and required to carry it to and from the dining hall. As I watched the breakfasters converge across the large main quad this aspect of it looked pathetic even at the time; but this was not the college's fault. Difficulties caused by rationing and the bad quality of the food did, however, create problems between the students and the college. So the students elected somebody they called the Food Representative, to meet weekly with the Bursar and discuss matters. They asked me to take this on. The Bursar was the Law Fellow, a red-faced butcher of a man called Vere Davidge. Although I went to him with only worthwhile complaints and suggestions, leaving aside all the petty ones, his way of dealing with them was to say whatever would be an extenuation of the status quo, regardless of its truth. I became sceptical of his explanations, and began investigating them, only to discover that they were improvised lies. Along with these he squirted out some obnoxious social attitudes. For instance, if the reason for some deficiency was a lack of staff he would say something like: 'We simply can't get the people. Now that they can get jobs at Morris's [motor works in Oxford] for more than we can afford to pay them, they won't work for us any more. What we need is a jolly good dose of unemployment. Then they'll come crawling back to us begging for jobs, and we'll be able to pick and choose the ones we really want, as we used to do.' His expressed attitudes to women and social minorities were in line with this. I found him more dislikeable than I can express, and at the end of a single term I resigned the job on the ground that he was impossible to have dealings with.

In the dining hall there was a separate table for the Scholars, who were still supposed to be some sort of academic elite, so when I was there I always had to sit and eat with the same people. This had the serious disadvantage that I never ate with anyone else, and I came more and more to resent this. I would like to have been free to eat with whoever I liked; but the rules would not allow that. Since I was in the college pretty well only to eat and sleep, this did a lot to narrow the range of my college friendships. The person of most interest to me at the Scholars' table was Ron Atkinson. He was one year ahead of me, studying PPE. Unusually intelligent, and confident of his intelligence, he was in no way nerdish, and yet seemed to do nothing for the whole of every day except sit in his room and read. I once asked him if he never felt the need to go out, if only for a change, and he replied: 'My idea of a change is to read a different sort of book.' I found him enthralling to talk to because he was the first person I met who was devoted to academic philosophy (he was to become a professor in it, first at York, then at Exeter). To my delight he started seeking me out to discuss philosophical questions. This was because the reigning orthodoxy of his student years was changing over to so-called ordinary language philosophy, in which the question was constantly raised: 'How do we ordinarily use this word? In what circumstances would anyone actually say such-and-such?' The point usually was that if this was not something that anyone would ever say, then asking what it meant was a vacuous question. It was Ron's opinion that because I was untainted by knowledge of what the philosophers were up to I gave undistorted and therefore useful answers to such questions. My long, absorbing discussions with him were my introduction to the basic ideas of linguistic philosophy, and also to logical positivism, against which the linguistic philosophers were starting to rebel. Both these sets of ideas seemed to me not just mistaken but obviously so, because contradicted by direct experience. But I found them fascinating none the less. There is no element of contradiction here – all my life I have had this reaction to certain thought-systems: for instance, I have never been a Marxist, yet I have always found Marxism fascinating. Perhaps the importance of getting clear, if only to oneself, why such systems are not valid is part of the fascination and the challenge, and explains why an engagement with them can help to advance one's thinking. I conceived the desire to learn more about academic philosophy. For an overview of it I read Bertrand Russell's *History of Western Philosophy*. It served as an introduction, though I could see even while reading it that it was idiosyncratic and inadequate.

Ron used to say that although philosophy was not my subject I was the only student in Keble with whom he could have an interesting discussion of it. I fear this may have been true. My reply was that it was unnecessary for him to confine himself to Keble: there were bound to be students in other colleges who were interesting to talk to about philosophy. But he never sought them out. However, I did. The Union was teeming with undergraduates studying PPE; and conversation at the Union tended towards discussion and argument whatever the subject; so I looked among the regulars there for people who found philosophy exciting. I also attended some philosophy lectures, and got into conversations after them with others in the audience.

Although I made my life outside Keble I was sufficiently concerned for my comfort there to secure, for my second year, the best rooms in the college. These were over the lodge, and for that reason bigger than the rest. With them came the best of the scouts, known to everyone as Harry. He belonged to the last whole generation of able British people whose lives were artificially stunted by a lack of educational opportunity. Distinguished to look at, intelligent, firm of character, he was much too good for his job. Although he became, in practice, my manservant, he remained independent-minded, and there was no chip on his shoulder. Another college servant of exceptional character, the only female scout, was an almost saintly middle-aged woman called Mrs Dunsby. She would do anything for anyone – washing, ironing, sewing, mending – without expecting reward. A shameful number of undergraduates put upon her. When I got her to do things for me I always paid her properly. An incident that speaks volumes about the relationship between the different social classes in the England of that day, now more than sixty years ago, occurred when I was walking down Little Clarendon Street and saw her standing in the road chatting to a friend. I stopped and said hello, and we talked for a few moments. As I then moved on she said, in front of the other person: 'Oh sir, it *is* kind of you to talk to me in the street.' To an unclouded eye it was plain that Mrs Dunsby and Harry were more impressive human beings than most of the people they served, the people they addressed as 'sir'. But in those days, surprisingly few people's eyes were unclouded in such matters.

The most dramatic thing that happened in Keble during the time I lived in college was that the wife of one of the professors ran off with J. B. Priestley, who was in those days a household name as a writer. She herself, Jacquetta Hawkes, also had a reputation with the general public, because as an archaeologist she had successfully popularised her subject on the BBC. She was a strikingly good-looking woman. For all these reasons her elopement received prominent and prolonged coverage in the national press. Her husband Christopher Hawkes was devastated. Not only was he bereft, he endured a cruel amount of public humiliation. His face and body seemed to collapse inward upon themselves. For months he crept silently around the college like the shadow of a ghost. People feared he might be on the verge of a breakdown, might even kill himself – his appearance suggested these fears. Seldom in my life have I felt so sorry for anyone. Suffering came out of him in waves – and they were not waves of self-pity. Perhaps because he was not self-pitying he eventually recovered, at least to outward appearance.

There was one thing about Keble that I never came to terms with, and that was the building. I had been horrified by it when I first saw it, and I never got over that reaction. It seemed to me monumentally ugly, hideous, gross, crass, an affront. It was built on a huge scale, as one of the largest colleges in Oxford, and the size compounded the offence. It vied with St Pancras Hotel as the apex of high Victorian vulgarity, and was built in garish red brick at a time when all other Oxford colleges were in grey stone. The whole place was a mistake. Inside, it was freezing cold, and not just gloomy but murky, as if those mock-Gothic windows had been designed to shed darkness in the interior. I lived in it for two years, and never ceased to be disturbed by it. This contributed greatly to a feeling that I did not belong there. The college I ought to have been in, I felt, was Balliol – and would have been but for an incompetent schoolmaster, who had forbidden me to apply for Balliol when I wanted to, and when subsequent events showed that it would have been the right thing for me to do. This feeling was so strong that twenty years later, when I became a lecturer in philosophy at Balliol, I felt I had come home as far as Oxford colleges were concerned.

It was a release for me when I moved out of Keble at the end of my second year. After that, except for tutorials, I rarely penetrated beyond its front lodge, where I had a pigeon-hole for incoming mail and messages. I still visited colleges where I had friends, mainly Lady Margaret Hall – girls, unlike boys, had to live in college for their whole time as undergraduates. There were also the chief party-giving colleges, which in those days were Magdalen, Christ Church and New College. My base, however, was 3 St John Street from then on, and my deepest-worn daily path was between that house and the Union.

Undergraduate teaching in Oxford was mostly college-based, so I went on being taught in Keble. Because I took two undergraduate degrees, and one of those was a combination of three different subjects, I received an exceptionally wide range of tuition. This was especially beneficial in Oxford, because of its one-to-one tutorial system. For each of my examination papers I had a different tutor, with whom I would spend an hour once a week for one or two terms. Meetings with a good tutor could be like facing a skilled interrogator – you could never get away with anything. The best I had in History was the great medievalist J. E. A. Jolliffe. For one of my earliest tutorials with him I left myself too little time to write my essay properly. In desperation I seized on one of the primary sources and paraphrased a whole paragraph of it, changing only the wording. While I was reading it aloud to him he got up from the chaise longue on which he always lay, said 'Don't stop', and went across to a bookcase. I flicked glances in his direction while continuing to read, and saw him take down the volume which I had imagined my rewording would disguise. He went back with it to his chaise longue, found the right page, and – to my mortification – followed the passage with his finger while I was reading. I felt such a fool I just stopped, waiting for the explosion. 'Don't stop,' he said: 'I want to hear you read it to the end.' Blushing lobster red, I carried on reading, drowning in humiliation. When I got to the end he snapped the book shut and said: 'Right. Now let's discuss it.' And that was that. He never uttered a word of condemnation, but he taught me a lesson I never forgot.

I knew, even so, that he had a favourable opinion of my abilities, because once, warning me against a mistaken practice of mine, he said: 'If you go on doing that, the examiners may put you down into the second class.' He was the person I most felt I was letting down when I made the decision about my relationship to academic work that rendered getting a second inevitable.

My two other History tutors in Keble were academic workhorses, one of them sound but narrow, the other a hack. However, for my special subjects I was farmed out to specialists in other colleges, and these were incomparably better. For the Italian Renaissance I was taught in St Hugh's College by Cecilia Ady, which brought me the pleasure of being one of the pupils to whom she dedicated her biography of Lorenzo de' Medici. For my special period of international history, 1871-1939, I went to Oriel College to be taught by Christopher Seton-Watson, a member of one of Oxford's leading academic families. Each of these gave me a grounding in the subject that stayed with me for the rest of my life.

When I turned to the study of Philosophy, Politics and Economics I moved on to a new set of tutors. Outstanding was my Philosophy tutor, Basil Mitchell. He was solid, thorough, and gave me the kind of painstakingly firm foundation that may seem old-fashioned but is actually the best way to begin almost any subject. My Politics tutor was M. R. D. Foot, who has since made a name as the historian of Special Operations during the Second World War. My Economics tutor was Maurice Hugh Jones. What he taught me was pure Keynesianism. But when he was away for a term I went to Nuffield College to be taught by Philip Andrews, who introduced me to right-wing economics, Hayekian, anti-Keynesian. I got the best of both worlds.

It is in tutorials such as these that the essence of an Oxford academic education lies. Your student essay is not just a gathering of material: you are always told to argue a case, either for or against something, and to base it on both evidence and logic. You are supposed to have mastered the evidence from reading the most important sources, which the tutor will have directed you to. When you have read your essay aloud to him, he will act as devil's advocate, and probe your logic, your arguments, your use of the evidence, and your conclusions; and you have to defend all these in face-to-face, one-to-one argument with him, falling back on whatever knowledge you have of the subject outside your essay. He will deliberately ask you questions which you will be able to answer only if you have read what you are supposed to have read. He may have written one of the books himself, may even be a leading authority on the subject, as Jolliffe was. You are alone in the room with him, and there is no escape. It is challenging in the extreme, and it stretches students to their limits. Those who find it most stretching (and therefore most stressful) are not the least good students but the best.

Three or four years of this add up to a mind-changing process for which I know of no equal in the world of higher education. It trains you in so many different ways simultaneously: to think for yourself, and to think critically and logically, yet always to base your opinions on evidence, not on emotion or empty logic; to work hard at your reading and master the facts, and then marshal them into a well-organized and well-argued case – and to defend this case against well-informed criticism. All this makes for a high-quality training not only for a politician, civil servant, lawyer, broadcaster or serious journalist, but also for people going into industry, commerce and finance. I feel myself to have been unusually fortunate in that I went through it in four subjects: History, Philosophy, Politics and Economics. It gave me an education that was broad without being superficial.

Because the tutorial was the focal point of the system, lectures played a comparatively unimportant role in Oxford. They were not even compulsory, and many students did not go to any lectures at all after their first term or two. It was normal for a course of weekly lectures to start off with a good audience which would then dwindle, week by week, until only a handful were left at the end of term. Occasionally it happened that an audience disappeared altogether, thus bringing the series to a premature end. In my day there were always a lot more girls than boys at lectures, and usually enough of the girls stuck it out to the end to keep the series going. While I was studying History I only once made it through to the end of a term, and that was the course on Hitler given by Alan Bullock, who was then in process of writing his classic biography. Dons, who could get approval to lecture on whatever they chose, often used a course of lectures as a way of organizing the material for a book – a sort of first draft – and the number and length of the chapters could betray a book's origin. (This was not true in the case of Bullock's work, which transcended such considerations.) Other than Bullock's, the most memorable lectures I went to were delivered by a visiting lecturer who was not an academic at all, the drama producer Tyrone Guthrie: he gave dazzlingly theatrical performances on the subject of theatrical performance.

I cannot bring this chapter to an end without saying an exculpatory word about Keble College. The ways in which I have criticized it express truthfully the feelings I had about it at the time, and I can attest that such feelings were shared by many of my contemporaries. But in justice to the college I must make it clear that it has long since ceased to be as it was then. All Oxford's colleges are perpetually changing. It is many decades now since the braying young men disappeared from Trinity; and Balliol has long since ceased to be the most successful college academically. (For many years now that reputation has rested with Merton.) Among the colleges, relative reputations rise and fall never-endingly, like shares on a stock exchange, Two or three will be at the top for ten or twenty years, and then slip away as others take their places. All this is natural. Keble has gone through at least two major transformations since I was there.

The egregious Davidge, whose son rowed for Oxford in three consecutive years, set out to make Keble the university's top rowing college. He took the cream of the oarsmen from the best of the rowing schools almost regardless of their academic qualifications; and Keble became Head of the River. It was in this position for many years, in the sixties and beyond. Sometimes half the university's boat-crew was from Keble. ('Eton and Keble' was the caricature designation.) Other sports in the college followed suit, and there came a time when a third of the university's rugger team, and a third of its cricket team, were from Keble. It had become the super-duper sporting college, even more than Brasenose had been when I was an undergraduate.

But alongside this came a rebellion from the brighter, younger dons against the lower academic standards that went with it. Low academic standards had always characterized the college, but now they were getting even worse. These Young Turks banded together, and resolutely took in from the schools only those applicants they deemed capable of getting second-class degrees. To do this they had to fight Davidge, and other members of the old guard, even some of the sportier young dons. But they had the active support of the head of the college, Dennis Nineham. Over a period of years they prevailed. The result was that Keble, having long been the outstanding sporting college, became also a good academic one. For a while it was both, and was among the better colleges in the university. This was a complete turnaround from what it had been when I was there. The churchy image had disappeared entirely, along with the reputation for low academic standards. Among Oxford colleges, the rise of Keble was the most outstanding success-story of the second half of the twentieth century.

During the years of Keble's rise I was in touch with developments in Oxford through contacts with other colleges. When I was forty I became a lecturer in philosophy at Balliol, and at forty-three a visiting fellow of All Souls, whose Common Room I belonged to for another five years. Later, also as a visiting fellow, I lived for a term each in New College, in Merton, and in St Catherine's. In Wolfson College I had a flat for three years, and am a life member of its Common Room. During that time I was elected to the Senior Common Room of St Antony's. Altogether, then, my involvement with Oxford has been sustained across many decades on an exceptionally broad front. As a result I now see the university from a quite different perspective from the one I had when I was an undergraduate.

I now see it as a world-class research centre, and also as one of the world's outstanding centres of scholarship. Undergraduates as a whole have little notion of such things. They see a university as not much more than a teaching institution – one that exists to teach *them*. (Nowadays, even a third of the students are doing research.) I must confess, though, that I too had that view when I was an undergraduate – and so did my friends. We thought the university was there to teach us. Actually, we thought the university *was* us. We had a distant idea that there were senior members of it who had international reputations, but we ourselves had not heard of more than a few of them, and the rest never impinged on us. Heads of colleges remained unheard of by us except for the heads of our own colleges plus, at most, three or four others. As far as we were concerned, such people were so remote as not to have a substantial existence. It never entered our minds that our conception of Oxford could be anything like as incomplete as it actually was.

In having remained in active contact with Oxford for most of my adult life, and being familiar with the perpetually changing character of it, my experience is unusual. Most of those who study there make only occasional brief visits to it after they leave. So their three or four undergraduate years remain with them as their only experience of it, which they then keep for the rest of their lives. Their conception of the university remains always as it had been when they knew it. And it is usually emotionally charged: a number of people think of those years as the happiest of their lives. Successes and failures back then preserve their out-of-proportion weight. In my eighties I still find that some people are impressed by my having been President of the Oxford Union. I have told already how the eighty-year-old Roy Jenkins regarded not having become President as the worst setback of his life. I have read that the dying Lord Curzon, who had failed to become Prime Minister at the point when he and almost everyone else expected him to, regretted more than anything else not this but the fact that he had failed to get a first at Oxford. In other words, some of the people who are among the most successful in later life are still never, in spite of their success, able to come to terms with their youthful failures at Oxford. This shows not only that those things had a disproportionate significance at the time but that they go on doing so throughout life. It is the same for the high points as for the low ones. The golden glow of those years never fades. Their magic is imperishable.

This must be, I think, because of the extraordinary formativeness of the whole experience. I have heard several people of outstanding achievement say that the most important single thing that ever happened to them was going to Oxford (or to Cambridge). I am inclined to agree. They usually say that it was this that opened up the rest of the world to them and was where they discovered themselves. Most of the other things they value followed from that. This is why what happened there goes on seeming so important, and *was* so important.

In my own case my feelings of that kind of indebtedness are to an extent shared between Oxford and Christ's Hospital. Coming from a poor, uneducated family, I was astonishingly lucky to find myself, at the age of eleven, a boarder in one of the truly great public schools, and this experience may have transformed my life as much as going to Oxford. Even so, there is no doubt which of the two I love the more: it is Oxford by a mile.

7

Vacations

One thing that always seemed odd to visitors, especially from overseas, was that Oxford University had more vacation than term. The three eight-week terms that made up the academic year resulted in students being 'up' for twenty-four weeks and 'down' for twenty-eight. There were six weeks of vacation at Christmas, six weeks at Easter, and four months in the summer. However, these vacations were not supposed to be for holidays. They were for reading. It was then that we were expected to get our solid reading done, away from all the distractions of student life. At the end of each term our tutors would give to each of us individually a list of the books they required us to read before they saw us again. They would, I think, have been surprised if we had read them all, but most of us read some of them. The theory, at least, was that you got the bulk of your reading done during vacations so that the terms could be devoted to writing essays and preparing for discussion meetings with your tutor, and perhaps going to lectures.

Few students succeeded in reading as much during vacations as they went down intending to. They had all the distractions of Christmas with the family, and Easter, and friends at home to catch up with, and old haunts to revisit. People in friendships that had formed at Oxford would go as house guests to one another's families in far corners of the country. Some went on visits to places of specialist interest, which might range from archaeological sites to jazz festivals. Those who could afford to made journeys abroad, particularly during the long summer vacation, or stayed with relatives or friends in other countries. There were some who were forced to get jobs, or did so because they felt they ought to – and this of course interfered with their reading. Tutors disapproved of it for that reason. Most students, however un-well-off, did not do vacation jobs. The assumption was that their families would keep them during vacations, and in nearly all cases they did. No matter how modest a family's means, nearly all managed to provide pocket money as well as keep. The assumptions behind this were strengthened by the fact that students did not become legally independent until they were twenty-one, so half of them had parents who were still legally responsible for them.

I was nineteen when I went up to Oxford, and had been in the army, but even so my mother was still my legal guardian for another year and a half after that. The first words she had said to me two years before when we got home after my father's funeral were: 'If you think I'm going to keep you at your age you're mistaken.' I had just had my seventeenth birthday. From then on I had no alternative but to be financially responsible for myself. For reasons I do not know how to explain, I carried on feeling that I ought to visit her, and I did so briefly at some point during most of my university vacations. She was living in Bristol then, so it meant I came to know Bristol, which I have always liked. But she never wanted me to stay more than a few days, and I did not want to either. As for money, there was no question of her giving me any. She did once lend me thirteen pounds, but she referred to it every time she met me after that until I repaid her. I was entitled to the maximum grant of £280 a year, in termly instalments, and that was my total income. My college scholarship was £100 a year, but this amount was deducted from my government grant, so being a Scholar made no financial difference. Grants were not intended for a student to live on all the year round: they were calculated only to keep him during the university terms.

What all this comes down to is that when I was an undergraduate I was one of few who received no support at all from their families, and had no home to go to, while at the same time having an income that it was impossible to live on. For a short while I struggled to make ends meet on what I had, but quickly found that this was literally impossible. Furthermore, not doing things that I could not afford to do meant missing out on too much of what made being at Oxford worth while, and half removed the point of being there. I realized that the only way to get through the university was to borrow money and pay it back afterwards. Since this made large-scale borrowing inescapable, it would be ridiculous to incur big debts and still miss out on valuable opportunities, so I took an 'in for a penny, in for a pound' attitude: I would borrow whatever I needed to live life in Oxford to the full, doing uninhibitedly all the things I wanted to do. Subsequent events bore this out as having been the right choice.

I borrowed from friends, ran up accounts in shops, and then – my decisive discovery – found a bank manager who would let me have an unsecured overdraft. He felt total confidence, he told me, that I would eventually repay, and of course I did. But it also turned out that he hoped to be one of the few non-university people to be given associate membership of the Oxford Union. He saw this as a way of getting the bank accounts of young men with promising futures. If he was gambling on me being a means of bringing it about, his gamble paid off, for when I became President of the Union I arranged it for him, in the hope that he would extend his invaluable facilities to my friends.

People who knew my circumstances sometimes assumed that it must be a perpetual struggle financially for me to get through university, but this was not so. Except for my first few months I was not unduly preoccupied by money, chiefly because I made no attempt to avoid spending it on whatever I really wanted. I never thought of myself as poor, merely broke, and for a limited period of my life. I sometimes had to juggle with money, simply to be sure of having what I needed when I needed it. But I became adept at that. The way was eased by my scrupulousness as a borrower. If I asked a friend to lend me ten pounds until the end of the month I repaid him at the end of the month regardless of circumstances. If I had no money then, I borrowed it from someone else. I have innumerable times borrowed from Peter to pay Paul. And never in my life have I left a bad debt. So people lent to me easily – it was safe, and cost them nothing. I felt no shame in borrowing, because it was forced on me by circumstances for which I was not responsible. Anyone else in my position would have had to do the same. The only occasions on which I felt embarrassment – and it happened only two or three times in the course of several years – was when I asked someone to lend me money and he refused. Then I felt humiliated. I would not have asked him if I had not been in need, and I would not have asked *him* if he had not been a friend, and if I had not known that he could afford it.

Because I was in this position, vacations were a bit of a problem for me. The problem was at its worst during my first two years, because I was living in college: students had to clear out in vacation, and I had nowhere to go. When I moved in to digs things became a lot easier. Landladies were only too pleased if you stayed in Oxford during vacations, because it meant that they went on getting rent for your room instead of its being empty.

For my first vacation, still addicted to being in London as much as possible, I found a room in a hostel of slum-like digs for London University students near Kings Cross. Life was bohemian in the true sense of that word – it made me think of *La Bohème* – and it could scarcely have been less like Oxford. But having experienced Basic Training in the army the year before, I had no difficulty in coping with it. I even found it intriguing. It was certainly an education. But I never went back to it. While staying there I paid a visit to an aunt and uncle in Southgate, further out on the Piccadilly Line, and they invited me to spend the following vacation with them. I did that. And that proved a disaster.

They treated me as a poor relation. When visitors called they would introduce me with such words as: 'This is Bryan, our nephew. We're letting him stay with us because he's got nowhere else to go' – and then perhaps give a laugh, ha, ha. But it was true, of course. And it was rubbed in every day, even when we were just among ourselves. Sometimes I could scarcely believe my ears at what they were saying. I realized that they were not unusual when I recalled that the Poor Relation was a perennial character in classic novels and drama, and that this was always how he or she was treated. It is, I fear, a human constant. When I left them I knew I would never spend another night under their roof, and determined to be as independent and self-sufficient during vacations as I was during terms.

In my next vacation, my first long summer vacation, I got a job with a travel agency as its representative in Brussels. For three months in the summer of 1950 I lived in a hotel in the heart of the city. There was not much to do in the way of work: it consisted mostly of seeing off the departing guests and meeting the arrivals. All were travelling by train and boat between Brussels and London, so departures were all after breakfast and arrivals all in the evening. Between, for most of the day, I was free. I would meet the arrivals on the station platform and take them to the hotel, where I saw that they were comfortably installed and had everything they wanted. I would sell them whatever optional day trips they chose – one was a visit to Antwerp and the Rubens house, one a day in Holland, one a day divided between Bruges and Ghent. I went on all these trips myself straight away, not just for their own sakes but to be able to sell them and answer questions about them. Apart from this, all I had to do was be available to deal with queries and sort out problems, which the guests would bring to me at my breakfast table in the morning.

The fact that I had so little to do did not trouble the travel agency, because I cost them nothing. The hotel provided my board and lodging free as their commission to the agency. (And, what is more, they were anxious to keep me happy, because they knew I made regular reports on the hotel.) As for my spending money, the guests bought their day trips from me with cash, and out of that I gave myself my wages and turned the rest over to the agency. As far as the agency was concerned I was all profit.

For that reason, no doubt, they left me alone as long as I did the job to their satisfaction. There was no one in Brussels to whom I was responsible. Messages from London about new arrivals took an impersonal form. The check on me was that when guests returned home they were asked to fill in a questionnaire, and this included questions about me. But it transpired that their answers were favourable.

For me it was a highly enjoyable summer, made so particularly because it was the summer of an abdication crisis in Belgium. The circumstances of King Leopold III's capitulation to the German invasion in 1940 had been such that he was widely felt to have betrayed his country. He was in Germany when the war ended in 1945, and did not dare to return to Belgium. Instead he went to Switzerland. It was not until the summer of 1950 that he said he was going to return. And this caused uproar. There were nationwide strikes, street demonstrations in all the major cities, big protest marches in the capital. I took part in these with friends I made in Brussels. It was the only time I have taken part in street demonstrations, or protest marches, and I did so with relish – I many times strode through the streets of Brussels as part of a vast crowd crying: *Le-o-pold au po-teau!* (*Leopold to the scaffold!*).

I will not attempt a description of these events here. A few years later, in my middle twenties, I wrote a book called *Georgette:*

A Novel in Three Acts, in which I described them as graphically as I could. This was my first adult attempt at a novel, and because of that I never sent it to a publisher, though an agent offered to handle it for me. When I look at it now it seems to me of publishable standard, so it may be published one day. As is the case with my other novels, the main characters and their actions are invented but the social setting is truthfully described, and I have tried to bring it alive. I think it contains a better description of that summer in Brussels than I could write today.

After my first year at Oxford I was invited increasingly often to spend parts of vacations with friends and their families, and this was something I enjoyed. It always resulted in my knowing the friend better: I understood so many more things about him after seeing him in the bosom of his family, and being able to relate his Oxford world to the background he had grown up in. I would see him in the round for the first time. In addition I took to visiting Paris, where my sister worked as a secretary in an American organization, and shared a flat on the left bank with an English girl. At first I stayed near her. She was able to find paid work for me teaching French to American children, and she also found me a room in a tiny hotel round the corner from where she lived. It was a room that was not normally used for guests, and to get to it I had to pass through a family's living quarters, which were hung impenetrably with the hotel's laundry; but they charged me only five shillings a night, and this included breakfast.

I still had friends in Paris from having been at the Lycée Hôche in Versailles three or four years before. That was when I had first acquired the skills involved in getting a lot out of Paris for little money. The city took on a special importance for me during this period of my life. It was where Caroline's family lived, so she went there during vacations. On one of my visits I stayed with them, but Caroline and I needed somewhere to make love, so after that I stayed elsewhere. There were various jobs in Paris at which I earned money, chiefly with a travel agency. Changes in my life since then have demanded so many long visits to other countries – Sweden, the USA, Germany, Austria – that in more recent years I have become almost a stranger to Paris, but in those days I knew it well, and felt at home there.

Once I had made the move from my college into digs I spent quite a bit of vacation-time in Oxford itself, being no longer under compulsion to vacate my room. Oxford was transformed into another world that I then became part of. Although nearly all the British students returned home, as did those from other European countries, most of those from more far-flung continents could not afford to do so more than once a year, if that. So the streets of Oxford became given over to young people from Africa, India and the Middle East. They frequented the cheapest eating places, as did I, and I got to know a lot of them. They introduced me to the British Council, which had its headquarters in Black Hall, an attractive seventeenth-century house in the centre of Oxford. The Council had been charged by the Government with the social welfare of foreign students, especially those from Commonwealth countries, so during vacations it turned parts of its roomy premises into a social club for them. From the first day of each vacation this would become the focal point of their lives in Oxford, and remain so until their colleges re-opened. I became one of the regulars there (I was a fanatical ping-pong player, among other things) and made many friends. The Oxford Union also remained open during vacations, with its two full-sized billiard tables; so for those few weeks nearly all my billiards opponents would be non-white. It was the first time in my life that I came to know non-white people as personal friends. During the terms we might see little of one another, but every vacation we would again spend time together. This was to have an unexpected consequence ten or more years later. The colonies from which most of them came achieved independence much sooner than they expected, and as Oxford-educated men they frequently found themselves in high positions in their home countries while still young. (They had often been older than their fellow students at Oxford to begin with.) When I became a television reporter in my thirties, and made repeated visits to third world countries – also to the UN headquarters in New York – I found myself over and again coming up against government ministers and senior diplomats who had been friends of mine in a different life that we had shared in Oxford. My favourite billiards opponent became an African Foreign Minister who represented his country at the UN, where at one time he sat on the Security Council. People like these trusted me, and opened doors for me that might otherwise have remained closed. As an already-existing international network of friends and acquaintances it was invaluable.

My second long vacation was my last before taking my first degree, which was in history. By this time the gaps in my work had become obvious to my tutors, who were worried that I would not do myself justice in the examinations. They tried to insist that I devote the whole of my vacation to essential reading, but I told them that this was impossible: I had to get a job. They asked me to see the Warden about this. He said the college would make me a grant for eight weeks of the vacation – the equivalent of a term – if I would promise to spend it doing nothing but read for my degree. I appreciated this, but felt I needed a change from Oxford, so I asked if I could make use of the grant in Cambridge – where presumably I could get digs at a similar rent, and permission to use the libraries. So in the summer of 1951 I went to Cambridge alone and spent two months there. I kept my word about working full-time for my degree, but I still read only things that interested me, and let the rest go. (When I walked into the examination room there were still two set books I had not read.) Each afternoon I took a break from reading to go for a walk, and each of my walks had a different object. In the course of eight weeks I got to know all the Cambridge colleges, and the town quite well too. It seemed to me the most beautiful town I had seen in Britain, and that is still my view. During that summer I developed a feeling for Cambridge that has never left me. I now consider it not only a more beautiful place than Oxford but a better university. In recent years I have spent time at two of its colleges, Peterhouse and Clare Hall, which has made me a Life Member. Because Cambridge is smaller than Oxford it has less going on; and given its geographical isolation it is less convenient a place to live in. But it is a more satisfying place to be.

The following year saw my last long vacation, after taking my history degree but before getting down to philosophy. It was the summer of 1952. I had arranged a job in Paris, but at the last moment it fell through and I was left stranded. I had no money, and my ever-accumulating debts were dangerously high. The prospect of four incomeless months of the vacation seemed to stretch ahead for ever. I grabbed at the only offer of work I was able to find immediately, a job as a waiter in a hotel in Stratford-upon-Avon. It was not one of the prominent hotels, of which there were several, but a formerly grand home that was now run as a hotel by its new owner. The building may have been grand but as a hotel it was amateurish. My arrangement with the proprietor (or rather his with me) was that for eight weeks I would work six days a week for my keep plus two pounds a week, and then, when I left – provided I stayed the full course – receive a bonus of £25. I had reached the bottom of the casual labour market. But I told myself that, at least, I would be able to see all the productions at the Shakespeare Theatre that summer. I did, and they included an unforgettable *As You Like It*, which I saw twice.

As I say, this period was the nadir of my experience as a casual labourer. What made it so was not the work itself, though that was arduous. The hotel's staff were put up some distance away, and I had to get up at six o'clock if I was to have breakfast in the hotel before serving it to the guests. I would then have a brief, awkwardly useless mid-morning break before eating a pre-lunch lunch. In the afternoon my break would be longer; but after that I would be on duty from before the first dinner guest until everything in the dining room had been cleared up after the last one left. I have always needed at least eight hours of sleep to function well, but I was rarely in bed before eleven, then up again at six. What made the experience a truly poisonous one, though, was the character of the owner. He was a Dickensian employer. Having trapped each of us in a version of the same financial arrangement (all the time I was there I never had enough money to leave) he would treat us shamefully. Towards the end of each person's period of engagement he would behave towards him or her in a humiliating way, as if defying them to walk out on him – in which case they would forfeit more than half their pay, which was what he wanted. Some did, even so. It was the young women who endured most. He would go to one of the unoccupied bedrooms, ring the bell for a maid, and then try to have sex with whichever one came. At the slightest foreshadowing of any ill-usage from him I would talk to him, preferably in front of other members of the staff, in a way designed to hurt without quite giving him sufficient excuse to sack me. He found this humiliating and he learnt to leave me alone. But only with the greatest of difficulty was I able to keep both my self-respect and my job. In my own eyes it was the lowest my social situation ever sank.

My position there was a world away from Oxford, where I was currently seen as one of the outstanding undergraduates, about to become President of the Union and perhaps a rather glamorous figure in my white tie and tails. It was a shocking but salutary immersion in life's realities. Personal ability and recognition without money (a common state for authors, of course, not to mention creative people of other kinds) are not defences against degradation. I hated everything about it, and it left a scar; but it was good for me to have the experience.

Taking one with another, the ways I spent vacations during my student years made a rich and many-sided contribution to my experience of life, and so to my education and personal development – more than if I had gone back each time to a normal home. On the other hand, I missed the sustenance of family life – which is why I relished so much the experience of staying with friends. My vacations kept my view of Oxford in balance: they reminded me how enclosed it was, and how different from the rest of life, though to do my friends justice they realized it too. Unlike them, though, I had no alternative world, and that made the whole thing more important to me, vacations and all. While I was at Oxford it was my life.

8

My Last Year

The majority of my close friends were in the same year as me, so after three years they took their degrees and left. It was as if half my world dissolved. Most of the departed either converged on London or returned to the background from which they had come – or took jobs abroad. The few exceptions, those who stayed in Oxford, were either studying for four-year degrees (the chief of these being in classics and the sciences) or starting postgraduate work. Of course, I had good friends in the year after mine, including one of my closest, Andrew Cuninghame; but Caroline and the Elringtons were in London now, as were most of the others.

Two powerful reasons induced me to stay in Oxford, one to do with academic work, the other with the Union. I had known all along that history ought not to be my special subject, fascinating though much of it was. I had tried to change to music, but not been allowed to. However, while studying history I had discovered philosophy, and found it intellectually exciting in a way that nothing else had ever been for me, or was ever to be again. Academically it was *me*. I realized I ought to have studied it from the beginning, and I decided I was not going to leave higher education while still on the wrong track. When I had taken my history degree I was going to get myself taught philosophy properly and professionally, and start it from the beginning.

Because several undergraduate degrees needed four-years of study, all those of us on grants were entitled to four years of undergraduate grant, provided we were working full-time for a degree. After four years, we could apply for more grant only if we were registered to take a postgraduate degree – which at that stage I was eligible to do only in history. To study philosophy at undergraduate level I could get a grant for only one year – and then only on condition that I took a degree. I decided to do this. In fact it was my only option.

At Oxford, unlike Cambridge, philosophy cannot be studied alone; it has to be taken as part of a package that includes at least one other subject, though within that package it can be the 'special subject'. My first thought was to take a degree in PPP – Philosophy, Psychology and Physiology. Candidates for this took only two of the three subjects, and I intended to take philosophy and psychology. I applied to the PPP School, and was accepted, registered, and became all set to begin. But then the head of it, a distinguished psychologist called Zangwill, told me it was physically impossible to complete the three-year course in one year, because nearly all the psychology consisted of laboratory work that dictated its own pace and could not be hurried. Two years might *just* be a possibility, he said, but one was certainly not. Reluctantly, I withdrew from the PPP School and arranged to take a degree in PPE – Philosophy, Politics and Economics. In those days, candidates for this had to take all three subjects – two examination papers in each – plus another two in specialisms of their choice. I chose logic and political philosophy. Now, at last, I could begin.

The other powerful reason for my wanting to stay in Oxford concerned the Union. In the middle of my third year Andrew and I had stood against one another for the Secretaryship, and I had won. This made it clear that if I stood for a higher office and got it I would then have a good chance of becoming President. But that would involve staying in Oxford for a fourth year. By the end of my third year I was emotionally committed to having a try, so I stood for the Librarianship and was elected. The Presidency was then the only step left. And I cared about it passionately. In fact, few things I have done in my life have mattered as much to me at the time as this did. Just as my commitment to studying philosophy would by itself have been enough to keep me in Oxford, so would my desire to be President of the Union.

This double intensity meant that in my last year I was motivated in a way I had never been up to that point. Here were two things both of which I was wholeheartedly committed to. And I had only this one year in which to do them. The rules of the Union precluded people from holding office after their fourth year. And in PPE I had no choice but to study a three-year course in one year, the same year. (I say one year, but it was an academic year, beginning in mid-October and culminating in examinations in early June – less than eight months later.) Obviously there would be no time for other activities. But this would be made easier by the fact that nearly all my closest friends were no longer in Oxford. In particular, Caroline was not there. In any case I had had enough of being an undergraduate. I had lived it to the full with my contemporaries, and hugely enjoyed it, but now they were moving on – and in my different way, so was I. Strictly speaking, I was no longer an undergraduate anyway: I was a graduate now, a BA taking a second degree. I began to feel a little above the fray, and a little fatherly towards the students coming up.

For my new degree I was going to sit eight papers. A normal student would have been given seven terms in which to prepare for them, his first two having been devoted to work for the so-called prelims. I was exempted from prelims, having passed them already in history, but I still had only three terms in which to prepare for eight papers. My tutors had a baffled confabulation about this, and came to the conclusion that there was no point in their trying to prepare me for more than two papers in any one term – and even this would be cramming. But that meant I would receive tuition in only six papers. They could see no way round that. They told themselves – and me – that it was not as bad as it looked, because there were two PPE papers whose ground I was already supposed to have covered for part of my history degree. There had been a political theory paper in history, and now I had chosen political theory as one of my two special subjects for PPE. Also, one of the compulsory politics papers was devoted to British political history from 1832 onwards, and I was supposed to have been given tuition in that for my history degree. So, they said, I could take those two papers as having already been prepared for. They congratulated themselves on their ingenuity in solving the problem, and were able to relax.

For political theory this attitude had substance. In the history degree there had been some set books that I had actually read: Hobbes, Locke and Rousseau. Furthermore, for history prelims one of my set books had been Aristotle's *Politics* and another Tocqueville's *L'Ancien Régime*, both of which I had read with unusual interest. I had read Plato's *Republic*, too, off my own bat. My special subject in history finals had been the Italian Renaissance, for which one of the set books had been Machiavelli's *The Prince*, and I had studied this with fascination (and, what is more, in Italian). I had a higher than average interest in political ideas, and on my own initiative I had given myself a grounding in Marxism and Burkean conservatism, these being the two political viewpoints opposed to mine that I found the most challenging. At school I had read John Stuart Mill's *On Liberty*, and had been permanently influenced by it, in fact was a devotee of its central thesis. Altogether, then, I had acquired quite a substantial knowledge of the subject. The trouble is, mine had been essentially a historical approach, and PPE required an entirely different approach. Candidates were expected to bring the logical armoury of twentieth-century analytic philosophy to bear on political concepts such as 'right' and 'rights', 'justice', 'duty' and the rest. Not only had I not been trained to do this, I regarded it as an arid exercise that left out most of what was valuable and important in the ideas themselves.

As for British political history from 1832, I had never been taught it at all. My history degree had required all candidates to study English history 'from the beginning', and examined them on it in three papers. The first paper combined Roman Britain, Anglo-Saxon Britain and the early medieval period; the second was late medieval and early modern; the third just modern. Students had a different tutor for each paper, and each tutor (rightly) would work his way through the period chronologically, starting at the beginning. There was never enough time to complete a period satisfactorily, and it was normal for a tutor not to reach the end of it. At his last tutorial he would say: 'We don't have time to cover the rest, but you'll find you've got a wide choice of exam questions on the period we've already been through, so you'll be all right.' And that's how it had been with me and the modern period of British history. The actual teaching I received, it so happens, came to an end with the Great Reform Bill of 1832, which is when the PPE period began.

Most students in those days would have studied nineteenth-century English history at school for their School Certificate, but I had not. Christ's Hospital, which taught the German language to nearly all its boys, was unusual in choosing the rarely-taken option of nineteenth-century German history to be a companion to the language; and I had had to study that. When I became a history specialist I was required to concentrate on medieval European history – it was in this that I had won my scholarship to Oxford. So whereas virtually all the friends I had at Oxford who were taking degrees in other subjects had learnt at school about Gladstone and Disraeli, Palmerston and the rest, I never had – and never did. On that subject I was left entirely to my own devices. In the event I read a couple of narrative histories, then a couple of biographies. But there was no foundation to any of it, no tutor, and no essay-writing.

However, the reason I was doing PPE was for the philosophy, and that was what I cared about. At the beginning of my first philosophy tutorial with Basil Mitchell he said: 'You see that waste paper basket in the corner?'

'Yes.'

'You see the open top to it?'

'Yes.'

'What shape is it?'

'Round.'

'You mean circular?'

'Yes.'

'Are you sure?'

'Yes.'

'How do you know?'

'I can see it. I'm looking straight at it now, and I can see that it's round.'

'You mean that what you're seeing *looks* round, does it? You have a circular visual image, and that means that the top of the waste paper basket is circular?'

'Well, no. The actual visual image I have isn't a circle, it's an ellipse.'

'So the top is elliptical, then, is it?'

'No. It only *looks* elliptical. I know it's *actually* round.'

'If it looks elliptical, how do you know it's round?'

'Because I'm familiar with waste paper baskets, and I know that ones like that have round tops.'

'That's completely different from what you said just now, when you said you know it's round because you're looking at it and can see it's round. Is there anywhere in the room from which it would look round?'

'Almost nowhere. Only from a point on a line rising perpendicularly from the centre of the opening. From everywhere else, if you can see it, it looks elliptical.'

'I don't suppose anyone has ever seen it looking round, do you? But tell me, if everyone has always and only seen it looking elliptical, why don't we say it's elliptical? Why do we say so firmly 'No, it's not elliptical, it's round.'? Why should a shape that it seems to have from only one sightline, and no other, be uniquely privileged in determining what shape we say it is?'

And so we were off. For nearly an hour he enmeshed me in simple questions about direct experience, and the problematic relationship between that and knowledge. I was enthralled. The questions were so basic. They were about immediate observation, head-on experience that I was having here and now; and about what I could claim to know on the basis of that. These are among the core questions of philosophy. And he plunged me into the middle of them in my first ten minutes. The examples he used were trivial, but he knew I would not be deceived by that. It is deliberate practice in philosophy to use trivial examples so that nothing of importance depends on the example. I realized straight away that I was in a minefield. Inferences that seemed self-evident turned out to be false, and half the explanations I offered were blown out of the water immediately by some devastating objection. I was told later that Basil had stolen this brilliant technique from a well-known philosopher of the day called H. H. Price; but I did not know that, and in any case it made no difference to me. By the end of the hour I had been knocked sprawling, and was all over the place, but also in a state of unprecedented intellectual curiosity and excitement. Then Basil, having spent most of the hour rubbing my nose in the problems, ended by telling me what I ought to read during the coming week in order to help me get a firmer grip on them. He also asked me to write something. I emerged from the tutorial trembling with impatience to get at the books. Nothing like this had ever happened to me before. There had been nothing like it in my study of history. The following week I went back with an essay brimming with ideas and arguments – only to have half of them shot down immediately by Basil, or carved up fastidiously. He was an excellent tutor. In this problem-led way he guided me through the reading of Descartes, Locke, Berkeley, Hume, and then a number of more recent philosophers. I went through a whole year of this highly intensive work with him, a kind of total immersion, and it was exactly what I needed. The ground we covered had to be selective, but Basil gave me a solid grounding in every area of it he chose, and I have felt permanently indebted to him for it.

In the Oxford of that day it was an incredible stroke of luck on my part to have a philosophy tutor who did not equate reality with what can be known, or with what is expressible in language. As a Christian, Basil believed that a great deal of reality was transcendental. I am not religious – if anything I am anti-religious – but I find that purely non-religious, purely rational considerations compel me to accept that much if not most of reality is permanently outside human understanding. So this was something I had in common with him. And, like him, I wanted to master the techniques of logic and philosophical analysis so as to help me maximize my understanding of what can be understood without taking the logically indefensible step of assuming that only what I can understand can exist. I wanted to be trained in the professional expertise of philosophy without being imprisoned in it. Fortunately, I succeeded in this. After that exciting year with Basil, culminating in a good degree, plus a later year of postgraduate study in Oxford under Peter Strawson, and then a further year of postgraduate work at Yale, I was deemed qualified for faculty posts in philosophy (which in those days did not require a doctorate). Thus philosophy replaced history as my field of academic expertise. It was one in which I was to be active for the rest of my life.

Two papers in basic economics were also compulsory, one in economic theory, the other in applied economics. As far as I was concerned, studying these was an accidental by-product of my commitment to philosophy, but it was a piece of good fortune nonetheless, and I remain permanently pleased to have done it. My understanding of politics was transformed by it. In fact I do not see how anyone ignorant of elementary economics can have a serious understanding of politics. This was brought home to me in practical terms when I became a Member of Parliament.

I was taught for only one paper in politics, and that was about the comparative institutions of Britain, France and the United States. This, though of permanent interest, gave me nothing like the illumination I was getting out of the others. Altogether, though, I came to realize that a degree in PPE was an excellent and modern-minded education. Coming on top of a degree in history it provided me with an exceptionally good grounding.

For the first term of my last year I was Librarian of the Union. This involved chairing the weekly committee meetings that bought new books for the library. I enjoyed this, and it gave me an incentive to keep abreast of the more serious book reviews – which probably also gave me touches of extra help in my academic work. I did this academic work for most of every day in either the Union library or the New Bodleian – a reformed character now. I took more of my meals in the Union than anywhere else. With Caroline no longer in Oxford, the Union was the focus of my everyday life. Most of my closest friends who were still in Oxford were there, so I would see some of them daily, and usually eat with them. It was a satisfying existence, though it had none of the adventuresome many-sidedness that had characterized my earlier undergraduate life. Quite apart from anything else, during my first couple of years at Oxford I would have been psychologically incapable of working as I was working now.

In the sixth week of that term the election of the next term's President took place. On the eve of polling day, as always, came the so-called presidential debate, in which the candidates for the presidency debated against one another. On this occasion the debate was broadcast nationally by BBC Radio. I think this may have influenced the outcome of the election, for I was lucky enough to hit form with the best speech I had made up to that time, and on this occasion it was heard not only by the 600 people in the debating hall but by people all over Oxford. The vote for me next day was some kind of record. In the Union's 128-year history only one President had received more votes, and he got a smaller majority, while only one other had had a larger majority, and he got fewer votes. I was inundated with congratulations, most to do with the broadcast. I also received letters from radio listeners all over the country. My election was reported in the national newspapers. In Oxford's little world, I was a star.

As I walked into the crowded Union bar next day, clapped on the shoulder at every step, a thought went through my mind so vivid that it has stayed with me ever since: 'I'm the same person today as I was yesterday, and I'll still be the same person tomorrow. The Union will still carry on just the same, too. And it'll always be like this, whatever I do in life. If I become Prime Minister, I'll still be the same person as I am now.' The thought was coloured with astonishment, and also an elusive sadness – I might almost say disappointment. I had previously assumed, unconsciously, that becoming President of the Union would be an apotheosis, would change *me* – that I would become a transformed person, a superior being. Perhaps this reflected the way I had looked at other Presidents. Although hyper-vivid, this new perception was also matter-of-fact, down to earth. It was my vision of a de-mystified reality. It was one of the formative insights of my life.

Two weeks later I moved in to the President's magnificent office and began preparing my programme for the following term. A year before, as President of the English Club, I had become used to talking to national figures on the telephone, inviting them to Oxford, and being their host when they arrived, so it came easily now. I had also to do something about the Union's internal organization. As an institution it was heading for bankruptcy. Although it employed a full-time staff of between thirty and forty people, and owned big buildings in the heart of Oxford, it had always been run amateurishly. For years, expenditure had been allowed to exceed income, and the overdraft had creepingly mounted, to a point now where the situation had become threatening. I set out to do some large-scale cost-cutting without diminishing the facilities.

Our large dining room had an excellent business, but was open only during term-time, which in aggregate came to less than half the year; yet we were paying full annual salaries to our kitchen staff and waiters. It had always been said that this was the only way of keeping them. Furthermore, because of a lack of proper control, they were surreptitiously plundering the kitchen's supplies, including the wines.

I gathered them together and spoke to them understandingly, giving in full the reasons for what I was about to do. Then regretfully I gave the statutory month's notice to all the waiters. This meant that they had to leave before the next term began. To replace them I hired waitresses who would be paid (well) by the hour. I went to great lengths to find confident, slightly motherly women who would be good with the undergraduates. In the event the young men liked them more than they liked the waiters, and the change was felt to be an improvement. At the same time I told the kitchen staff that they would continue to be paid full-time salaries for less than half-time work but only on condition that wholesale piracy of the kitchen's provisions ceased. I told them I would have the new situation monitored, and any individuals caught transgressing would be dismissed. There was unabashed vocal protest at this. 'Traditional perks' was the cry: the perks had always gone with the job, and were part of the pay. The chef in particular was used to taking whole sides of beef home, and keeping a well-stocked wine cellar. But I was firm, and they gave in, as I knew they had to – nowhere else could they have expected to get a full year's salary for a half-year's work. Between them and the waiters I saved the Union a small fortune, enough to balance the books, while actually improving the quality of the services to members. The staff in the rest of the building, who worked all the year round, rallied to me with enthusiasm in all this, having always resented the inequitable situation enjoyed by their colleagues in the kitchens and dining room. Throughout my term of office I received noticeable loyalty from the staff. Eighteen months later my reforms were pushed radically further, with equal success, by Michael Heseltine.

An important aspect of the Presidency of the Union was that it gave its holders what, for most of them, was their first experience of running an organization with a sizeable paid staff and a substantial budget. But it was – as running a staff and an organization usually is – a demanding job, and for periods a full-time one. I could not expect to do it and also write two essays a week. So when the term began I asked my tutors if I could be excused essays, just for this one term. I would, I said, do as much reading as I could, and see each of them once a week for interrogation, discussion and guidance; but I could not manage to write essays. My economics tutor exploded. How the hell could he be expected to prepare me for a three-year degree in one year if I was not even fully available for one of the terms? It was a good question. But I was unbudgeable, and our friendship returned after a while. My other tutors accepted the situation without demur. As a variation in teaching method it turned out to have its advantages, because it meant we spent the whole of our time together discussing the work of really important writers, as against spending most of it discussing my essays. There was something altogether more mature about these discussions, and I benefited greatly from them.

But I was, for the whole of that year, working at the top of my bent. I drove myself to the limit, and then kept going. I was conscious of the strain – on one occasion I took it out disgracefully on Caroline – but I knew it was only for one year, and I knew I could handle it. (So could she.) Never again, though, have I experienced such a level of work-stress. After my thirties I doubt whether I would have been able to sustain it. But I think I got more out of it than out of any other year's work I have ever done.

I embarked on that year expecting to have almost no social life except for hosting a weekly dinner party at the Union; but that turned out not to be so. Simply because I was the President of the Union I was invited to parties every day – and all sorts of other University events, too, all over Oxford, often by people I did not know. Although it was impossible to go to most of them I was at liberty to go to those I felt like. So this became my chief way of giving myself a break. Furthermore, after a by-election in the first week of my term as President, Andrew was elected Secretary, and became my right-hand man. He lived an active social life not only in Oxford but also, through his mother, in London, and he included me in both. So in the event I had as much social life as I could take, at the same time as I was doing as much work as I could take.

I was also having the experience, within the confines of my little world, of being famous. It was soon to be extinguished when I left Oxford and emerged into a wider world in which I was unknown; but for a short time, in Oxford, I had it. I was not to have it again until I appeared regularly on television several years later. The scale then was different, but most of the symptoms were the same, and I suspect they always are. A lot of people wanted to meet me, or get to know me better, or make use of me by enlisting my support for their pet causes. Old acquaintances whom I had not seen for years got in touch out of the blue, and tried to re-establish our friendship. Women, some of them attractive, showed interest. Ever so slightly, I was treated with more respect – it was a small difference, but noticeable: people listened more attentively to my opinions, laughed longer at my jokes, were more ready to accommodate themselves and their arrangements to my convenience. I was constantly meeting new people, and inevitably this meant spending less time with old friends. But my horizons expanded. All these are standard by-products of fame, familiar from all the stories one hears and reads about it. Inevitably, the experience is enjoyable for those who are not alarmed by it, but it can still be corrupting. The ego gets used to being massaged and wants more of it. I enjoyed it, I have to say, though with a certain detachment. I had other, more serious things to do at the same time, and these involved hard work, which kept my feet on the ground. Even so, going from this into the big wide world was to be a harsh as well as salutary experience. I remember bumping into the actor Charles Hodgson, who had gone down before me after being successful at Oxford, and asking him what going down was like, and he replied, in the words of a then-popular song: 'Baby, it's cold outside.'

The aspect of my little bit of fame that I enjoyed most was having attractive women stand round me at parties. I flirted with them harmlessly – unless Caroline was with me. She was amusing on the subject of the relationship that she was seen to have with me when she visited Oxford. At the Union, she said, both members and staff treated her as if she had some sort of semi-official position – the President's mistress, she said, as in a Latin

144

American republic. She enjoyed that. She was edgy, though, about my receiving so much female attention when she was not with me. I was faithful to her, and it would not have entered my head to be otherwise; yet at the same time it is true that the chief object of her suspicion was someone who, in later years, had an intimate relationship with me. So it may well be that her radar was picking up on *something*.

The young lady in question was Robin Burke. She had been born in India, as one of four daughters, to an English mother and an Indian father. When partition (which was then recent) had come, her father, a Christian, threw his lot in with Pakistan. He became one of the new country's leading diplomats, which meant working in ever-changing postings in a variety of countries across the world. To provide Robin with a stable education he sent her to school in England. My last year at Oxford was her first at Lady Margaret Hall, where she studied English. During vacations she remained in Oxford most of the time, but had to vacate her college room, so she came to live in 3 St John Street. So when Caroline came to see me during vacations she found Robin living in the house. And Robin was exceptional in ways that included being exceptionally attractive.

She was tall, well built and good looking. Because of her European mother her appearance was not so much Indian or Pakistani as Mediterranean – Spanish, you might say. But even more striking than her looks was her personality, which bubbled with vivacity. Without any effort, she was lively and amusing for most of the time. This went with unusual warmth, and a high level of emotional intelligence. Never had I met anyone so perceptive about the feelings of others: it was as if their detailed reactions were a language giving her messages, so that she knew what was going on inside each person. She always seemed to be accurate in her predictions about how they would behave, even when she differed in this from everyone else. I took to her enormously, despite her being so young – she was eighteen, while I was coming up to the ripe old age of twenty-three.

The arrangements in the house meant that Robin and I had breakfast together every morning, with a couple of other people; and lunch on Sundays; and would bump into each other constantly in our comings and goings. Before long we were special friends. In one way, Caroline's suspicion that there might be (or might be about to be) something between us was right – there was indeed a special feeling, though at that time it was not sexual. It was a friendship that was to be lifelong, to pass through widely differing phases and survive them all, with never a break up to the present day.

9

Going Down

When my term as President of the Union ended there was less than three months to go before my final degree exam, after which I would be leaving Oxford for good. I was ready to go. Whereas I could not have borne to leave at the end of my third year, during my fourth I had found my feet, and was beginning to want to move on. I was not expecting to get a good degree in PPE, but since I had been studying philosophy for its own sake and not to get a degree, I tried to feel stoical about that. Basil Mitchell had given me a first-rate introduction to the subject, and this was what I had always cared about. Even so, I did not relish the thought of getting a third. But the possibility now stared me in the face. I saw myself as battling against almost impossible odds for a second-class degree.

There was a general feeling around me of things drawing to an end. Those of my closest friends who were still in Oxford – Andrew Cuninghame, Richard Cavendish and others – were taking their finals too, so the atmosphere in which all of us lived was valedictory. Oxford had been an epic experience for us all, for some the most shaping experience of their lives. Our feelings about its passing were in proportion. It was the end of a shared world. We knew that the friendships between us would last, but we also knew that the rest of our lives would lead most of us in different directions.

A lot of my friends were clear-headed about their immediate aims: they wanted to go into the Foreign Office, or the Treasury, or to be lawyers, doctors, academics, or whatever. They knew what they wanted to do next. But I was surprised at how many did not. This is another way of saying that there was nothing in particular that they wanted to do next, and I found that hard to understand. I was full of will, and I knew what I wanted: I wanted to write books and go into politics. However, in one important respect I was in the same position as those who did not know, because there was no job I wanted, and yet I had to get one. Writing my first book was bound to take some time, especially if I had a full-time job; and I could scarcely expect to live on the income from books until I had written some. Similarly, I would get no income from political activity until I became a Member of Parliament, but I could not expect that to happen for some years. So although writing and politics were both time-consuming occupations in which I had a powerful urge to sink myself, I would have to do yet a third thing to earn a living. I mistakenly supposed that it would not matter much to me what this was, provided it was not unpleasant and enabled me to do more important things. I would not be looking for a career in it: on the contrary, I would leave it the moment I could afford to, and the sooner the better. It would be no more than a stop-gap, albeit possibly a long one.

As the French say, it's the provisional that lasts. Had I but known it, this problem was something I was going to have to grapple with for most of my life. I did not go into the House of Commons until I was forty-three, and then left at fifty-three. I did not earn enough money to live on from my books until I was in my mid-sixties. However, in my early years, with the optimism of youth, I took it for granted that these things were going to happen sooner than they did. There were then, just as there are today, people who had become successful authors or Members of

Parliament while still young, and I took it for granted that I was going to be one of them.

I thought, again mistakenly, that for an aspiring writer the most congenial sort of job would be a writing job, and therefore journalism. So I wrote to *The Times*, and was given an interview in its offices by a well-known figure of the day called A. P. Ryan. He told me that so many already-experienced journalists were trying to get on to *The Times* that the paper had no need to train beginners. This, he said, was so with all the national newspapers. If I could acquire a year's experience on a provincial paper, and then come back to him, he thought he would be able to find me something.

I actively disliked the idea of taking a job outside London. But it would be for only a year. So I wrote to what was then *The Manchester Guardian*. It was the newspaper I had long been reading every day, and I felt myself already in a relationship with it. I took the train to Manchester and was interviewed by a journalist whose work I knew well. From the interview it seemed – and he said it was – touch and go whether they would offer me a job. But in the end they did not. So I gritted my teeth and wrote to the other prestigious provincial paper, *The Liverpool Echo*. Its editor told me he was about to come to Oxford, and would interview me in his old college. There he told me he thought I might be a decent catch for his paper, but the snag was that as soon as they had trained me I would leave and go to London. This was spot on. I did not admit it, but I could not deny it. He added that this was so obvious that he doubted whether any provincial paper would employ me. It was catch-22.

I started writing to the weeklies, and to magazines. I had some interviews that resulted in near-misses: Kingsley Martin, Editor of *The New Statesman*, asked me twice to go back and see him, so I must have come near getting a job with him, but in the end it did not come off. All this was taking time – time up to and beyond the end of term – so when the term ended I still had no job. Meanwhile there was the small matter of my final examination.

Having taken a degree the previous summer I had been through the process already, so I was nothing like as scared of it as most of the other candidates. I was surprised how relaxed I felt. I was able to perform up to the highest level that my truncated preparations would allow. After the written papers I was summoned for an oral examination, the so-called viva. For most candidates vivas were a formality, and lasted only a few minutes, because the marks awarded to their written papers placed them unambiguously in this or that class, so the result was a foregone conclusion. Only in borderline cases, when the examiners were unsure in which class to place a candidate, were vivas long and significant. When several minutes of mine had gone by, this fact itself, and the ongoing intensity of the questioning, made me realize that I was being given a long viva. Immediately I assumed I was on the borderline between a second and a third.

I sat alone on one side of a long table opposite a row of examiners, two each from Philosophy, Politics and Economics. After a quarter of an hour's interrogation they asked me to go out of the room while they discussed me. Eventually they called me back, and grilled me for another quarter of an hour. Then they sent me out again – and then called me back for yet another quarter of an hour. Finally they let me go. I told all my friends I was being viva'd between a third and a second. When, some time later, the printed results came out it appeared, as I believed, that I had scraped a second. But what had actually happened, unsuspected by me, was that I had been viva'd for a first. I had missed a first by a hair's breadth. I learnt this from Basil Mitchell, to whom, as my tutor, my marks were later sent by the examiners. He told me I had come as close to getting a first without actually getting one as it was possible to come. Many years later, I learnt that during the breaks in my viva one of the philosophy examiners,

Peter Strawson, had been arguing that I should be given a first, but the other would not agree to it.

With the academic year over, and my exams behind me, I was no longer a student at Oxford. Since entering a public school at the age of eleven I had lived in institutions – first a boarding school, then the army, then university. Now, for the first time, I was without a support system. I was an independent adult of twenty-three with nothing but his own resources to sustain him. And I had no resources. In fact, my resources were negative. I was up to my eyes in debt to every imaginable source of loans and credit: several friends, several shops, my college, my landlady, and above all my bank. In those days the normal starting salary for fresh graduates was four hundred pounds a year, although management trainees in industry would often be paid four hundred and fifty. My debts added up to more than that, so it would take me several years to pay them off. I did not resent this: I had contracted debt with my eyes open, knowing what I was doing. But now had come, as people say, pay-back time. I calculated roughly that if I could live on three-quarters of a slowly rising salary I might hope to pay the debts off in something like five years. It was a formidable prospect, and I was a little daunted by it, yet I did not see it as an excessive price to pay for the four years I had just spent in Oxford – which had unquestionably changed my life permanently, and for the better. I would far rather have Oxford and the debt than no debt and no Oxford.

I stayed on in 3 St John Street because I had nowhere to go. My landlady, the sainted Mrs Slay, told me that I could chalk my rent up on her slate until I found a job. She had known me for two years, and knew that, short of premature death, nothing would prevent me from paying her in full. But I was now under pressure. All my attempts to get the sort of job I wanted were failing. And I never did, in fact, become a writing journalist, in the sense of earning my living at journalism. Unrealized by me at the time, this was a stroke of luck, because when I did start writing occasional articles for national journals I found that I did not enjoy it. It did not come naturally to me. I found myself to be a natural book-writer, not a natural article-writer; a long-distance runner, not a sprinter. I would have detested having to write articles for a living. And it might not have been good for the real me that was a writer.

I needed a job desperately. I had no money, and no possessions except for my clothes, gramophone records and books. I could live only by increasing my debts. There is danger in such a situation, for if you plump for something bottom-of-the-barrel out of sheer desperation you may find that it itself becomes a handicap, and hampers you, and makes your situation all the more difficult to get out of. You cannot even easily look for a job if you are already in a job. I was aware of this, and tried to cope with it by making as many different job applications simultaneously as I thought I could handle. When I think now of some of the jobs I applied for I am amazed. It is difficult to know which to pursue when you do not want any of them. The most embarrassing question that was put to me in interviews – and it was put often – was 'Why do you want this job?', because the truth was that I did not want it, and would rather not have had to apply for it. But I usually managed to come up with a more acceptable reply.

I had interview after interview. My success at Oxford meant nothing in the outside world, or at most very little. People forget that success as an undergraduate cannot possibly have anything to do with degree results, because these do not exist until after the end of the final term. In any case, having two second-class degrees gives a greater impression of ordinariness than having one, and is not at all the boost to a CV that some people might imagine. And having been at Keble was a handicap in those days. One member of a BBC interviewing board said: 'I see you were at Keble. How did you manage to become President of the Union?' The same prejudice was hinted at in three or four interviews, the implication always being that if I had been any good I would not have been at Keble. I was told subsequently by another member of the BBC board that the interviewer had specifically given that ground for vetoing my being taken. There were other interviews in which it became only too often obvious that I was not going to bring the kind of commitment that the interviewers were looking for. In Shell-Mex House one of them said: 'What it all comes down to, Mr Magee, is: Are you prepared to live Shell?', to which I could only reply: 'No, I'm afraid I'm not. I'm sorry.'

Weeks went by, and began to turn into months: July passed and we were in August. Summer would soon be behind us. Over and again I was the runner-up in an interview, but missed the job. It was a long time before I realized what was going on. I had grown up in meritocratic institutions. In Christ's Hospital, and then the Intelligence Corps, and then Oxford, how well an individual fared depended on his abilities, not on his connections. But England as a whole was not like that. What still mattered most in the outside world was who you knew – or rather, who your parents knew. As, one by one, my friends told me about the jobs they were getting, I began to notice that this one said he was going into a firm in which a godfather of his knew somebody; that one said he was joining an organization in which an ex-boyfriend of his mother was important; and so on and so forth. The connection was often at two removes: someone knew someone who knew someone. There was an acquaintance of mine whose father's doctor had become a family friend, and my acquaintance was offered a job by a firm in which another of the doctor's patients was a senior executive. That was how England operated in those days. If an undergraduate told a group of friends that he had landed a job in such-and-such an organization, one of the group would always ask: 'Who do you know there?' People would say: 'There's no point in my applying for so-and-so – I don't know anybody there.' The $64,000 dollar question was always: 'Who do you know?' The

153

penny dropped in my head about why I was so often coming second. It was that I did not know anybody, and interviewers were trying to ease someone else into the job. If I was the runner up, it meant that they thought I was the best of the candidates interviewed, and would be offered the job if anything went wrong with the easing process. This made me despair. If being the best candidate was not enough, what could I do? I was at the mercy of opportunity, and opportunity depended either on connections I did not have or on the accident of someone dropping out. It was to be the case that two of my first three jobs after leaving Oxford were jobs I got because someone dropped out.

Of course, I was not the only one in this situation. I had seen some of Oxford's outstanding personalities go down in previous years into similar circumstances. But I had supposed them to be victims of bad luck, and had acquired no deeper understanding until it happened to me. What I am talking about was not, or was not directly, a question of social class. Nepotism was the key, and that is not the same thing. When nearly all the good jobs went to mediocrities for disreputable reasons, other people who wanted those jobs and would have done them better did not get them, regardless of their social class. Oleg Kerensky, who had been educated at Westminster and Christ Church, and lived in Belgravia with a prominent and prosperous family, was unemployed for a whole year, despite innumerable interviews. Dick Taverne, who had been head boy at Charterhouse and taken a first in Greats at Balliol, took a job as a night watchman while he read for the Bar. Robin Day, after failing as a barrister, was in a worse situation than mine, and reached the point when he was sleeping on a friend's living-room floor and insulating his shoes with newspaper. In August 1953 (the month that was also my lowest) he put England behind him in despair. In the autobiography he published thirty-six years later he wrote:

> On that August day in 1953 at Waterloo station, the girls in the
> group which had come to say goodbye to me were in tears. …
> I had failed. I was quitting. It was a miserable moment in my
> life. I could not see a glimmer of hope. … I was now going to
> a badly paid and inferior job in America with no prospects and
> no future.

All these people proved their ability eventually, not least Robin,
who returned to England and became famous. But some of the
people I knew who went abroad in such circumstances never
returned. Ours was the last university generation to emerge into
what was still, predominantly, a pre-meritocratic England. The
Angry Young Man movement, with everything it implied,
followed us immediately in the middle fifties, precisely because of
these circumstances. Later in my twenties, when I was living in
London, half the new friends I made had been through a period
of this sort – and were now demonstrating, having at last been
given a chance, that they merited the opportunities that had
previously been held back from them. The mediocrities whom
they squeezed out of the way were, in parallel, the first whole
generation of mediocrities in Britain to be mortally threatened by
meritocrats. Inevitably, they too were resentful. Many of them
went on to live lives of decline and failure which otherwise they
would not have had – and they knew it. For them, too, it was
difficult not to be bitter.

When I was at my lowest in Oxford I began to understand why
so many of my contemporaries took a path that I found
disappointing. We had come from an almost infinite variety of
backgrounds, but as students we had transcended our
backgrounds. Again, this was not a matter of social class. Some of
us, regardless of class, had grown up with conventional parents
while others had parents who were radicals; some came from
religious families, others from secular ones; some had grown up

imbued with tolerant values, others with judgemental ones; some were used to being convivial, others independent; this person had a military background, that a business one, another an academic one. This person had lived all his life in a London suburb; another in an industrial northern city, another on a farm. We came from an extraordinary variety of worlds. And in almost every case those worlds had left their mark on us, given us some of our limitations. One of the most valuable things we did for one another in our relationships was to break through those limitations. The daughter of the manse and the rackety jazz pianist became lovers; the nouveau riche was best friends with the Quaker; each took the other into a new world; and that was how the best of our student circles swept us along.

From a position that transcended all these backgrounds, each of them looked small and cramped. I had taken it for granted that, having developed beyond them, none of us would ever go back to them. At the very least, I thought, we would always live in a world that included one another. Many of my contemporaries had already headed for wider horizons, especially those who had grown up in the provinces and now lived in London. But I was astonished at how many did not. Instead these returned to the limited background from which they had come. I have already described the dismay I felt when Caroline, a revolutionary from upper-middle-class bohemia, returned to live in that background after Oxford. I had had the same disconcerting experience with other friends. A Quaker friend returned to his narrow Quaker world. And so on. I could scarcely believe it. I felt betrayed. It was as if, for them, the Oxford experience had counted for little, and they were turning their backs on everything we had meant to one another.

I, of course, had nowhere to return to. My friends *were* my world, so I felt their defalcation keenly. But now, for the first time, I began to understand what was going on. To live without any world at all, without any stable background to relate to – as I was now doing for the first time in my life – was exceedingly difficult, and alarming. I began to realize that if I had had somewhere to go, I would probably have gone there, if only as a temporary expedient. And this is how some of the returnees did behave: they re-emerged. But others got stuck, and slowly lost their vitality, like flies on fly-paper.

This was a stressful and dark period of my life, which it is still painful for me to think about. I kept having my hopes raised by my interviews and then dashed by what came of them; and, as the Old Testament says, hope deferred maketh the heart sick. But in the end, as was probably bound to happen sooner or later (though it did not feel like it at the time), I was offered a job. Three big things about it are in line with everything I have said. First, the opportunity came via someone I knew who was putting himself out to help me personally. Second, when it was made firm, that happened because another person dropped out. Third, the job was not in England.

I had registered with the Oxford University Appointments Board, whose function was to help graduates find jobs. The Board had a bad reputation: in fact it was said that no one ever found a worthwhile job through it, because the real job-getting procedures by-passed it. Even so, I had registered with it as part of the all-inclusiveness of my job hunt. When I was interviewed there, one of the two people who ran it – a man called Escritt – told me with much approval that he had been educated at Christ's Hospital and Keble like me. He was the sort of person who saw me as a fellow spirit on those grounds, and he set himself to make a special point of helping me. Some of my interviews had already come to me through him.

The job was in Sweden. An organization that ran extra-mural teaching from Lund University wanted to give a one-year contract to a native English-speaker who would give classes in the English language and lectures on English literature. The eye-catching thing was the pay, which was made up of sums from different sources and totalled something like three times a normal English starting salary. Sweden in those days was far more prosperous than Britain, and salaries were much higher. When Escritt put the proposal to me, the first thing I said was: 'But I don't have a degree in English, nor any qualification to teach it.' He said: 'Nonsense. You've been President of the Oxford University English Club. You're a published poet. You've got two Oxford degrees. You'll have been sent to them by Oxford University. They'll believe they're really getting something.'

I was torn. I did not want to work abroad – because of Caroline, and also because of a deeply felt desire to live and work in London. However, after all these months of applications and interviews I had not received a single offer, not one – and it might be months again before I did. For several days I stewed over it. I tried to think it through systematically, examining the factors one by one. I knew that if I had managed to get a first-class degree I would not even have considered this job. With a first and the Presidency of the Union under my belt I would have been bound, I thought, to be offered a worthwhile opportunity sooner or later, no matter how long the wait. But that is not how things were. And they seemed perfectly capable of going on indefinitely as they were. So this opportunity was a real one. Going to Sweden would mean being separated from Caroline for another year. But I had already felt willing, with huge reluctance, to spend that year in Manchester, and even in Liverpool. In Sweden I would at least get to know a new foreign country, and learn a new language. I had little idea of Sweden, simply that it was North and cold. My mental image of it was too faint to be either favourable or unfavourable. I had not heard of any town in it except Stockholm. When, later, I told people in Lund that I had never heard of Lund until I went there, they thought it was some kind of supercilious English joke and did not believe me; but the truth is that scarcely anyone in England to whom I said I was going to Lund had heard of it.

The negative considerations almost carried the day. I did not want to go abroad at this juncture. On top of a continued separation from Caroline, and my passionate love of London, was the fact that if I left England I would feel I was running away, bolting, chickening out – even worse, being *forced* out. I would be leaving England because it could find no place for me. Everything inside me rebelled against that. And yet, in spite of this inner rebellion, I was in a despairing state of mind, the lowest I had ever been. My lack of self-confidence was extreme. I could see no alternative. What tipped my decision was this lack of alternative, plus financial considerations. I calculated that if I could keep my standard of living in Sweden close to what I had been used to in Oxford I would be able to pay off most of my debts in a single year. This prospect would not in itself have been enough to decide the battle that was raging inside me, but given the other factors it settled the outcome.

I talked all this through with Caroline. I expected her to oppose my going, but she did not. She was as torn as I was, but for a different balance of reasons. She feared the effects of our continued separation more than I did, but the prospect of getting out of most of my financial troubles in one year seemed much more imperative to her than it did to me. I had always accepted my five-year plan more equably than she had. To her, the financial consideration seemed the dominant one, whereas for me the dominant consideration was the absence of alternative job-prospects, plus a growing anxiety that had been building up inside me to a point now of desperation. I had come to feel that I must take any chance that was offered. Caroline, as I have said, was more fearful of what this could mean for our relationship. She did not say to me but to Mrs Slay, who repeated it to me, that what

Sweden meant to her was beautiful blondes and Free Love. She was not confident of my ability to say No to either.

The employing organization in Lund paid a barrister in London not only to draw up the job contract but (strangely, it seemed to me) to interview the applicants and make the choice. So for my interview I went to the Inns of Court. Eventually I was to find myself going there again to fix the practicalities of travelling to Sweden and starting work.

I had taken it for granted that my employers would pay my fare, but this turned out not to be the case. They expected me just to turn up in Lund on a particular date, by which time they would have engaged a furnished room for me to rent and would start paying me. So I had little alternative but to tell the interviewer I was broke and ask him to lend me the money to get to the job he had just given me. He was taken aback by this, but he coughed up. For years afterwards, especially when I became well known on television, he enjoyed telling the story.

The head of my college, Harry Carpenter, asked me to see him before leaving Oxford, so I did. He told me he was pleased that I was going to Lund because it had a distinguished international reputation in theology. He also remarked that I had done well by the college in becoming President of the Union, and that I must have worked hard to get such a good degree in PPE. Never had he talked to me so benignly. He then quizzed me about my finances. He knew I owed the college a lot of money, and asked about other debts. I felt unable to tell him about the huge amounts I owed to my friends, and to the bank – these were private matters, I felt, which I was unwilling to discuss: they were for me to cope with. But I did tell him about my several-months' arrears of rent to my landlady, and my bills at the bookshops. He said Keble maintained a special fund for students in need which would pay these; and he would see to it that my debt to the college was also cancelled. This was wholly unexpected, and it made a significant difference to me. I was surprised and grateful. Then he asked if this would put me 'completely in the clear on this side of the water', to which I untruthfully replied that it would. This was false pride, but I could not bring myself to say otherwise. In any case, I did not believe the college would be willing to pay *all* my debts – their extent would have shocked the Warden. I was more than pleased with what he had given me, and more than happy to leave it at that.

I made the journey to Lund by the cheapest route, by ferry to Esbjerg then across Denmark by train to Copenhagen, then a ferry again to Malmö, and then a train to Lund. I was in a new world. Entirely unrealized by me, it was a world that was to be part of my life for the rest of my life. I have been in Denmark and Sweden every year since then, and I now have a whole family in Sweden: a middle-aged daughter, three grown-up grandchildren, and an increasing number of great-grandchildren. None of these would exist at all if that London barrister's first choice had not dropped out, or if I had been given the first-class degree that I missed by the breadth of a hair. It is a terrifying illustration of the radical contingency of our lives, of our very existence.

So ended my four years at Oxford. My friends, like me, went out into unpredictable lives, and some to early deaths. Many of the people I have named in this book are dead now, including those who were closest to me – Caroline, Andrew, Chris Elrington, Philippa, Oleg Kerensky, Bernard Williams, Tyrrell Burgess, Richard Cavendish. Others, still alive, are among my closest friends – especially Robin and Richard Sarson. Yet others have been good friends for more than half a century. As a matrix of friendship Oxford has been beyond compare: what it created turned out to be rich, nourishing and lasting. Although my readers may find themselves wondering how life turned out for some of them, few would wish me now to embark on their successive life stories. In spite of that, though, I do want to say a word about Caroline.

She and I were not only lovers but good friends until the day I left England. However, her forebodings were correct. In the circumstances of my life in Sweden I found it impossible to remain faithful to her for a year. I became involved with someone else, and then with someone I eventually married. But so did she. At first *both* of us got involved lightly with other people, expecting to return to one another; but then each of us moved on from that first infidelity to something more serious; and then the gap between us changed its character. There was never a break, never a conscious separation: we drifted away from each other in countries a thousand miles apart. By the time we realized what was happening it had happened. We both realized, in retrospect, that the bonds between us had loosened during the year when she was in London and I was in Oxford. We had each half-realized that at the time, without wanting to acknowledge it. When eventually we talked these things over, there was no disagreement about what had happened, and no inclination to blame.

I never met the man Caroline married. He was Lukas Heller, a German-born Englishman who wrote films – mostly, though not exclusively, for Hollywood – the best-known being *The Killing of Sister George*, *The Dirty Dozen* and *Whatever Happened to Baby Jane?* He and Caroline had four children, whom I saw from time to time as they were growing up. Luke's work took him abroad a good deal, and on those occasions Caroline would sometimes telephone me, and we would meet. There was never any sex between us – my life had moved on too, and I was involved elsewhere – but a good deal in our complicated relationship remained the same. There was a palpable feeling of intimacy between us, a field of force which we were both aware of. We discussed it sometimes, without really understanding it. Whatever it was, both of us found it unique.

One day, Luke went off with another woman, leaving Caroline with the four children. She made a half-hearted attempt to revive her relationship with me, but half-hearted it remained. It was as if we were revisiting a house we no longer lived in. Too much else had changed. Our relationship became sexual again for a short time, but it was never the same. We found ourselves unable to turn that kind of love on and off like a tap or a switch. In fact my involvement elsewhere survived through it, and carried on. Eventually Caroline married for a second time, a younger man.

But still the sense of there being a unique bond between us persisted. We went on meeting, always with long gaps in between, and a something between us was always there. When Caroline died of cancer at the age of fifty-nine she told her husband in her last days that she wanted me to speak at her funeral. He asked me to do that, but I said I could do it only if I spoke truthfully about our relationship – which with his full knowledge and permission I did. It was an extraordinary occasion, described by one of the mourners as 'transcendental'. There was a large crowd, and I believe most people there must have found my contribution surprising and, to say the least, unconventional. One or two, I know, were shocked and disapproving. But it was what Caroline had asked for. And I felt a need for it too. In ways that only she and I understood – and I am not sure that we understood it either – we had had a unique importance in each other's lives.

The first of the Sherlock Holmes short stories begins with the sentence: 'To Sherlock Holmes she is always *the* woman.' To me, Caroline was for many years *the* woman. Neither of us escaped the feeling that we ought to have spent our lives together, even though each of us knew that for this to have happened, and to have worked, we would need to be different people. Genuinely, inwardly, neither of us blamed the other for the way things turned out, because at each point we had both been responsible for it, and accepting of it. The 'ought to have been' and the 'is not' co-existed.

But each remained the other's 'might have been', with a vivid reality that neither of us could let go of.

Whether Caroline could have lived a fulfilled life with me I have no way of knowing, but I doubt it. As things were, she did not have a fulfilled life. At Oxford she was every bit as outstanding in her generation as Shirley Williams had been in the one before, and Margaret Thatcher in the one before that; and she had the personal endowment to become, as each of them did, a national figure. She was as striking a personality, as naturally gifted and intelligent, much more beautiful, and with a more effortless charisma. She should have begun by becoming, like them, a Member of Parliament. Politics was her metier, and it would have been astonishing if she had not reached the top level of it. But she did not try. And I believe that the key to this is the radical but hidden self-doubt that had revealed itself to me in connection with her speech at the Oxford Union. She possessed all the abilities it required – and she really did have them – but at the same time, concealed, she had an incapacitating fear that it was not so, a fear that she would be inadequate and would fail. Why the prospect of failing was so terrifying is itself a question, perhaps the key question – for, as Noël Coward once brilliantly put it, the secret of success is the ability to survive failure. I think it was because the high expectations that had been placed on her all her life were intolerably stressful: at home, as the oldest of five children, she was very much the star of the family; and at university, a star again, she was hailed on all sides as a future public figure of national fame. But inwardly she feared she was not up to it. That she felt this did not occur to others, so gifted was she, and so confident did she appear. The jobs she opted for in her subsequent life were trivial by comparison with her ability. They were not even suited to her gifts. The truth is that after Oxford she never allowed her potential to be challenged.

The price she paid was ruinous. As her daughter Zoë Heller wrote in the pen-portrait I quoted earlier: 'In mid-life, she was plagued by a sense of having squandered her education and talents … From time to time, these feelings would overpower her and she would succumb to long, inky-black bouts of despair.' She knew that she had let her life go by without even trying to fulfil herself. And there was no one else to blame. But instead of galvanizing her to action, this fact resulted in devastating depression. It was only the existence of her four children that gave her any feeling that life was worth living.

She sought psychiatric help, but it was of no use, and she gave it up. What she needed was not therapy but a life. And she could no longer see how to get one. In this regard she was a severely damaged person. I have never known anyone so gifted so damaged. But the damage had been there through all the time I had known her, deep down and covered over, invisible to anyone but an intimate. It is possible, I suppose, that if she had continued to be partnered and supported by someone who understood her she might have sailed magnificently through life in the way she sailed so magnificently through the Oxford Union debate. But I do not really believe it. In a public career she would have had to face more alarming challenges than that, and anything much more alarming would have got the better of her, with or without support. All the abilities she needed to meet it would have been there except for the confidence that she had them.

Book Two

The Turning Point

to
Gunnela
with all your children
and their children
with love

1

I knew next to nothing about Scandinavia when I went there in the late summer of 1953 at the age of twenty-three. To most English people at that time, 'abroad' usually meant parts of Europe south of us. This applied to me too. I had been to school in Versailles for a while, and knew Paris quite well. I had spent a year in Austria as a teenage soldier in the British army of occupation. As an undergraduate at Oxford I had taken vacation jobs in Belgium. And that was the sum total of my experience of the world outside England. I had never been in a country with higher living standards, and did not know there were any apart from Switzerland and the United States. I thought of England as being comfortably in advance of those other European countries which so recently had been either defeated by us in the war or occupied by the Nazis – and then liberated by us.

I was fresh out of Oxford, and on my way to take up my first job. An adult-education organization whose offices were in the University of Lund in Sweden had given me a one-year contract as an extra-mural lecturer in English language and literature. I had no academic qualifications in these subjects, but knew a great deal about them compared to most foreigners. As for teaching, I hoped it was something I would improve at as I went along. I already had a little experience of teaching French to American children, so I had been broken in to language teaching. Altogether, I was hopeful about my ability to do the job. But as regards the whole area of the world I was heading for and would be living in, there were only two or three thoughts I could muster about any Scandinavian country.

Finland was the home of my beloved Sibelius, and it had fought with a courage that was still legendary against a Russian invasion under Stalin, when Stalin was Hitler's ally. Norway had provided us with Ibsen and Grieg, and sailors in London pubs. I had acquired a love of Ibsen's plays, but the picture of Norway these projected was gloomy. Denmark had a livelier image, partly because of Hans Christian Andersen, but also because of the unique way in which the country had defied Nazi occupation and helped its Jewish population. Then, in the middle of those Scandinavian countries, came Sweden, a blank. It had been neutral in the war, and had therefore rarely been mentioned in the newspapers. It had produced no music that I was aware of having heard, no plays I had seen, no books I had read. I had seen one Swedish film, and the language had sounded to me surprisingly like English without the intelligibility. Sweden's society had a reputation for being 'advanced', which I took to include socialism and fashionable modern design. I knew that Lapland was partially in Sweden, and imagined that so northern a country must be so cold that the people there would dress like Eskimos for half the year. When I talked to my friends about the fact that I was going there I found that scarcely any of them knew more than I did.

I had been asked to make my way there by boat and train, because that was the cheapest way and air travel had not yet become the norm. The first leg of the journey out of England was an overnight ferry from Harwich to the Danish port of Esbjerg. I had twice before boarded a boat in Harwich, a troopship bound for the Hook of Holland, to meet up with a troop train down the

Rhine Valley into Austria; but now I linked up with an ordinary train across Denmark. At some point inside the country, to my surprise, there was another quite long boat trip between two land masses. And at Copenhagen there was to be a third boat trip to the Swedish port of Malmö – of which I had not previously heard. This was unlike the continental travel I was used to: all this sea, all these boats.

By the time I got as far as Copenhagen my muscles were cramped from the journey and I was in need of stretching my legs. When an announcement came that the train would remain in the station for another hour and a half I decided to get out and look at Copenhagen, if only for an hour. By sheer good luck I turned to the right outside the station, and soon found myself in one of the city's two main squares, with a marvellously Nordic statue of two Viking warriors blowing colossal horns. (For many generations these horns have resounded every time a virgin crosses the square.) In order not to risk losing myself and being late back for the train I decided to keep walking in a straight line, so I ambled across the centre of the square into the street directly opposite. Unknown to me, this was Copenhagen's most famous shopping street, Strøget – actually three linked streets with three different names. I walked the full length of them, and found myself in what is in fact (though again I did not know it) Copenhagen's other main square. By this time I felt that the time had come to turn back. So I strolled back along Strøget, then across the first square – using up the time that remained by poking into its sides – and finally back to the train. By the happiest of chances I had spent my hour in the heart of Copenhagen.

The boat to Malmö arrived late, so by the time I got to its railway station the train for Lund, standing at the far end of a very long platform, was on the point of leaving. It was making about-to-go noises, so I ran the full length of the platform shouting 'Hey! Hey!' at the top of my lungs, hoping to be heard by the driver, whom I had seen getting into his cab. Unknown to me, the sound I was making was the commonest of all words of greeting and parting for Swedes, so to everyone in the station I looked as if I was sprinting along the platform bawling farewells at the departing train. It did indeed leave without me. I minded missing it because I was due to be met at Lund. It was late in the evening, and I had visions of being stranded for the night in a foreign city, whether Malmö or Lund (where I did not know what address I was to be taken to), in a country I had never before set foot in, where I knew not a soul, and spoke not a word of the language. But there was another train, and I got to Lund. There, waiting patiently in the deserted station, was Harald Wohlstad.

Harald was the local boss of the organization that was hiring me, a stubby figure dressed with informal formality in a light brown suit. One thing about him that was evident straight away was that he was sensitive and unassuming without being weak. He took me to a furnished room nearby that he had hired on my behalf; and there he left me to sort myself out and get a night's sleep. In those days trunks travelled separately from their owners, and mine was due to be delivered the following day, so there was not much sorting out for me to do. Next morning Harald came to collect me and show me round Lund, then take me to his office. My professional life in Sweden had begun.

But my trunk did not arrive. It contained all my worldly possessions except for books and gramophone records, which I had left with friends in England. It had done this for several years now, so it was the worse for wear, with locks that no longer fastened and a leather belt strapped round it to hold it together. Harald made telephone enquiries which revealed that the trunk had not been transferred from one train to another in Denmark when I had. It must now be standing abandoned and alone on an open-air ramp in an uninhabited plain on Denmark's central island. 'Typical Danes,' muttered Harald with satisfaction. He was surprised at his success in tracking it down but thought little of my chances of getting it back unpilfered-from. Yet I did. And that set a pattern for something I found in all Scandinavian countries from that day to this: an unsurpassed level of public honesty.

Harald loved Lund, and showed me round it with pride. It has distinctive charm – much smaller than Oxford, its central streets are cobbled and have an atmosphere that characterizes many little old cathedral-and-university cities in Europe. The cathedral itself was built in the twelfth century. Although it is renowned for its architecture I thought the exterior ugly but found the interior attractive – simple, golden, honey-coloured, austere and yet warm. To one side of the cathedral buzzes the main square of the modern town. The older of the streets converging on this are lined with old-fashioned shops and cafés. The other side of the cathedral, much quieter, is where the university is. This, founded in the seventeenth century, acquired what are now its dominating buildings in the nineteenth, and is separated from the cathedral by a small park that functions as a quadrangle for the university. This is called Lundagård. (The word 'gård' in Swedish means a court, in the sense in which Cambridge colleges have courts; and there is also a word 'lund' meaning a copse or grove; so 'Lundagård' means Lund's copse, and also a university court consisting of a tree-grove.) It is the heart of academic Lund, with university buildings scattered among its trees, continually criss-crossed by scurrying students and academics – a bumping-into place for the preoccupied. Overlooking it from one of the streets that enclose it is the university's premier coffee house, also called Lundagård.

Harald showed me round all this as if he were the father of it all – the university, the cathedral, the town and me – explaining everything, and pointing out whatever might later be of use to me. It would never have entered his head that I had not previously heard of Lund, but he became increasingly short in his answers as, each time he mentioned a famous Swedish figure of the present or past, I asked: 'Who is he?', for I was indeed anxious to learn. In particular it irked him that I had not heard of the many people whose statues and busts he showed me. He was beginning to regard me as someone of culpably defective general knowledge. This came to a head in front of the full-length statue of Tegnér (1782–1846), one of the greatest poets in the Swedish language.

'Here,' he said with a flourish of the hand, 'is Tegnér,' and stepped aside for me to admire.

I looked with genuine interest at the statue, but then asked: 'Who was he?'

Harald was startled, incredulous. 'Well – *you* know, he said. 'Tegnér.'

'I'm afraid I don't know who he is.'

'Everyone's heard of Tegnér.'

'I honestly don't think they have, not outside Sweden.'

'Nonsense. He's internationally famous. Everyone has heard of Tegnér.'

I wanted to amend Harald's view of me, and persisted: 'I'm sure you'll find that even well-educated people in England haven't.'

'Rubbish,' he said, in tones of finality. 'I'm quite certain they have.'

And that was that. He really did believe that, even if I hadn't heard of Tegnér, every other educated person in Britain had. It was I who was ignorant. I could see that, if I went on insisting, it could only strengthen this view, so I was silenced.

However, a few months later I was comforted to learn that when Thomas Mann had given a lecture at Lund University he had begun a sentence with the now-notorious words: 'As your great poet Jeremias Tegnér wrote ...' Even I now knew that the poet's name was Esaias.

My third night in Lund remains unforgettable as one of the most terrible nights of my life. By this time I had carried out a reconnaissance of the new world that was to be mine. I had done a lot of shopping in the main streets of the town, and settled into my living quarters. I had met two or three times, in Harald's offices, some of the people I was going to be seeing a lot of from now on. And when I went to bed on that third night and switched the light off I was overwhelmed by a sense of the inadequacy of it all to sustain me. The feeling seemed primarily physical. I was being stifled. I was struggling for breath, there was not enough oxygen. I needed more life than this: more demanding and engrossing work, a wider field of operation, bigger people as my colleagues and associates, a town to live in where the performing arts were alive. But I was trapped. I had signed a one-year contract. And I did not have enough money to leave – I had even had to borrow the money to come here. And even if I did leave, there was nowhere to go. I had no home in England, and had come to Sweden because I was unable to find a job in England after months of searching. This was the first and only job I had been offered. If I left, where would I go, where would I stay, what would I do – how would I get the money even to live day by day, let alone make a journey?

Inside me a violent rebellion broke out against my whole situation. Every point of my consciousness was seized by the thought *I don't want to be here.* This intensely personal rejection was accompanied by a more impersonal thought, at an almost equally high voltage: *I ought not to be doing this: I'm wasting my talents and my life.* The violence of the whole experience was extreme. All my insides were in turmoil now, in uproar. The tension bordered on the intolerable. I fought to master it with every resource I had. But for most of the night it was as if a civil war was waging inside me. I lay there in the darkness believing I was having a nervous breakdown: I simply could not come to terms with the position I was in, and felt as if I were disintegrating under that inability.

Dawn edged into the room from behind green curtains, but even in that light I was still in the same state as I had been all night. I began to feel as if I were going off my head. Then, from somewhere deep inside me, a primal instinct of self-preservation emerged and began to make itself felt. *I can't allow myself to be defeated by this. I need to be bigger than this. I need to be bigger than anything that can happen to me. I've got to get on top of it – then stay on top of it. I'm here now for a year, and if I'm to survive that year I can't let these thoughts keep coming back. I've got to drive them out and keep them out. I must take each day as it comes. It's the only way to get through. I must never again let myself think like this. I've got to master my own thoughts, stay on top of them, all the time.* Slowly, the tide turned. The feeling of violence in the tension remained extreme, but little by little I began to feel I was getting on top of it. By the time I heaved myself out of bed into full daylight I felt I could just about face the day. But then when I saw my face in the bathroom mirror I got a shock I shall never forget: it was a pallid green, with the skin tightly drawn over the features, scarily tight, and with deep black circles under the eyes.

When I went into Harald's office later that morning I knew I looked a terrible sight. I still had that tight feeling in my face, as if my skin were shrinking and squeezing my eyeballs out. Harald took one look at me and said, 'What on earth is wrong?'

I told him I had had a sleepless night, caused by an unusually violent stomach upset, with repeated vomiting.

'You look to me as if you're seriously ill,' he said. 'You ought to see a doctor. Let me arrange it for you.'

I refused. I said I was sure the trouble was over. I knew I would be better soon. I knew I had no need of a doctor.

My appearance must have been exceedingly abnormal, not to say alarming. Harald persisted in quizzing me. He looked so disbelieving of my answers that I suspected he might be getting an inkling of what was wrong. But I was not going to admit it, not even to myself, still less discuss it. I had already begun the process of putting my whole self in to the repression of the truth, as if my sanity was going to depend on it. Nothing would shift me now.

But I did say to Harald that I wanted to pay an immediate visit to Stockholm, some hundreds of miles away. The real reason, which I did not divulge, was that I had an overwhelming desire just to get out, to be somewhere else, like a claustrophobic compulsion: a compelling and immediate need. There was still a week to go before the teaching term began. I had been expected to spend that time settling in, getting to know my colleagues, being briefed by them on what I was going to teach, and above all preparing my first classes. I put it to Harald that I had done the first three of these four things already, and could do the fourth during a visit to Stockholm. To get any serious understanding of Sweden, I said, it was essential to have at least an acquaintance with the capital city. And it would be impossible to acquire one from Lund once I had started teaching.

Harald seemed to perceive that going to Stockholm was a necessity for me, and that my sudden insistence on it was connected with my abnormal state, and that he was going to have to go along with it. But still he did not understand it. He agreed, though, and gave me an advance on my salary for the purpose.

2

In area, Sweden is about twice the size of Great Britain, but when I first went there its population was smaller than Greater London's – less than eight million. Fewer than a million were in Stockholm. The rest lived in much smaller towns. If there is such a thing as a typical Swede he is a modern man who lives in a small town. Although the country extends well up into the Arctic Circle, and is about a thousand miles long, most of the population is concentrated in the southern part, and enjoys a mild climate relative to its latitude. The summers are particularly beautiful – sunny and warm without being humid. For me there is no more enjoyable weather than a Swedish summer.

Going to Sweden was the first time I had been in a country with higher living standards than Britain. Everything seemed of higher quality, more 'modern', cleaner, more comfortable, more reliable, and worked better than I was used to. But so used to this also were the Swedes that they took it for granted. Good design, especially, was the norm. More or less all furniture and all interiors were 'modern', as was cutlery, crockery and glassware. This assumption of the ordinariness of modern design looked incongruous to me until I got used to it – for instance the sight of old ladies sitting chatting together on avant-garde chairs. The food was fresh-tasting and delicious (as food in England was not, usually, at that time). The coffee was of a standard I had not encountered – it was as if I had never tasted coffee before; and for a long time I drank huge quantities of it. As time went by I found the basic social services, such as education and health, to be of a higher standard than Britain's. So also was the level of a number of personal qualities that are specially prized by the British – fairness, decency, honesty, truthfulness, consideration for others (though the Swedes scored very much lower on tolerance and humour). It was altogether a salutary experience, and made a permanent difference to the way I perceived my own country. For the rest of my life I was to see Britain in a more realistic light.

Two things that made a difference to the way I experienced Sweden were that I was living in a university town and that I was close to Denmark. Sweden has two ancient university towns, Uppsala and Lund, and they are hundreds of miles apart. Uppsala, in central Sweden, is not much farther from Stockholm than Oxford is from London, and has a similarly symbiotic relationship to the capital city. Lund, however, is down in the south, in a part of Sweden that belonged to Denmark until 1658. (Lund cathedral was in Denmark for 500 years. Indeed, in the 12th century Lund was the capital of Denmark.) Lund University can almost be said to have been founded to celebrate the union with Sweden. Not surprisingly, especially in view of the distance from Stockholm, people in that part of Sweden still think of Copenhagen as their metropolis. I thought so myself when I lived in Lund.

At that time Lund was a town of thirty thousand. The nearest place for large-scale shopping was Malmö, easy to get to, a town of a quarter of a million people, the third largest in Sweden. Even so, the big, exciting city was Copenhagen, across the water. Although we were in Sweden, and Copenhagen was the capital of Denmark, we lived in its magnetic field. It was our hub, and was referred to as such constantly (whereas people rarely went to Stockholm, and seldom mentioned it: some had never been there.) This closeness has been intensified since by the building of a bridge linking the two countries. Swedes who are within easy reach of the bridge can now go into Copenhagen for an evening. And

Copenhagen has always been more fun to visit than any other Scandinavian city.

Stockholm, however, is more beautiful. That was what struck me first. In its particular way it was the most beautiful capital I had seen up to that time. Unlike the others, its beauty consisted not in its buildings, or streets, or squares, but in its vistas. It was built between a large lake and the sea, and included many islands. It derived unique character from wide views of capital-city buildings in amongst the waters, and waters in amongst the capital-city buildings. On my first visit it seemed to be all bridges and islands, and from each I got a different view. As for the buildings, in the old town there were ancient churches, twisting medieval streets, and stylish eighteenth-century dwellings, not least the royal palace. More modern parts of town had more modern buildings, the showpiece being the town hall, in an outstandingly beautiful setting on the shore of a great lake – there again it was the setting that was beautiful rather than the building. Visually, Stockholm was a different sort of town from London, Paris, Vienna and Brussels; and those were more like one another than any of them was like Stockholm. The broad openness, the bright aqueousness, were quite unfamiliar to me as features of a capital city. Here was mostly water, sky and space; and I found it exhilarating. The newness of the experience helped to take me out of myself. And just to tap into a capital city restored me to a more balanced, assured and settled frame of mind.

For cheapness I stayed in a temperance hotel run by the Salvation Army – basic, but at the centre of things. From there I went immediately to the Royal Opera House to see what was on, and found they were performing Wagner's *Tristan and Isolde* in Swedish. By this chance I saw Birgit Nilsson's first ever performance of Isolde. At that time she was not much known outside Sweden, and her name meant nothing to me; but it was obvious at once that she was going to be an international star. I was to go on seeing her for the rest of her career, including several more performances of Isolde, though never again in Swedish. Her Tristan on that first occasion was another Swede, Set Svanholm, and I had seen him sing the role in London opposite Kirsten Flagstad – whose successor Birgit Nilsson became as the world's leading Wagnerian soprano. It was strange for me at that time to hear the opera in Swedish when I did not understand a word. The language struck me as agreeably liquid for singing; but I missed the definition and bite of German consonants, which are intrinsic to a fully authentic Wagner sound.

I spent a day visiting the island which is home to Skansen, an open-air museum of Swedish houses, churches and buildings of every kind. From each part of Sweden, and dating from every century, these structures have been dismantled at their point of origin and reassembled here to show the story of Swedish society's development and history in the language of buildings. It is a fascinating place to visit, especially for someone who is about to start living and working in Sweden. It gave me my first perception of the country's history.

There is a zoo on the same island, and also a pleasure garden. In a restaurant overlooking the pleasure garden I had a dinner of snaps and elk steak. This made me feel I really was in Sweden. After that I watched Zarah Leander, one of the most popular of all Swedish singers. She had reached the height of her fame before the Second World War but was now under something of a cloud because of her comings and goings to Germany during the war, when Sweden was neutral. Not only did she sing in Nazi Germany, she was on friendly terms with some of its leaders. Even so, in her native Sweden she still commanded big audiences in spite of the shadow across her past.

I quickly discovered that anything to do with the Second World War was a delicate subject in Sweden. The Swedes were resented by the other Scandinavian peoples for having stayed out of it.

Denmark, Norway and Finland had all been invaded by totalitarian dictators, and the first two had suffered prolonged military occupation by the Nazis. To escape the same fate, the Swedish government had bowed to a German demand for transit facilities through Sweden for troops and supplies destined for Norway. Norwegians saw this as the Swedes facilitating the Nazi occupation of Norway to save their own skins. As the biggest and richest of the Scandinavian countries, Sweden was bound to be resented by its neighbours in any case, but because of the events of the war the hostility was doubly strong. The other countries not only envied Sweden's prosperity but regarded it as having been gained and sustained at their expense. It took many years for these feelings to fade.

I got a great deal out of this first visit to Stockholm, not only in making the acquaintance of a beautiful town but also in getting to understand more of Sweden. It was on the two long train journeys between Lund and Stockholm that I had my first prolonged view of what the country mostly consists of: endless pine forests interspersed with lakes. Sweden has a hundred thousand lakes, and the biggest of them are among the largest in Europe. Not all, but a majority of Sweden's significant towns are beside water, whether seacoast or lakeshore. And throughout the whole society there is a feeling that real life is lived close to Nature. This feeling persists even in the hyper-modern society that Sweden has become.

3

Returning to Lund from Stockholm, I plunged into my new job. I taught every afternoon and evening but had my mornings free. Most of the teaching was in Lund, in small weekly classes held in seminar rooms of the university. One of my groups, self-organized, consisted of wives of academics, most of them in their thirties – bright and attractive, fun to teach. I also had one or two private pupils; and I gave a series of fortnightly lectures. The lectures were about British writers of the twentieth century, and attracted a lot of university students. All my teaching and lecturing was in English, of course, so all my pupils were, and had to be, advanced enough to cope with that.

On two evenings a week I took a train to Malmö, twenty minutes away, and taught larger classes of young adults there. And one whole day a week I spent in Helsingborg, more distant. There I taught in the business college during the day, and divided the evening between private lessons and a lecture to a literary society. Two of those lectures I remember with special pleasure, about the two parts of Shakespeare's *Henry IV*: I devoted weeks of preparation to them, marinading in those marvellous plays.

As with all teaching, the early stages were the most demanding. Once you get into your stride as a teacher you can legitimately use in one class material that you have used already in another, or can deliver to one audience a lecture prepared for another. After your first year you may re-use whole courses, because you now have different students. But when you are starting from the very beginning, everything has to be developed from a blank sheet of paper. It was especially difficult for me, because I was teaching a language to people whose own language I did not understand, and I was never able to translate for them, or make comparisons.

My first personal relationships, after those with my teaching colleagues, were made with my pupils. Many of these were in my own age group, or only a little older: in one or two of my classes I was the youngest person. After a while some of the younger ones, when leaving a class in the afternoon, would invite me to go with them to a café. Then some of the older ones started inviting me to their homes, perhaps for an early lunch before my teaching. There were some among the women whom I found attractive. If one of these came up to me with a question after a class I would suggest we go somewhere else and discuss it over a cup of coffee. Altogether I found the level of female attractiveness disconcertingly higher than in England. The fact that I was teaching these women made me an object of interest to them, and caused some of them to want my approval. I was a newcomer in Lund, and that added to people's interest in me, as did the fact that I was an Englishman living on his own. All these things caused some of my students to cultivate my friendship, so eventually I had quite a number of relationships outside working hours.

However, all this took time. And it got off to a slow start. Meanwhile I was lonely. I found myself dropping into Harald Wohlstad's office every day just to have a few minutes of chat with his staff – in particular with the secretary of the outfit, a woman called Rut Friberg, who ran most of it most of the time. In my early days I met the two young British university lecturers in the English faculty of the university, together with their wives. One of these couples, Bill and Doreen Nash, were to become the closest of all my personal friends in Lund, and showed great hospitality and kindness to me.

But loneliness was a serious problem in my first couple of months. Never before had I lived alone. In fact, since the age of eleven, I had lived a communal life: first at a boarding school, then in the army, then at university. I was used to being surrounded all the time by people with whom I had personal as well as institutional relationships, some very close. Now I was in a foreign country where I had arrived not knowing anyone, and did not understand what anybody said unless they were addressing themselves to me personally and in English. One often hears it said that all Swedes speak English, but that has never been true, and was a great deal further from the truth then than it is now. In those days well-educated professional and business people knew some English, and of course those making a study of the language, but few others were capable of having a conversation in it. Their English was like the French of most English people: although they learnt it at school, they could manage only a simple exchange, and were lost in any real conversation. For me it was isolating, because it so drastically limited the number of people I could communicate with. In any group of which I was not the centre of attention I had no idea what was going on. Everyday activities such as shopping and travelling on buses were heavy going and accident-prone. All this gave me a feeling of separateness from the society I was in: it made me feel an outsider, as indeed I was. The truth is that, deep down, I did not want to be there at all, and at the core of my feelings there was a kind of alienation. I overcame most of it during the course of my year in Sweden, but I never got over it entirely.

I made active efforts to learn Swedish, having started already in England. As soon as I had got the job I bought and began reading a book called *Teach Yourself Swedish*. It was deeply old-fashioned. After only a few pages I knew the Swedish words for 'lice' and 'geese' because, like their English counterparts, they are irregular plurals. It was like learning Latin. Even so, I persisted in studying this book during my early weeks in Sweden. It gave me the basic grammar, and some useful vocabulary. But I never had any lessons in Swedish from a teacher. What I was mostly doing was picking it up by ear as I went along. Naively, I expected to become better at it slowly and steadily, but this is not what happened. My ability to *understand* Swedish grew in that way, but not my ability to speak it. For weeks, which then began to turn into months, I was unable to say much more than 'How do I get to ...?' and 'Can you please tell me ...?' and 'Can I have ...?'. I understood more and more of the answers without myself being able to respond much. I felt increasingly blockaged and frustrated, and began to fear I might never learn to speak. Suddenly, after about three months, it was as if a dam broke, and I seemed to pass overnight from not being able to talk to conversing volubly. I was astonished to hear what was coming out of my mouth. I have since discussed this with language specialists in Oxford and learnt that it is what normally happens when a language is learned under such conditions – it is, for example, a common experience among immigrants to Britain.

Because I learnt Swedish largely by ear I have always been bad at writing it. I am capable of mis-spelling even the commonest words. But I became, eventually, able to get along in the spoken language for everyday purposes. It has been invaluable to me ever since.

My early inability to speak the language was not the only cause of my loneliness in those earliest months. My work situation also contributed to it. On weekdays I was free in the mornings, when all the people I knew were working; but in the evenings, when they were free, I was working. By the time I finished teaching, around ten o'clock, they were either going to bed – Swedes do that earlier than British people (and get up earlier) – or, if not, were unready to receive a visitor, and still less to embark on a social evening. For quite a while it was difficult for me to share my leisure time with anyone at all, except at weekends. Then I would visit Bill and Doreen Nash, and guzzle my starved self on their generous presence. On weekday nights there was nothing for me to do but go back to a solitary room. Cafés were near the point of closing. There was nowhere to get an alcoholic drink, because alcohol could be bought only in government-owned off-licences, and they were closed in the evening. My adrenalin was running from teaching, and I would be incapable of going to sleep for at least another couple of hours. There was a radio in my room, but I could not understand any of the talk on it, and others in the house would be disturbed if I played music. Two things alone existed for me to do: think and read.

Increasingly, I felt sex-starved. I had been used to a happy sex-life in England with my devoted girlfriend Caroline, but I was now completely deprived. Caroline had approved my coming to Sweden, because it promised to pay me so much better than a job in England that in a single year I could expect to pay off all, or nearly all, the debts I had incurred to get through Oxford. I had come out of desperation, but there had been no dispute with her about my coming. When we parted we were still not only lovers but the closest of friends. Both saw our separation as a desperate temporary expedient, and took it for granted that our full relationship would be resumed as soon as I got back to England. But now the negative reality of what this involved, a sexless year, stretched out in front of me like the Sahara desert. When I found myself contemplating it the fingertip of a deep dismay touched my heart.

The problem was made all the sharper by the fact that I was surrounded by attractive women. I had only to walk along any of the streets in this university town to be passed by girls who would be thought beautiful in England. More female students than males attended non-compulsory lectures, so each time I stood up to give a lecture I would find myself gazing across a sea of female heads, gazing up at me with expectation. There were lots of attractive blondes in each of my classes, and I could not help noticing that two or three of them had shown signs of interest in me. To say of any that they were throwing themselves at me would be a ridiculous exaggeration; it was not like that; but there were a couple who, whether consciously or unconsciously, were showing oblique signs that hinted in that direction. I knew that if I made approaches to them they would respond.

The inevitable happened. I became involved with two or three of my students. It never occurred to me – nor did it to them, I believe – that these relationships were anything but transitory. The fact that it was all so superficial made it easy for me to have more than one such relationship at a time, and also to tell myself that none of them made any real difference to my wholly different relationship with Caroline. At this point in their lives none of these girls were thinking of marriage: they would, I am sure, have been surprised if I had mentioned it. (It might even have put them off.) So I happily embraced the good fortune that had fallen into my lap, and was grateful for the difference it made to my life. But naturally I did not tell Caroline. And I felt guilty. But I was driven by need and loneliness – not only the need for sex but also for human closeness and warmth. And I told myself that these harmless flings would secure rather than endanger my relationship with Caroline, because they would remove the danger of getting involved more seriously. There was no question of getting *permanently* involved with any of these girls. And they were making my separation from Caroline bearable. I relaxed into their arms. This turn of events, coming when it did, was liberating. As far as sex was concerned I had always been a one-woman-at-a-time man, and was to be so again for many years, but just for that brief period I gloried in an abundance of sex with beautiful women. Psychologically, I believe, it compensated me for my rejection by England, and my other deprivations and maladjustments. Here I was wanted: I had everything I could ask for, my cup was running over. It did a great deal to reconcile me to being in Sweden, for only in Sweden could such a thing have happened to me at that time.

One of my students, a middle-aged doctor, drove me in his car round the southernmost province of Sweden, called Skåne (pronounced Skaw-ne). It is prosperous farmland, much of it flat like neighbouring Denmark. He took me to see the country houses, which the Swedes call castles, as the French do. In some cases he knew the families, and they showed us round. These castles are a well-known feature of Skåne, and some are beautiful. Virtually all are still lived in. The main towns of Skåne include Lund, Malmö and Helsingborg, and these were all now in my home territory. Skåne had enjoyed peace for generations, and there was something attractive in a social atmosphere that reflected that. The town I found most charming was Helsingborg, with its air of relaxed elegance that made me think of France. It lies on the coast at the narrowest point of the sound between Sweden and Denmark, with Elsinore two and a half miles away on the Danish side. The castle at Elsinore, the setting for Shakespeare's *Hamlet*, was built in Shakespeare's lifetime, so when that play was written the building was a new one. I have paid several visits to Elsinore and its castle, and become familiar with the stretch of Danish coast between there and Copenhagen.

Slowly the culture of that part of Europe seeped into me. I got to know not only locations but the way of life, and began to read about them and their history. If a small country has only one writer of global reputation then every educated person in that country will have read his work. In Sweden the example is Strindberg. To my surprise I discovered that much of his writing is satirically funny. Somehow that has got lost in traditional English translations, with the result that the English think of Strindberg as darkly tortured, as well as slightly mad, which indeed he was. Denmark can boast two world figures in literature, Hans Christian Andersen and Kierkegaard. It was a bizarre experience for me to spend time in a country where every educated person has read Kierkegaard.

Before I understood any of the Swedish language I saw a performance in Malmö of Pirandello's play *Six Characters in Search of an Author*. I expected to be bored, but I understood a surprising amount of what was going on, and found it riveting. It gave me an interest in Pirandello that has never left me. Since then I have seen a number of classic plays in languages I do not understand, and have nearly always found them interesting. Once I attended an uncut performance of *Hamlet* in Serbo-Croat, all five hours of it, in the castle of Dubrovnik. I bought an aisle seat beside an exit so that I could slip out when I felt I had had enough, but I stayed through to the end with total absorption. In Malmö I saw *The Marriage of Figaro* in Swedish. It was a good performance, full of verve. During an interval one of my companions asked me who could possibly be interested in this old-fashioned stuff. At first I assumed he was making a joke and responded accordingly, to his confusion. I was to become familiar with the fact that by quite a number of intelligent Swedes only what was contemporary, modern, up to date, was considered worthy of attention.

The fact that I had my mornings free enabled me to do two things that mattered more to me than my job. The first was start to write a novel. I had had a volume of teenage poems published, but this novel was my first adult book. I was not to get it finished until three or four years had passed, by which time I was living in London. Then, no sooner did I begin offering it for publication than I changed my mind and withdrew it – mistakenly, I now think. It is called *Georgette: A Novel in Three Acts*, and when I stop writing new books I shall offer it to a publisher.

The other thing I did was resume, after what had been only a brief interruption, my studies in philosophy. I had just taken a degree at Oxford with philosophy as my specialism, in the famous PPE course (Philosophy, Politics and Economics), so I had already received a full-scale introduction to the subject. But I viewed the philosophy being published by the current stars of Oxford as shallow. Their approach was that of linguistic analysis. It seemed to me that no problem of substance could be solved by this approach. To do them justice, the linguistic philosophers thought so too. But their claim was that philosophy did not have profound problems of its own, only puzzles. Rightly seen, they believed, philosophy did not concern itself with first-order problems. Its task was to address itself to statements made by others, and subject these to critical analysis – analysis of language, of concepts, of logic, of method, and so on. Thus all philosophy ought to be the philosophy *of* something – of knowledge, of morals, of politics, of science, of mathematics, of logic, of history, of art, of religion. Philosophy in and by itself, so to speak, had no problems other than those of its own methods. Its task was to sort things out, clear things up. When it had done its job, whatever *philosophical* problems there had seemed to be would have dissolved. 'Not solved but dissolved' was a mantra. I disagreed with all this. It seemed to me that human beings confront philosophical problems of the greatest magnitude, and that these are not merely puzzles about language and method but are problems of substance about reality, including the realities of what we ourselves are. Throughout the past, philosophers have addressed themselves to such problems. Only recently and locally had they stopped doing so. The university syllabus had introduced me to some of the greatest figures of the past. Now I wanted to find out who and where the living philosophers were – if any – who were carrying on the great tradition.

The first I stumbled over was an American woman called Susanne K. Langer. She had published a book, *Philosophy in a New Key*, in which she attempted to explain the significance of music by applying to it a profound insight that she had gained from Wittgenstein's *Tractatus*. (Wittgenstein in turn had got this from Schopenhauer, but Langer did not know that, nor did I.) Scarcely had I read this when she followed it with a new book, *Feeling and Form*, in which she extended her theory of music to cover all the arts. Her work excited me – it even ignited in me a desire to visit an American university, somewhere where such things were taken seriously by philosophers. It also sent me back to Wittgenstein, whose *Tractatus* I bought in Lund and read again three or four times.

My life was now full. Even so, apart from my mornings, it was not satisfying. I found teaching easy, and was considered good at it, but the kind of teaching I was doing was not a substantial enough occupation. Few of my students were intellectually serious about their work. They spoke English quite well already, and attended classes chiefly because they wanted a congenial leisure pursuit that would be of use to them, and in which they would make friends among like-minded people. This is true, I suppose, of most adult education – the motivation is more social than intellectual. There is nothing wrong with that – on the contrary – but for me such teaching was too light an occupation. The only important thing I got from it was money. Earning money had never been a primary motivation with me, but at that juncture of my life it had particular importance. I had borrowed large sums to get through Oxford, and had done so willingly, prepared to spend several years after graduation working off my debts. But here in Sweden, incomes were surprisingly much higher than in pre-affluent, still-austerity Britain, and I was being especially well paid.

This was partly because I received not a salary but separate fees for each bit of teaching. These came from different sources: Lund, Malmö, Helsingborg's business college, its literary society, private pupils, and a separate fee for each lecture. In addition I was in demand for extra teaching and lecturing; and because it came easily, the only limitation on how much I could do was my time. It is astonishing but true that during that one academic year in Sweden I earned something like four times as much as I could have expected to earn in the same period in England. It enabled me to pay off nearly all my debts. My Swedish employers made it clear to me early on that they were pleased with me, and would be asking me to renew my contract, but I never considered that as an option. I was determined to return to England after one year almost clear of debt, and hurl myself into the job market there yet again. It seemed to me a necessity for my whole life to secure a foothold in England, which up to this point I had failed to do.

Meanwhile, I did what I could to enjoy life in Sweden. Apart from girlfriends, the Nashes were the focal point of my social life. Their inner circle consisted of a charismatic and unusually intelligent young doctor called Nils-Magnus Ohlsson and his wife Irma, plus a young woman student of English called Berit Aspegren. The half-dozen of us spent innumerable hours together. Outstanding in my memory is a visit we made to Copenhagen during the run-up to Christmas, when that wonderful town was at its most attractive. When Christmas came we celebrated it twice. Like most continental countries, Sweden holds its chief celebrations on Christmas Eve – Christmas Day there is rather like a Boxing Day in England. So on Christmas Eve we all celebrated in Swedish style at the Ohlssons, with their Swedish friends. And next day the English colony in Lund, plus the Ohlssons and Berit, gathered at the Nashes, and we celebrated an English Christmas.

Nils-Magnus was an attractive personality, and I liked him particularly. But he may have been a touch too self-confident: not many years later he died from the side-effects of his researches into radiation. I have remembered him ever since as somebody special. At the time of our friendship I realised that Berit was in love with him; but I do not think he was unfaithful to Irma, who was if anything a stronger personality than he was.

Winter descended, and we all settled down into Scandinavian gloom. The reason for the depression the rest of the world associates with Scandinavians is not the coldness of their winters but the darkness. Even in the very south of Sweden it does not get properly light in January until late in the morning, and then starts getting dark in mid-afternoon. On some days there seem to be only about four hours of daylight. It feels like living in a cave, or a tunnel. Everyone gets depressed. That is when people start hitting the bottle – or, if they are going to, commit suicide. It is why Swedes burst into joy when spring comes, like a liberated population, and why they worship the sun almost primitively in summer. I felt these things with them, and know from inside what they are like to experience.

When my teaching began again after the Christmas break, at the lowest point of the winter, I had a strange but decisive experience. It happened in Malmö. As I was stepping down from the tram that I always took from the railway station to my classes, a thought out of nowhere lit up my mind with unnatural brilliance. '*I ought not to be doing this*'. It was not a rebellious thought, like those tortured and agonizing thoughts I had gone through during my third night in Sweden. It was not a howl of rejection. It was sober and calm, factual, objective, detached. From that moment my attitude to being in Sweden was transformed. I was not rebelling against it, as I had done at the beginning, but nor was I trying to repress my alienation, as I had been doing ever since. Suddenly I was outside it all. I saw with matter-of-factual simplicity that the job and the life were not for me. I did not belong in it. As soon as I was able to get away from it I would. And until that time I would float along in it in as unpressured a way as possible, doing what was expected of me but without investing any of my self in it.

And that is what I did. Whether my students noticed the difference I have no way of telling, but I doubt if many did. Having taken so easily to teaching I had become confident in my classes, and was assured. This did not change. So my guess is that a few of the more intuitive students may have felt there was something different about me while the majority did not.

The new term in January saw the beginning of two new classes for me. In one of them, in Lund, I saw the most beautiful woman I thought I had ever seen. I do not believe she can actually have been that: I suspect my vision was distorted by sexual attraction, which was intense and immediate. But she was certainly beautiful: others thought so too. Her name was Ingrid Söderlund. She worked as an assistant in one of the university's life-science laboratories. Her English was good, though she had been outside Scandinavia only once, and then to Germany. When we first got to know each other she told me she was a year older than me, but later I discovered she was two years older. This may suggest she had her eye on me early on. But the truth is that, whereas with other students who became girlfriends, the first intimations of attraction came (whether consciously or unconsciously) from them, with Ingrid this was not so. From the moment my eye fell on her I knew I was going to do everything I could to make love to her, whereas she was later to say that her response to me was not at all instantaneous in that way. By the end of the first class she was thinking merely that I was 'quite nice'.

After our third class I went up to her as everyone was leaving and engaged her in conversation about something she had said. I did not attempt to leave with her, but remarked that it might be interesting for us to meet sometime to discuss the point further, to which she agreed. After the following class we left together.

After that, our relationship developed quickly. Soon we were on the brink of going to bed together. What took us over the brink was something shamefully cheesy on my part, the conscious use of a ruse from Puccini's *La Bohème*. Ingrid was in my room until late one evening, and when she started gathering the contents of her handbag to go home she could not find her door key. We began looking for it, and I did in fact find it, but slid it unnoticed into my pocket and pretended to go on looking. She stayed the night. Next morning I found the key. I have seen productions of *La Bohème* in which it is hinted that Mimi might have misplaced the key deliberately, or might have seen Rodolfo find it. But these are conjectures. We shall never know.

From the beginning, my attitude to Ingrid was different from my attitude to other women. I was not in love with her, but I found her more irresistibly attractive than any woman I had ever met. My other involvements in Lund, which were unserious, lapsed, and I became addicted to Ingrid. I wanted to make love to her at every possible opportunity, and did so, passionately. This had an arousing and involving effect on her, and I believe she gradually fell in love with me. We became a couple. When neither of us was working we were usually together. Soon other people began to treat us as a couple.

My furnished room was too small for this way of life, and in any case was not sufficiently private. I found a self-contained flat in the street overlooking the university's main buildings, on the old campus. It was right in the middle of town yet deserted at night. Ingrid kept her flat, so both of us were free, and we were no longer conducting our relationship under the eyes of other people.

Inevitably, this had implications for my relationship with Caroline – with whom I really was, or had been up to this point, in love. My previous flings in Sweden had not been public, and were so shallow that they left my feelings for Caroline undisturbed. But now things were different. There was a wholesale investment of my sexual libido in Ingrid, and we were going around together as a recognized couple. This could only have the effect of dislodging some of my attachment to Caroline. It was inevitable, and I felt it happening – I could feel the ground shifting under my feet. I had not seen Caroline for five months, and events were now carrying me bodily away from her. In theory – especially since I did not suppose myself to be in love with Ingrid – I could have brought the new relationship to an end right then. But this was more than flesh and blood could do, especially as I knew that Ingrid was emotionally attached to me. It would have been opting for isolation when I did not need to, and the loneliness would have been not only for me but for Ingrid too. I never seriously contemplated it. But I knew that my relationship with Caroline had been radically altered, and I was no longer sure what it would be when I returned to England.

In the here and now Ingrid was at the centre of my life. To look at she was classically Swedish – tall and slim, long boned, a natural blonde. Her face had unusual features: her eyes were of an intense light blue, her nostrils slightly flared, and her lower lip so full that she tried to make it appear smaller by covering only part of it with lipstick: she painted a carefully shaped smaller lip on to the bigger one. She was the oldest of four siblings, who were close in age and came from a rather old-fashioned, prosperous family with a substantial house in a village between Lund and Malmö. Her father was the government official responsible for inspecting butter coming into Sweden through the port of Malmö, vast quantities of it from Denmark. During the Second World War he had wanted the Germans to win, and from the moment Ingrid told me that, I was resolved not to meet him if I could avoid it. In this I was successful. She invited me to her family home only when he was away. Her mother had recently died, and Ingrid was dreaming about her a lot. Sometimes in these dreams her mother would berate her for the immorality of her relationship with me.

Increasingly attached to Ingrid though I was, I was still determined to leave Sweden as soon as I could be free of my job.

There was no acceptable future for me in Sweden. However, now that my commitment to Caroline was being undermined I found myself tinkering with an alternative to going straight back to England. I was in a state of intellectual excitement over my studies in philosophy, and I began to wonder what it would be like to pursue these full-time in a sympathetic environment such as I could have some hope of finding in an American university. At Oxford I had heard of postgraduate fellowships to the United States, some for only one year, and I knew individuals who had had them. I began to wonder if one of these might be the thing for me.

I realize as I write these words that they will come across unsympathetically to some of my readers. But in those days my commitment to the further development of myself and such talents as I had was something that was taken for granted in a man. Men followed their work, went where the opportunities were, and women accompanied them. This was expected even by most women, although they may not always have liked the consequences. It was certainly taken for granted by me, and I think I was normal in this respect, not unusual. During the years I had spent in Oxford, no one of either sex would have dreamt of expecting a man to subordinate his career to his relationship with a woman. It was the woman who adapted herself to the man's career. She went wherever it took him, and they lived as it dictated – or else accepted the necessity for the two of them to be apart, as Caroline had done when she endorsed my coming to Sweden. That is how things were in those days. The important but difficult thing for today's readers to understand is that this was internalized by both sexes.

I made enquiries, and discovered that Commonwealth Fund Fellowships were being advertised for British citizens to study for two years at one of the great American universities. I put in for one. In due course I was informed that I had been short-listed, and was told to fly to London for an interview. I assumed that the fact that the selectors were paying my air fare from Scandinavia plus a couple of nights in a London hotel meant that they were fairly sure they were going to give me a fellowship. So I began to adjust my mind to the prospect of spending the next two years in the United States.

Going to London meant seeing Caroline, and explaining what I was doing, with all the implications this would have for our relationship. How on earth was I going to explain an application to spend two years in the United States? I could see no way of doing it that did not involve telling Caroline about my relationship with Ingrid. On the plane to London I tried to prepare myself for a doubly agonizing encounter with the person who still mattered more to me than anyone else.

The plane was diverted to Hamburg, where I had to change to another, so by the time I met Caroline at Heathrow she had been waiting there for two or three hours. The Commonwealth Fund had booked me into a hotel in Gloucester Place, so she went there with me. In my room we had what was far and away the most significant meeting we had had since becoming lovers. In some ways, it was less difficult than I had feared. It emerged that she was involved with someone else in a light-hearted, uncommitted way, and had every intention and expectation of returning to me – an exact counterpart of what my behaviour in Sweden had been before meeting Ingrid. Those relationships of ours were like wartime relationships, and we confessed them sheepishly to one another. In her case, she said, it was because she had taken it for granted that I would do the same, and she had felt there was no danger. This made it easier than I had expected for her to understand that with Ingrid things had gone further. She said she had been afraid of that too, and appeared now to be grimly accepting of it. To my surprise she was not recriminatory. Rather, she talked as if the way things had turned out had been inherent in the situation, and was partly her fault. It was a blow but not a surprise. In spite of all this, the feeling of intimacy between us in that room was palpable. I remember thinking that it was not our relationship that we were losing but its future.

When the talking was done there was an unspoken question of whether to make love. It would have been the natural thing to do – indeed, it seemed unnatural not to – and we wanted to. Yet after what had happened it would have been confusing. Indeed, we were confused already. And we did not make love, for the first time since we first had. That in itself, I think, clinched for both of us the realization that our relationship of old was at an end.

After that meeting, which was a milestone in both our lives, we continued to see one another, but always with gaps in between. In an odd sort of way we remained the closest of friends. There was something unique about our friendship – an intimacy, an intensity – that never died. To the very end she felt, as I did, that there was something between us that was forever near the centre of each of us, and touched us to the heart.

I did not get one of the Commonwealth fellowships that I had flown to London to be interviewed for. A few years later I discovered why; and it is a story worth telling, because it illuminates something that was affecting my life more generally at that time.

I later got to know a man called Gorley Putt, Director of the Commonwealth Fellowships, who had acted as secretary to the interviewing board and been present at all the interviews. He told me that when those of my year ended there had been a spontaneous outburst of approval from the interviewers for the whole short-list of candidates – a chorus which the chairman, Oliver Franks, cut short with something like the following speech: 'Gentlemen, it's an exceptional year. In any other year, each of these candidates would be an obvious choice for a fellowship. But the fact is, we've got to drop some of them. Let's address ourselves to the question in that form: not who to pick, but who to drop. If we discuss it in terms of who to pick we shall be here all night, because they all deserve to go. Picking deserving candidates is not our problem. *Dropping* deserving candidates is our problem. If we face it head-on in those terms – who to drop – we'll get to a conclusion sooner. Has anyone any suggestions about who we can drop?'

There was a long silence. The interviewers rubbed their chins and looked again down over the list of names. Then a voice said: 'I see that every candidate except one has got a first class honours degree. What about dropping the one with a second?'

There was another silence. Gorley Putt, telling me the story, said he was taken aback by such a suggestion because he thought the candidate with a second was the best candidate. And so, it emerged later, did a couple of the others. But the board had to make unpalatable decisions. A quiet, reluctant mutter of acceptance came from somewhere. The chairman promptly declared the suggestion adopted, and moved on.

'So,' said Gorley Putt to me, 'you were the best candidate, and the first one to be dropped.'

I tell this story now to illustrate the fact that not getting a first class degree changed the course of my life during the years after I left Oxford. If I had had a first I would not have gone to Sweden. Or, given that I did spend a year in Sweden, I would then have gone to Princeton for two years. My being viva'd for a first after doing a three-year degree course in one year may have been, as it was described, the outstanding individual performance of my exam year, but it nevertheless left me with the label 'second-class' round my neck, and no one knew the story behind it except for a few insiders at Oxford. For several years when I was a young man this tipped the balance of opportunity away from me, and large-scale chunks of my life were altered by it, even to the countries I lived in. It unquestionably gave me a different life from the one I would have had. The change was not entirely for the bad. It forced me to go my own way more than I would have done otherwise, developing intellectually with an unusual degree of independence outside the mainstream of academia. This had big advantages. I was nothing like as influenced as I would have been by the intellectual fashions of my generation. What the bottom line is in the profit-and-loss account, I am not sure. I doubt whether, in the long run, I have been all that much worse off. But my life has certainly been very different.

Because I had been too confident of getting a Commonwealth Fellowship I was all the more cast down when I failed to, and became depressed. A period of stress followed. First I started to suffer piercing headaches, then I had problems sleeping. Night after night I would find myself still awake at three o'clock, and would get up, read for an hour, go back to bed and fall asleep at last, only to wake again four hours later red-eyed and exhausted, underslept, headachy, nervy. I had two alarming experiences – or rather the same experience twice – for which there are no words. Sitting in my flat talking to someone, I suddenly felt my stable state of mind liquefy and start flowing away from me, out of control. It was terrifying. It lasted only a matter of seconds each time, but each time I believed I was losing my mind, and was left shaking.

It was obvious that all this was due to stress caused by my inability to accept my life as it was. When the symptoms showed no sign of diminishing I realized that I was in danger of some sort of breakdown, and that the only way to avoid it was to change my life. I worked out a plan and embraced it with therapeutic intensity. I would get myself to a good American university, and there I would try to follow a path in philosophy that consisted of what I really did think and believe, independently of the current orthodoxies of Oxford or anywhere else. However, my only chance of doing this was *through* Oxford. So at the end of the current academic year I would return to Oxford to pursue philosophical studies there of my own choosing, at postgraduate level, while applying for a fellowship to be held the year after that in the United States. I could not take it for granted that I would get what I wanted. I was no longer on any degree ladder, and I was in a foreign country. There was also the question of my second-class undergraduate degrees. I had used up the normal entitlement of grant by taking two degrees (the earlier being in history) and would not necessarily get any more. It was clear, too, that I was likely to miss the application deadlines both for more grant and for registrations in the following academic year. So I decided to do these things in a freelance way, off my own bat. I would get a paid job in Oxford for a year, and make all necessary arrangements for study on the spot when I got there, and pay for them out of my salary.

I had landed my present job in Sweden through a man called Ewart Escritt on the Oxford University Appointments Board. He had taken a special interest in me, and now I wrote him an explanatory letter asking if he could find me a non-academic job in Oxford for the coming year. He did, although I have no memory of how long it took – it certainly did not happen immediately, and I think it may have happened after my return to England. This would not have influenced my behaviour in any case, for I was set on my course. I was determined to do what I was determined to do, and went ahead as if it was what was going to happen.

6

My sexual intimacy with Caroline being at an end, my relationship with Ingrid acquired greater importance as the only such relationship I now had. It was not casual or shallow, in fact it filled a great part of my life. It was my compensation for everything else: for being alienated from being in Sweden, and for being emotionally detached from my job, which I was carrying out with professional competence but on automatic pilot, longing for it to end.

But what, when my job did end, of my relationship with Ingrid? Time was passing, and the end of the academic year in Sweden was beginning to appear on the horizon. What would I do when it arrived – turn to Ingrid and say Thank You Very Much and Goodbye? Impossible. Yet what were the alternatives? It would be irresponsible of me to persuade her to accompany me to England. I had nothing there – nowhere to lay even my head, let alone hers: I might have to sleep on somebody's floor for a while. There might be no job for me on my arrival, and no certainty of an income. I could not ask her to leave her home country, her job, her flat and her family, for that. There was no certainty about my future in the longer term either. I had hopes of getting myself to America, but hopes is all they were. I had failed in my only attempt so far. But then again, what if I did succeed in getting to America – and had brought Ingrid to Britain? Would I abandon her in Britain? That would be worse than leaving her in Sweden. I thought long and hard about all these things. I even considered asking her to marry me – to throw in her lot with me, come hell or high water. But

211

then I barked my shins on the fact – which I had never disguised from myself – that I was not in love with her. What if I married her and then, at some future time, fell in love with someone else? Would I abandon her *then*? If not, to marry her now would be to give up, for ever, the possibility of an in-love marriage. I could not bring myself to do that. With great difficulty, I came to the conclusion that when I left Sweden I would have to leave Ingrid.

She and I had never discussed these things. Throughout the period when I was going through these anguished thoughts I made no reference to the fact that the end of my time in Sweden was approaching. Having no idea myself what I was going to do, I did not want to be asked. To my surprise but relief, Ingrid made no reference to it either.

When finally I came to the decision, I thought the only possible thing was to tell her straight away. The alternative would be to carry on with our seemingly carefree relationship until the day of my departure and then go. That would be bizarre – mad, in a way, because a denial of reality, and in any case wrong. I simply had to tell her. But it was fearsome to contemplate. By this time I knew, or thought I knew, that she was in love with me. There would, I expected, be terrible scenes, harrowing dramas, floods of tears, and a lot of new problems.

I told her I had something difficult to tell her, and would find it easier if we were walking out of doors rather than sitting indoors. Out we went, then, and without any conscious thought pointed our steps in the direction of the Botanical Gardens. When we got there we found an isolated bench and sat on it side by side. We seemed to have the whole garden to ourselves. It was a dull, heavy, chill, grey afternoon, with the thinnest of drizzles relentlessly drizzling.

She knew, I said, that my residence permit and my job in Sweden would both be coming to an end quite soon. I would not, I said, be attempting to renew either. I was going to return to

England. But I had nothing as yet to go back to – nowhere of my own to stay, no job, no income, and my future was totally uncertain. In these circumstances I could not ask her to come with me. But this meant that when I left Sweden our relationship would, in effect, have to end.

Her reaction took me completely by surprise. In a steely, subdued-angry voice she said: 'Why are you telling me this?'

It seemed to me only too obvious why I was telling her this. Knocked off balance, I said: 'I felt you had a right to know – to know exactly what the situation is.'

'But I do know,' she said, her anger still held down but slowly rising. 'I know everything you've just told me. Why are you saying it?'

'Well,' I said, disconcerted, 'I've been terribly unsure myself what's going to happen. I thought you might be unsure too.'

'Why should I be unsure? What is there to be unsure about?' She was getting angrier and angrier.

'Well,' I said, 'I couldn't just take it for granted that everything looks the same way to you as it does to me. You might – I don't know – have been thinking along different lines.'

'What lines? What might I have been thinking?'

'Well,' I said desperately – and unwisely, 'given how the two of us are together, I thought you might have wondered whether I was – well, perhaps – possibly going to ask you to marry me.'

'*Marry?*' Her anger exploded at last like a hand grenade. She shouted the word. 'Have I ever said anything to you about marriage?' She was still shouting. There was no one else around.

'Well, no.' I was struggling against a wholly unexpected turn of events. To my incredulity I was being made to feel *presumptuous*, of all things. 'But given that we're lovers, and how happy we've been together – and for some time now – it wouldn't have been unreasonable if the thought had crossed your mind. I just wanted to … I only thought …'

Resentment rose up my throat. My intentions had been honest and compassionate, but here she was shouting into my face with uncontrollable rage.

I floundered on: 'You may not have thought about marriage,' I said, 'but I did. I thought about it very hard. But in the end I had to decide not to ask you.'

'You don't want to marry me.'

'No. You know how I feel about you. But I don't want to marry you.'

'Well,' she said, still seething and bristling: 'there isn't anything more to say, then, is there?'

Indeed there was not. We got up off the bench and made our way back to my flat in fraught silence. I was disoriented. Only once before had I seen her blazingly angry, and then not as angry as this. One day she had crashed into my flat in a towering rage and stalked around me shouting, without my having the faintest idea what it was all about. It emerged that we had been separately to the same public entertainment the previous evening with different people (I had been with Berit Aspegren), and she had thought I was ignoring her. The simple truth was that I had not known she was there. I would never have ignored her. And there could have been no possible reason for me to do so. She refused to believe me at first, but I persuaded her, and she calmed down. On that occasion what had made the biggest impression on me was the colossal size of the rage that had blown up out of nothing at all, a rage that I never really understood. Now something like it was happening again.

I understand these things so much better now than I did then. When Ingrid and I were in the Botanical Gardens I thought she was outraged because she saw me as patronizing her by telling her what she already knew and had learnt to accept. I was upsetting a hard-won equilibrium. I was thrown out of gear, but at the same time felt a kind of relief that nothing like the scene I had been dreading had occurred – the tears, the protestations, the pleadings, with her begging me either not to go or to take her with me. It now seemed that what was going to happen was what I had considered impossible. We would simply carry on as we were until the time came for me to leave, and then I would leave. This was the easiest option for me, self-evidently. A burden was lifted from my shoulders, I thought. I had just been wrong in thinking that anything needed to be said.

7

The academic year always ended in May, to free everyone for as much as possible of the precious summer. In the past, students had been needed at home during that season to work on the land, many in quite distant parts of Sweden. Among those now graduating there were displays of rejoicing that included rituals of long tradition, such as marching around the town several times in endless processions, singing arm-in-arm. These long ago absorbed the age-old public celebration of the arrival of summer, and there was something primitive and powerful about it all. Ingrid and I were spectators-cum-participants, because we each knew many of the people involved and were invited to a lot of their parties. For us too it was a time of ambiguous and heightened emotions. We were soon going to have our own goodbyes to make to one another.

For me it was not altogether the end of my academic year, not just yet. I had two tasks still to perform. One was to run a two-week summer school at St Andrews University in Scotland, for teachers of English in Swedish schools. The other, immediately after that, was to run a summer school in English on the Swedish island of Öland, in the Baltic Sea. I knew that I was going to have to be at both of these without Ingrid, and that when I finished in Öland I would then have to leave the country, because my work permit and residence permit would both have run out. My journey back to England from Öland would be via Copenhagen, so we arranged for me to break it in Lund and be with Ingrid one last time for a couple of nights. Strictly speaking this would mean being in Sweden illegally during those days. But I knew the authorities would treat this as insignificant. They would certainly make no attempt to prevent my leaving the country, still less punish me.

In due course, then, after St Andrews and Öland, I was with Ingrid again in Lund. It was a month since I had seen her. She seemed turned in on herself, in a way I could not quite fathom. I could tell it was not to do with our parting – I now knew her well enough to know that by itself this would produce a different reaction. I tried to make her open up about what was wrong. For a while she stonewalled. Then she came out with it. She was pregnant.

I was shattered. Stunned. *Now*, of all times. She said she had wanted to let me go back to England without telling me. I asked how she could ever have intended such a thing. What had she thought she was going to do? She said she was going to wait for me to leave Sweden and then kill herself.

I did not (and do not) believe she would ever have done that, even if she believed it when she said it. But I knew I could be wrong. I needed to keep her at my side for the time being. In any case, there was no question of my leaving her as she was. The whole situation was impossible. I was in Sweden illegally, not now allowed to do a job or even remain in the country. There was no avoiding going back to England. But that meant I would have to take Ingrid with me. In order to do what? My whole being rebelled against marrying her, and rebelled even more against being forced into a marriage by shotgun. Yet before I could separate myself from her I would have to dispel the possibility, distant though it might be, of her committing suicide. The only way out of the impasse was an abortion. Then my insides rose in revolt against that too. I have always looked on abortion with revulsion: it is killing something living, and human, a human life that is potentially independent. But I could see only those three alternatives: to abandon Ingrid pregnant, to marry her, or to have an abortion. I wanted, violently, to hurl all three away from me.

In language as considerate of Ingrid's feelings as I could make it I poured all this out to her. She said she could not bring herself to have an abortion. I said it was the only one of the only three alternatives that would enable us to carry on with the rest of our lives. Hateful though it was, I said, we were forced into it. Still she said No. I reminded her that her intention had been to kill herself, which would automatically have killed the child as well. But my words rolled off her.

Inside myself I believed that whatever she said we would end with an abortion, because it alone would resolve everything. Any of the alternatives would blight, indefinitely, the ongoing lives of one or other of us, probably both. Because this was so, I believed that when it came to the point I would be able to pressure her into accepting it. When we went to bed that night I had a horrifyingly clear view of the immediate future. We would go to England, where I had already arranged to stay in London for a short time in the flat of some friends who were away on holiday. From there I would make contact with people I had known in Oxford who had had abortions, and find out who to get in touch with. Ingrid and I would then go through with it. Then she would return to Sweden. I was not under any illusion that this was going to be easy. I was in turmoil at the prospect: it was something I would have to force on myself as well as on her. But I believed it was what we would do.

I lay in bed in the blackness confronting this, trying to steel myself to face it. Suddenly I was engulfed in tears. They were not, as I would have expected, tears of guilt or remorse, they were tears of grief. I was overwhelmed with devastation at the death of this unique life that would otherwise be my child. The loss was inconsolable. In the same moment, I had a profound insight into the absolute wrongness of killing a human life. My weeping was convulsive, uncontrollable and noisy. Beside me in the darkness Ingrid kept asking desperately: 'What's wrong? What's wrong?' I could not answer. This got her into a distressed state. At last I managed to croak: 'The abortion'. She misunderstood me. She thought I was weeping so convulsively as a reaction to her refusal to have an abortion. She threw her arms round my neck and said: 'Stop, stop. I will have it. Don't cry like that. I'll do it.' And this made everything worse.

With both of us now apparently accepting the same course we crossed Denmark two days later and took a boat for England. The only thing I remember from that voyage is the two of us standing on the deck at the ship's rail looking down into a pool of blood on the deck between Ingrid's feet. She had haemorrhaged.

We installed ourselves in my friends' flat, and I tracked down an abortionist in south London who was also a qualified doctor. In those days abortion was a criminal offence, unless it was needed to save a woman's life. Doctors (or anyone else) found guilty of carrying it out were sent to prison. Because of the great demand for it, though, and the scarcity of doctors who would do it, there were unqualified abortionists all over the country who did it for the money (as indeed did the doctors). But quite a few of those were dangerous. The whole activity was shrouded in essential secrecy. But it went on extensively, at all levels of society. Social researchers believed that the proportion of families in Britain containing a member who had had an illegal abortion must be something like one in five.

When Ingrid and I went to the doctor he opened the conversation by trying to persuade us to have the baby. He carried on about this. I began to realize that what he was doing was preparing a defensive position for himself. This was confirmed later, when I learnt that it was standard practice for abortionists, so that if they found themselves in a criminal court they could say: 'I didn't want to do it, and I tried to avoid it. These people came to me in desperation, begging for an abortion, but I did everything in my power to persuade them to have the child instead. Nothing I said made any difference, though. I was confronted with a desperate woman. It seemed to me that her health might be at risk, perhaps even her life. So in the end, with the greatest reluctance, I helped her.' Ingrid and I, if questioned under oath in a witness box, would have had no alternative but to confirm such words as true.

The doctor's apparently relentless attempts to dissuade us re-aroused Ingrid's true feelings, until she was in a distressed condition again. She started to say she agreed with him, agreed with every word he had uttered. She began to weep. Then she shouted that she did not want the abortion and never *had* wanted it. She became hysterical. The scene was like the most horrific of nightmares. The doctor was seriously discomposed – this was not what he had intended, and not what he expected. He tried to soothe Ingrid and calm her down. He said there was no question of his doing anything there and then, while she was in this emotional state. She must go away and compose herself, and then come back to him another day when she was calm. I could see from his face that he was frightened. A hysterical woman could land him in gaol if she were to say he had performed an abortion on her that she had told him she did not want … I realized he would never be seeing us again.

I too had passed a tipping point. The doctor, no doubt out of long experience, had said all the right things about why we should have the baby, and all my own horrors of abortion had been activated. To these were added my feelings for Ingrid in the state she was in – the fact that my own revulsion at abortion had been re-aroused meant that I empathized all the more intensely with her. I could not now, simply could not, go on trying to force her into it, whatever might be at stake. So like both the other people in the room I changed my mind, and decided not to go through with it.

As soon as Ingrid and I were outside in the street we just stood and clung to one another, and the question of abortion was never again mentioned between us.

In that case, what were we to do? Ingrid said we would have to get married. I said No: it would destroy my future. For a week of the most extreme emotional stress we tried to thrash it out. I thanked God that before any of this had arisen I had told her bluntly that I did not want to marry her, so I was not now in the position of saying this for the first time. That would have been intolerable – even ignominious as well as horrifying. But she insisted, now that I had stopped pressing for an abortion, that marriage was the only course. In support of this she said all the things that a woman of her generation would naturally say in her situation. For her there was no countervailing course, and also no snag about marriage. The fact that I so totally did not want it did not count as one. In her present position marrying me would give her everything she wanted. It began to dawn on me that this might have been what she wanted all along. However, I felt and expressed an iron refusal to be shotgunned into a marriage which she had always known I was adamantly against. I could no more have backed down on this than I could have gone ahead now with the abortion. My situation did not correspond to hers: for her there was one alternative that offered everything she wanted, whereas for me they were all repugnant. After much discussion it presented itself to me that the least worst course of action would have to be something like this. The fact that Ingrid was going to have the baby meant that her pregnancy could no longer be kept from her family. They were a well-off, mutually supportive one who made free shared use of a large family home. So for Ingrid accommodation presented no problem. She could go to her family home to have the baby, and then carry on living there for as long as she chose, being well looked after, surrounded by people who loved her. In Sweden there was nothing like the stigma attached to illegitimacy that there was in England, though in neither country was there the general permissiveness of today.

Ingrid fought against the idea, and put her heart and soul into trying to persuade me to marry her. I was not to be shifted. We then found ourselves in a new impasse. The time had arrived when we had to leave my friends' flat. The pregnancy was not yet visible, and would not be for some time, so Ingrid decided to go back to Sweden to do things she would have to do, whatever her future, such as prepare her colleagues in Lund for her forthcoming absence from her job, and tell her family she was pregnant. So we parted for the time being, the future of both of us undecided. The level of conflict between us was still rising, though.

When Ingrid returned to Sweden, and I had to get out of my friends' flat, my most immediate needs were to find somewhere to live and to earn some money. So I went to Oxford to find out about the job Escritt said he had found for me. It was with the British Council on a one-year contract. The content of it was as follows. Professional people from all over the world were continually making short visits to the University of Oxford for work-related purposes. If a new operation was developed at the Radcliffe Infirmary, surgeons from other countries would come to watch it performed, and then perform it in their own country. A foreign academic writing the first-ever biography in his mother tongue of a classic English author would come to England to examine the relevant documents and meet acknowledged experts on his subject. During my year the senior army officers who ran Egypt's prisons made a fact-finding tour of England's prisons, including Oxford's. The university's leading scientists were visited by a never-ending stream of foreign experts, as were the leading figures in economics, politics and law. Such visits could occur in any subject. Not all of them were funded by the British Council, but many were, and even when the Council did not fund them it tried to facilitate them. I was to be their man for this in Oxford, with the job description of Visitors' Officer.

The flow was enough to keep me occupied. I would be given advance notice of who was coming, when, for how long (usually three or four days), and for what purpose. This would give me time to set up meetings with the people they wanted to see. It was also part of my job to find out through these primary contacts if there were other people in Oxford who could be of use to the visitor, perhaps unknown to him, and arrange meetings with them too. I would host the visitor during his stay to the extent of supervising his hotel accommodation, and going with him to the meetings I had arranged. Often I would take him out to dinner or to a theatre one evening. I performed the same role for the foreign visitors of the Central Office of Information, which had no office of its own in Oxford. In the course of a year this gave me dealings with a great many interesting people from abroad, and also some of the most creative people in Oxford.

I did the job from an office in St Giles, one of the most attractive streets in central Oxford. The British Council occupied Black Hall, an imposing seventeenth century private house with a garden. (The philosopher John Locke used to visit a young woman there who was keen on him.) I had a light, spacious office on the first floor, and shared it with my secretary, Imogen Mais. She was eighteen, and my first secretary. I was never to have a better one, and we became good friends. Her father, S. P. B. Mais, had been a household name in the England of my childhood as a broadcaster and popular author, but was now already a living figure from the past.

For my living quarters I had the amazing luck to get a room in the house I had lived in for two years as an undergraduate. This was only a few yards from the Randolph Hotel, where most of my British Council visitors stayed. The largest room in the house, which until then had been the dining room, was newly converted into a bed-sitting-room, and I was its first occupant. The relief of being in familiar surroundings, with people I had known before I went to Sweden, was indescribable. But I said nothing to any of them about my current Swedish problems. I was in a state of confusion and distress about them, too desperate to talk. I conducted my relationships with other people on automatic pilot, and got on with my job.

Although the job was a worthwhile one, and quite educative for me, it made no demands except on my time. I found it effortlessly easy to do, and this made it ideal in my present situation. The fact that I was in stress and turmoil throughout that year made no difference to my effectiveness in the job. I even found it therapeutic to have other things to do, and things to think about. These considerations gave additional boost to my resumption of my studies in philosophy. I made application to be a doctoral student, and received a form asking me who I wanted to supervise me.

Among Oxford philosophers who were currently practising, the one who seemed to me the best was Peter Strawson. But he had not published anything on the subject I was writing my thesis about. Scarcely anyone had. There was no book in the field, and in the back numbers of academic journals only two articles by a little known young Oxford philosophy don called Iris Murdoch. Someone pointed her out to me at a party, and I thought her dramatically ugly, though for that reason intriguing-looking. I needed two names for my form, so I put down Strawson as my first choice and Murdoch as my second. I got Strawson. When his teaching turned out to be of the highest class I was grateful for my good luck, but in after years, when I came to know Iris, and she had made an international reputation as a novelist, I could not help wondering what it would have been like to be taught philosophy by her.

My new life in ultra-familiar Oxford had a strange feel about it. I had previously lived there for four years, since when only one year had elapsed, so I still had friends and acquaintances all over the place. Being such a recent President of the Union I was still an *ex officio* member of the committee that ran it, and was now invited to attend its meetings. The new President was Michael Heseltine, who was bent on solving the Union's long-term financial problem by converting its capacious cellars into a nightclub. This was controversial, but I was in favour of it, so he and I were allies in that cause. In so many different ways – through wide-ranging friendships, through being taught philosophy again, through living again in my old digs in St John Street, through being involved again with the Oxford Union – I was transported back into Oxford's familiar embrace. Yet this was happening to an external me, the me on the outside, the me on automatic pilot. The inner me was tortured with uncertainty, wracked with anxiety about what lay ahead, felt trapped, did not know what to do, was wrestling with alternatives all of which were intolerable.

Ingrid's return to Sweden shifted our situation into a new phase for her. She was living in the bosom of her family now, and they were adamant that she and I must get married. In their minds there was no alternative. When she told them it was what she wanted, but I refused to agree, they remonstrated with her for being feeble. She must *make* me agree, they told her. It was up to her to get me to see that it was the only thing to do. She must assert herself – not just sit there a thousand miles away from me throwing up her hands. She wrote me letters full of nothing but this: we had to get married. I wrote letters back saying I was not willing to do it. Hers changed into bitter denunciations, a recycling of what her family were saying to her about me. These letters had the inevitable effect of making relations between us worse, and agreement between us more difficult to achieve. Then suddenly, one dark evening in early November, when I was walking past the main university building in Broad Street on my way to my first supervision with Peter Strawson, there was a sound of running footsteps behind me, a voice at my back shouted '*Hey!*', a hand grabbed my shoulder, and there stood Ingrid. She had arrived from Sweden that day and, not finding me in my digs, roamed the streets of Oxford looking for me – and, miraculously, saw me.

Strawson was expecting me in a matter of minutes, and this was my first supervision with him, so I told Ingrid I could not talk to her now, but would be with her in little over an hour. She thought I was trying to escape from her, and was scared she would not see me again. This shocked me into a realization of how far her family had poisoned her mind against me. At no time in my life would such behaviour have been a possibility for me. I firmly directed her to the Randolph Hotel, and went to the supervision.

With many people, intellectual activity is made impossible by extreme emotional turmoil, but I have never been like that, not entirely. The turmoil is real enough, and in this case was extreme, but a certain amount of thinking went on alongside it. When I walked into Strawson's room my feelings were in a state of volcanic eruption, and I could feel my body trembling; but I was still able, if only just, to cope with Strawson. His teaching method was one of naked aggression. He asked me what I wanted to do, I told him, and he then launched into an all-out, bare-knuckled, no-holds-barred assault on the whole undertaking, while I fought for its life. By the end of the hour I assumed he was going to disallow my project, but to my astonishment he finished by saying that he thought it a good one. He had been making certain, he said, that I understood what the most formidable criticisms of it would be, because my thesis would need to bring forward effective answers to those criticisms. He said he thought I would make a good job of it, and wished me well. We fixed our next meeting.

Given the state I had been in when I arrived, I was now at the limit of the tensions I could tolerate. It was as if I were living to the maximum of what I could bear on all fronts simultaneously. My path now lay directly from Strawson to Ingrid.

At the Randolph it emerged that Ingrid's family had sent her to confront me – without warning me, in case I tried to escape – with an absolute insistence that we get married. I said that this tactic was misconceived on their part, and counter-productive. I could not be bullied and intimidated in this way. If I were to marry her it would be because I honestly believed it was the best thing to do in the circumstances. I had no desire to escape responsibility for the child, but marriage was a different matter. I asked Ingrid to get her family to stop interfering – they were making matters worse between us. I told her I would put her up at the Randolph for that night, but as far as I was concerned she should return to her family next day. Today needed to be wiped out of our minds. We must start again, the two of us, and try to find a course of action we could agree on.

After I had booked her in to the hotel she came out with me to the front steps. There she exploded into hysterics. To Beaumont Street at large she shouted: 'You are abandoning your child,' over and over again, the same words. I put an arm round her shoulders and tried to comfort her, saying – also several times – that there would be no question of my abandoning the child. She sat down with fierce defiance on the outer steps as if expecting that I would try to move her away from there, and carried on shouting, the tears streaming down her face. Something she let slip caused the possibility to cross my mind that she had allowed herself to get pregnant in order to make me marry her and was now hoist with her own petard – and panic-stricken at the failure of her stratagem. I was later to find that this belief was held by most of my Swedish friends who knew her. I always defended her against it, but the truth is that after that evening at the Randolph I was unsure myself. The important point, though, is that it did not make any difference now. Once we were in the situation that we were now in, what I did would not be affected by that consideration. From now on it was questions about the future that mattered, not questions about the past.

If Ingrid tried to get her family to stop interfering she was not successful. After her return to Sweden they took matters into their own hands. I received a letter from her brother telling me it was my duty to marry his sister. I replied that marriage between his sister and me was a matter for his sister and me to decide, not one in which he could expect to have a say. Ten days later there was a knock on the door of my office, and in walked a priest from the Swedish church in London. He had come to Oxford to see me without prior arrangement, as requested by Ingrid's family. Since I was sharing the office with Imogen it was impossible to talk there, so I took him on a long walk across Oxford's main park. He said what he could have been expected to say, in reply to which I said what I could be expected to say – including that the matter was one for Ingrid and me to decide, and that I was finding it increasingly difficult not to be antagonized by the attempts of third parties to interfere.

It was this last consideration that caused me to decide on unilateral action, while I was still unalienated. This turned out to be the decisive turn of events in the whole story. I accepted, finally, that agreement between Ingrid and me was never going to be reached. And this meant that I alone had to decide what was to be done. The only honourable course was to impose a settlement that I truly believed to be equitable, one not favouring myself but demanding equal sacrifices from each of us while making equal concessions to each of us.

The way to arrive at this, I thought, was to identify what was absolutely non-negotiable for me – what I would never give way on in any circumstances – and give way on everything else. This would give to Ingrid the maximum she could possibly have. By this stage nothing could have persuaded me to live with her, or be her provider, but in return for those things I had to agree to whatever else she wanted. For instance, I would contract a legal marriage with her. This would achieve several significant goals. Ingrid would not be an unmarried mother. I would publicly acknowledge our child as mine and accept legal responsibility for it. And the child would not be illegitimate. These may seem trivial points to make now, but in those days they were important in a way that made a difference to people's lives – a serious difference to child and mother.

I said all this to Ingrid as persuasively as I could. We were well into November now, and the baby was due in February. (It must have been conceived in May, at the very end of my time in Lund.) I proposed to her that I should come to Sweden immediately after Christmas, while still in the Christmas break from my job, marry her there, and return to England. Although I made it unambiguously clear that I was never going to live with her, neither in England nor in Sweden, she jumped at the suggestion and undertook to make all the arrangements for a civil wedding in Malmö – not in Lund.

9

Michael Heseltine had been suggesting that he and I should find an evening when the two of us could have a leisurely dinner together. In those days there was no such thing in Oxford as a good restaurant: the best hotels were also the best places to eat. (This was true of Britain as a whole, outside the main cities.) The Mitre in the High Street was considered best for eating, though the Randolph was best for staying at. However, the cognoscenti, who like to be different, would tell you that the *really* best food was at the Royal Oxford Hotel, near the railway station. Michael and I, being well-known characters around town, thought we would have a better chance of not being noticed if we went to the Royal Oxford. So there we went.

In those days a good meal meant large amounts of rich food and the wines to go with them. We did ourselves so well that I wanted my coffee black at the end of it. For an hour or two after we finished eating we sat talking, and as we did so I drank cup after cup of strong black coffee. I had never done this before, and I think it may have been connected with the state of stress I was in. When finally we broke up and returned to our digs I found myself unable to sleep. For hours, literally, I lay wide awake, my overstimulated mind abnormally and nastily alert. Everything in my head was unnaturally light and bright: I have since heard this described as 'white logic'. It was accompanied by a tension that made it both inescapable and sinister. What obsessed me was my inability to come to terms with what I was doing in my relationship with Ingrid. I had told her I would legally get married to her – and, having given my word, neither then nor at any subsequent time did I consider breaking it – but I could not come to terms with it. I had forced myself to do it, but it was intolerable to me. Yet the alternative – not marrying her – would be worse, both for her and for the child. As for my relationship with the child, the more I thought about it the unhappier I became. I would visit him or her regularly in Sweden, and he or she would visit me regularly in England. But the fact remained that we would be living a thousand miles apart, in different countries, and this was not good for the child (nor for me). Yet, again, the alternative was worse – the only way I could live with the child would be to live with Ingrid, and that was not tolerable. So even though we had eliminated the worst alternative of all, abortion, I was still trapped between alternatives none of which I could accept. They were incompatible both with my conception of myself and all my hopes for the future – the sort of person I was.

I became more and more stressed until, some time after three o'clock, I decided to switch on the light and read, hoping this would help. The book I was halfway through was Gertrude Stein's *The Autobiography of Alice B. Toklas*. I read a page or two – then something happened that words will for ever be unable to describe. The tension in my head went beyond the bounds of tolerance. It broke free of its constraints and spilled over into the rest of my being, flooding and filling me. I could not withstand it. I had to get away from it, get away from *myself*, get away, get out, not be there. Without having decided anything I leapt out of bed and started putting clothes on. My whole body was shaking so much that I had the greatest difficulty getting my arms into my sleeves and my legs into my trousers. Because of this I dressed to the minimum – a shirt unbuttoned, a pair of trousers half done up, a pair of shoes without socks. As I hurtled out of the room I grabbed the jacket off the back of the door with a gesture of habit and put it on when I got out into the street.

It was the dead of a November night, about a quarter past three, dry and cold. The street was dimly lit, silent and deserted. I was under a compulsion to keep moving, move strongly and vigorously, not let the tension that filled my whole being close its grip on me and shut out rest of the world, not let it shut me in, keep a chink open that I could move into, and keep on moving into that chink. I strode round the corner into Beaumont Street so that I would have wider views into other streets, all of which were empty. My heart was thumping against the inside of my chest in a way I had never known before, like someone banging hysterically on a big wooden door, *Bang, Bang, Bang, Bang, Bang, Bang* at immense speed and with huge force, as if it was out of control and about to burst. At the same time I was gasping noisily for air in a way that was also out of control and hyper-fast, gulping it in with huge breaths and puffing them out immediately. I realize now that I was hyperventilating. My face felt inflamed, my whole body like a radiator on maximum heat and about to explode. My state of consciousness was one I had never experienced, uncontrollable terror. I thought I was going to stop, end, burst. I was at the same time overwhelmed by a sense of isolation and loneliness. Then from out of sight, in St Giles round the corner, came a sound of human footsteps. At once I made for the sound, to see another human being. He was on the other side of the street, a man in a dark overcoat walking away from me under the gaslight. Without crossing the road I half-followed him, from a distance, keeping him in view for as long as I could. When he disappeared I had to strike out harder, more energetically, be extra on the go, *walk, walk, walk*, into that chink, not daring to risk losing it. I kept going like this for hours. Round and round the central streets of Oxford I went, the same streets over and over again, never pausing, my body so hot I kept my jacket and shirt wide open to the cold night air, desperately trying to get cooler. But my body went on feeling as if it was on fire, my heart went on pounding, my breath went on coming in noisy gasps, and I went on being in a state of uncontrollable terror, convinced that everything was about to end the next instant in some sort of explosion of myself. The one thought in my head was: 'I've gone mad.'

Dawn began to break. I was in St Giles for the umpteenth time when a policeman came on the scene, my first of the night. When he saw me he walked towards me as if he wanted to have a word with me. I turned towards him with gratitude. When he got near enough to see me clearly an expression of surprise took hold of his features.

'Are you all right?' he said.

'I think so,' I said, my voice trembling and cracking on every word. They were the first words I had uttered after several hours, speed-walking on overdrive.

He came right up to me and peered into my face.

'Are you sure?'

'I think so.'

'You don't look it.'

'I'm worried about something.'

'I should think you are.'

Just talking to him made me calmer, more in possession of myself. Having to direct my attention outwards took me out of myself a little, and had an immediate therapeutic effect on me.

'What's your name?'

'Bryan Magee.'

'Where do you live?'

'Just round the corner, in St John Street.'

'Oh? Why aren't you at home?'

'I needed to walk. I've got to think something over.'

'Hmm ... Will you be going back there?'

'Yes.'

'Now?'

'Well, I ...' I did not actually know when I would be going back.

'Is your front door locked?'

'Yes.'

'Do you have the key?'

'Yes.'

'If you don't mind, I'd like to stroll round there with you now and see you in at your front door, just to make sure you get home safely.'

'Why?'

He smiled in a compassionate way. 'Actually,' he said, as if telling me something in confidence, 'I just want to make sure you live there.'

'Why?'

'I've only got your word for it that you do. Look at you. Bare-chested in this weather, no proper coat, clothes all undone, no socks. You're obviously in a state. For all I know you could have broken out of somewhere. I want to be sure, that's all.'

You could have broken out of somewhere. With a shock I realized that this was how I looked. Now that daylight was coming I did not want to be seen in the street as I was. Now was therefore the time to return to 3 St John Street. I gestured so to the policeman, and we walked together round the corner to my front door. While I was letting myself in he uttered kind, encouraging words, but I have no memory of what they were: my mind was focusing forward to the fact that I was about to go back into the solitary room that I had been hurled out of by terror a few hours before. I was still in a state, as the policeman said, if not as bad as at the beginning. At least I was improving. As I climbed the stairs I concentrated on trying to do it quietly, so as not to disturb anyone in the house. My whole body was suddenly invaded by extreme exhaustion, the weariness of having just walked miles and miles at a cracking, unremitting pace. I felt at last as if I could sleep, must sleep. I wanted to drop. Once into my room I got out of my clothes and into bed in seconds, and went straight to sleep. It was a tense, unrelaxing, semi-conscious sleep. But it was, if only just, sleep.

10

I have no memory of whether I went to my office the next day. It is just possible that I did, though I find that hard to believe. I know I told people there and in St John Street that I had had a totally sleepless night, disturbed by repeated bilious attacks brought on by a huge and over-rich dinner. If anyone had heard me moving about in the night it was because I had kept going to the bathroom to be sick. If I now looked terrible, this was the reason.

If I did miss a day, it was only one. What I was determined to do above everything else was survive, not go under, not fall to pieces, hang in, hang on. Yet something irretrievably terrible had happened, something radically different in kind from the whole of my experience of life up to that point. There is no language to describe it, and there never will be. I had been mad.

Panic attacks returned immediately. In the subsequent days they kept coming back, each accompanied by a pounding heart, a desperate gasping for breath, a hot and bright red face, and a conviction that this time I really was going mad. When I felt the onset of one I would make some excuse to Imogen and leave my office, to have the attack in solitude and secrecy somewhere else. It was usually an hour before I came back. It seemed to me of supreme importance that no one else should know what was happening. I wanted, above all, to return to normal, and this would be made much more difficult, if not impossible, if other people knew what was going on.

I had phobic attacks of other kinds, especially claustrophobia. It was impossible for me to be in a room if its door was closed, or in a room with a low ceiling. I even found it impossible to walk along a path between a wall and a fence. Any position where I was hemmed in so that I could not get out of it easily – and immediately – became impossible for me, or at the very least a terrifying challenge. Travelling in a car was difficult: I had to fight against claustrophobia all the time I was in it. I would sit there twanging with tension, more and more sweat bursting out of me, first of all on my forehead, then on my face and neck, then from the rest of my body, and my clothes would start sticking to me. I would have to make any excuse to get out of the car. Soon I was avoiding cars altogether.

I developed vertigo. If I was above the ground floor of a building I could not look out of the window, not even a window in my office. If I stood on a table, or a chair, my head swam. If I was going down stairs I had to avoid looking down, and I would feel my way down by the banisters while looking to one side.

I was unable to cope with ordinary stress of any kind. If I tried at my job to deal with more than one thing at a time, or worked for several hours without a break, or sat up late at night and let myself get tired, there would always be a panic attack. Any form of strain whatsoever, any challenge, induced one, as did any confrontation. These terrors dominated my life. Coping with them was my overwhelming concern. I began to learn and adopt strategies for avoiding them. All this was accompanied by dissimulation, attempts to conceal from everyone round me what was happening. It is impossible for me to know how far such attempts were successful. My guess is that they were partly so but not entirely: I think the people close to me knew I was desperately worried about something but had no idea what it was. They could certainly not have had any conception of the earthquakes taking place inside me. By that age I had developed a confident-seeming social manner which had become habitual and unconscious, and this took over automatically when I was with other people.

Those who have never experienced neurosis of this kind are inclined to believe that coping with it is a challenge to one's strength of character – one needs to take a firm grip on oneself, pull oneself together, assert control, not let things get on top of one. To think like that is to misunderstand the situation entirely. One can no more will such things not to happen than one can will oneself not to have chicken pox – or, when one has chicken pox, will it to go away. Willing plays no part in the matter. The mechanisms of cause and effect are outside one's control. It is like being at the steering wheel of a car whose steering has stopped working. One is in the driving seat but powerless to direct the vehicle, swept along willy-nilly, hoping not to be destroyed in the smash-up that one anticipates at every moment.

Even farther from most people's understanding is the actual feel of such experiences themselves. Fear in a panic attack is not normal-fear-but-more-so. Vertigo is not an intenser version of the insecurity and vulnerability that are natural to people at extreme heights. Claustrophobia is not a stronger version of the feeling of being trapped and stifled that most people are capable of feeling in a tightly packed tube train. This is the mistake most commonly made by people (including some who have researched and written on the subject) who have not had the experiences themselves: they take them to be over-the-top, out-of-control intensifications of experiences everyone has. The misunderstanding is encouraged by the fact that, since no words exist to describe the private experiences of the neurotic (nor could there be – an intelligible private language is impossible) there is no alternative but to take words from the public language of the emotions. The reality is that the inner nature of such experiences is different in an incommunicable way. The nearest thing to them in the experience of the non-neurotic is the all-consuming terror of the most extreme and horrific nightmare. But of course the neurotic is awake, and knows himself to be awake. So there can be no question of his waking from his nightmare. Nor, in the instant, is there any way of escaping from it. The fear (to use that word) is not fear *of* anything: it is causeless, nameless, free-floating yet all-engulfing terror of a most extreme, very terrible kind. The neurotic knows perfectly well that it is irrational, but that knowledge does not make things easier for him to bear, it makes them harder, because it makes him think he must indeed be going mad.

In those last few weeks of 1954 my overriding concern was to remain sane and alive, not to follow any of the alternative ways out of these seemingly intolerable forms of consciousness. I came as close to having a breakdown requiring hospitalization as it is possible to come without having one. What kept me going, and kept my nostrils out of the water, was a fixed idea that nothing must now prevent me from flying to Sweden (which I could not do until the Christmas break) and marrying Ingrid, since I had given my word that I would, and for the sake of the child.

I was unable to sleep at nights, and it was this that drove me to see a doctor, to ask him for sleeping pills. In reply to his questioning I poured out an account of my symptoms, then of their cause. He was much taken aback. But he listened. At the end of it he said doubtfully: 'You don't want to see a psychiatrist, I suppose, do you?'

No such thought had crossed my mind. Ignorantly but truthfully I said: 'No. I want to deal with this by myself.'

He nodded approvingly, and prescribed barbiturates. These helped to tranquillize me. They did not stop the panic attacks from coming, but they made them easier to deal with when they did, and they also helped me to sleep. Without any doubt at all it was they that saved me from a complete breakdown.

Throughout this time I assumed that freeing myself of these nightmare symptoms was going to be a matter of weeks, after which I would be back to my normal self. When they went on longer than this I was dismayed, but still saw it as a matter of months. It was to be a very long time before I understood that I had changed permanently – that I was never going to be the person I had been before. Throughout that early but still seemingly endless period of almost unremitting struggle I thought of myself as fighting to get 'back to normal'. The months turned into years, during which all my hopes, all my efforts, were devoted to 'getting back'. And I believed I could. If I had known from the beginning that I was never going to 'get back' I would have sunk into the most despairing of depressions, perhaps have been suicidal. It was the illusion that I could get on top of it all and put it behind me that saved me.

When I was small my father was a lover of boxing. He got special satisfaction from talent-spotting among young boxers. Nothing pleased him more than to identify a teenager in a local tournament as a possible future champion, and then follow his career through, seeing all his fights till he reached the top. It was like picking winners among the horses. Some would make it but the majority did not. He used to say that one of the things that made these youngsters extra-good was their unqualified self-confidence. They were not frightened of anything. Every time they stepped into a ring they felt an absolute assurance that they were going to win. This itself was one of the reasons why they did win, though of course they needed to be outstanding boxers too. If, he said, this came unstuck for them only once, and they were given a bad beating, you could write off their championship prospects for ever. Their early promise would never return. They would never be the same again. This was because it would never again be possible for them to feel unqualified self-confidence. Not only did they now know from personal experience how bad a bad beating could be, they also knew every time they stepped into a ring that it could happen to them this time unexpectedly, as it had happened before. They could never again be unselfconsciously certain of themselves.

Something of this sort happened to me. Before November 1954 I confronted life with extraordinary self-confidence. I just *knew* I was going to be successful in the things I most seriously wanted to do – not necessarily immediately, but in the long run. Reverses could only be setbacks, and I would overcome them eventually. In the very foundations of myself I knew I was bigger than anything that could happen to me. Therefore everything was bound to come right in the end, no matter how far away that end might be, or how serious the setbacks were along the way. In November 1954 all that came to an end. From then on I knew I could be overwhelmed. And I knew how unimaginably horrific it was. Short of that, I also knew that if I strained my resources too far I would be incapacitated by panic attacks. I have had to conduct my life ever since on those terms. The panic attacks never ceased, but because I learnt to heed their warnings, and never again attempted to drive myself through them, I have never broken down to the point of having to opt out of normal life – have never been hospitalized, or unable for more than a matter of hours to do my work. Attacks became fewer as the years went by and I became more experienced at dealing with them; but they never disappeared. Also, the whole range of other phobias stayed with me – claustrophobia, vertigo and the rest, and I have had to live with them too. I deal with them chiefly by shunning situations in which they occur, for there is no question of my being their master once they do. The fact that so many people are intolerant, because uncomprehending, of some of the forms of behaviour that this gives rise to is beside the point, because I do not have the option of ignoring phobias, nor does anyone else who has them. Because of this my inner self-confidence (I am not talking about a social-behaviour kind of self-confidence) has never returned to what it was, or even to a level that would count as normal among people who have never had such experiences.

That first and worst cataclysm of November 1954 came about because I was in a situation in which all the options open to me, including that of doing nothing, were incompatible with my moral sense, my sense of my own integrity. There was none that I could go along with and carry on being myself, remain whole. Whatever I did or did not do would have been bound to break the dykes of my mind. After that experience, in order to preserve my sanity and possibly my life I could never allow myself to get into such a situation again. One cannot live a life worth living without moral risk or moral danger, but in all such situations I never again allowed every single option to close. I always kept a path open, however narrow the slit, that I could pass through in an ultimate extremity without self-destruction. So long as I was able to preserve my inner wholeness I knew I could face any threats from outside; but a split inside, divided against myself with uncontrollable violence, would destroy me, and I now knew that. I had to live without ever again getting into a situation whose moral prohibitions were more powerful than I could ignore.

I arranged with Ingrid that I would fly to Sweden on Boxing Day and marry her in Malmö the day after. She undertook to make minimal arrangements, with only the two of us there. The officials in attendance would act as our witnesses.

Engrossed as I was in a struggle to get back to 'normal life', I did not want anyone in Oxford to know that these things were happening. This feeling was contributed to by the peculiarly uptight state I was in. I simply told friends that I would be spending Christmas in Sweden. The only two people in Britain who knew what was really going on were the couple in whose flat Ingrid and I had stayed in London. They were going away for Christmas, so by arrangement I moved in to their empty home on Christmas Eve, spent Christmas Day there by myself, and flew to Sweden on Boxing Day.

The desolation of that Christmas Day is something I shall always remember. I had imagined making positive use of it. I needed a break and a rest, so I thought a day doing nothing, not having to respond to other people, would do me good. I would get up late, then loaf around playing records, reading, listening to the radio. At some point I would go out for a walk. It would all be restorative. I would unwind. I had barbiturates with me in case there should be a panic attack, and to help me sleep. It would set me up for the challenge I would have to face in Sweden.

When it came to the day I was engulfed in loneliness and isolation. I felt as if I were in hiding (as indeed I was). My knowledge that it was Christmas Day brought imagined laughter from the other side of the walls around me, where people crowded together celebrating, full of good cheer, warmth and togetherness. I tried to read, but could not concentrate. When I tried to play music it impinged on my sensibilities like a dentist's drill hitting a nerve and was so insupportable I had to stop.

The ground floor flat was alongside the River Thames at Upper Mall, in Hammersmith. So when I looked out of the window there was no movement, no people or houses, but instead an empty expanse of wintry water. At low tide there was a dirty little beach of shingle and mud just across from the window. Bleakness could scarcely have been bleaker. It was distilled dreariness of spirit.

I went out to walk, walk, walk – inland, so to speak, to get away from the icy river. The streets were deserted. Through all the windows I could see groups of rosy-faced people partying, and hear their muffled noises. All this gave me a craving for contact. I found myself approaching a church, and from inside it the sound of singing came towards me – a carol service. Fearfully wondering whether I would be able to endure the music (I have always loved Christmas carols) yet desperate to be with other people, I went in and melted into the congregation. That service brought me inexpressible comfort at a time when I was at the end of my tether – though neither the stress nor the comfort had anything to do with religion. They made it easier for me to get through the rest of the day, though this was still exceedingly difficult.

Two days later in Malmö, Ingrid and I were married. The ceremony, if it can be called that, was performed by the Mayor in his magnificent office overlooking the main square. He was Munck af Rosenschöld, scion of an upper class family such as one is seldom aware of in social-democratic Sweden, and Mayor of Malmö for a quarter of a century that included most of the Second World War. Two members of his staff were called in from their offices to be witnesses. With Ingrid seven months pregnant, and me looking white-faced, hollow-eyed and hunted, the truth of the situation must have been obvious, though I expect these people were used to it. When, at the appropriate moment, the Mayor asked me to produce a ring and place it on Ingrid's finger I was thrown into confusion – I had given no thought to a ring. Feeling a fool, I mumbled that there was no ring. He in his turn was taken aback, as if he had never encountered *this* situation before. No ring. He turned to one of the officials and asked if, since a ring was called for at this point in the procedure as laid down by law in print, we could be a hundred per cent certain that a marriage without it would fully meet legal requirements. The official reassured him that it would. So we went ahead. Ingrid emerged from the town hall as Mrs Magee – or rather, since we were now in Sweden and had married under Swedish law, Fru Magee. In the Swedish language the word 'magi', which Swedes pronounce in the same way as they do my name, means 'magic', so the name is a doubly unusual one to have.

Ingrid thought of herself as having succeeded in getting me to marry her, and felt it as a triumph. Contrary to everything that had passed between us, she started saying that the logical and natural next step would be for her to come to England and live with me. Nothing in the world would have got me to agree to that. I was rock-like in my refusal, and insisted on sticking to the agreements we had made. I was, though, full of shame at not having given Ingrid a ring: after all, one of the reasons I had married her was so that she would not be seen by others to be having an illegitimate baby. I did not have the money on me to buy a ring before I left, but as soon as I got back to Oxford I bought one and sent it to her. To mail it safely through the post, and so that she would not have to pay customs duty on it, I buried it in a roll of newspapers (for which there was a specially cheap postal rate) and mailed it like that.

Ingrid bombarded me with letters about how, now we were married, with a baby due in two months, we should live together.

When that failed, she pinned her hopes to the arrival of the child changing my mind. Within hours of Gunnela's birth on 16 February 1955 she wrote to me. My response was to want to go to Sweden at the first opportunity to see Gunnela, but not to move one inch nearer to living with Ingrid. I wanted passionately to get to know Gunnela, and visit her regularly, and have a continuous relationship with her, but not to live with Ingrid. When Ingrid finally saw that I was immovable she became vengeful. Unless I agreed to live with them, she said, she would refuse to let me see the child. This flagrant use of Gunnela as a weapon revived suspicions that the child might have been a weapon all along. But I quelled these suspicions, not as being unfounded but as being irrelevant to the situation as it now was. My response was to use the only weapon I now had, and say I would contribute financially to Gunnela's upbringing only if I was allowed to see her. Ingrid could, of course, challenge that in a court, but the same court would rule that I must have access to the child. The fact that I was living a thousand miles away, in a different country, meant that I would not be able to see her often, but two meetings a year were an absolute minimum – one visit by me to Sweden, and one by Gunnela, with Ingrid, to Britain. I desperately wanted Gunnela to grow up knowing England, and feeling at home there. But Ingrid was as adamant as I was. She went on maintaining that she would not let me see Gunnela unless I lived with them, and I went on maintaining that I would not send her money unless I could see Gunnela. This impasse lasted a couple of years.

I knew that the courts of either country would settle it in my favour, but I did not want it settled in that way. What I wanted was for Ingrid to agree of her own accord. I was pretty sure she would eventually do so, though I knew it would take time. And that is how things turned out. One of the reasons why I was willing to wait was that I thought then (foolishly, it now seems to me) that until Gunnela could speak she and I would not be able to interact much, or have much of a relationship. On what were bound to be flying visits I would be able to do little more than gaze at her. Only when she was able to speak would we be able to communicate and relate. And by that time, I believed, Ingrid would come round to accepting the desirability of my seeing her.

The fact that we were log-jammed for so long had great side-effects on other aspects of our lives. Since, if I was not seeing Gunnela, it would make no difference whether I was in Britain or the United States, I renewed my applications for a one-year fellowship to America. Having already a record of failure in this regard, I was none too optimistic. But this time I was luckier. I received notice of election to a fellowship at the University of Indiana. It had recently become famous internationally for its unprecedented studies in sexual behaviour, published by Professor Kinsey. On that day I happened to be seeing my doctor, and when I told him about it he thought the conjunction of me and Professor Kinsey's university hilarious. It did not enter my head that I would receive more than one such offer, so I sent an immediate reply accepting this one. The next day came an offer from Yale – a one-year research fellowship with complete freedom to devote myself to my own work, and no duties. Self-evidently I preferred Yale. So I telephoned the University of Indiana in order to withdraw my acceptance before it could reach them through the post – only to be told that the person who would open the envelope when it arrived was at that moment attending a conference in an Oxford college. I went straight round to see him. I expected him to be understanding and sympathetic, in view of the naturalness of the step I was taking, but he was not like that at all. He was bitterly resentful, and argued that I was under a moral obligation to keep to my written word, even though not a soul had received it or even knew of its existence except for him – and he only knew of it because I had just told him. But I stuck to Yale. And Yale was where I spent the next academic year.

12

I carried on in Oxford from February to September 1955, in a world of emotional turmoil compounded of repeated panic attacks and my hideous relationship with Ingrid. I slept only fitfully, in spite of the barbiturates. Each morning I would be torn with great difficulty out of a belated, troubled sleep, my eyelids hot, my whole body aching with exhaustion. I went to my office every day, and performed my undemanding job adequately. But I felt strained and drained the whole time – and probably looked it, too, though I did everything I could to cling to normality. When I dealt with other people I was on automatic pilot. Surviving was all I now cared about. I wanted to get back on top of my circumstances, however long that might take. So I avoided anything that would add to my problems. Although to outward appearance I was living a life that looked at least partly normal, my inner life was dominated by a neurotic onslaught and my all-out fight against it. Behind my face, the facade I presented to others, a completely different life was going on. The world external to myself was a long way away.

Things were actually to carry on like this throughout the rest of my twenties. But since then nothing as bad has happened again. So I have lived since the age of thirty with an ever- diminishing neurotic handicap which has nevertheless always made itself felt, demanding to be taken into account, a permanent presence. Because I have striven always to live as normal a life as I can in this respect I have rarely talked about these things to other people. It is my hope and belief that only those closest to me are aware of them. And, after all, not all their side-effects are bad. Concealed neurosis is not uncommon, and my experience of it has made me perceptive of it in others, and much more sympathetically understanding of it than I would otherwise have been.

Transporting my life to America in September 1955 did nothing to effect a cure, but it did me an enormous amount of good nonetheless. It immersed me in new and surprisingly congenial surroundings, and did a lot to take me out of myself and get me interested in other things. I once published a whole book about that year, so I need not go into details here. While I was there I kept a diary, and when I got back to England I submitted this to a publisher. He said he would publish it as a book if I would take it out of its diary form and recast it as a continuous narrative. I did this, and the book was published in 1958 with the title *Go West Young Man*. It is essentially a work of social observation, a detailed and (I hope) accurate report on a year during which I travelled all over the United States. It tells where I went, what I saw, who I met and what I thought about it. But it is all about America. There is nothing in it about my private life: nothing about the situation I had left behind me in Europe, or the ongoing inner struggles I was having, the panic and phobia attacks. For that matter there is not even anything about the work I was doing at Yale. This last gap, if gap it is, was filled by a chapter called 'A Yale Education' in a later book, *Confessions of a Philosopher*. So only the private-life omissions have remained unwritten, and only these are relevant here.

My going to America brought home to Ingrid that there was never going to be any question of my living with her. Her declarations that I was never, ever going to be allowed to see Gunnela acquired a vindictive edge. Halfway through the academic year a request came for me to call in at a lawyer's office in New Haven, the town in which Yale is situated. There I was told that Ingrid was pursuing me for money through the American legal system. I explained to the lawyer that I would be perfectly happy to send her money if she would agree to my seeing my child. Meanwhile my motto was 'no taxation without representation'. He told me that any court in the US, as well as in Britain or Sweden, would uphold my right to see Gunnela. He must have reported this back to Sweden, because I never heard any more about it. When, a long time later, I reproached Ingrid for the self-defeatingness and nastiness of this move she said it was her family who had done it, and that she had not approved of it. Whether this is true or not, I do not believe she can ever have told her family the whole truth.

My psychological problems simply continued in the US. With experience I was becoming more skilled at dealing with them, and more used to living with them, but the attacks themselves remained the same, and were as frequent. They brought with them new physical symptoms. I began to get piercing, burning pains in my stomach, and to feel bilious. I took myself to the university's clinic and was diagnosed as developing a stomach ulcer. The doctor questioned me about the stress I was under, assuming at first that this was academic, so I told him something of my situation. He told me that free and confidential psychiatric help was available to members of the university, and advised me strongly to take advantage of this. By now I had come to realize I needed it, and was altogether more sophisticated in my attitude to such things, so I followed his advice. However, by the time I saw a psychiatrist at Yale most of that academic year had gone, so there was not a lot he himself could do. But he had acquired enough understanding of my problems to put me in touch with a psychiatrist to see as soon as I got back to London.

I was thenceforward to receive talking-therapy, on and off, for a number of years, from various psychiatrists. I always steered clear of medication-based therapies, except for taking sleeping pills and tranquillizers. Occasionally I would have a crisis, during which I would take drugs to get me through the crisis, but the drugs then were not associated with courses of therapy, and I never took them for long. I might have survived some of those crises without drugs, but I doubt whether I would have survived them all – I would either have broken down completely or, there is just a remote possibility, have killed myself. It was from my talking-psychiatrists that I got the drugs.

When I was seeing a psychiatrist I would go once a week, or once a fortnight. About the medical efficacy of it I have mixed feelings. It certainly helped me, but I suspect that this came from the opportunity to unburden myself to someone intelligent, understanding and non-judgmental, and had little to do with medical science. During my worst years, the second half of my twenties, I was kept going by the conviction that I could, should, and must get over my neuroses if I was to have a life. My whole conception of my future – which had always had a powerful influence on me – was at stake. To lose control and go completely to pieces would be, whether I killed myself or not, to lose my life, the totality of all my hopes. Other people had already begun to wonder about my career. As I approached thirty it came to my ears that some of my contemporaries at Oxford, where great things had been expected of me, were beginning to ask what was going on – or rather, what was not going on. Why was I not bounding up the ladder of success? When they met me, it was said, they found me nerveless and unengaged, quite unlike my former self. Some, I was told, suspected I had sacrificed my interest in a career to my interest in women. (There was a sense in which, unknown to them, this was true, but involuntarily on my part, and not in the sense in which they suspected it.) I never did fulfil their expectations. But the expectations were for success in politics, and I believe that what I have done is more worthwhile than that. One of the most gifted of my contemporaries, and also one of the most successful, Nigel Lawson (who was Chancellor of the Exchequer in the twentieth century for longer than anyone else) said to me after his retirement from politics that, as between writing books and being a politician, I had made the right choice, a choice which he now wished he had made. This was to become my view too, soon after I entered the House of Commons. Once I had seen politics from close to, I realized that writing books was a more valuable thing for me to do with my life.

During my adult lifetime the psychiatrist best known through his books and broadcasts to a general educated public in Britain was probably Anthony Storr. I wrote a favourable review of his first book, *The Integrity of the Personality*, but I had an important criticism about which Anthony wrote me a letter. From that grew a lifelong friendship.

He said to me on one occasion that no patient ever got what he went for out of going to a psychiatrist, but he did get something else instead of such value that he kept going back. He first went seeking a cure for his neurosis, but what he got instead was an increase in self-understanding that changed his life and helped him live with his neurosis. This certainly applies to me. My gravest regret – and indeed it is great – is that I was eighty before I gave serious time and attention to Attachment Theory, and it is there that I found the key to how my emotional development had been damaged by my relationship with my mother. I had been steered away from it decades before by people who had told me misleadingly that it was all about the psychology of children.

13

When I returned to Europe from the USA in September 1956 I told Ingrid that I was going to insist now, and through the courts if necessary, on seeing Gunnela regularly. She went on resisting, but her resistance weakened rapidly – she had been warned professionally, I believe, that she was bound to lose any legal battle we might have. Even so, because of all this, it was not until the summer of 1957 that I saw Gunnela for the first time. By then she was two and a half years old. And of course it was longer than that since I had seen Ingrid. The two of them met me off the boat-train in the Central Station of Copenhagen. We had, at long last, reached the agreement I had always wanted us to have: that I would send regular payments to Ingrid to help support Gunnela, and would see her at least twice a year, once in Sweden and once in England.

The experience of seeing my own two-and-a-half-year-old child running around and talking was the most extraordinary one I have ever had. She was magical. My interest in her was unbounded, and I had to make a conscious effort not to be overwhelming. She was wary of me at first. Then a hint of hostility crept in to her attitude – I think because I was for the time being displacing her as the chief focus of Ingrid's attention. I had appeared out of the blue, and was now centre stage. But this was something I could not help. It was in the logic of the situation.

We spent a day or two in Copenhagen, much of it in Tivoli. This is the most delightful of all pleasure gardens, cunningly attuned to adults and children alike, amazingly variegated and extensive. It has every sideshow from a lucky dip to a scenic railway; its eating places range from a hot-dog stand to a luxury restaurant, its theatre from pantomime to an international concert hall. Clowns on stilts pick their way along its paths, towering like skyscrapers over the children; toytown bands march across it; miniature trains chug round it. To spend a whole day in it is one of the easiest things in the world to do, and one of the most pleasurable. It is greatly loved, not only in Denmark but across northern Europe, and much imitated in other cities. (Originally, I believe, it was modelled on Vauxhall Gardens in London, which were internationally famous for two hundred years between the seventeenth and nineteenth centuries.)

From Copenhagen we took a boat to the island of Bornholm, which, though just off the coast of Sweden, belongs to Denmark (as the Channel Islands, off the coast of France, belong to Britain). There we spent a week or ten days. Gunnela's hostility to me reached its peak on our first day there, when she threw all my belongings out of the hotel window into the street. After that our relationship improved. There were two reasons for this. First, she was an ice-creamoholic, and I indulged her (with Ingrid's permission) by buying her more ice cream than she was usually allowed to have. So she began to look on me as a source of forbidden pleasure. Second, when we were out of doors I carried her on my shoulders, and she found sitting up there exciting. As soon as I put her down she would beg to be taken up again. She was not yet talking in sentences, but the words on her lips most often were '*Pappa bärar*' ('Daddy carry') and '*glas*' ('ice cream').

At that age children are able to interrelate with grown-ups but are not self-conscious about it. There is something awe-inspiring about the resultant naturalness, spontaneity, openness, innocence. Every movement and every word are 'pure'. Such children are like creatures from another order of existence. It is, indeed, pure magic. This phase does not last long, and may have passed before their third birthday, but for a short period they are numinously attractive. When Gunnela did not know I was looking at her I would watch her for long periods, feeling I had never seen anything so wonderful in my life.

Ingrid and I fell into a habit that continued for the rest of her life. When we were talking alone together (having, for instance, put Gunnela to bed) we spoke English, because Ingrid's English was better than my Swedish; but when Gunnela was present we spoke Swedish, so as not to exclude her from the conversation. When I was alone with Gunnela I had no choice but to speak Swedish, since that was all she understood. This meant that I talked with Ingrid each day in roughly equal proportions of English and Swedish. I was intrigued to discover that although I always had clear, indubitable recollections of what she and I had said, I often could not remember whether we had said it in English or Swedish. It shows that we human beings can understand and remember the meanings of words independently of the words themselves.

For the first couple of nights, after Gunnela was in bed, Ingrid and I stayed in our hotel room with her, chatting in low voices or reading, or playing cards. By the third night we were finding this boring, and wanted to go out and have dinner at some nice little restaurant nearby. We waited until Gunnela was in a deep sleep, then checked that all the windows were closed and fastened from inside (our room was one floor up). Then we double-locked the door, and slipped guiltily away. It was no more than a hundred yards to the restaurant; but neither of us enjoyed our dinner much: we were anxious about Gunnela. When we got back, the first thing I did on entering the room was look across to the bed beside the window where we had left Gunnela sleeping – only to see the bed empty and the window wide open. My terror in that instant was unique – it is identified ever since with a literal feeling for the phrase 'my heart leapt into my mouth'. I ran round the bottom of the beds to get to the window and look out – but there on the floor, between the open window and Gunnela's bed, lay Gunnela, curled up, peacefully asleep. To say I was overwhelmed with relief is the biggest understatement in this book. But feelings of guilt were almost as overwhelming. We lifted her back into bed, and of course we asked her about it next morning, but she remembered nothing at all. As far as she was concerned she had gone to bed in a normal way, and woken up next morning as usual, with no memory of anything in between. Our conjecture was that our closing all the windows had caused the room to become stuffy on that warm summer night, and this had half-wakened Gunnela, who had got up in a drowsy state and opened a window, then relapsed into unconsciousness before getting back to the bed. The design of the window was such that, having opened it, she could easily have fallen out of it.

During the years before writing these words I have thought about this incident a lot, because one like it has had international publicity. A British couple on holiday in Portugal, with a beautiful blonde daughter not far from Gunnela's age at that time, had left her sleeping in their hotel while they went for dinner in a nearby restaurant – whereupon the child was abducted, presumably by or for a paedophile, and never seen again. The couple, the McCanns, were cruelly criticized in the media for leaving their daughter in these circumstances. But I know that I could have done the same, because I have. What happened to the McCanns is unimaginably appalling, and I know that there but for the grace of God go I.

In the early autumn of 1957, Gunnela and Ingrid came to London. From the beginning the dominating problem was that Gunnela could not communicate with anyone: she did not understand a word anybody said, and the only English person she met who could understand her was me. When my friends were with her, all they could do was stand smiling down at her, and say nice things that they knew she did not understand. Both sides found this awkward, embarrassing, and painfully self-conscious-making. After a few visits Gunnela refused to go on meeting people like this, saying she simply could not cope with it, and she would never again meet my friends. Ingrid demanded that I teach her English, but this was absurd: I could not teach a small child English in a week or ten days; and in any case our overriding need in that time was to communicate, which was possible for us only in Swedish. The only person with a full opportunity to teach Gunnela English was Ingrid, but she refused to consider it.

From Gunnela's first visit to London a charming photograph survives of her, Ingrid and me feeding the pigeons in Trafalgar Square, all of us looking sparklingly young. As the three of us were walking away from that scene and up the bottom of Lower Regent Street – Ingrid and I on each side of Gunnela, holding her by her two hands – we passed three young women who seemed to be secretaries having their lunch hour together. The moment they were behind us they broke into a loud, enthusiastic chorus – all talking at once, and oblivious of the fact that we could hear – about what a wonderful-looking family we were. I thought: 'if only they knew'.

For many years the pattern stayed the same. I would travel to Sweden every year, and was met in Copenhagen by Ingrid and Gunnela. We would spend a couple of days there – the first day always in Tivoli, then visits to places such as the zoo (the biggest and best in Scandinavia), or an out-of-town pleasure garden in Bakken, or the horse races at Klampenborg, or the art centre at Humlebæk. Then we would cross over to Sweden, either for a short holiday somewhere we had never been or to their home in Malmö. Quite early on, the two of them went to live in Helsingborg, which I liked as much as they did, and then we would often be happy to stay there, enjoying the town, and taking trips across to Elsinore.

However, on each visit there was always a crisis in my relationship with Ingrid. The better we all got on together, the more bitterly she would reproach me for not living with them; and when the time came for me to leave there would always be a hysterical outburst, in fact a terrible scene. On one such occasion she started shouting that her life was not worth living, and she was going to put an end to it – and what is more, she shouted, she had the means to do so. She leapt up to the bookcase on the other side of her living room, and with a single gesture swept the books from the top shelf and brought her hand down holding a Luger – just about the biggest pistol there is, with an enormous barrel. Without a flicker of conscious thought I was across the room like a rocket and wrestled the pistol from her. I looked to see if it was loaded, and it was.

I stayed very late that night, calming Ingrid down. When I felt it was safe to go, I did not dare to leave the pistol, even though I had unloaded it, for I could not be sure she did not have more bullets in the flat. So I took the gun with me. Because it was too big to go in any of my pockets I walked along holding it under my overcoat. As I made my way back into the centre of town I mulled over the question of what to do with it. To take it back to England would be illegal, and in any case purposeless; and there was the danger of being caught with it in Customs. If I left it in my hotel room there would be a police investigation. My first positive thought was to throw it into the sea – but if, however unlikely, I was seen doing that, it could again lead to police enquiries which would get Ingrid or me into serious trouble. I took it for granted that her possession of the gun was illegal, and was deeply disturbed by the fact that she had taken the time, and gone to the trouble, to get it. On consideration I decided to hand it over to the police without naming anyone other than myself. It was indeed the right thing to do, but the way I did it was unbelievably thoughtless. All I can say in my own defence is that I was in a state of inner turmoil.

Seen from the point of view of the policeman on night duty at the central station, what happened was that at the deadest hour of the night, about three in the morning, an obviously stressed young man strode purposefully in, walked straight up to him sitting at his desk facing the door, and drew a Luger out from under his overcoat. In that instant I saw from the expression on his face that he thought I was going to shoot him. When, instead, I laid the gun on his desk it took him some minutes to get over his shock – and then over his relief. I felt a fool, and was profuse in my apologies, which helped to fill in the time before he was fit to deal with the situation. I told him I had taken the gun away from someone to make sure nobody got hurt, but I did not want to get anyone into trouble by naming names. I assured him firmly that no crime had been committed. I gave my name, and that of my hotel, and told him when I would be returning to England. I never heard any more about it.

When Gunnela was still quite small she started asking me: 'Why don't you live with us? Other children's fathers live with them – why don't you live with us? Don't you *want* to live with us? Don't you like us?' I never found an answer to this. It was only because of my deep feelings for her that I was with her at all, against Ingrid's prolonged refusal. Ingrid still did not want me to see Gunnela. But I never said this, or criticized Ingrid to her in any way. There was no way of explaining such a situation to a small child. I did everything I could to communicate my love for her in word and deed, but I could see she felt rejected by me. Her attitude was full of conflicting elements. As her father I mattered to her, and she wanted to have a relationship with me that was denied her by the situation. It made her feel rejected and frustrated, and she blamed me for it, and wanted to reject me in return. 'Love-hate' would be too strong an expression, but there was a powerful 'push-pull' in her feelings towards me. Before one of my visits she said to Ingrid: 'I'm longing for him to come, but I don't want to see him.' One of the most heart-breaking moments I had with her was when she was very small, and the two of us were at the zoo, looking at a buffalo calf with its mother. She looked at them for a long time, then said: 'Where's the father?' After a quite long further reflection she murmured: 'Perhaps he lives in England.'

On most of my visits I would at first find her resentful, even sometimes rejecting; but then she would soften to the point where we were getting along well – until the time came for me to leave, and then she would become distressed, and resentful again. Throughout the whole time we were apart I would write a message to her every day on a postcard, so that she would know I thought of her every day. In addition to that, the content of the messages kept her in touch with where I was and what I was doing. When possible I chose postcards with pictures that showed either the places I was in or something to do with my activities there.

On her yearly visits to England, Gunnela's refusal to meet people had the consequence of enclosing the three of us in a little bubble of our own. There was plenty in London for us to do, but Gunnela's social experience of people in England remained close to zero, for although the years were going by she still knew scarcely anyone except for me. And the only home she knew was my flat. When she was eleven she came without Ingrid for the first time, but then she brought a friend with her, so the two of them did everything together and spoke only Swedish. At thirteen she was stricken by a serious eating disorder, sadly common among adolescent girls; and from then on she refused to come to England at all. The disorder lasted for the rest of her teens, and then she got over it completely, but she did not come to England for something like thirty-five years. Throughout that period I went to Sweden every year. But now I was seeing her only once a year instead of twice.

I had so much wanted us to have a good continuing relationship that the reality of it disheartened me. Ingrid was pleased by it, though, and in the earlier years kept saying that it was a good reason for me to stop coming. But I could never have given up on it. First, I could not have borne not to know my child. Second, I was convinced that when she became a mature woman she would wish to have had a continuous relationship with her father, and would want that relationship in the present to be a good one.

14

In the last few pages I have telescoped a story that was spread over many years. It had some unwelcome side effects. The chief was that my relationship with Gunnela and Ingrid remained in a separate compartment from the rest of my life, which I shall tell the story of in the rest of this volume. Most of my closest friends, old friends whom I saw frequently, never saw them. Once a year I would disappear to Sweden and come back with stories about them, but that was all. It appears that for some of my acquaintances the situation seemed to have a mysterious aspect. There were rumours that I was not really married at all, and had a secret child in Sweden, and that I was deliberately keeping her a secret from everyone in England.

For me the situation was the direct opposite. My relationships in Sweden were central to my life. I wrote to Gunnela every day. As a freelance writer and broadcaster, always self-employed, I needed to earn enough money not only to keep myself but to send monthly payments to Ingrid. In lean periods that was sometimes difficult, but never once was I late with a payment, which took priority over everything else. My Swedish commitments were something I lived with all the time. Whatever else I might do or not do within any given year I had to go to Sweden. Helsingborg, Malmö and Lund were among the places I was most familiar with.

To my surprise, my command of the Swedish language remained at the same level from one year to the next, despite the fact that I had no use for it in between. I would have expected it to rust, but it was as if I kept it clean in a box, and took it out whenever I needed it. Never having had any lessons, I made grammatical mistakes, and of course had a foreign accent; but everyone understood what I said, and I could get along quite well in ordinary life: I could communicate with Gunnela, play games with her and teach her things, chat with the neighbours, do the shopping, and so on. The thing about my Swedish was that it was everyday, domestic. I had difficulty discussing a film, and could not have taken part in serious talk about politics, music, or ideas. Although I have read innumerable Swedish newspapers, I have never read a book in Swedish.

When Gunnela was small she enjoyed teasing me about my faulty and foreign Swedish, and she got pleasure from correcting me. This became a game between us, in which I encouraged her. I took it for granted that when she started to learn English at school she would try talking English to me, but this turned out not to be so. On the contrary, she seemed to assume that I would seize the opportunity to get my own back, so she went on talking to me in Swedish. Since everyone who knows a foreign language can understand it better than he can speak it, when Gunnela's English became better than my Swedish we were able to enlarge our communication in a different way: I spoke English to her and she spoke Swedish to me. We would carry on the liveliest of conversations in two different languages, not only face to face but on the telephone. Other people found it bizarre, but it was so habitual to us that we ceased to be aware of it. We continued to do that for many years, until Gunnela was about fifty. Then one day she started, without explanation, talking to me in English. I felt it as some sort of acceptance, and, as such, a landmark. I was so pleased that I did not want to ask her why she had done it.

Until Gunnela was nineteen she was a British citizen. But she has always thought of herself as Swedish (so have I) and as soon as the law allowed her to change her nationality she did. At around the same time she became a student at Lund University, studying social psychology. As soon as she began living away from home I made my monthly payments directly to her. But it was only during vacations, which she spent at home, that she could get much time to spend with me, so when I visited her I continued to see Ingrid.

During Gunnela's last years at Lund University she became involved with a young Chilean, Santiago Mateluna, a refugee from the Pinochet regime. One day she telephoned me to tell me she was pregnant by him. It came as rather a shock to realize that I was going to be a grandfather. I had recently turned fifty, which was bad enough in itself. But I sincerely congratulated her and said how pleased I was for her – but then made the mistake of asking if she was considering getting married. She was scandalized. '*Married?*' she said, in tones of scalding contempt. 'No one gets married nowadays – except for a few priests.'

Thus Jenny, the first of my three grandchildren, came into the world. Because Gunnela was still unmarried, Jenny's full name was Jenny Magee. A few years later, Gunnela and Santiago married and had two more children, whose names were Josefin Magee Mateluna and Niklas Magee Mateluna.

When Gunnela began living with Santiago my visits to Sweden changed their character. Ingrid was no longer around. She lived by herself in a little town called Skanör, a coastal resort a long way south of Malmö by bus. Gunnela and Santiago lived in Malmö, so that was where I went for my annual visits. Each of these would include a day trip by all of us to Skanör, but this was now my only contact with Ingrid – one day a year.

I got to know Malmö well during those years – its hotels, restaurants, shops and parks, and all its places of cultural interest – but I never liked it. Its streets were eerily empty in the evenings, in fact there was no vitality to its social life. The blood was sucked out of it by the proximity of Copenhagen. In recent years it has become livelier as a result of a new bridge that joins southern Sweden with Denmark, and a sharp rise in immigration – livelier but rougher, still not an attractive city, though there is now more to enjoy.

Suddenly, more than twenty years ago now, Ingrid died. She was fifty-eight, and apparently in the best of health, when one day she felt horribly ill. The doctor who saw her rushed her into the local hospital. There she relapsed into a coma. In that state she was taken by ambulance to the major teaching hospital of Lund University. And there she died. In three days she had gone from being apparently normal to being dead. It transpired that she had contracted a viral infection of the bloodstream. I had never heard of such a thing, though needless to say I have heard of it again since. I was stunned. For Gunnela, who had grown up as an only child in a one-parent family, it was traumatic.

Ingrid left everything she had to Gunnela, including the house in Skanör. Gunnela and her family moved in to it, and have lived there ever since. So for decades now my annual visits to Sweden have been to Skanör. To vary this experience and also broaden my knowledge of Sweden I long made it a custom to visit other parts of the country either before or after my time in Skanör – each year a different region. This gave me great pleasure in itself, as well as being an eye-opener about the country at large.

The town of Skanör was important in the Middle Ages because its position on the coast enabled it to dominate much of the herring trade. From those centuries there remain an attractive old church beside the sea and the moat of what used to be a castle but has now disappeared. Today's Skanör is still prosperous, though partly as a holiday resort and partly as an unusually attractive place to live for retired people. These two functions dominate the local economy. The holidaymakers are of two main kinds. There are day-trippers from Malmö who come to spend the day on the beaches, which are among the best in Sweden. And there are longer-term, better-off vacationers catered for by a couple of good hotels (at one of which I stay) plus a couple of first-class restaurants, some expensive boutiques, several golf courses, several horse farms and a marina. Because this region has the mildest climate in the country vacationers come from other parts of Sweden, and many own summer homes there. A noticeable minority come from northern Germany, directly across the water. These find that their only way to communicate with the Swedes is to talk English. The public manners of the Germans are not always as courteous as they should be, and this is obtrusive because the Swedes are well mannered. So Germans are not popular with the locals. But they contribute to Skanör's prosperity.

Today all this is a long-standing part of my life, and Skanör a place that I return to every year. In many years the best weather I experience is the time I spend in Sweden. Summer there, although short, can be ideal – as warm as the best of English summers without the humidity: blue, cloudless skies and brilliant sunshine, clear and invigorating, day after day.

As for my family relationships, all the clichés about grandparenthood have turned out to be true. It has been an unmitigated pleasure for me. I am good friends, in different ways, with each of my grandchildren. Until they started learning English at school they spoke to me only in Swedish, but from then on we have talked English. Both Jenny and Josefin came to work in England during their gap years. The older they grow, the more of a family we become. Within this family I am now a great-grandfather, for Jenny has four children – William, Viktor, Gustav and Karl. There are probably more great-grandchildren still to come. It will always give me pause that none of these human beings would have existed if I had not taken that job in Sweden – and nor would any of their descendants, to the end of time.

Book Three

My Second Go at Life

to
Isobel

1

Guinness is Good for You

My university education came to an end when I was twenty-six, in the summer of 1956. I was in the United States, at Yale, and was being pressed to stay there and launch myself on an academic career. But I had a daughter of a year and a half in Sweden, whom I had never seen. I also had a long-standing desire to become a Member of Parliament. I needed to return to England.

From my teens onwards I had known, with a definiteness that now surprises me, the work I wanted to do in life: I wanted to write books and be a politician. It had never occurred to me to be a career academic. Only a chance combination of events had kept me so long in the university system. Like other members of my generation, I had had to do a period of military service (which for me included a year in Austria) between school and university. Then, at Oxford, circumstances pushed me into a false start in what I knew at the time was not the right subject for me, so after taking a degree in Modern History I took another in Philosophy, Politics and Economics, to put me back on the right track. I had developed a passion for philosophy, and wanted to study more of it; so after a year of language teaching in Sweden I had returned to Oxford for a year of postgraduate study in philosophy, and then followed that up with another year of it at Yale. Now, however, I felt that the time really had come to launch myself into what I looked on as properly adult life, life outside the university.

The jagged edge of the reality confronting me was that neither of the two kinds of work I wanted to do – neither writing a book nor being active in politics – would bring in any money at all for a couple of years at the very least; and I had no money of my own; so I would have to do a third kind of work at the same time to earn my living in the present. This problem was to plague me for most of my adult life. Not until my sixties did enough money come from my books to live on, even modestly, so – except for the nine or ten years when I was a Member of Parliament and had a salary – I was always having to spend at least half my working time doing work that I would not have done had I been free. And however interesting it was, it always took me away from what I really wanted to do, the thing I regarded as 'my real work'. It is this that makes my career so many-sided: in addition to writing and politics I have been a broadcaster on television and radio, a music and theatre critic, and a teacher in universities and schools. But all those other things were done because I had to keep myself while writing books, and for that reason alone. If I had had a private income I would not have done them.

When I confronted this situation for the first time in 1956 I had no idea it was going to be with me for most of my life. My reasoning went something like this. Although I need to get a job, as soon as I can leave the job I shall, so there is no point in concerning myself with its long-term prospects. I shan't be wanting a career in it, but just to be kept while writing, and perhaps while writing only my first book. I shall leave the job instantly if that first book is financially successful. I shall not be looking to the job for my primary work-satisfaction, so provided it is tolerable I do not greatly care what it is. That being so, the obvious thing is to look for whatever job will earn me the most money while giving me maximum time for writing. Such a job is more likely to be in business or industry than in public service or any of the professions, because pay in the former is higher.

As soon as I got back to England I found out which of the publicly reputable companies paid its new recruits the most. I came up with a short-list of four: Shell, Fisons, the Metal-Box Company, and Guinness. I wrote to all four, three interviewed me, two offered me jobs, and Guinness took me.

The beer made by Guinness was at that time the best-selling beer in Britain – millions of bottles a day. This was remarkable for more reasons than one. First, the beer itself was jet black and had a strong, bitter taste. Second, unlike the other major breweries, Guinness did not own any pubs but sold its product through outlets owned and run by its competitors, who were compelled to stock it because of the public demand for it. There were two Guinness breweries, one in Dublin and one in Park Royal, west London. The one in Park Royal was the largest brewery in the world outside the United States. The rest of the business was on a like scale. Sales were international: the company owned seagoing tankers, and had its own docks in Dublin and Liverpool. It had maltings in East Anglia, and hop fields in Kent and Sussex, where it owned whole villages. It spent more money on advertising than any other company in Britain – and needed to, its outlets being controlled by its competitors. Everything it did was marked by quality as well as scale. It paid the highest salaries of any brewery, and therefore, at least in theory, got the best staff. It treated its employees munificently, not only in housing, cars and pensions but in other ways too. Its advertising was justly famous – its chief slogan, 'Guinness Is Good For You', was known to everyone, and was usually quoted approvingly. The beer itself was pure: nothing went into it other than malt, hops, yeast and water – the blackness came from the fact that the malt was deep-roasted. The most prestigious prize in contemporary poetry was the Guinness Prize.

When I joined the company it had just published the first *Guinness Book of Records*, which itself was to break records.

For all its size, the Guinness Company had remained a family business. Across a period of over a hundred years the family had become not only wide ranging but socially grand, with an accumulation of titles. As their friends put it, they were now members of the beerage. The whole thing got under way in nineteenth-century Ireland, and from those origins the firm developed what was basically a colonial structure. Although the family was Irish, they were members of the Protestant Ascendancy, and took to educating their sons at Eton and Oxbridge. As the firm expanded they took on people to work alongside the family who were not unlike themselves – mostly not Irish, but always public school and Oxbridge, and (I believe) not Catholic. So the company was run by Anglo-gentlemen, and it was not possible for the home-grown Irish Catholics who constituted the bulk of the workforce in Dublin to work their way up into that elite. They could rise to highly paid positions just a little short of it, but the elite reproduced itself by recruiting directly from outside. The situation was parallel to that in which very young men from British public schools and Oxbridge went out to distant colonies and exercised power over large adult populations.

The top management of Guinness liked to have what they regarded as one such young man standing by in the wings, having been through their own special training course, ready now to step in to the next junior vacancy to occur among them. Before they took me on it had been Chris Chataway, Olympic runner, world-record holder, best known as a helper to Roger Bannister – he had been one of the two athletes who paced Roger in the first-ever under-four-minutes mile. Eventually he had come to the conclusion that Guinness was not good for him, and had left to be, together with Robin Day, the first newscaster on Independent Television, which had come into existence the year before. (Chris was the first of the two to appear on screen.) The men who selected me to replace Chris expressed their regret that, unlike him, I did not have an Oxbridge blue, but they said the presidency of the Oxford Union was an acceptable second-best. This was not the first time I had got a job in that sort of way. I had got my teaching job in Sweden (which had been recruited in London by an Englishman, a barrister at the Inns-of-Court) because the first choice for it, a rowing blue, had dropped out. Values of that kind were common in the Britain of the 1950s.

At Guinness all the members of the top management elite, and only they, were called Brewers, and this resulted in Gilbertian titles such as Brewer in charge of Transport, Brewer in charge of Advertising, and so on. I was taken on as a trainee Brewer. My starting salary was £1,200 a year, at a time when the usual starting salary for management trainees in a decent company was £450. (My student grant at Oxford had been £280 a year.)

The training course lasted six months, and took me through every stage in the making of the beer. It had been designed for members of the Guinness family, and began with the most menial tasks of all, so that all their lives they could say they had done them. On my first day I swept the floor of the brewery. I did this for only one day, and the chief point of it was to meet and talk to the other cleaners, learn their names, and eat and drink with them. Whenever I passed one of them subsequently there were always smiles and greetings on both sides. And so it went on, through tasks of ever-increasing difficulty, spending whatever time on each was necessary to learn it and get to know the people doing it. At first it was pure manual labour, some of it very hard. For a week of night shifts I worked in a gang of men stripped to the waist in a temperature of 120° Fahrenheit, in thick steam inside a copper vat the size of a house, from which boiling liquid had just been drained away. We had to scrub the internal walls with copper-wire brushes before the steam evaporated, knowing that if we touched any of the exposed piping it would scald the skin off our backs. After two or three weeks of other jobs of this kind I was sent to East Anglia to learn how barley is transformed into malt; and from there to the Sussex hop fields to learn about hops. After that I returned to Park Royal to be taught how these ingredients were made into beer. Then I took responsibility (under supervision) for the process itself, keeping colossal quantities of beer under minutely detailed and endlessly checked control through three days and nights, to ensure stability of the product. As with nearly all jobs, there is vastly more to it than anyone who has not done it imagines, or has enough knowledge to imagine.

As part of all this I was given a training in tasting. For this I went to the laboratory, and on day one was confronted with a long row of burettes, each containing Guinness. I was invited to taste and comment freely on each in turn. Most tasted fairly alike to me, though there was one without much flavour, and another that was too bitter. I probably singled out two or three more. After being told that my performance was average, I was taken through the burettes again, slowly, and it was explained to me that this example had been stored at too high a temperature, that one had been slightly adulterated, and from this other one the yeast had not been extracted sufficiently at the end of the brewing process. Because live yeast is used in the production of Guinness, the perfect condition of the beer has a lifespan, and it can be too old by significantly differing lengths of time, each of which has a different taste. After each explanation I was made to taste again, and again, then again, looking always for the differences I had missed the first time.

Next day I went back and confronted the same row of identical-looking burettes, but in a different order. This time I did surprisingly much better than the previous day. We had the same careful explanations and repeated tastings. This process carried on every day for two weeks, occasionally with new samples thrown in. By the end I was identifying correctly, and with accurate explanations, all but one or two. Between some of those that had tasted alike two weeks before the difference was now so obvious to me that I was at a loss to understand how I could have failed to perceive it. It was a revelation of how an average palate can be trained not just to discriminate between tastes but to identify correctly the differing *causes* of the different tastes.

The brewery had simple rules about its employees' access to the beer. Everyone, without exception, could drink as much as he or she wanted to on the premises, but drunkenness was a ground for instant dismissal. And no one could take any beer away. The firm was zero-tolerant about this, and it worked. New arrivals who had no taste for Guinness usually acquired one, and almost everybody, even the teenage girls, drank it, but in moderation. It was freely available in the canteen, of course, but the tea ladies also trundled their trolleys round the offices offering a choice of tea, coffee or Guinness. In each office the bottom drawer in the filing cabinet, always deeper than the rest, was kept stacked with bottles. In those days, when the British drank their beers at room temperature, there was no problem about refrigeration.

When I had completed my course of training I was a fully fledged Brewer, and was given a handsome pay rise. The situation now was that when the next Brewer retired, or died, or became too ill to work, other Brewers would move up, and a vacancy at the lowest level of the elite would be created for me to fill. Meanwhile I was expected to keep myself appropriately occupied and out of others' way.

Having been trained so thoroughly in the brewing process itself I set out to teach myself something of how the other departments worked For a couple of weeks I became a fly on the wall in each of them in turn: the laboratory, Accounts, Advertising, Sales, Transport and the rest. I visited, or revisited, the company's operations in other parts of the country. Because of my status I had chauffeur-driven cars, and stayed in the best hotels, so everything was done in comfort. When I was at Park Royal I lunched with the other Brewers in their special room. I got on well with nearly all of them, but it was borne in on me that they and I had little in common, actually. Apart from work they were interested chiefly in such things as golf and bridge, and a range of outdoor sports from shooting to sailing. Their social life consisted mainly of pursuing these activities with like-minded people, often one another, as did their holidays abroad. None of this held any interest for me. I had an entirely different, essentially metropolitan relationship with leisure. I lived in central London, just off Portman Square, and went to theatres, concerts and opera, and to drinks parties and dinner parties with friends, most of whom I had met at Oxford and were now in a wide variety of different London jobs. Alongside this I had been drawn into political activity by the British invasion of Egypt during the Suez crisis, and also the Russian invasion of Hungary, both of which happened in September 1956. I opposed both with a passion, and went to some of the many protest meetings that took place. From the responses to me of the other Brewers it was clear that most of them thought I was quite an interesting sort of chap, and perfectly acceptable, but not really one of them. There were one or two who were against me from the start, but that was for a particular reason.

By sheer bad luck my first day at Guinness had been the day after Britain invaded Egypt. People all over the country were talking of nothing else – and so were the Brewers when I went to their room to be introduced to them at my first lunchtime. After the introductions, and a few polite exchanges, they returned to the subject of the war, retaining an awareness of me as a required focus of polite attention. Every one of them was in favour of the invasion. With most there was no triumphalism: they expressed regret, in the reasonable-sounding language of practical men. But two or three of the less mature ones were cock-a-hoop, whooping with delight and saying things like: 'It's time we gave those gypos a good kick up the arse.' The person who was looking after me turned to me, still nominally the focal point of the group, and said: 'You're not saying anything. What do you think?' I said: 'I'm appalled.' There was a silence. Someone said: 'Why?'. So I said, briefly, why. The atmosphere became one of paralysed embarrassment. An older Brewer made a diversionary remark, deliberately, and restarted the conversation on a different subject. The most egregious one of the cock-a-hoopers, seeing that this was happening, snorted ostentatiously and stalked out of the room. He never talked to me again all the time I was there.

One or two of the others disapproved of me from that moment. But the rest did not have the kind of attitude to politics that would lead them to hold such a thing against me. They were not all that interested in politics, except when it affected them personally, whereas they were dedicated to maintaining good relations among colleagues. Most were pleasant to me always, from then on, and did everything they could to make me feel one of the family.

When I became a fully-fledged Brewer an attempt was made to persuade me to live at the brewery. There were dozens of buildings there – some enormous, with interconnecting roads – and one was like a small country house, with valet, housekeeper, cook and servants, for the use of Brewers when for any reason they wanted to stay at Park Royal. It also provided accommodation for guests if they were grand enough – members of the Guinness family often entertained there – and there were frequent dinner parties and receptions. One unmarried Brewer lived there already, and attempts were made to get me to do the same. Without saying how adamantly against it I was, I turned the proposal down. I was happy to stay there when it suited me – when I was working on night shift, for instance. But to live there permanently would put me at arm's length from my real life in central London. The other

Brewers had difficulty in understanding my objections. Most of them lived just outside London to the west, either in the country or in the stockbroker belt of suburbs and exurbs, and they had no problem in going as often as they chose to what they thought of as social occasions in central London. They did not see why I could not be driven to theatres, restaurants, meetings, or anything else I wanted to go to. What was my problem?

Although I upheld my refusal to share the Guinness-family comfort in the bosom of the brewery, there was one experience that I believe fell into my lap because of my perceived membership of that elite. We were now in 1957, and the last year in which there were debutantes was 1958. Every year till then, young ladies of eighteen were presented at court in May, and were deemed at that point to have 'come out'. This was celebrated in a series of coming-out parties that went on for a number of weeks – each debutante threw one, and the others would be invited, so there were several a week. I believe it was this that was the origin of the London Season, because it meant that upper-class families from all over the country had to be in London at the same time and stay there for the same number of weeks. Coming-out parties were balls that lasted through most of the night, and took place either in private houses with rooms big enough to hold them or in the ballrooms of flagship hotels, the two favourites being the Savoy and the Dorchester. Since they went on for so much of the night, it was necessary for youthful guests to eat a good dinner beforehand. However, almost anyone with a house big enough to seat that many for dinner would be using the space for the ball. So the ball's guest-list would be broken up and distributed among a mass of separate dinner parties held by the mothers of the other debutantes, nearly always in their own homes. When those dinner parties came to an end, their guests would converge on the ball.

These arrangements required co-operation among the mothers (always referred to as the Mums), not only about dates and dinner parties but also about guests – bearing in mind that few of the male guests would be personally known to their hostesses. It mattered very much to the Mums who these were, because, historically at least, the ultimate aim of coming-out balls was to find a future husband for each of the debutantes by the end of the season. This was less pressing now than it had once been, but was still in the minds of most of the Mums, who deemed it essential that young men invited should be 'suitable'. Nearly all of these were in their early twenties, two or three years older than the girls. Few were from Oxbridge. Most lived in the country and worked on family estates, but a number worked in the City. Noisier ones were usually Guards officers. There was a sprinkling of one-off individuals, including suitable foreigners, who fitted into none of these categories. Each Mum made her own list of the young men to invite to her own ball, but in addition she would give many dinners in her home for the invitees of other Mums, who would provide the names of those to be invited. Inevitably, in these circumstances, the young men were avidly discussed by the Mums, who compared lists, so a name that appeared on one would start popping up on others. This is what happened to me. In the period May-July 1957 I was invited to a great many coming-out balls. So, as people used to say, I did the Season.

This occurred when I had just become a fully-fledged Brewer, so I was no longer tied by duties at Park Royal. It was easy for me to stay up half the night and then get to the brewery only just in time for lunch the following day, without anyone caring or even noticing. As was normal, I was being invited to dinner parties in the houses of people I had never heard of, who had little idea who I was, and then going on from them to balls in the houses of other such people, or in grand hotels. At twenty-seven I was a few years older than most of the young men, but there were enough like me (many of them foreigners) for me not to stand out as an oddity. Also we were all dressed alike, in white tie and tails. I still had mine

289

from when I had been President of the Oxford Union four years earlier, and could still just get in to them.

No one other than the ball-givers and the dinner-party-givers was expected to provide any entertaining at all, so the cost to me of this whole way of life was no more than taxi fares. At first I found it fun – then it palled. I found myself meeting the same people in different houses evening after evening, and they were not the most interesting company available to me in London. By the standards to which Oxford and Yale had accustomed me the girls were uneducated, and too often unintelligent, and on top of that, at eighteen, callow. The only subjects most of them wanted to talk about were clothes, horses, other members of their family, and young men. I had a good enough flow of conversation about a couple of these. As a soldier in Austria I had been taught to ride by a toothless old Russian who had been a cavalry officer under the last of the Tsars. And my father, whose greatest interest in life had been horse racing (of which he possessed an encyclopaedic knowledge) had taken me to the races with him throughout my childhood. But the only interest any of the girls had for me was their attractiveness, which in some cases was considerable. I found that being a few years older than most of the other young men was an advantage with the girls, but the men themselves were at a stage of development which I had left behind, and their company was not very interesting for me. Their standard complaint, like mine, was that the only subject of conversation that they had in common with the girls, apart from themselves, was horses, so on that we were together. After a honeymoon period, which I enjoyed, I stopped accepting most of the invitations.

Another motive I had to stop was that I was now in a position to give time to my writing, and this had been my ulterior motive all along. I began work on a book about America that was published the following year under the title *Go West, Young Man*. During my time at Yale, a year before, I had travelled all over the

United States. Much of this travel was a response to speaking invitations organized by such bodies as the English-Speaking Union, which provided me with hospitality in private homes. Everywhere I went I was a house-guest; and I had these experiences in different kinds of home, and in many different states. Even more of my travel, over longer distances, was done independently, just to see the country. For that, when I was paying my own expenses, I travelled not by plane or train but by Greyhound Bus, or in car-shares with students. I had little money, and stayed in the cheapest acceptable rooms – or, to save the cost even of that, I would sleep on an overnight bus, or in a bus station. I lived on the cheapest food, in the cheapest eateries. So I saw the country at many different social levels. Throughout all this I kept a diary. At first my intention was to publish it. To that end I did a lot of editing work on it: I tried to improve the writing, cut out the less interesting passages plus everything that smacked of repetition, and tighten the whole thing up. In this form I submitted it to a publisher. He said he would publish it if I would agree to recast the diary form into a continuous narrative. So I did that too.

The discussions all this involved me in with the publisher, and with the literary agent who took me on, brought me up against the brute fact that there was no prospect of such a book bringing in the kind of money I needed to live on. Like nearly all aspiring writers I had been unrealistic, because ignorant, about this. I now had to swallow, and digest, the realization that it would almost certainly be years – and several more books – before there was any likelihood of my earning a living from writing. This caused me to look at my situation with Guinness in a new light. There was an emptiness about it that I was beginning to find oppressive. It was not caused solely by the fact that I had no real job to do: it concerned also the sort of people I was associating with at Park Royal, and the environment there as a whole. Furthermore, when a specific job did come along, the department it was in would be decided not by me but by chance. If it was in Advertising I might find myself working for years in advertising, which I did not want to do. It could be in Sales, and that would be worse. Accounts might be more interesting, but Transport might not be. I lacked the qualifications for anything senior in the laboratory. I viewed my position with dismay.

I realized now that I had been wrong to suppose that I would not mind how I earned my living so long as I could write. I wanted to work at things that interested me, and with people who interested me. In the absence of those, I was surprised at how little difference it made to me that I was paid well. I would rather have been paid half as much for a job I enjoyed, with people I found congenial. Never again was I motivated by money, beyond the need to earn the necessary minimum.

At that time I was sharing a flat with Tyrrell Burgess, who worked on *The Times Education Supplement*. That whole paper was anonymous in those days, and Tyrrell occasionally got me to write pieces for it. These were usually brief reviews of some kind, including music reviews. Writing them took me into a wholly different world. A couple of Tyrrell's colleagues became lifelong friends not only of his but also of mine: their interestingness as people was independent of the jobs they were doing. That sort of working environment inhabited a different universe from the Guinness brewery at Park Royal.

Slowly, and with embarrassment, I arrived at a decision to leave Guinness. By September I had made up my mind. I had made all the arrangements for a holiday abroad then in any case, and I felt an obstinate refusal within myself to come back to Guinness when the holiday was over. I went to see the Managing Director, the man who had carried out the very first interview of me and been my key contact ever since. He was not pleased. Our conversation went on for most of an afternoon, and was a turning-point in my life. He began by offering to raise my salary, and asked how much

I wanted. I said that it would be nice to have more money, but this was not the issue. He then suggested that I take longer holidays, or more holidays, or both. I said the same thing about holidays. He offered me a car. I said I did not want a car – I did not yet have a driving licence, so a car would be a nuisance. He was nonplussed. He sat back in his chair, looked at me evenly, and said (I do not remember his exact words): 'Do you realize that you already have what most people spend all their lives working to attain, and never achieve? You're in the top management echelon of a world-famous company, and yet in spite of that you're in a position where you can take things easy. If you wanted to, you could play golf several afternoons a week, take frequent holidays abroad, be driven everywhere in chauffeur-driven cars. We'll pay you any salary within reason, and give you whatever else you want. Nobody's going to query your expenses. For most people this comes only as the reward of a lifetime of work. It comes at the end, if it comes at all. And you've got it now.' There was a long silence, during which he still looked nonplussed. Then he said: 'What on earth do you want?' There was another silence. Then he said: 'If you leave here you'll have to get another job, I take it. How can you expect things to be better for you there than they are here?'

I tried to explain, but it was impossible without saying superior-sounding things, which I had the good sense not to do. When we were discussing my relationships with my colleagues he said: 'We know you're different in some ways from the rest of us, but there aren't many who mind that. People enjoy your company, that's the main thing. As long as you're competent, which you are, being different won't stand in the way of promotion. In fact it'll help it.'

I found this conversation permanently educative. When we were discussing the fact that I did not pursue the same leisure activities as my colleagues, and therefore did not spend any of my leisure time with them in the way they did with one another, he asked: 'What's your idea of the perfect way to spend an evening?'

'Oh,' I said, 'the same as most other people's – a comfortable time sitting around with old friends, drinking and talking, when the atmosphere's just right.'

He looked at me with amazement. 'What?' he said. 'You mean not doing anything else for a whole evening but just drinking and talking?'

'Yes,' I said, wondering what else he could have in mind.

'You're quite mistaken,' he said, 'if you imagine that's what most people like. A whole evening of nothing but talk is a terrible strain. Most people need something to do. I'm the same. I can talk for a bit, but then I want to do something – dance, or play cards.' Then he added: 'You're more different from other people than you realize.'

After, in the end, he had accepted the fact that nothing was going to prevent me from leaving, we switched our attention to the practicalities.

'There's no point in your coming here any more, other than to say your goodbyes,' he said. 'I hope you'll do that, though. We're only under obligation to give you one month's salary, but we'll pay yours till the end of next month.'

I hesitated, then plucked up courage and took a plunge: 'I'm about to go on holiday now, and shan't be back till mid-October. So I won't be able even to start looking for a job till then. And I'm not going to find one in a fortnight. Then, when I do get one, I shan't be paid till the end of *that* month.'

My undeclared reason for saying this was to get the maximum time to work on my book. To my astonishment he replied: 'I see that. It'll take you several weeks to get a job, presumably. All right. We'll pay your salary to the end of the year.'

My heart leapt, although I tried not to show it. More than three months of freedom to work on my writing, and on a Guinness salary! I could never have expected such a thing. As it turned out, I was to have an even greater stroke of luck. Shortly before Christmas, Guinness announced that they had had an unprecedentedly good year and they were going to pay a Christmas bonus of three months' salary to every employee whose name was on their books on 31 December 1957 – the last day on which my name was on the books. So they kept me for more than half a year of full-time writing, and in comfort.

To this day the year I spent at Guinness is the only experience I have had of working in manufacturing industry. I remain permanently pleased that I did it. I learnt so much at every level, from the long hours of manual labour in gangs of men on night shift to sitting in on confidential decision-making discussions among top-level management with millions of pounds at stake. The intensive six-months' training course with which I began had been cleverly devised to give members of the Guinness family a proper understanding of their own business, and it did the same for me. But another thing it taught me was that the whole world of industry, even at its most civilized and quality-conscious, is not one that I want to live in. Even so, it did me a world of good to live in it for a year, and learn about it from inside. Apart from anything else, it inoculated me against the ignorant prejudices that someone of my interests and political opinions could have developed against big business and the people who run it.

When I went to Guinness it was to fill a vacancy created by the departure of Chris Chataway. In after years I got to know him, and discovered that he had become dissatisfied for much the same reasons as I had. He had also, as I was to do, followed being in Guinness with a career in television, and then followed that by becoming a Member of Parliament. The fact that we both followed the same path points up the mistake Guinness made in recruiting us. We were both destined to be – in our different ways, and at different stages of our lives – public performers and minor celebrities, and Guinness took us on because they wanted a star within the firm. The trouble was, the kind of person they had in mind was not going to remain in the firm, and after us they stopped looking in that direction. Instead they gave their own middle-ranking people a proper chance to get to the top. This was in line with changes that were beginning to take place at that time in Britain as a whole.

Mention of television prompts me to add a tailpiece to my Guinness story. I had renewed my passport while I was there, and where the form asked me to fill in my profession or occupation I wrote, accurately, 'Brewer'. The passport was valid for ten years, so throughout the subsequent period when I was flying round the world as a television reporter I did so on a passport that said I was a brewer. It was an Open Sesame. Innumerable times I have been slapped approvingly on the shoulder by officials in foreign countries and pushed on ahead through Customs and Immigration with the same joke, accompanied by drinking gestures and laughter: 'We know already why you are here. You have come to try our beer.' My designated profession was one that received instant and automatic approval almost everywhere. On one or two occasions, in communist countries, it was suspected of being some sort of front or cover, for they knew I had done my national service in the Intelligence Corps. Occasionally I found myself being questioned in detail about brewing in what was obviously an attempt to catch me out. But I passed all such cross-examinations with flying colours.

2

Running for Parliament

Finding myself unexpectedly free in October 1957, I attended an annual conference of the Labour Party for the first time. I had been a member of the party for a couple of years now, but for half that time I had been in the United States, so I had little direct experience of the party's inner workings. Its annual conference, which is held every October, was in Brighton that year, and I went for all of its five days. Over the next twenty-four years I was to attend about twenty such conferences, all of them in Brighton, Blackpool or Scarborough. They are the only occasion in the year when the whole Labour Party comes together, one delegate from each constituency plus all the important trade union leaders, the Members of Parliament, and delegates from affiliated organizations such as the Co-op and the Fabian Society. Members of the public are allowed as spectators, and there is a huge media presence in and around it all. In those days any resolution passed by conference with a two-thirds majority automatically became party policy, and no other body or person within the party had the power to make official policy, neither the leader nor any other group.

It was in Brighton in 1957 that I actually *saw* the Labour Party for the first time. It was a lowering experience. It was like travelling on a time-machine back to the 1930s. There were plenty of individual exceptions, of course, but for the most part the delegates were figures from the past, stale and old-fashioned in thought, outlook and utterance, even in appearance. Worst of all were the trade union delegates, middle-aged and elderly men whose attitudes had been fixed between the wars. They did not just assume, they positively asserted, that society was the same in all essentials as it had been twenty years before – so all the solutions to social problems that they had proposed before the war were still valid. They occupied whole blocks of seating, row upon row of them wearing pre-war-looking suits, the sort of suits my family's shop had sold in Hoxton when I was a child. There in front of my eyes they incarnated the poverty-stricken England of the 1930s, and were massively complacent about it, giving off an air of immobile stolidity. Their speeches were as antediluvian as the rest of them, a stew of out-dated and largely irrelevant attitudes.

The delegates from the constituency parties were not, in the main, quite like that. They tended to be schoolteacher types, or local government workers. They were out-dated in a different way. Their speeches gave off the musty aroma of Marxist assumptions, and in many of their attitudes they were archaically to the left of the trade unions.

The first thing I realized about the Labour Party when I saw it all together in one place for the first time was that it no longer represented (if it ever had) the people it imagined it represented. The country had massively changed, and left it behind. The party was out of touch now with a changed reality not only in Britain: almost all references to Soviet Russia and other communist countries were friendly, and rested on assumptions about the nature of those societies that were grotesquely at odds with what was now well-known truth.

Everything I found myself confronted by was self-contradictory. Here was the party of progress being blind to progress, denying that it had occurred. The party of the future was stuck in the past. The party of change had not changed. Its members, declaring themselves democrats devoted to freedom, were in the same speeches declaring solidarity with the most hideous totalitarian dictatorships in the world. The whole organization was moribund. Only two futures were possible for it: either it would have to reform itself drastically, and bring its outlook into line with the world around it, or it would decay and be replaced by another party. I believed very strongly that the country needed an up-to-date party of the democratic left that could be elected soon, and there seemed no time to start again from scratch with a new party. So from late 1957 onwards I joined with others who shared these views within the Labour Party to fight for its modernization. We formed various groups over the years, and tried to exercise influence within the trade unions and the Co-op as well as in our constituency parties. We published articles, pamphlets and books. We stood for election to a wide range of offices. My contribution included fighting two parliamentary elections in the next three years, then writing a book, *The New Radicalism*, which was published in 1962. In the very long run our struggle was successful, but it was to take decades rather than years – with the result that many of us, including me, eventually turned aside from this fight to pursue other activities. We even made an attempt to found a new party.

At Brighton in 1957 the most violent conflicts between the old and the new took place over two issues: nationalization and nuclear disarmament. On the first of these, the old-fashioned left wanted to nationalize nearly everything; but 1957 saw the beginning of a long campaign by the recently appointed leader, Hugh Gaitskell, to wean the party away from commitment to public ownership as a universal principle and to accept the need for basing industrial policy on the realities of each industry. This was to result in acceptance of a mixed economy, part publicly owned, part private. The left saw this as a betrayal of the fundamental principle of socialism, and conducted an all-out campaign against it. As for nuclear disarmament, everyone wanted that, of course, but there was a disjunction of opinion about how it could be achieved. Some demanded that the West should simply renounce all nuclear weapons and disarm unilaterally. This, they said, would be the morally right thing to do, and would set an example to the rest of the world. The opposing point of view, which included me, was that the nuclear powers should try to achieve disarmament by negotiation, multilaterally, step by step, in such a way that the Soviet Union never held a clear advantage in nuclear weapons. In this, we thought, lay the only hope of maintaining the stability of the world, its peace and also the security of the democracies, while still working towards disarmament. For the West to disarm unilaterally would leave the Soviet Union with a world monopoly of nuclear weapons. The results could only be catastrophic. Communist Russia had never disguised its espousal of violence as a political means in its determination to help communist governments into power everywhere. It had already done this wherever it could, which was throughout Eastern Europe and in Asia. When those of us who were multilateralists voiced this argument, the unilateralists responded with their famous slogan 'Better Red Than Dead'.

In all the years I was involved in this dispute I never encountered a rational case for the unilateralist option, or at least one that did not rest on either pacifist or pro-communist assumptions. No such case existed. The main appeal of unilateralism was to the violent revulsion we all felt against the idea of using, even possessing, nuclear weapons, a revulsion which in some people expunged rational thinking. It was, as Aneurin Bevan famously described it, 'an emotional spasm'. Characteristic of the old left were not only this sort of self-indulgent emotionalism but also wishful thinking based on two out-of-date assumptions, one that communist regimes were morally benign, the other that

Britain was still in a position to give a lead that the rest of the world would follow.

Characteristic also of the way people on the left held their views was that, lacking rational arguments, they did not attempt to argue rationally. This may also have been connected with an attitude to politics that was in many ways religious. Their automatic response to opposition, even to ordinary criticism, was moral indignation. They proclaimed that people who did not agree with them must be enamoured of nuclear weapons and blind to the dangers of their possession, and denounced such people as 'warmongers', even 'homicidal maniacs'. The emotional state into which they lashed themselves when they engaged in face-to-face controversy was nearly always one of extreme anger and moral outrage; and their protest marches ran on the fuel of righteous indignation. The satisfaction many of them so visibly got out of this was so great that one could not help suspecting – in the absence not only of rational argument but also, usually, of political effectiveness – that as far as they were concerned this was the main object, an end in itself. For them, politics was protest – rallies, petitions, marches, shouted slogans, shouted speeches. It had little to do with accepting responsibility and getting something actually done, still less with running a society. They conducted internal party controversy on other issues with the same kind of passion: nationalization, the role of the trade unions, Britain's membership of Europe. This meant that the party was in a perpetual state of civil war. In these battles I fought actively for the right of the party against its left. For a short time in the early stages I was inclined to suppose that, when all was said and done, there was something to be said for the left as being, so to speak, the party's conscience; but I soon discovered that this was the opposite of the truth. The most reliable thing about the left, after its irrationality and its irresponsibility, was its hypocrisy.

Among the pleasures of being at annual conference was that of seeing the leading personalities of the party in the flesh, and in action. Several I had heard speak, and sometimes met and talked to, at the Oxford Union, but here they were all together. The outstanding personal drama of that conference of 1957 was the public repudiation by Aneurin Bevan of his role as the leader of the dissident left, throwing in his lot with Gaitskell by becoming deputy leader of the party and shadow Foreign Secretary. The issue over which he did this was nuclear disarmament. In an unforgettable speech he pointed to some of the glaring flaws in the unilateralists' case (which he had hitherto espoused) and said that when he became Foreign Secretary the chief negotiating weapon he would have for achieving nuclear disarmament would be Britain's possession of nuclear weapons. He could say in effect to other countries: 'We'll give up our nuclear weapons if you'll agree to give up yours. Or at least, to begin with, we can both agree not to develop them any further.' However, if Britain had already given up its nuclear weapons in return for nothing at all, he would be left with nothing at all to bargain with. There would then be less hope of securing disarmament from others. In a phrase that has since gone into the *Oxford Dictionary of Quotations* he said that in those circumstances the party would be sending him 'naked into the conference chamber'. Many on the left were beside themselves with anger and hatred of him for saying this, regarding him as a Judas, and calling him this to his face. More than two years later Bertrand Russell said to me: 'Aneurin Bevan considers it more important that he should become Foreign Secretary than that the human race should survive.'

As with all conferences, the most enjoyable activities were not part of the official business. Brighton is, after all, a seaside holiday resort, and many of the people who, because they were at conference, were staying in hotels, saw this as the partial equivalent of an annual holiday. They would bring partners or friends with them to Brighton, and in the hotels in the evening there was a party atmosphere in a double sense of that word. In overflowing bars and noisy lounges a great deal of fun was being had. Sexual adventure was rife, in addition to politicking. In amongst all this, anonymous delegates would be hobnobbing on terms of evanescent equality with nationally famous politicians and media personalities. Wheeling and dealing, not to mention self-promotion, proceeded nakedly, with individuals in pursuit of political support for this and that, trying to get publicity for themselves or their good causes, or finagle jobs, or get women into bed. Constituency parties looked for candidates, and candidates for constituencies.

In a crowded bar I saw a friend who shouted across a sea of heads at me: 'Have the people from Mid-Bedfordshire found you yet? They're looking for you.'

I looked back at him blankly, and shook my head.

It turned out that a small group from Mid-Beds had come to the conference in the hope of finding a parliamentary candidate. Their constituency, a Conservative seat, consisted of 250 square miles of villages, none of which contained anyone they considered of sufficient calibre. So they were in search of an acceptable outsider. He would have to be someone prepared to fight hard and lose. This suggested a young man eager to win his spurs. They had made overtures to my friend the previous evening. He declined their approaches, so they asked him if he could suggest anyone else, and he suggested me.

Eventually the Mid-Beds people found me. Their leader, the Chairman of the local Labour Party, was a retired brigadier from the British army in India, Brigadier Jones. His family and friends called him 'O', the initial of a Christian name which he refused to divulge. (I still do not know what it was.) Others addressed him as 'Brig', and referred to him as 'the brigadier'. He was now a market gardener and pig breeder. The constituency Labour Party's social life was organized from his farmhouse, more by his wife than him. The Conservative member of parliament they were fighting was Alan Lennox-Boyd, the Colonial Secretary in Harold Macmillan's cabinet. Lennox-Boyd had supported the fascists in the Spanish civil war and coined the notorious phrase 'gallant Christian gentleman' for the fascist dictator Franco – still in power then and long to remain so. Having – an extraordinary coincidence as far as I was concerned – married into the Guinness family, he was familiar with the whole Park Royal set-up, knew all my senior colleagues there, and had often stayed in the Brewers' house I had used. We had other things in common, too – for instance we had both been President of the Oxford Union. The prospect of running against him in a parliamentary election appealed to me, and I said I would be willing to stand.

But of course I had to be selected first, and for that I needed to submit myself to an open and competitive selection procedure. This culminated in a selection conference in the spring of 1958. There were other aspirants, but the Joneses bent their backs to get me preferred. During those intervening months they invited me to the constituency many times to address meetings in different places, and to get to know key party workers; also to get to know the constituency itself. Its economy depended primarily on market gardening for London. The Joneses – with whom I always stayed – educated me about this, both the work and the business, in their own market garden. Their strategy was to get the members of the selection committee to incline towards me before seeing the other candidates. It succeeded, and when the selection conference came I was picked. One of the five others on the short list was the twenty-eight-year-old Betty Boothroyd, who was then working in the House of Commons as secretary to a Labour MP. In the long run she was to prove herself a person of formidable character and ability. Thirty-four years later she became the first-ever woman Speaker of the House of Commons, and is now an OM. But there was no sign of this in 1958. She came across then as mincing and ingratiating, immaturely trying to exploit her femininity. Having written those harsh words, though, which are true of her behaviour at the time, I must add that before she and I got to know each other sixteen years later in the House of Commons she had matured beyond all recognition, and I developed both liking and admiration for her.

Another person on the short list was a middle-aged local man who had become rich in the timber trade and had donated a lot of money to the local party. I was told later that he finished his speech to the selection conference by listing all his advantages over the other would-be candidates through having been born in the constituency and lived there all his life. He ended with the words, on a throwaway cadence: '– and I have the wherewithal.' This was imitated with much delight afterwards. He was so disgusted at being passed over by his long-standing friends – and in favour of an outsider of barely twenty-eight who, until a few months previously, had never set foot in the constituency – that he resigned from the Labour Party forthwith. I never saw him again.

For the eighteen months between then and the general election of 1959 Mid-Bedfordshire was the alternative focus of my London life. I spent at least every other weekend there, and often went for an evening during the week, travelling on trains from St Pancras. There were seventy-two villages; and in those days few people had cars, so the villagers did not travel around the area in the easy way they do now, but stayed mostly in their own villages. Each one had its local Labour Party, with Chairman, Secretary and Treasurer, and held regular meetings. If these were small enough they would be in somebody's living room, but otherwise they were in the village hall or local school. I set out to spend at least half a weekend with the members of each village party, during which I would visit some of their homes and a housing estate or two, and then be taken to a nearby market garden, or factory, hospital, fire station, or old people's home. In the evening I would address a public meeting, to which plenty of villagers would usually come who were not party members. The local newspaper would report these visits, both before and after, so the content of my speeches was read all over the constituency. By the time of the general election I knew the constituency in detail.

I had a full-time agent, Jim Shaw, a middle-aged northerner. He was small, bald-headed, sparky-eyed and grittily humorous. Part of his job was to make the arrangements for my visits, then meet me off the train and drive me around. He himself had come to the constituency only recently, so by accompanying me in my efforts to meet all the members he was making their acquaintance himself. Always at my elbow, with his grass-roots knowledge of internal Labour Party affairs he was invaluable to me. At first he drove me in his own car, but when I arrived on the scene the constituency decided to buy a party car. I had not yet learnt to drive, so they asked me to take lessons and get a licence. Meanwhile they bought the car. Their idea was that Jim would drive me until I was able to drive myself. However, I failed the driving test, and the rules of the test would not allow me to take it again until six months had passed. As things turned out I was to fail it again, and again a third time. So throughout the whole of my period in Mid-Bedfordshire, Jim was landed with the job of chauffeuring me around in a car that had been bought for me to use.

Like all organizations, the local party depended on a small number of individuals. I was blessed in these: they were people of good will and good sense, none of them unreasonable, and certainly none dedicated to making trouble within the party – so different in this respect from many of the activists I had seen at work in Brighton, and from the Labour Party nationally as I was to see it in the 1970s and '80s. Together we fought an enjoyable campaign, and even began to feel we were getting somewhere. The whole experience was a fundamental one for me – as Winston Churchill wrote, 'no part of the education of a politician is more indispensable than the fighting of elections'. It taught me reality at the grass roots, and not only political reality. In becoming knowledgeable about the internal workings of the Labour Party I visited hundreds of ordinary families in their own homes, many on council house estates, and became thoroughly familiar with the level at which most of the population of Great Britain was living at that time. I got to know each individual village, and many of its inhabitants, with their homes and shops, and also their market gardens, their factories and brickworks, their police and fire stations, their hospitals and old people's homes, their local schools. I became familiar with local government and local services. Those 250 square miles are the only part of rural England I have ever got to know in such a detailed way. It was a slice of life in every sense – a slice of England's life, as well as of mine. The more I learnt, the more I realized that the sort of people who were my friends in London were ignorant about most of it, as I had been. And this was as true of those who voted Labour as the rest.

A lot of my day-to-day life in London remained unconnected with all this. Even so, I carried on with my driving lessons, and did the perpetual homework of keeping up with current affairs, in the hope of being able to give sensible answers to questions. I was an active member of my own local Labour Party in St Marylebone. In London I met nationally prominent members of the Labour Party, and managed quite often to persuade them to come and speak in Mid-Beds. Naturally I tended to invite those I liked, and some became friends. The Shadow Colonial Secretary of the day was Jim Callaghan, so I invited him to have lunch with me to brief me against my Mid-Beds opponent, the Colonial Secretary. I also met, for a similar purpose, Richard Crossman, who I looked on then (and have done ever since) as the most brilliant debater I have heard.

If someone had said to me then that Jim Callaghan was a future prime minister I would not have been able to see it. He was not a lightweight, but nor did he appear to me a heavyweight. He was like one of those impressive actors in the London theatre who make successful careers playing important but supporting roles. I saw him as a figure of substance who compelled attention and had acquired a name, but not a leading figure. I liked him, and respected him, and we were friendly acquaintances from then on. But I always felt him to be lacking something. It may be that the venue I chose for our first meeting was misplaced, the Oxford and Cambridge Club in Pall Mall. Unknown to me then, Jim had a chip on his shoulder about not having been to university. His sense of inferiority about this was excessive, and was never assuaged. When, eighteen years later, he became prime minister, and was taken to task by one of his cabinet ministers (who told me the story) for not having given junior ministerial office to me and an MP who has spent most of the time since then as a Harvard Professor, he replied: 'They make me feel as if I've just come down from the trees.'

In the Oxford and Cambridge Club a member I bumped into occasionally was Clement Attlee, who had been prime minister of the first post-war Labour government and was now in retirement. I asked him if, when the General Election came, he would speak for me at my eve-of-poll meeting, and he did. Although he was to live for another ten years, this may have been his last public political speech.

All over Britain during 1959 political opinion seemed to be moving towards the Labour Party. Opinion polls did not play the role then that they do now, but in all political parties, the press, and among the public generally, the expectation grew that Labour was going to win the General Election. In Mid-Beds we even began to think we might have a chance of winning – a feeling that was strengthened when we discovered that the local Conservatives were afraid of losing. During the three weeks of official campaigning I addressed packed meetings, sometimes three in one evening in three different villages. People unable to squeeze in had to stand and listen from outside the open doors. And when Lennox-Boyd spoke in the same venues he drew small audiences. All this encouraged illusory expectations.

There were many people in London who, when they heard I was standing against Lennox-Boyd, told me that as well as having a wife and children he was an active homosexual. At first I was sceptical, but it was true, and I came to realize it. Since actively homosexual men in those days were sent to prison if caught, a gay cabinet minister was a serious liability who was running hair-raising risks. Perhaps in Lennox-Boyd's case the danger was part of the attraction, for he would visit illegal clubs in central London with male prostitutes wearing make-up, and would even travel in taxis with them (as one taxi driver told me from experience). Some years later the veteran Conservative MP, Angus Maude, told me that he and some of his senior Tory colleagues had been to see the prime minister of the day, Harold Macmillan, to tell him about this, because it looked to them as if Macmillan was about to make Lennox-Boyd Foreign Secretary – whereupon the government might at any time be engulfed in scandal, not to mention the possibility of blackmail. I never breathed a word of this in Mid-Bedfordshire, and it remained unknown there throughout the twenty-six years that Lennox-Boyd was its MP. I am certain my local supporters knew nothing about it, because if they had they would have been the first to tell me, and would have made delighted jokes about it. Lennox-Boyd won his lifelong game of 'Chicken'. He got away with it. The true story came out only after his death. But his activities cost him the Foreign Secretaryship. He may have considered it a price worth paying for so many years of hairsbreadth escapes – not to mention thrills and excitements far more earthy than that.

On polling day in my constituency, when the candidates were driving around all day in an attempt to visit every polling station, I found my car approaching Lennox-Boyd's on an open and deserted highway. I flagged him down, and we got out and talked together at the side of the road by ourselves.

He said: 'Now that neither of us can do anything about it, tell me honestly what you think has happened.'

'Well, to be absolutely honest with you,' I said, 'I think I may have won.'

'I think that too,' he said, quietly but firmly.

In fact he won comfortably, as did the Conservative Party nationally. Everywhere, people had turned out in multitudes to listen to Labour Party speakers and then voted Conservative. Their behaviour fooled everybody's expectations. It is interesting to speculate why.

The 1950s was the decade in which the majority of people in Britain emerged from poverty into comparative affluence. The full employment that had been created by the Second World War was maintained after it by governments of both parties, on the basis of Keynesian economic management. After nearly twenty years of it the population was beginning to acquire consumer durables on a large scale. It was during the fifties that most people acquired television sets; and they could now see the possibility ahead of getting cars, taking holidays abroad, and even owning their own homes. They had moved into this position latterly under a Conservative government. It was at a local meeting of the Mid-Bedfordshire Conservative Association that Harold Macmillan made his famous remark (another that is now in the *Oxford Dictionary of Quotations*): 'Let's be frank about it; most of our people have never had it so good.' By contrast, the Labour Party was giving out the impression of disliking the new-found prosperity. Its members talked about it disparagingly, as if it were something they were against: 'materialism', 'consumerism', 'the consumer society'. Having come into existence to abolish poverty among the masses, the Labour Party disliked mass prosperity when it came. Not only had the Labour Party lost contact with its reason for existing, and with the aspirations of the people it was supposed to represent; it was actively coming out against those aspirations, uttering public insults about them. And now that most people had television sets for the first time, for the first time they were able to see and hear national political figures discussing these matters. What they saw made them unwilling to entrust the future of their new and still insecure affluence to the hands of a sneering and condescending Labour Party.

As for me personally, my hopes were shattered overnight. On polling day I had imagined being a Member of Parliament the next day, and embarking on a lifelong career in national politics. When the next day came I was unemployed.

The count was a new experience for me, and I found it intriguing. Because of the far-flung nature of the constituency it did not begin until the day after polling day. Ballot boxes that had been sealed under police supervision and brought to a central point overnight were emptied out on to long tables in a large public room. Along both sides of the tables sat tellers appointed by the candidates, each teller having to work under the eyes of another from a different party, so that the votes and the counting were cross-checked. These tellers were required not to stray from their places. By law the only persons free to move about among them were the Returning Officer in charge, the candidates and their agents. Anyone else had a right to observe, but it had to be from a safe distance, in this case in a cordoned-off area from which the counting tables could be clearly seen but not reached. A platform was offered to the spectators so that they could overlook the room, and many of my supporters were sitting on it.

To my incredulity, I saw most of the leading local Conservatives wandering round the room, laughing and joking loudly, chaffing with Lennox-Boyd and his agent, and with people they knew among the tellers. I drew the attention of the Returning Officer to this. He said all of them were people he knew personally. They always did this, he said.

'Perhaps,' I said. 'But they're not supposed to.'

'Well,' he said, 'not theoretically, I suppose. But they wouldn't dream of doing anything improper. It's perfectly safe.'

I looked at them. They were all middle-aged or old, expensively dressed. Most were local landowners, or retired army officers, some of them accompanied by colonial-looking wives. It was obvious they regarded the law as something for other people, not for them. It was clear that they were used to behaving like this.

I said to the Returning Officer: 'I'm sorry, but I must ask you to make them withdraw to the platform and sit down. Also to be reasonably quiet.'

He looked embarrassed. 'I can't very well do that,' he said. 'They've always done it, and they're not doing any harm. It's a sort of tradition with them. It's all part of their big day. They'll be having a great celebration this evening.'

'Look,' I said. 'You can see my supporters up there on the platform, obeying the law. If you don't make these people do the same, I shall bring an official complaint against you for conducting the count unlawfully. The room is full of witnesses to the fact that this is so, and you will have no defence.'

Contorted with embarrassment, he went over to Lennox-Boyd and his group, and conferred deferentially with them in hushed, mortified tones. Consternation broke out. They all looked across the room at me. There was much hesitation, then more murmuring. The situation seemed insolubly difficult. Then the Conservative agent began, stutteringly and apologetically, to round up his supporters and usher them, objecting, to the platform. There was a lot of *sotto voce* huffing and puffing. One of the supporters, a retired-colonel type with bulging eyes, broke away from the rest and came striding across to me, bearing down in what was obviously meant to be an intimidating manner, and barked directly into my face: 'What precise clause of what precise law is it you have in mind?'

I looked at him evenly. 'Don't be a bloody fool,' I said quietly. 'Go to the platform and sit down.'

For a moment it looked as if his bulging eyes would bounce out of his face. Then I saw him realize that he had no choice but to obey – and how mortifying that was for him. His whole manner collapsed, and he slunk away, almost invisible.

The result was announced outside, in the open air, but it was given to me beforehand by the Returning Officer. As the candidates then lined up for the announcement I was engulfed by a feeling that my life had nowhere to go. The bottom had fallen out of my future. This was an over-reaction to exhaustion and disappointment, above all to the climactic ending of weeks of stress. In that instant I was lost to my surroundings and anything to do with the election. I was sunk deep in the emptiness of the time ahead of me. It was a moment of despair – but only a moment. I came to my senses immediately, pulled myself together, and was never to feel like that again. But unfortunately for me, the local newspaper had taken its photograph in that moment. When it was published a few days later it showed me standing in the row of candidates scowling with a face as black as a thunderstorm, like a demon in hell's torments. It made me look like the worst loser anyone could imagine.

A month later, after everyone had had time to get back to normal, there was a meeting of the local General Management Committee. The Labour Party's rules, very sensibly, prohibited the immediate re-adoption of a candidate, requiring instead a cooling-off period with time for reconsideration on both sides. In spite of this I was unanimously asked to stay on as the parliamentary candidate for Mid-Bedfordshire. I demurred. The next general election would not be for another five years, I said, and the fact that we had not won this one, when our hopes had been at their highest, meant that we might not win the next one either. And I was serious about wanting to be an MP. So with genuine reluctance I felt I had to keep myself free to stand for a more winnable seat. They said that, since the rules would not permit them to adopt a candidate for some time anyway, they would leave the offer to me open.

After the election, it came to light that Lennox-Boyd had not wanted to stand at all, and had told his colleagues he was going to retire. However, because Labour had been expected to do so much better than it had, the local Conservative Committee had feared that an unknown new Conservative candidate might possibly lose the seat for them – and if the election was tight nationally this might even have national implications. So the prime minister had persuaded Lennox-Boyd to run with the promise that if the Conservatives were returned with a majority that could withstand the loss of a single seat he would, after not more than one year, give Lennox-Boyd a viscountcy. This promise was kept. A year after the 1959 general election there was a by-election in Mid-Bedfordshire. Every section of the local Labour Party nominated me as its candidate, so at the selection conference, which the rules of the Labour Party required, there was only one candidate. My Conservative opponent was Stephen Hastings, who beat me easily, and was still in the House of Commons when I arrived there in February 1974. We left at the same time, June 1983.

When our two candidacies were announced for the 1960 by-election we felt we would like to get to know each other. We agreed on the telephone that our more crudely partisan supporters on both sides would take it ill if they knew that the two of us were meeting in London, so we kept it a secret. This enabled us to talk with total candour. He told me he was astounded to discover that not even the most sophisticated of his local Conservatives knew about Lennox-Boyd's homosexuality, even after twenty-six years. He gave me credit for this, and said it made him feel safe in entrusting me with the secret of this meeting. I found him agreeable company, a slightly Bertie Wooster-ish figure but a brave one, with endearingly dotty right-wing views. He was involved with British intelligence, and was later to convince himself that Tony Benn and other loony lefties in the Labour Party were part of a conspiracy manipulated by Moscow – and that their opponents inside the Labour Party such as myself were brave British patriots fighting for their country.

Standing in a by-election was an altogether different experience from fighting the same seat in a general election. I was a news item of national interest, and received coverage in the national media. All the newspapers sent reporters down to Mid-Beds, and I was interviewed by the BBC. Prominent politicians arrived every day to support me. On the other hand, paradoxically, the local electorate were less interested than they had been in the general election. This time, as far as they were concerned, it was not a question of choosing a government but merely of choosing a local MP – and it was obvious anyway that the Conservative was going to win. There was little personal enthusiasm for Stephen Hastings, because the locals had never heard of him. They knew me, but they also knew I was going to lose. My meetings in all the familiar venues were even smaller than Lennox-Boyd's had been the previous year. In the village of Old Warden half a dozen ancient and bemused rustics turned out to be addressed by Denis Healey, Tony Crosland and me. I do not think I secured even all of their votes.

As presented in the media, the campaign was lively and interesting, but on the ground there was something forlorn about it. An unusual report in *The Times*, although secured by deception, captured something of its true spirit. At the general election the tycoon Robert Maxwell had been the Labour candidate in a neighbouring constituency and had fitted out a caravan as his mobile headquarters – office, living room and kitchen all in one, covered on the outside with giant Labour posters, just right for country electioneering. I borrowed it from him for my by-election. A *Times* reporter talking to me in my campaign headquarters, and seeing this caravan parked outside, was greatly taken by it, and said: 'Let me see you using it.'

'There's no engagement to take it out for,' I said.

'Oh,' he said, 'you can just take me out on the road with it as if you were going somewhere. I want to see it in operation.'

'But that wouldn't be 'in operation',' I said. 'I don't go out and just wander around in it. I go on planned expeditions to pre-arranged events, with back-up by other people.'

'But it doesn't matter, just for me to see it.' He had a light in his eye. I thought he was seeing the caravan as a toy he wanted to play with.

My agent intervened. He assumed that any publicity was good publicity, and said to me: 'Go on, why don't you take him out in it? He just wants to see it. Nothing's due to happen till after lunch.'

Not wanting to rebuff my agent in front of the journalist I called for a driver and set off.

When we were out on the open road the reporter said: 'Do these cooking facilities work?'

'Yes.'

'Do you have any food?'

'Yes.'

'Why don't we stop and have lunch, then? It'll be fun.'

So we stopped and had a convivial lunch with the driver.

A couple of days later an article appeared in *The Times* that drew an achingly lonely picture of a stationary, isolated caravan on an otherwise empty country road, with little puffs of smoke coming out of its chimney, and inside it was me, all by myself, not going anywhere, frying up a solitary lunch. As journalistic practice it was scandalous. It was partly just plain untrue, and the rest deliberately misrepresented. And it had all been set up by the reporter. Yet there was an elusive grain of truth in it.

This by-election was my first experience of being an object of interest to the national media, and of dealing with journalists and broadcasters from the receiving end. I learnt that you must never trust them, and never do anything merely because they ask you to; and never assent to words that they put to you in the form of a casual question, for instance formulations uttered with apparent innocence by an interviewer. Such people are never following your agenda, always following their own. You must not expect anything else, however friendly they may appear. You cannot use them for your purposes without being used by them for theirs, and this will usually involve your being set up. It may be worth it to you in order to achieve your ends, in which case all is well, but if not, your only recourse is to have nothing to do with them. It is a mistake to imagine that you can get what you want out of them without being betrayed.

A tailpiece to the story of my connection with Mid-Bedfordshire is my farcical history as a car-driver. After failing the test for the third time I had no intention of taking it again, and said so to the examiner who failed me. But he talked me out of that. He said if I let him put a date down for my next test in several months' time, I would be sent a reminder in the post a fortnight beforehand, and if I still did not want to do it I could ring up and say so. I let him put my name down. Between my third and fourth tests I did not drive at all, and forgot about it. But when the reminder came in the post I felt there was nothing to lose by trying, so I took the test for a fourth time. It so happened that my candidacy in the forthcoming by-election was now being regularly referred to in the national media, occasionally with a photograph.

When I began the test my car was parked between two others.

'Drive out,' said the examiner, 'then straight ahead, and I'll tell you what to do.'

I reversed, and with a *crunch!* hit the car behind.

I looked at the examiner, despairing.

'Go on,' he said casually.

'Surely there's no point in us both wasting the next hour,' I said.

'Go on,' he said in a hard voice.

I drove forward, clipped the bumper of the car in front, and drew out of my parking space.

From then on I made one error after another. The worst was when the examiner told me to reverse round a corner: driving backwards, I went right out on the wrong side of the road, on a sharp bend, and it was the purest of good fortune that nothing came the other way. Finally, when I had to end by parking the car in the space from which I had begun, I once more hit both the car in front and the car behind.

As I put the handbrake on I turned to the examiner with an extravagant gesture of comic despair. Without any change in his expression he said: 'Congratulations, Mr Magee, on passing your driving test.'

I assumed this to be a joke, and laughed. But something about his demeanour made the laugh gurgle to a stop in my throat.

'You don't mean it,' I said.

'Yes I do,' he said. 'And may I also wish you the very best of luck in your by-election.'

I assumed instantly he must be a fanatical Labour Party supporter. But when I told the story to my friends they all said he was obviously a Conservative.

I told the Mid-Bedfordshire Labour Party that having passed the test only at the fourth attempt, and never having driven alone, I did not possess sufficient confidence to drive alone around the constituency, for if I were to cause an accident it would get huge local publicity and might wreck our chances in the election. They accepted this. By that time they were used to having me driven everywhere by the agent anyway, and it was going to be only for another three weeks.

The truth, however, was a lot worse than I had told them. In the course of learning to drive I discovered that I was lethally dangerous. On every occasion when I took a car out – even on my successful test – I did something that could have got me and my companion killed. This had nothing to do with lack of confidence – I was blithely confident. My problem was keeping my mind on driving. Although I was not absent-minded in any other activity in my life, I could not keep my mind on driving. However hard I tried, my thoughts wandered, and I would speed over crossroads without looking, drive through red lights, perfectly relaxed and happy, my mind a thousand miles away. Only my companions had saved me by frantically recalling me to myself with shouts and yelps, sometimes grabbing the steering wheel. If I were to drive alone it would be a short time only – a matter of weeks at most, more probably days – before I had a crash. Out of pure self-preservation I decided never to drive.

3

Young Man in London

In America in 1956, during my year at Yale, I began to think seriously for the first time about living in London as an independent adult. It had to be London, no question about that. I would not have considered life in Britain based anywhere else. (That was true until my late sixties.) Even so, although I had friends in London I had nothing else – nowhere to live, no job, no more personal possessions than would fit into a large suitcase. Also, I would be arriving without money. So I really would be starting from scratch. My mother, with whom I was on bad terms, had remarried and was living in Bristol. My sister, my only sibling, was living in Paris. I had no near relations in London, despite being a Londoner. But I was twenty-six now, and wanted to embark on adult life in my home city.

I did not want to live alone, however, so I tried to think of someone to share a flat with. This was difficult. I had spent two of the last three years outside England, and during that time my friends among my contemporaries had made their own living arrangements with their (often my) friends, or partners, or wives. None of those I knew now wanted an additional flatmate. So it needed to be someone who was not living in London but would move there with me. And of course it had to be someone I could be reasonably sure of getting along with. After a number of exploratory letters I found the right person in Tyrrell Burgess. Up to that point he and I had been friendly acquaintances rather than friends, but as a result of what ensued we became close friends for life.

Tyrrell had been two years behind me at Oxford, which is a big gap between students, and although we were in the same college I had moved out of it into digs before he arrived. It was really through the Oxford Union that we got to know one another. At the end of my term as President he was elected as Secretary for the following term, and became President a year after that. Through this connection I recommended my digs in Oxford to him when I left to go to Sweden. When I came back, a year later, he was still there, so we then lived in the same house for a year. Now, in 1956, he was teaching at a public school in Bedford, but was coming to the conclusion that schoolteaching was not, after all, the career he wanted. Near the end of that academic year he was offered a staff job as a journalist on the *Times Education Supplement*, and he decided to take it. This meant he wanted to move to central London. He and I agreed by correspondence that when one of us found a flat we would share it.

At first, when I arrived in London from Yale (having crossed the Atlantic a second time on the *Queen Elizabeth*), I lodged in West Kensington in the flat of a lifelong friend, Richard Cavendish, and his wife Mavis. I had been their best man when they married. It was from their home that I did my job hunting, while Tyrrell and I both looked for a flat. I found the job at Guinness, and we found the flat just off the bottom of Baker Street, near Portman Square. It was actually the top half of a small house, in a short street called Robert Adam Street, which was blocked off at one end by the Wallace Collection. It had previously been occupied by a lady of the night, who had moved on to more ample surroundings. For a while we still received telephone calls for her, and whenever a stranger's voice asked if Carmen was there we replied: 'Carmen is Bizet'. On one occasion I was got out of bed at three o'clock in the morning by a man at the front door who, confronted by me in

322

pyjamas, asked if I could tell him how he could get into the church next door.

Since neither Tyrrell nor I owned any furniture we rented the flat furnished. It was, I confess, dowdy. One cleaning woman who came to be interviewed by us turned us down on the ground that it was against her self-respect to work for people whose home was inferior to her own. But it was comfortable. And the location was marvellously convenient. We were close to the tube stations of Bond Street and Marble Arch, from which I could travel directly to Guinness, always in the opposite direction to the crowds since I was going out of central London in the mornings and coming back into it at night. We were only a couple of hundred yards from Oxford Street at Selfridges, with its prodigious food hall. And on the other side of the Wallace Collection lay Marylebone High Street, our village, a neighbourhood shopping centre of character and charm. We lived in that house for two and a half years, during which nearly all the events recounted so far in this book occurred. Since that time I have felt that this is one of the parts of London that belong to me, and I have always especially liked Marylebone High Street.

Scarcely had Tyrrell and I moved into our flat together than Britain invaded Egypt, and the Suez Crisis broke. This pushed both of us into political activity. We added our mite to the biggest of all the protest meetings, a sea of humanity in Trafalgar Square that was addressed by Aneurin Bevan – who, as usual, rose to the occasion. We had both been inactive as members of the Labour Party, but we now made contact with our local constituency party in St Marylebone and started going to its meetings. Bewilderingly soon, the Russians invaded Hungary. We believed that British aggression had provided a degree of cover for the Russians' aggression, and had helped to precipitate it by making it politically less costly for them. We joined the main public protests against the Russian aggression too, including another great rally in Trafalgar Square.

During the week or so when the western frontiers of Hungary were not under the control of any authority, something like a tenth of the population fled the country. Families scattered, and many fugitives arrived in the countries of Western Europe with nothing but the clothes they stood up in. Tyrrell and I heard an appeal on the radio for anyone in London who had a spare bedroom to make it available for transient refugees, if only for a night or two while more permanent arrangements were made. We took in a couple of such guests who passed quickly through; but then we had one who stayed for a year. He was Paul Wonke, an eighteen-year-old student of architecture from Budapest. His family had been scattered: his mother and older brother were in Holland, his girlfriend in Switzerland.

Even during Paul's first days, Tyrrell and I had no alternative but to go to our own jobs each day, so he was left to his own devices in central London. He was sturdily independent, though, and refused to accept money from us, though I think he was given a little by the organization that had sent him to us. He wandered around with a purpose, looking for free art galleries and museums. In one of the private galleries he saw an exhibition of the work of Graham Sutherland, where he found himself riveted by one of the lithographs, and stood in front of it for a long time. The owner of the gallery came over and said: 'You seem to be fascinated by this one.' They got into conversation, in which it emerged that Paul had just arrived from Hungary as part of the diaspora that was being covered by the world's news media. The owner was so moved that he gave Paul the lithograph. I was in the flat when he got home with it. My immediate thought when he walked in holding it was: 'Christ, he's stolen it.' He then told me what had happened – and finished his story by saying wryly: 'I have no underpants, and I have an original Graham Sutherland.'

During the year Paul was with us, Tyrrell and I were plugged in to a whole world of young Hungarians in London. One of the salient features of the Hungarian rising of 1956 was that the activists in it were mostly young people who had grown up under communism and had no adult experience of anything else. Obviously it had failed to indoctrinate them. Those who fled to the West were mystified by the illusions about communism that they met on every side, even in otherwise intelligent people – in fact *especially* in intelligent people. But they got used to it. They were adaptable as individuals, eager to work and use their initiative. Several of those I met, arriving with nothing, became millionaires. Most were successful in one way or another. The joke went round that a Hungarian was someone who walked into a revolving door behind you and came out in front.

When a new academic year began in the autumn of 1957 Paul went to Liverpool University to study architecture, and there he qualified. We retained contact: I was his best man when he got married (having been reunited with the girlfriend in Switzerland), and then I was godfather to their first child. We were part of his world now, and he of ours.

I had known two or three middle-aged Hungarians in London before all these young ones arrived, but they were not the same kind of people at all. They were leftovers from the old Hungary who had been living in London since the communist takeover of their country after the Second World War. The two groups had a huge amount in common: their mother tongue; their knowledge and love of Hungary and its cultural heritage; their anti-communism; membership of an international network of exiles who had been driven abroad by the same tyranny. Yet in spite of this they did not care for one another. The newly-arrived tended, on the whole, to be modern-minded people of an egalitarian and socially liberal outlook, and they fitted in effortlessly with liberal-minded people in England. Those who were already here tended to be older and old-fashioned, conservative, class-conscious and snobbish, and to belong to a largely vanished world. They were most at home with those elements in England that were also old-fashioned, class-conscious and snobbish. The diaspora of which they felt a part consisted not of a nationality but of a class, and a class not only from Hungary but from all the countries of Eastern Europe. There were innumerable counts and vons among them, with a good admixture of barons, and even a number of princesses. Strangely enough, I knew this world, and then got to know it ever-increasingly well in what was left of the fifties, and throughout the sixties. This was through my relationship with someone who played an important part in my life then, Nancy Cuninghame, the mother of one of my most loved friends at Oxford.

Her son Andrew and I had been especially close as students, fellow spirits. This relationship was interrupted by my years in Sweden and America, although in Sweden I had stayed once near Stockholm as a house guest with Nancy and her Swedish second husband, Jan Killander. Her first husband, Andrew's father, had been a baronet and a military attaché, and in the courts and capitals of Europe between the wars Nancy had revelled in the life of a titled diplomat's wife. Their social world was a cosmopolitan one of individuals in or near government and politics; of daily lunch parties, drinks parties, dinner parties and receptions, often in beautiful surroundings and always with a plenitude of servants; of comfortable outings to cultural and sporting events; of *sub rosa* sexual networking; of polyglot jokes and gossip. She loved these things, and loved sharing them with other people. I have never known a better hostess, nor one who took more trouble, though it never showed. This kind of social life was her element, and she created it round herself wherever she went. She was a positive snob but not a negative one – she was automatically interested in anyone titled, famous, rich, or powerful, but in no way prejudiced against people who were none of those things. If she liked them she was just as caring and attentive.

About titles her snobbishness was comic, despite the fact that she herself knew that it was, and that her friends kept teasing her about it. I once saw a cousin to whom she had given a handful of letters to post riffle through the envelopes and say, with a straight face: 'Nancy, there must have been some mistake; there's one addressed to a "Mr"', to which she replied, with an equally straight face: 'It's a bill.' It was as if she had remained in touch with every titled person who had ever crossed her path. Half the princes and barons of Eastern Europe, many of them now old and broke, were lavishly entertained by her. I lost count of the princesses I met in her company. As for mere counts, they were two a penny. But of course, all these people were human beings too, and really just like anyone else. The comic-opera world of their imagination, in which some of them still lived, could actually be quite charming. Several were warm hearted, and many were good and true friends to Nancy. Some were much loved by her.

About her own title she behaved disgracefully. When her husband died (and passed his baronetcy on to Andrew when Andrew was still at school) she married a Swede called Jan Killander, yet she went on calling herself Lady Cuninghame. When her friends took her to task for this she said she needed the title for her job. She made a living letting flats fully furnished in the style of sumptuous stage sets. She had half a dozen of these, in central London, and typically she would let each for three or six months to a visiting film actor, or a third world politician, or head of an international company. Often, at the end of a let, she and Jan would move into the newly-vacated flat and restore it to its pristine condition before letting it again. She was wholly professional in this, down to the smallest of details, and she worked hard at it – and made a lot of money. Over the years, I stayed as their guest in most of these flats – as well as in their homes in Stockholm and central Mallorca – and never have I experienced more relaxed luxury, or been better looked after.

To explain how all this became one of my worlds for such a long time I need to fast-forward my story for a single paragraph. Andrew died shockingly young of a blood disease, while still in his twenties. Nancy was distraught. Because I had been so close to him she wanted to keep me near to her – and so, without consciously realizing she was doing it, she began to look on me as a kind of substitute for Andrew, a sort of surrogate son. And I – because I had no functioning family of my own, and got on so well with her (and perhaps because I had never experienced a mother's love) – allowed it to happen. I would be automatically included on all family occasions – if I held back, Nancy would say firmly, 'You're family.' When invitations were received from other people she would ask if I could come too, and soon I was being invited separately. I started spending my Christmases with them.

There are many ways in which my relationship with Nancy contributed to my education in life. One is that for a period of many years, whenever I was *en famille* with her, I was experiencing a variety of upper-class life from the inside, together with the operetta-like, Ruritanian extension of it that existed among some of the European émigrés. It is, I think, a possibility that it was through her that my name got on to the Mums' lists of Debs' Delights in 1957, although Andrew was still alive at that time, and it was perhaps too early in my relationship to Nancy for that to be very likely. When I came to write my novel *The Story of All Our Lives*[1] I drew on her in creating the mother of my central character, although the central character himself was nothing like Andrew.

Of course, Nancy's world was only one of several that I lived in, and it was never the main one. The one I lived in most was the

[1] Originally published as *Facing Death: A Novel* (London, 1977: Kimber).

world of my contemporaries, many but not all of them from Oxford, a world increasingly diversifying as time went on. I also had my Guinness world, and my Labour Party world. I was beginning to enter the literary world, and was soon to be part of the television world. My flatmate, Tyrrell Burgess, worked in journalism and education, and people from his worlds came into my life. Two of my friends were hospital doctors, two architects, two worked in London University; another was in advertising, one in the City, one in the Foreign Office, one in the newly-born computer industry. From all these would come invitations to meet their other friends. The different worlds overlapped, and people moved between them – we were young, full of energy, and most of us had several interests. Few of us had much money, and our dinner parties were often the cheapest imaginable – a mountain of, say, risotto to be shared by everybody, with plentiful cheap wine, the bottles having been brought by the guests. To our drinks parties we each took a bottle; the host would provide several, and the party would go on for half the night, usually with dancing in the early hours. For most of us there was a kind of bliss about it all, because we were young. For a tragic few, things went seriously wrong: a botched abortion, a breakdown, a slide into alcoholism, a suicide. Every now and then some such terrible thing would blacken our sky. We would be truly, horribly appalled. But then we would carry on, because there was nothing else we could do. And the drama, whatever it was, would slide into the past and become part of our collective memory, the shared folklore that made us a group of friends.

Some were keen on indoor games. These enthusiasts would get the rest of us involved – chiefly in poker, Monopoly, or The Game (a form of charades that was especially popular with actors). For me the centre for these activities was the home of a couple called Val and Robin Schur. This Robin was my old friend Robin Burke from Oxford. Her husband Val had arrived in Britain from Vienna in the 1930s with a refugee mother, an archetypal Jewish Mum whom even the rest of us addressed, and referred to, as Mamma. The circle that gathered around them included several people who were to have interesting futures: the poet Donald Michie and his black wife Daphne, Michael Heseltine, and Sasha Moorsom, who was to marry Michael Young and become the mother of Toby Young. From those early days I remember especially the subtlety of Sasha's humour in The Game – while Robin chiefly recalls my noisy altercations with Michael Heseltine over the Monopoly board. Poker I loved, though instead of getting better at it I got worse. They were marvellous evenings. Because of them, most of the people who were friends of Val and Robin became friends of mine.

Most of us were keen on theatre, and many were music-lovers. We went to as much in the way of plays, concerts and operas as we could afford – and always in cheap seats so as to be able to go more often. The year of my return to London from America, 1956, marked a turning point in the London theatre: it was the year of *Look Back in Anger* and all that followed from that – the so-called Angry Young Man movement. Most of us were sympathetic to this epoch-making play: we did not share its one-sidedness, but we welcomed the way it broke out of the straightjacket of traditional theatre. Actually, traditional theatre continued perfectly happily alongside it, and we went on enjoying that too. Three of the greatest classical actors of the century were at the height of their powers: Laurence Olivier, John Gielgud and Ralph Richardson. Shaftesbury Avenue never stopped being a provider of high-quality light entertainment, most of it conventional. And the fact that all these contradictory things were going on at the same time was part of the marvellousness of living in London.

Unlike before the war, music in London was now as rich as the theatre. With two recently founded symphony orchestras – the Philharmonia, with first Karajan and then Klemperer as chief conductor, and the Royal Philharmonic with Beecham – London was in the astonishing position of having five orchestras of international class. (The other three were the London Symphony, the BBC Symphony, and the London Philharmonic.) There was also a new concert hall, the Royal Festival Hall. With these to bring them, the world's best performers came before us in a never-ending stream. As for opera, in the whole of Britain there were only two full-time opera companies that had their own theatres, and both were in London: Covent Garden and Sadler's Wells. Two of the finest productions I have ever seen were staged at Covent Garden in the late 1950s: Berlioz's *The Trojans* and Verdi's *Don Carlos*. The latter, directed by Visconti, introduced a new conception of acting to the operatic stage, namely good acting, and was rightly remembered for ever after as a turning point. Of special interest to me were the annual cycles of Wagner's *Ring*, which I saw every year, sometimes twice. Even during my first parliamentary election campaign I managed to give myself those four evenings off.

I have told earlier how, when I gave up working for Guinness in September 1957, the firm went on paying me for six months. During that period, and then beyond, I finished my book *Go West, Young Man* and went on to write my novel *To Live in Danger*. I worked every day in the library of the Oxford and Cambridge Club in Pall Mall, walking there through the streets of Mayfair and St James's after breakfast, varying my routes to keep the walks interesting. I got to know every street, almost every shop, in those parts of London. Street prostitution was rife, and the same girls would accost me regularly on the same street corners, until they accepted the fact that I was not in the market; then we might stand and chat for a moment. I think I got a mild erotic charge out of knowing them and talking to them. It also contributed something to my knowledge of the ways of the world. But I would never have dared to go with any of them – I had a terror of venereal disease. In any case, I was seldom without a girlfriend.

The Oxford and Cambridge Club is a palatial establishment at the end of Pall Mall, near St James's Palace. I had joined it when I was a student – to help it entice young members who it hoped would stay for life the club waived the entrance fee for students, and charged them only a nominal annual subscription (I think it was a pound a year). For me it was an invaluable base in the heart of London where I could work in the library and have meals, or just relax in comfortable surroundings, read all the newspapers and magazines for nothing, make telephone calls, receive mail, cash cheques, entertain guests, play billiards, and get my hair cut. I have always found a London club an indispensable facility, and over the years have belonged to several – there are about forty of them altogether. The Oxford and Cambridge has one of the biggest and best of the libraries, and for a couple of years it was my chief place of work. I eked out my Guinness salary for a great deal longer than the six months it was nominally for. When finally I was forced back into earning money I did so by part-time teaching, so as to continue writing. When my finances got run down to a level at which I found it too expensive to eat in the club I would go out to one of the nearby workers' cafés, the so-called greasy spoons. I was already familiar with these from my years of eating in them as a schoolboy.

In those days an honours degree qualified someone as a schoolteacher, and I already had friends who earned money by what was called supply teaching. In a vast area like London, with hundreds of state schools, there are some teachers every day who do not turn up for work, for whatever reason, and therefore there is a daily need for last-minute stand-ins. These are supply teachers. They hold themselves ready at home until a certain hour, to be telephoned and sent immediately to schools that need them. They may teach just for a day, but possibly for much longer: the need is unpredictable. It is ideal work for an indigent writer, because it keeps his wolf from the door without being a full-time job – and on any particular day he can always say No if he wants to, or not answer the telephone. The schools who have the greatest difficulty in keeping staff are the problem schools, so they are the ones that make most use of supply teachers. I did not teach in them only, but I taught in many. The worst was in Bell Street, off Edgware Road. The oldest pupils were no more than fifteen, but a number of the boys were already in organized crime, usually involving drugs, and a couple of the girls were pregnant. Keeping order was a Herculean task, and getting all the children interested in the same thing at the same time bordered on the impossible. Teaching in Bell Street was itself an education. In fact, I found supply teaching educative altogether, because I taught in a diversity of schools, and in many different parts of London. The most satisfying was a technical school beside a bridge near Victoria Station. Many of the boys in the leaving class were good at mathematics and technical drawing but were incapable of writing a letter of application for a job. They were powerfully motivated to learn, though, and I enjoyed teaching them. But the headmaster was suspicious of me. He considered it fishy that someone with a university background of Oxford and Yale should be doing this job, and he thought there must be a skeleton in my cupboard.

Supply teaching was quite a common experience for my generation of university graduates. People who did not think of themselves as teachers, and had no intention of becoming teachers, would do it to earn money while looking for a different sort of job, or between jobs. There were others for whom it was part of a way of life based on something else – not only writers but also actors, musicians, painters, and artists of other kinds. Val Schur had done it. Tyrrell Burgess had too, and had taught in Bell Street.

Although Tyrrell and I were sharing a flat we had our separate lives and went our separate ways for most of the time. Usually I had little idea what he was up to. However, there would be evenings when neither of us was up to anything in particular, and we would go to one of the nearby pubs together. These took their last orders at eleven o'clock, a time at which we would not normally want to stop drinking; so at that stage we would move on to the Savile Club, of which Tyrrell was a member. This was in Brook Street, a short walk from our flat. We would find there a room full of people drinking and talking, often grouped round one of the exhibition-talkers of the day, the most notable of these being Compton Mackenzie and Gilbert Harding. There we could go on drinking for as long as we liked.

After I had been visiting the Savile for a couple of years as Tyrrell's guest, some members became so familiar with me that they assumed I was a member. Others thought I ought to become one and pay a subscription. I did, and am still a member more than sixty-five years later. The Savile has accompanied me through life and given me a great deal of pleasure, so perhaps I ought to say just a word about it.

In the late nineteenth century, when clubs like that were largely the preserve of establishment figures and the well-to-do, a need was felt for clubs which people who were neither of those things could comfortably belong to. Writers, in particular, felt the need – actors already had the Garrick. So the Savile was founded. It was mainly, though not exclusively, for writers and people interested in the arts. The eating and drinking were simple and cheap. Oscar Wilde described it as 'a real republic of letters: not a sovereign among 'em.' Over the years it widened out. For instance it found itself the main club for people in the British film industry. Being within walking distance of Harley Street and Broadcasting House it acquired many doctors and psychiatrists, and became the BBC's main club. Being only a few yards from Grosvenor Square it picked up members from the American Embassy. A strong interest in the arts was still its most obvious characteristic when I joined it: the men of letters embraced half the leading novelists of the day, including William Golding (who was to win the Nobel Prize for Literature) and such personalities as J. B. Priestley and C. P. Snow. The visual artists included Henry Moore, the composers William Walton, the actors Ralph Richardson. The atmosphere was easy-going and relaxed: as one member put it, when members who were eminent came into the Savile they hung their halos with their coats in the entrance hall. Today most of the members are in business of some kind, but have an interest in the arts; and there are many professional people. But there is still the same relaxed atmosphere. Whereas going to the Garrick Club, of which I have also been a member for some decades, is like going to a lively party given by friends, being in the Savile is more like being at home with one's family, if not always one's favourite members of it.

When I joined the Savile I had just started to work in television – in the next chapter I shall tell how this came about. My office at Oxford Circus was only a few minutes' walk from the club, so I went there for lunch on most days. This meant that I quickly came to know the other regulars. Some became friends, and one in particular, a psychiatrist called Anthony Storr, a lifelong friend. After lunch I would usually play snooker before returning to my office. Savile Snooker is a variant of the standard game designed to make it faster, and more fun for below-average players. The outstanding exponent of it was Stephen Potter, who was then at the height of his fame as the inventor of such concepts as gamesmanship and one-upmanship, words that have entered the English language. He wrote best-selling books about them. He was also an exceptional games player who frequently made hundred breaks at Savile Snooker. I played him many times, but it was necessary for him to give me gargantuan starts if I was to have any chance at all. He would then deploy with uninhibited ruthlessness the wiles of gamesmanship of which he was not only a master but the inventor, and I had to thicken my skin against his psychological onslaughts if I was to stay in the game. It was immense fun. Often my visit to the Savile was the most enjoyable part of the day.

In the late 1950s, which were my late twenties, a way of life formed itself around my activities which was to remain mine for several decades: living in central London, chiefly concerned with writing books and with politics, but having to earn my living doing other things too; marinading in music and theatre, also reading, while being involved in a many-sided social life, and having a special love of parties. The ingredients were constant for many years, although the proportions varied with circumstances.

The adversity that caused me the greatest upheaval during those years was Andrew's illness and death. He had Hodgkin's disease, a cancer of the lymph glands. I knew a long time before he did that he was going to die, because Nancy told me. Rightly or wrongly, she decided that he should remain ignorant of it for as long as possible, to enjoy his life to the full (which he certainly did). When he fell in love and told his mother he was going to get married she told the girl he was dying, but neither of them told him. It was a bizarre, agonizing situation; harrowing in the extreme: all those of us closest to him knew he was going to die, and soon, but he had no idea. Like the others, I tried to spend my time with him doing whatever it was he most wanted to do; but I could not stop myself from being distressed in his company. When finally he knew he was about to die he faced it not only with courage but with a kind of constructive resignation. I did not believe I could have done the same, and it made me feel inadequate. His death was a loss I have never ceased to feel. Years later, when I became a Member of Parliament, I realized what a high-quality politician he would have made. His death was a loss to society as a whole as well as to those who loved him.

Tyrrell and I began eventually to feel we could afford something better than living in a dowdy flat, with furniture that was not ours, and we started to look around for a flat we could furnish for ourselves. We found it in The Little Boltons in SW10, near the bottom of Earls Court Road. It was a semi-basement flat, currently lived in by two of my friends, Liz Clunies-Ross and her husband Beverley Cross. Liz owned the house, and wanted to let her flat to someone she knew rather than a stranger, so Tyrrell and I took it over in February 1959. Each of us assumed he was likely to marry before long, so we agreed that whichever of us married first could keep the flat, if he wanted it, and the other would then move out.

Scarcely had we arrived when, in the course of putting down carpets, we uncovered dry rot in the floorboards of the two biggest rooms. For quite a while the flat became uninhabitable – not only because two floors had been taken up but because the rot, once it had been fully uncovered, stank. At this point Tyrrell set off on a long journey, which had already been arranged, through the coastal countries of East Africa, starting from Nairobi and finishing in Cape Town. Nancy invited me to move in with her and Jan at number one Hyde Park Street, an address that was already playing quite a part in my life. I remained there until my own flat was habitable again. When I returned to it so did Tyrrell, with a girlfriend he had acquired on the boat from South Africa. She did not move in with us immediately, and I stayed in The Little Boltons for most of 1959. When I did move out, it was to a flat nearby. That area of London was to remain my cabbage patch for the next forty years.

The best thing for me about being in The Little Boltons was that I was now just round the corner from Val and Robin Schur, whose home was the hub of some of my most enjoyable activities. I found myself falling in love with Robin. But I had already made it a rule (which I held to for the rest of my life) never to initiate

337

advances to the wife or partner of a friend. And Robin made none to me. Instead I formed an attachment to an Indian girl, an unemployed actress who worked in a nearby coffee bar called The Troubadour, which was like a little local club to us all. Beautiful though she was – and she had the most beautiful body I have ever seen – she was nearly always unemployed as an actress because she had no acting talent whatever. Her attempts at it were beyond hopeless. Even when we played The Game, every other player was better than she was.

Tyrrell's girlfriend, Joan, moved in with us in the summer of 1959. They decided to get married, so it was settled that I would move out. But a general election was now expected in the early autumn – during which I would be in Mid-Bedfordshire full-time for a matter of weeks, and therefore not able to cope with flat-hunting or moving into a new home – so it was agreed to delay my removal until all this was out of the way. Meanwhile the three of us lived together happily; and we have remained good friends all our lives.

Eventually, with the election over, I found a new flat. This time, for the first time, I lived alone. Robin's marriage to Val had come apart, for reasons that had nothing to do with me, and this gave me hopes for a new relationship with her. If that had happened, and lasted, my new-found flat would have been only a temporary home, and that is how I thought of it at first. But, as the French say, *c'est le provisoire qui dure* (it's the provisional that lasts). I was never to marry again, and that flat was my home for most of my adult life: I was twenty-nine when I moved into it, and seventy when I moved out. I loved it from the moment I saw it. But at first I assumed I could not afford it, and turned it down. During the subsequent weeks of looking at other, inferior flats, I found myself more and more regretting that I had not taken this one. I had started work in a temporary job at the lowest level of television, a job without security, but I now told myself that if I could manage to go on doing part-time work in television I would be able to afford this flat in a year or two's time. Meanwhile I would pay the rent out of the overdraft that was then a permanent feature of my life. Six weeks after seeing the flat I went back to it, thinking that by now it must surely have gone – and it had not. To this day I do not understand why. It was one of the greatest pieces of good luck I have ever had: for forty years I lived in a flat that I positively, actively liked.

It was mainly to do with the size and shape of the rooms – unusually large, high ceilinged, pleasingly proportioned, beautifully light. There were only two of them. The flat had a wide entrance hall, a large kitchen, and a bathroom with a separate lavatory; but even so, the fact remains that it was basically a two-room flat. I made one of these into a study-bedroom, spacious and private, with a large desk by the window and an enormous bed against a distant wall. The other became a living room for a life I shared with friends. It had comfortable armchairs and a window seat, a sofa that turned into a double bed, walls covered with bookcases, and a record player. All this was on the first floor of an Edwardian mansion block whose internal walls were so thick I could play *Götterdämmerung* in the early hours of the morning without the neighbours hearing. I never had to worry about any of the problems of being a householder. If anything went wrong I rang for a porter. If he was unable to fix it, the agency that ran the property took care of it. The whole block was well managed: the central heating never failed, nor did the lifts; hot water was on tap twenty-four hours a day. It was not until I moved to Oxford in my seventies that I had to concern myself with such things, and I hated having to do so. By purest chance I had been protected against them for most of my life, yet no such considerations had been in my mind when I moved into my London flat.

The flat was in Marloes Road, just off Kensington High Street. Although only three hundred yards from Kensington High Street tube station, it was in a quiet enclave, with its own side street of shops. This gave me the best of two worlds. I relished the villaginess of the enclave (the locals referred to it as 'the village') but Kensington High Street was within a stone's throw. Earl's Court Road was not much farther away, in another direction. Three tube stations were within less than ten minutes' walk, so the tube became my daily lifeline. The character of Kensington High Street was transformed during the time I lived there. At first it was suburban, royally so, the most splendid of suburbs. But long before I left, it had become an organic part of central London, the second busiest shopping street in Britain after Oxford Street. Even so, the villaginess of the small pattern of streets and shops near my flat stayed the same, and I always derived pleasure from that. I constantly saw some of the same people in the village when I first arrived without knowing who they were, though naturally I noted the attractive women: and forty years later some of the same people, including the attractive women, were still brushing past me in the same streets and shops, having grown old along with me. And I still did not know who some of them were.

1959 was a turning-point in my life as a whole, but this appears only in retrospect. It was then that I started living alone for what was to be the rest of my life. It also launched what turned into a career in television, though again, at the time, I had no idea that this was going to be. What I did feel at the time was that time was passing me by. My next birthday was going to be my thirtieth, but I had no feeling that my life was going somewhere. I had published my first book, and finished writing my second. I had fought my first general election. But these experiences only confronted me realistically with how far away I was from being either established author or a Member of Parliament – and how un-automatic the achievement was of either aim. I seemed to be little further ahead than when I started. And soon I would be thirty.

This feeling of life passing caused me to think of taking specific steps to do the things I most wanted to do, and not just go on assuming that they would happen in some indefinite future. For instance, I had always wanted to go to the Bayreuth Festival, and also the Salzburg Festival; but I had never done anything about it; so in 1959 I went to both. In those days there was no problem about getting even the less expensive tickets for such things, if one was willing to book them well in advance, which I did. Having got the tickets I was struck by an idea. I wrote to *The Times* and asked if I could review both festivals for them. They said they had someone going to Salzburg but not to Bayreuth, and they might be prepared to consider an article about it from me. However, their response was carefully guarded. They said I could not regard myself as representing *The Times* in Bayreuth, nor could I say to anyone there or anywhere else that I was writing for *The Times*; but if I cared to telephone a review from Bayreuth they would consider it on its merits, without any obligation to publish. Encouraged by this, I wrote to *The Guardian* asking if I could review Salzburg for them, and they responded in exactly the same terms. So another of my new beginnings in the year 1959 was that my career as a published music critic began, with reviews of the Bayreuth Festival in *The Times* and the Salzburg Festival in *The Guardian*. Both newspapers sufficiently liked what I wrote to commission new articles from me, and the following year I went to Bayreuth for *The Guardian*. For several years I reviewed music festivals annually for *The Guardian*, going to a different one or two each year, in new places. I chose them myself, and it became my way of taking a summer holiday. It was also those two initial 1959 reviews that led John Christie, the founder of Glyndebourne, to invite me to a private dinner party at his house in 1960, during the intervals of which we went into the family's box in the theatre and saw *Don Giovanni*. I have been to Glyndebourne every year since, and seen every new production since 1973. Altogether, life opened up for me in 1959. And the process was stimulated by living alone for the first time.

4

Starting in Television

When television began it had no alternative but to recruit people from other professions. Chief among these were radio, the film industry, newspapers and associated news organizations, magazines, the theatre, and advertising. So the professional background of everyone who worked in television in its earliest days was rooted in something else, and this meant that the person had been trained to think in other terms. For some time this affected the way the medium was used. What was essentially a staged variety show would be put in front of cameras; what were essentially radio discussions were held in front of cameras; and so on. No one had yet begun to conceive the programmes in terms of the new medium itself. It took a while for this to happen.

The first individual I knew personally who went straight from university into television and was never anything but a television animal, without any admixture even of radio (as everyone had who came from within the BBC), was Jeremy Isaacs. His career was getting under way at the end of the 1950s, as a trainee producer with Granada in Manchester. His chief interest was current affairs, and he believed that a television debate should be the confrontation of two points of view in televisual terms, not just in words as on the radio. If two people were going to argue for different solutions to a social problem, each should make a television report or mini-documentary that put his case, and these should be considered side by side. We should not have, as we were having, two men sitting in armchairs in a studio conducting a purely verbal dispute in front of cameras.

He proposed to his bosses that he should be allowed to make a regular series in which the same two protagonists – one left-leaning, the other right-leaning – confronted one another over a range of questions of the day. It would have to be fortnightly, because of the time required for filming. And because the two presenters would be making their films simultaneously, the series would have to employ two film crews. The costliness of this was the chief obstacle from the beginning. Jeremy proposed to offset it by having unknowns as the two protagonists: if the series succeeded, they would become well known, but before that they would be cheap to hire. As part of his attempt to convince his superiors he conducted screen tests to find good presenters. He invited me to go to Manchester for one of these. In the end, the presenters he came up with were me and Michael Heseltine, both of us still in our twenties.

We were asked to make a pilot programme on the subject of the housing shortage, which was currently seen as a national crisis. Michael filmed a report arguing that the only effective solution would be a market-based one while I filmed a report arguing that what we needed was more social housing. The resulting programme was well received in-house, and was thought to demonstrate that such a series could succeed. There remained, however, the objection that it would be unusually expensive to make. It could pay its way only if it were transmitted over the whole ITV network rather than just in Granada's local region – and even then provided only that the public viewed it in sufficiently large numbers. Granada's first task was to persuade the other ITV companies to take it.

Granada asked me to stand by while they engaged themselves in this process. They assured me that they had decided definitely to have me in the series if it were made, and asked me to keep myself available. I told them this would be a problem for me, since I needed to earn money doing *something*, if not this programme. So they paid me a retaining fee. I could scarcely believe my luck. For a young writer to be paid *not* to get a job is an ideal solution to his problems. I began writing *The New Radicalism*, my best book up to that time, a call from inside the Labour Party for a fundamental rethink of its ideas. Writing it mattered a great deal more to me than working in television, so I hoped that Granada would never reach a decision.

After several weeks, someone from Granada telephoned me to say that, since they were paying me quite a lot of money, they thought they might as well get something in return for it while at the same time giving me more experience of being in front of cameras. A non-networked magazine programme was being transmitted in Manchester on three evenings a week, and they wanted me to be in it on one of these evenings and conduct a live interview. I could scarcely say No.

On the first and every other weekly occasion a chauffeur-driven car collected me from my flat after lunch and drove me to Heathrow. There I boarded Granada's private plane, which shuttled between London and Manchester every day. At Manchester airport I was met by another chauffeur-driven car which drove me to the studio. There, on the first occasion, I interviewed a young man for three minutes about tiddlywinks. The world tiddlywinks championship had just been played in Manchester, and I was scooping the first interview with the new world champion. Having myself played the game as a small child, and enjoyed it, I was able to enter into the spirit of the thing. It was my first experience of appearing on television.

Eventually the Granada management decided not to go ahead with Jeremy's idea. My perfect arrangement was at an end. Naturally I was disappointed; but by this time I had made a good start on my book, and accumulated some money – and even enjoyed a bit of fun on the side – so I felt I had done reasonably well out of it. Most important, I had glimpsed a far more rewarding way than supply teaching of earning money without having to take a permanent job. I began to make enquiries about other possibilities in commercial television – there were, after all, several companies.

Eventually something came to my ears. One of the companies, Associated Television (known as ATV, which tended to get confused with ITV), had a long-running fortnightly series whose success was raising a problem. In those days all programmes were transmitted live, and the people working on this one needed a holiday. The company decided to take the whole series off the air for three months, during which time the people working on it could go away for a holiday and then do some fresh thinking. Meanwhile the gap was to be filled by a quite different series of six fortnightly programmes. To put this together they would need to bring somebody in, but only as a stop-gap – once his series had finished there would be nothing for him to do. When I heard about this I rang ATV and asked to be considered for the job.

At my interview, the new series was explained to me. It was called *Right to Reply*, and the basic idea was as follows. Individuals are constantly being attacked in the press – not only politicians but also the heads of companies and public services, authors (by book reviewers), actors (by critics); in fact individuals in most walks of life. Each of the programmes would take a good current example of this and give the victim a chance to answer by confronting him with his critic on television. This confrontation, and the resultant altercation, would be the programme. What was needed was for someone to pick the subjects, engage the participants, and provide a briefing on both to the man who had been engaged to present the programmes on the screen. This was William Clark, a staff journalist on *The Observer*.

I was taken by the idea, and thought I could see how to make it work. I had had experience, as President of the Oxford Union, of engaging national figures to clash publicly with one another, and choosing the issues for them to do it over. There were other applicants to be interviewed, though, and I was asked to telephone in on Monday to be told the decision.

On Monday I rang, to be told by one of my interviewers that they did not think I was the right person for the job.

Something inside me refused to accept this.

'Who have you given it to?' I asked.

'No one as yet,' he said. 'We didn't think any of the people we talked to were quite right. We're still looking.'

'Well I'm convinced you're wrong about me,' I said. (This was out of character.) 'I know in my bones I can do it. How can I convince you?'

He explained regretfully that he and his colleagues had discussed me thoroughly before coming to their decision. It was not possible to reopen the question with them.

I still refused to take No for an answer. And I managed, somehow, to keep him talking at the other end of the line. Finally – I could hear from his voice that he was doing it just to get rid of me – he said wearily, and with no note whatsoever of encouragement: 'Well, if you like, you can have a think about what subject or subjects you would choose if you were preparing a programme for us today, and ring me about it tomorrow. But I honestly can't see that it's going to make any difference. I can't ask my colleagues to spend time on you again.'

I was making this telephone call from the Oxford and Cambridge Club, which takes all the main newspapers and magazines. I went straight to these and started ransacking them for ideas in every field – news, current affairs, films, popular music, sport, politics, the arts, business, television itself. I spent hours at it, and telephoned the next day with not just one or two ideas for programmes but with a dozen, all of them issues that were receiving lively treatment in the current press. I could hear from my interviewer's reaction at the other end that he was highly impressed.

'Could you put those on paper straight away and let us have them in tomorrow morning's post?' he asked.

'Certainly.'

I got the job. The individual I had talked to on the telephone turned out then to be my boss. He told me that he was as much impressed by my pertinacity as he was by my ideas, because it would be as indispensable in the making of good programmes.

When I got down to serious work on the series I was surprised by the extent to which, new to television as I was, I was left to my own devices. Programme ideas came only from me; and although I had to have them cleared before turning them into programmes, this became a formality. Three days before each transmission I would go to William Clark's flat in Albany and brief him, leaving the documentation with him. On transmission day, a producer who was otherwise unconnected with the series would come into the studio and direct the cameras.

I soon learnt why the point about pertinacity had been stressed. The chief problem in making the programmes was that, whereas an individual who had been attacked would often leap at the chance to reply, his attacker would rarely be willing to confront him on television. It was difficult in the extreme to persuade the critics to take part. Only rarely did I get my best ideas as far as the screen. Normally I had to move down my list to my third or fourth choices, sometimes lower. Even so, the programmes came out well, and the series was a success – viewers had no awareness of what was *not* being put on. ATV changed its mind about regarding the series as a stopgap, and wanted to keep it going as a regular feature. They asked me to stay on and run it on a regular and increased salary.

Doing it, I had found – once I got on top of it – that making this fortnightly programme required an amount of work from me that I could fit into one week if I organized myself properly. This meant I could turn it into a half-time job while being paid full-time – and, what is more, paid at a salary higher than most of my contemporaries were earning. So I changed my mind about not getting a regular job, and grabbed the opportunity with both hands. It launched me on a career in television that was to last for four decades. Such a career was totally unlooked for by me when I began it: I merely had the good luck to light on it. Given that I needed to earn money, this way of doing it suited not only my needs but my talents. I was good at it. And it provided me with worthwhile experience of a sort that being a writer alone would not have yielded.

The fact that I began in television as a behind-the-scenes programme-maker had lasting effects on the way I used the medium. The occupational vice of performers – on television just as in film and theatre – is to care too much about their own performance compared with the programme, film or play as a whole, and to see everything out of proportion, whereas from the beginning my primary concern was with the whole thing. This remained so after I became a performer. In subsequent years my chief successes in television were series in which I was responsible for everything, not just for my own performance on the screen.

I began working in television in 1959, and was in on the early years of ITV, which started in 1955. Until then the BBC had had a monopoly of television in Britain – and there was only one channel. Because the new commercial companies were profit-driven they avoided the bureaucratic structure of the BBC, which consisted of a skyscraping pyramid of committees, administrators, managers and controllers soaring up into the clouds over the heads of a lowly layer of programme-makers. The structure of the BBC has been top-heavy and wasteful from the beginning in a way that has nothing to do with the making of programmes.[1] By contrast ITV, aside from the people who actually made the programmes, employed only enough personnel to do the jobs that were necessary. They hired these people as individuals, usually signing them up on short-term contracts to avoid building unnecessary staff structures. Throughout my broadcasting career I was never on anyone's staff, but was always self-employed, a freelance contributor, first on short-term contracts and then, as far as ITV was concerned, with no contract at all, working on verbally agreed terms. The personal relationships involved could not have been more civilized. In ITV I never found myself in a hierarchy, and there were scarcely any committees. The internal structures were tiny compared with the BBC's. Inside these new companies the atmosphere was also entirely different from the BBC's: cost-efficient in method and structure; modern-minded instead of old-fogey. Those of us working in them knew one another, and talked freely together on equal terms, as fellow professionals.

One of the bonuses of working in television is that you have lively and stimulating colleagues. Several of the young people I got

---

[1] John Sergeant, who was Chief Political Correspondent of the BBC for the last twelve years of the twentieth century, wrote in his memoirs: 'There was a strong body of people who made the programmes, and a distinct and quite separate line of managers who contrived to lead interesting lives without ever having to connect directly with the stressful business of broadcasting. They spent their time producing endless reviews on the future of the BBC, in writing needlessly complicated memos, and in working out reasons why various posts should be filled, or not filled, depending on the ebb and flow of management thinking at the time. There was a clear gap between programme makers and management.' He called this superfluous management 'a parallel BBC'. It was very much bigger, and more highly paid, than the body of programme-makers.

to know in ATV in the late nineteen-fifties were to have distinguished futures. Christopher Morahan became, and was for most of a long life, one of the best directors in the British theatre. Mary Selway became, for an equally long period, the doyenne of casting directors in the British film industry. (Her mother lived in the flat above mine in Marloes Road for many years.) Neville Sandelson became the owner of Putnam's publishing company, and then a Labour MP. Julian Grenfell became an international figure in the World Bank as Lord Grenfell. Gordon Reece went into public relations and achieved widespread fame as the man who carried out a successful makeover of Margaret Thatcher's public image – lowered the pitch of her speaking voice, softened its tone, darkened the colour of her hair, and improved her dress – in return for which she made him a knight. The company itself, ATV, was the most showbizzy of the ITV companies. It had been created by its chairman, Lew Grade, who was the nearest thing in Britain to an old style Hollywood tycoon – little and fat, double-breastedly suited, big cigar, self-confident vulgarity, exclusively concerned with showbiz and money: a doer, effective and shrewd, sentimental. For him there were only two kinds of programme: light entertainment and culture. He regarded himself as knowing all about the former and nothing about the latter. The Independent Television Authority required him to put on a certain proportion of 'cultural' programmes, so he complied without the faintest pretence of being interested. I realize now that this was why I was left with such freedom to run my own show. I once talked to him about it, and he used the phrase '... cultural programmes like yours'. I said: 'Oh come on, Lew, you can't call the programmes I make cultural,' and he replied: 'Well you certainly can't call them entertainment.'

When *Right to Reply* had run its course I was kept on as a maker of one-off documentaries. My job now was to think of subjects, write scripts, lay on the ingredients (a presenter, interviewees, filmclips, graphics, and so on) and hand the complete package over to a producer/director who would then bring the programme alive in a studio in two days without having been involved with it before. My screen credit was Editor. The programmes were, I believe, quite good of their kind, though not particularly special. However, I was still learning. Then along came a much bigger project.

Ever since my year in the United States, 1955-56, I had been struck by how mistaken the image was that most British people had of America. It was based largely on Hollywood films and television programmes, plus popular culture, magazines, and the behaviour of American tourists and troops abroad – and then, on top of that, a huge dollop of resentment against the country's overwhelmingly preponderant wealth and power. The publication in 1958 of my book *Go West Young Man* established me as someone familiar with contemporary America, so I now proposed a series of calculatedly unglamorous documentaries about it. The point was to present reality as it was for most Americans. What was your life like if you were a suburban housewife in New Jersey, or a farm labourer in Kansas, or a car-factory worker in Detroit, or someone with a black face in the Deep South, or a retired elderly couple in California? I proposed a series, *Main Street USA*, in which each programme would be built round the daily life of such a person, in locations spread across the country geographically. I worked on it on a fifty-fifty basis with a producer called James Bredin, who knew the United States well, and who contributed as much to the series as I did.

Jim and I travelled all over the United States twice. The first time we were in search of the all-important individuals, plus the film locations to go with them, and gathering the detailed local information we were going to need. On that journey there were just the two of us. When we got back to London I wrote the scripts for six programmes. Then we went out again and travelled round the same itinerary with an American film crew. This time Ian Trethowan (who was later to become Director-General of the BBC) accompanied us as the presenter and interviewer. In the course of preparing the scripts I wrote out lists of carefully worded questions for him to ask in his interviews, and he adhered entirely to these. He also stuck to the introductions and linking passages that I wrote for him in full. He was a good performer, and did it well. But I could not help wondering: 'What do we need Ian for? Every word he is uttering is mine. Why don't I do it myself?' It was this experience more than any other that made me decide to move from being behind the cameras to being in front of them.

When I told my bosses in ATV that I wanted to work in front of the cameras they were dismayed. What I was already doing for them had a monetary value so much greater than what they were paying me that they wanted me to go on doing it. They said, with total frankness: 'You're too valuable to us as you are. We don't want to lose you. And what reason have we got – or have you got, come to that – for thinking you'll be good in front of the camera? Ian was first-class, but what evidence is there that you would be? You know perfectly well that we prefer to hire well-known people to do that, and we engage them ad hoc to suit each programme or series. However, we'll be only too happy to increase your salary substantially for doing what you're doing' – which they did. But they made it clear that they were going to offer me no escape route from my existing job.

From that moment I felt I was being exploited and held down, and I became determined to move. So I kept my eyes alert for possibilities. One day a veiled entry appeared among the small ads of *The Spectator* saying that a current-affairs television programme was looking for a new face as a junior reporter. It gave only a box number, with no mention of the programme or the company. But being in the business I was able to uncover the fact that the programme was *This Week*, ITV's flagship current-affairs programme, which came from Associated Rediffusion in Kingsway. As an experienced programme-maker I did not want to send a job-application to an anonymous box number and have my name considered on equal terms with applicants from outside the industry. So – taking a leaf out of the book of my snooker opponent, Stephen Potter – I behaved with calculated gamesmanship. I telephoned the Editor of *This Week*, a man called Elkan Allen, and told him I had seen his advertisement in *The Spectator*. I indicated briefly what my television experience was and invited him to come and have lunch with me at the Savile Club to see if there were any possibilities for me. He was audibly taken aback. Then he laughed at my cheek, and accepted the invitation.

When we met, he said he was making a short-list of applicants, and would screen-test all of them at the same time. In view of my experience, he said, he would certainly include my name on the list, but he could not promise me more than that. He gave me the date on which the screen tests would be held, and said I should simply turn up at Associated Rediffusion at ten o'clock on the morning of that day.

When I arrived at Television House I was the only applicant to do so. Elkan Allen was in Viet Nam with his *This Week* team. Another producer, David Hennessy, was hauled out of his office to explain and see if he could help me. He said that the other applicants for the job had all been written to, but because there was no letter from me on the file no one apart from Elkan Allen had known about me. And no one knew when he was coming back. On his return he would be so busy with his Viet Nam material that it was unlikely he would have time to carry out screen tests. David was charming and apologetic about it – and then began to look thoughtful. He asked me to accompany him to his office.

He was, he said, about to need a reporter and interviewer himself for a series he was preparing. Would I be interested in having a try-out, only on probation? His series was nothing like as imposing as *This Week*, which was nationally networked at a peak hour and had an eight-figure audience. His was going to be fortnightly, transmitted between eleven o'clock and midnight, and screened only in the London region. It was to be called *Questions in the House*, and its basic idea was to build programmes around parliamentary questions, usually about social problems, and usually filmed in the constituency of the MP who raised the question. I would visit the constituency with a film unit and shoot a mini-documentary which could be about, shall we say, the decay of a fishing town or a holiday resort, or the conservation of an offshore island, or the tearing down of a church or hospital, or the building of a motorway. The programme as screened would include an interview with the MP, either filmed by me in his constituency or carried out live in the studio. If it was done in the studio the interviewer would be either me or the front-man of the programme, a well-known *Observer* journalist called Kenneth Harris. David Hennessy made it clear that he himself would choose the subjects and the participants, without consultation with me, but that once he had done so he would give me a free hand with both the filming and the interviewing.

So I became a television interviewer. The fact that Elkan Allen had forgotten about me, and left no instructions for me to be informed that the screen tests had been cancelled, told me that I was not in his mind as a possible member of his team. So I no longer expected to be offered a job on *This Week* – in which case David's offer was my only hope, which is why I took it. When Elkan returned from Viet Nam he made no attempt to talk to me, even though I was now there working from an office on the same corridor. He never explained or apologized, or even said hello.

So my first filmed television reports, and my first serious interviews, were for *Questions in the House*. One of the programmes I recall most clearly was a charming and very English little documentary about the struggles of the small-boat building industry on the Isle of Wight. This subject conveys the flavour of the series as a whole.

When I had for the first time the experience of sitting in a darkened viewing theatre looking at the rushes of my own filming I was greatly put out. I did not care for it at all. In the same way as hearing a recording of your own voice for the first time is like hearing the voice of a stranger, so seeing yourself moving around on a big screen for the first time is like seeing a stranger. We do not look like what we think we look like. The experience is quite different from looking at photographs, because on film we are living and moving, talking to other people, reacting to them, walking about, getting into and out of chairs or cars, climbing up and down stairs; and this enables us to see our own behaviour, how we act and react, our changing facial expressions, our body-language. What I disliked about myself was the smoothness, especially in reaction to other people. I was sometimes urbane to the point of blandness. This was not how I felt inside, not at all. On the contrary, I was full of inner uncertainties, and I had always assumed that these showed. When I saw myself in action on the big screen I realized that, unconsciously, I had developed a protective outside. It was self-evident to me that I needed to be less afraid of letting my feelings show, even letting my insecurities show. I must stop being so goddamned smooth. I did not care much for the interviews, either, for similar reasons. They were too polished. They needed more bite, more edge, and they needed to engage more, dig more deeply into both the subject-matter and the person being interviewed. For this they needed to come from somewhere deeper inside *me*. This again needed to show. At least a compensation about my inner insecurities was that they made me uninhibitedly self-critical; and this launched me on an attempt to improve myself as a performer. All the time I worked in television I went on getting better. As a result, I was an unrecognizably better performer in later years than I was at the beginning.

After a few months on *Questions in the House* I was asked to leave it and join *This Week*, and this was specifically because of my more engaged way of coming to grips in interviews. Control of *This Week* had now moved out of the hands of Elkan Allen into those of a duumvirate, Cyril Bennett and Peter Morley. These two particularly liked my interview of a retired naval commander, a holder of the Victoria Cross and man of authority, in which I had said to him easily and pleasantly at one point: 'You're quibbling now, Commander Roberts.' What they wanted, they said, was someone who could say things like that to people like that without appearing offensive. They wanted me to do it (when justified, of course) to national political figures, which in those days was not the usual thing.

In television terms their invitation offered a breakthrough – regular exposure to a nationwide audience in a weekly series at a peak hour, accompanied by worldwide travel and a leap in pay. But I was working now on my book *The New Radicalism*, and that was where my heart was. I asked Cyril and Peter if I could work for them half-time, be available for six months of the year, in periods of their own choosing. They said No. Their programme was at the mercy of news over which they had no control, and they were all the time having to make instant responses to the unexpected, with whatever resources they could muster. They needed me to be available either always or not at all. On this they were unbudgeably firm.

To begin with they offered me a one-year contract. I screwed up my courage and took the plunge. I reckoned that if, in a year, I won my spurs as an international reporter, I would be able to negotiate a part-time contract. If not, or if I did not want to go on with it, I would have earned what by my standards was good money, and would be able to have a long and uninterrupted spell of writing. What actually happened was that during that first year I made enough of a reputation for other television companies to start trying to lure me away from *This Week* with offers of up to twice as much as I was currently earning; so that when the time came for my contract to be reconsidered I was able to show these offers to Cyril and Peter. I told them that if they were willing to go on paying me exactly the same as I was already earning I would work for them half-time. They laughed, and caved in gracefully. I stayed with *This Week* on that basis for several years. At first I worked a regular three weeks on and three weeks off, but both sides found this unsatisfactory, so we changed it to six weeks on and six weeks off. This became our standard arrangement. When eventually I left the programme it was because I wanted to give myself totally, and without any ifs or buts, to writing the novel that was published as *Facing Death*, and is now *The Story of All Our Lives*.

In these circumstances I published five books between 1962 and 1966. They were *The New Radicalism* (1962), *The Democratic Revolution* (1964), *Towards 2000* (1965), *One in Twenty* (1966) and *The Television Interviewer* (1966). In the last of these, half the book was about the craft of television interviewing and half about how a programme like *This Week* is made.

During my regular six-week periods of work in television I was a general reporter, ready to go anywhere at a moment's notice and cover anything. But there were two areas in which I specialized: America, and the liberation of the British colonies in East Africa. Because the United States was the most powerful country in the world it was the most prolific source of news stories. There was one year when I went there about every six weeks. Among much else, I attended the crucial party conventions, covered the Cuba missile crisis, and was at J. F. Kennedy's funeral. When it was a matter of gauging popular feeling, the grass-roots knowledge of 'ordinary' America that I had developed through making the series *Main Street USA* was invaluable. It enabled me sometimes to make accurate predictions that were contrary to 'informed' opinion. The earlier series had made me familiar with a small town called Salina, in Kansas, which was almost the geographical centre-point of the United States; and now, from other parts of the country, I would make telephone calls to my contacts there – even go there if I could make the time – to discuss the stories I was working on. In 1964 I flew directly to Republican Salina from the Republican Convention in San Francisco which had selected Barry Goldwater as presidential candidate, and it was partly on the basis of what I found there that I wrote an article for *New Society* on the plane going home in which I predicted that Goldwater would carry only some five states. I was laughed at for this prediction, but he did in fact carry five states. Not the least eye-opening of my contacts had been an undertaker in Salina with a name like Jerry Murgendorfer who told me that he, who had voted Republican all his life, could not possibly vote for Goldwater. When I asked him why not he said in an outraged voice: 'That guy says exactly the same things about foreign policy as I say, and I don't know a goddam thing about it.'

This episode illustrates something that was of fundamental importance to *This Week*. It was not a 'news' programme but a 'current affairs' programme, in other words its remit was not to report the news but to interpret it and comment on it. That distinction was vital as far as I was concerned, because it fitted my talents. My fortes were explanation and comment. I would not have made a very good news reporter.

In the African colonies my chief focus was the liberation movements, who were obviously about to come to power. I found the local representatives of the colonial powers hopeless at forming relationships with the leading figures in these movements, despite the fact that they were soon going to be the government. Whenever I arrived in a colony with my film unit I would go to the British authorities to register my presence, and ask for whatever help they could give me; but when it came to putting me in touch with the individuals who would soon be running the country they were useless. Once, at a Governor's dinner table in his private residence, alone with him and his wife, I asked him in confidence for his personal evaluations of some of the leading local African politicians. He looked embarrassed, and was silent. To explain his silence his wife said: 'We don't know them. And to be frank I wouldn't have any of them in the house.' It was only through the local United States mission that I was able to make personal contact with them, win their confidence, and get them to talk to me. Although it is difficult to find out what is really going on in the internal politics of dissident groups, and who the individuals are who really matter, the Americans were well informed and anxious to have good relations with whoever was going to be in power. They were invaluable to me; and having registered my presence with the British I would often work unobtrusively via the Americans. As a result I formed long-running personal relationships with some of the most interesting and influential of the African leaders, notably Julius Nyerere, Kenneth Kaunda and Joshua Nkomo. I interviewed them in their own countries and on their visits to London, before and after they achieved independence. Off the record they would occasionally talk to me with startling candour, knowing they could trust me.

At that time, the colonial liberation movements and their well-wishers, of whom I was one, believed that with independence their societies would be launched on a road to democracy and prosperity. As things turned out, the opposite happened. The tragedy of Africa was that the independence movements became, almost without exception, socialist movements, so that when they achieved power they set up centrally planned socialist economies, and those – as they did everywhere else – failed. In the process they impoverished their societies, bred corruption, and destroyed personal freedoms. As a result, Africa was the only continent in the world whose societies actually moved backwards during the second half of the twentieth century. The main cause came not from outside but from within: it was bad government by Africans themselves. I did not, I have to admit, foresee this development. It was always clear to me that communism would be a catastrophe for Africa, but I believed it would be avoided (as indeed it was) and that a slow, bumpy improvement would take place under well-meaning, left-of-centre governments. It has been a nightmare to see a liberation that I so warmly welcomed lead to destitution and tyranny.

A reason why I knew that communism would be a tragic mistake was that I had seen what a failure it was in Eastern Europe. I was the first British television reporter to be allowed in to Hungary after – and it was several years after – the uprising of 1956. I also visited East Berlin, and filmed in Poland – where, for the only time I was aware of, a honey trap was laid for me (which indeed looked delicious, but which I did not taste). In my book *The Democratic Revolution*, published in 1964, one section was headed 'The Abandonment of Communism'. In it I stated that in the communist countries the communists themselves knew that communism was a failure, and understood that genuine progress for them meant not building a new kind of society but becoming more like the West. They were, I said, already embarked on such a course without publicly acknowledging it. No one else at that time was saying these things, but – perhaps for that reason – nobody took much notice of what I published. It was to be decades before these elementary truths were generally recognized as such in the West.

Not much more than half my television time was spent abroad. The rest was devoted to covering domestic affairs in Britain. All the country's leading politicians came into our studios, many more than once, and I interviewed most of them. Nearly always our most illuminating discussions were not those we had on the screen but those we held in private, behind the scenes after the programme, when we would sometimes sit up drinking into the small hours. Home truths and indiscretions came pouring out, and I acquired a fairly detailed knowledge of what was going on behind the facade of government, and also behind the facade of opposition. The most dismaying individuals among our guests were some of the leaders of the big trade unions, who exercised enormous power in society without having any of the necessary sense of responsibility to go with it. Their basic attitude was summed up by one of them called Alan Fisher. When it was put to him that what he was doing was harming society as a whole he said: 'It's not my job to think of society as a whole, it's my job to look after the interests of my members.' In private some of them were so puffed up with a sense of their own importance that they looked like pouter pigeons: they said the most skin-crawlingly vain things. I developed a contempt for some of them beyond anything I have felt for any other public figures. They were inflicting such damage on our society during those years, and felt nothing but overweening pride in themselves for having the power to do it. The politicians, on the other hand, although a lot of them were little men pursuing mistaken policies, had far more sense of responsibility. They took an altogether less piggily self-interested view of society. They were doing the best they could in difficult situations, and this made them aware of their own inadequacies. In private, at least, the politicians, unlike the trade union leaders, talked turkey with us, not bullshit.

This Week covered not only high politics but social problems – health, housing, transport, education and the rest. I made what were often, in effect, documentary programmes about such matters, thinly disguised as current affairs programmes. For each of them I did some conscientious preparation, hiring acknowledged experts as consultants whose task was not only to point me to the best materials and check the accuracy of the programme but also to give me tutorials on the main issues. I became quite well informed about the condition of England. Altogether, working on *This Week* gave me a massive education about Britain and much of the world. From my present standpoint, however, I still had a lot to learn. I had not yet grasped the connection between markets and political freedom, or even between markets and economic efficiency, so I was much more of a socialist then than I am now. Nearly all of us working on the programme were socialists of some sort, and in most cases publicly so. I had recently stood for parliament, twice, as a Labour candidate. My fellow reporter, Desmond Wilcox, had come from the *Daily Mirror*, and was a populist socialist. The most frequent of our outside contributors were James Cameron, the best loved left-wing journalist in the country, and Paul Johnson, Editor of the *New Statesman*. When we wanted to call in a specialist we used the experts on the staff of *The Observer*, the Sunday newspaper of the left. Our formulation to ourselves of what we were trying to do was to interest the readership of the *Daily Mirror* in the content of *The Guardian*. Given all that, I assumed that sooner or later a Conservative newspaper would blow the whistle on us, but none ever did. It has to be said that we were much more even-handed and objective in those days than broadcasters are today. Our professional ethics were quite different: all of us would have considered it unacceptable to spin our presentation of events in the direction of our own opinions, whether individually or as a group. Even so, and inevitably, our opinions did influence us, not so much in what we said as in the subjects we regarded as interesting, and chose to cover. But then, as now, people further to the left of us believed that the capitalist class was manipulating the public's perception of politics through the media, which was flatly contrary to our direct experience – and ours was the most-watched current affairs programme on television. Never in all my years in television did anyone from outside the working team of any programme I worked on try to exercise political influence over it, or try to suggest what it should say, or what questions it should raise. We would have sent them packing if they had. Then, as today, the bias that actually existed among programme-makers was predominantly left-of-centre.

The only Conservative on *This Week* was its presenter Brian Connell, a person of brutishly right-wing views who was, however, good at the job. For some reason he became convinced that I not only wanted to supplant him in it but was trying to. So frightened of me did he become that he tried to get me dropped from the programme. There was a double irony in this. First, Cyril Bennett and Peter Morley had already sounded me out about whether I would like his job, and I had said No, because it would require me to be in the programme every week. Second, they had then decided to drop him anyway. They were thoroughgoingly professional in their attitudes, few people more so, and they appreciated Brian's skills, but he grossly and grievously abused their goodwill. Each time he lost a professional disagreement with them, he would go around slagging them off to other people as 'those two Hebrews' and 'those Israelites'. It shocked everyone. And of course it got back to them. In spite of their and my alienation I played a key role in getting Brian's contract renewed for another year. I did it because I could see no one available who would do the job as well as he did it – I had suggested Robin Day, and Cyril and Peter had tried to get him, but the attempt failed. Typical of the absurdities of office politics (in which I have all my life refused to involve myself) is that during his last year Brian Connell, sensing correctly that there was imminent danger of his being sacked, made extreme efforts to get me dropped from the programme, when in fact it was only because I had turned his job down and then fought to retain him in it that he was there at all. His behaviour towards me was so treacherous that when his contract came up again for renewal I made no move to save him, and he was finally dropped.

I now behaved as Cyril and Peter had: I acknowledged that Brian was superb at his job, but I found him personally intolerable. The programme carried on without a presenter at all – neither I nor anyone else took over Connell's role. A decision was made to give showing things happening priority over talking about them, and to bring in the necessary minimum of talk as an off-screen voice-over. For the rest of Brian Connell's life he told anyone who would listen that I had destroyed his television career. And he could never again talk to me straight, or even look me in the eye.

Over the years a lot of interesting people worked for *This Week*, and it retained the biggest audiences of any current affairs programme on television. Overlapping with me was Robert Kee, the best reporter I ever knew, and an unusually attractive man. Either shortly before or after me were Jeremy Thorpe, later to be leader of the Liberal Party; Michael Heseltine, later to be deputy prime minister; and Ludovic Kennedy, the country's leading exposer of miscarriages of justice. When it came to a talent for the medium of television itself, the most gifted was Cyril Bennett, who emerged as the undisputed leader of the programme. With characteristic wit Peter Morley said to me years later, talking of their duumvirate: 'I flapped and Cyril flew.' Cyril seemed to know with unerring rightness which stories to go after, and when, and how much screen time to devote to each one, and which reporter to allot to it, and which director. He knew when to leave them alone to get on with the job and when to interfere to improve what they were doing. I have never known anyone with such a gift for thinking creatively in terms peculiar to the television medium itself. I was once in a cutting room having just returned from some dictatorship with a heap of film shot under draconian restrictions, and was finding it impossible to put together in a shape that was coherent and at the same time illustrated the things I wanted to say. It was transmission day, so I faced a crisis. In desperation I asked Cyril to come and look at the film. He told me that another crisis had just blown up which required him to stay at his desk to receive an urgent telephone call. Without moving he said: 'Tell me what footage you've got. Describe it to me.'

I did.

Then he said: 'What do you want to say?'

I told him.

'Well,' he said, 'don't start with what you intended as your establishing shot, start with such-and-such a shot, because that can be made to support another point about so-and-so that you wanted to make. And if you begin your commentary with that point instead you can appear to move naturally from there to such-and-such a point, which would be well supported by the last piece of footage you mentioned. After that you can easily go to ...' and so he went on. In pure imagination he cut my chaotic heap of film to match what I wanted to say without having seen any of it or been to the country concerned. I went back to the cutting room and did what he suggested, and it all worked. I was thought to be good at that sort of thing myself, but Cyril was in a completely different class from me.

He was a Cockney from the East End, with the classic accent and little formal education, and he was almost embarrassingly ugly, like a bulky black toad. Although he was highly strung he was tough, and his toughness was real and not just a protective front. He was effortlessly funny. According to him he had an archetypal Jewish mother, who became a character in all our lives.

'Cyril, I worry about you. When are you going to get a proper job?'

'I've got a proper job, Mum.'

'You tell me you work in television, but I never see you.'

'I don't appear on the screen.'

'Do you operate the cameras?'

'No.'

'Or the lighting?'

'No.'

'Or the sound?'

'No.'

'Do you look after the studios?'

'None of those things.'

'Are you a scriptwriter, then?'

'No.'

'Well what else is there?'

'I've explained to you what I do, Mum, but you never seem to understand.'

'You're right, Cyril. I don't understand. None of it sounds like work to me. You don't do anything anyone can put their finger on. You can't be very important. I know they're paying you well, but that's because it's television. It won't last. I'd be happier if you got a proper job.'

Cyril taught me more about television than anyone else ever did. I had run a successful series myself, so his teachings were masterclasses, and they raised my skills from a decent level to something higher. Making television programmes of quality can be done only with experience. But the matter is one on which most people are like Cyril's mother: they do not understand what is involved, even after it has been explained to them. When, after Cyril's death, I was awarded the silver medal of the Royal Television Society for a series of my own, it was to him that I owed it more than to anyone else. If I got into serious difficulties with a programme I would sometimes think: 'What would Cyril do?' During the years when I worked for him I developed a feeling akin to love for him, for he was a warm and remarkable human being. He died young, in his forties, by falling from a window. There were suspicions of suicide, and the newspapers speculated to that effect, but when I looked into it seriously I concluded that what happened was almost certainly an accident. That was also the coroner's verdict. Cyril, one of the most influential people in my life, leads a colourful afterlife in my memory.

A specifically television personality in a quite different way, also on *This Week* in my time, was David Frost. With *This Week* he was not successful. He arrived as a trainee, not having worked in television before; and it soon became evident that although he had talent it was not for what we were doing. When his first independent film was made on location, featuring a comprehensive school in the Midlands, Cyril came to me quietly and said that David's material was unusable. Would I be willing to go back to the school and remake the programme? He would say to David and the headmistress, and anyone else who asked, that the film stock had been defective, and that David was now tied up on another project (which Cyril saw to it that he was), so there would be no embarrassment for anyone. At the end of David's period of probation he was dropped. Yet within a few years he had acquired more fame and money through television than any of us. He had found out what he was good at. And, most importantly, he was the first of us to act on the perception that the commercial value of what we, the programme-makers, were doing was several times what we were being paid for it. We were all freelance, but while the rest of us worked on a series of short-term contracts, David turned himself into a production company, and sold services from one company to another at something like their commercial value. Of course he always needed to be sure that there was a demand for what he was offering. That made him a crowd-pleaser; and I have never cared for his programmes. But he handled himself astutely. Other performers, including me, benefited from this financially, because he pushed fees up to a more realistic level for all of us.

The way of life that went with being a nationally networked performer on ITV was enjoyable for a young man with the energy for it. During the first ten or fifteen years of commercial television, before the accountants moved in, the companies behaved as if they had a licence to print money; and those of us who were in the public eye, and therefore most in demand for jobs, lived the life of Riley – not on our fees but on the perks we got. Our expense accounts seemed almost unlimited: the companies told us behind their hands, but explicitly, that they would rather give us money in the form of expenses, which were tax-free to them, than as fees, which were not. (I suspect also, looking back, that it made it easier for them to keep a tighter lid on the salaries they were paying to their other employees.) In addition to out-of-pocket expenses, I spent half my working-in-television time abroad, staying in the best hotels in whatever country I was in, and wining and dining my contacts there in the best restaurants (and doing the same again when they came to London). I hired chauffeur-driven cars uninhibitedly, always flew first class, and would hire private planes if the situation called for it, as often it did in Africa. Social invitations poured in for no better reason than that I appeared on television. There were only two channels, so audiences for each were much bigger than they are now, and performers better known for doing the same things.

It never occurred to me to think that any of this had made me special. In fact it never occurred to me to think that what was on television mattered particularly. I seldom saw it myself, and working in it was always something I would rather not have been doing. If I had not needed to earn money I would have immersed myself in writing books and in music, theatre, politics, philosophy, and personal relationships, and in freely directed travel of my own choosing. However, given that I had to earn a living, and found myself doing so in television, it was not difficult to enjoy it. It put me in an unusually privileged position to enjoy also the social life of the decade that turned out to be the most socially extravagant of my adult lifetime: the sixties. There were parties galore, and at those given by producers or directors there were beautiful actresses. I went through a phase for some years of having flings with them. I joined the White Elephant, a luxurious restaurant-cum-club in Mayfair aimed at theatre, film and television people and the sort of high-society types who want to mix with them. When London became Swinging London, in the middle and late sixties, there were few parts of it more swinging than clubland round the White Elephant. I have always been blessed with reserves of energy, and during my thirties I took in copious draughts of this life along with my other lives, while still managing to do my work successfully. Apart from freedom and independence there was little more I could have wished for.

There is something classic about my experiencing, in the middle of all this, intimations of mortality. It was as if I woke up one morning to the fact that I was halfway through my life, exactly halfway through the threescore years and ten that I had always thought of as my ration. It had whizzed past, yet I knew that the second half would pass more quickly than the first. However long I might live, death was inevitable. I did not believe in God or an afterlife, so I assumed that this life was all I had. And *this*, I thought, is what I am doing with it. The books I was writing, after *The Democratic Revolution*, were little more than journalism in stiff covers. My love relationships were no more than enjoyable affairs. The world events I was reporting disappeared into nothingness as fast as I reported them. Everything vanished into thin air, nothing stayed, nothing had permanent meaning or value. And looming over it all, bound to come, was death, the permanent nothingness of everything. I became inwardly distraught at the thought.

Within this overall perception there were some especially nasty moments. For instance, having landed in Zanzibar for the third time, I was walking down the steps of the plane when I was overwhelmed and frozen in my tracks by a sense of *déjà-vu*. In that moment I felt I was going for ever round and round a merry-go-round, and was overcome by a sense of pointlessness. I knew I had to stop. I knew I had to get off the merry-go-round.

As far as television was concerned, my first reaction was to change the subject matter I dealt with, away from public affairs and towards the crises of private life – no doubt because I was going through one myself. I made documentaries about alcoholism, drug addiction, prostitution, abortion, adultery, homosexuality, psychopathic violence. My concern in all of them was to put the unadorned truth about such matters on television for the first time. I treated them with unsensational candour, which had never been done before in broadcasting. As a result, I found myself among the people who spearheaded the change in public attitudes that characterized the sixties. In response to the pleading of my publisher I turned the research I had done for two programmes on male and female homosexuality into a book, *One in Twenty*, which attracted great attention and was later credited with helping to bring about the change in the law that decriminalized homosexuality.

Alongside these programmes, to which Cyril Bennett always gave the necessary support, I had been having a long-running dispute with him about the range of *This Week*'s coverage. I thought it unduly narrow. As I put it to him, if the Italian prime minister visited London we treated it as an important event, whereas if Stravinsky presented us with a new opera we took no notice of it; yet the Italian prime minister and his visit would be soon forgotten, whereas Stravinsky would long be famous, and his opera would go on being performed in London – not only performed but written about in newspapers and books, and discussed by broadcasters. We ought to treat it as news when it was new, I said. In fact, a new opera by Stravinsky was more worthwhile news than most other news. The doings of great artists in general were among the most important human affairs, and we should treat them as such on television. I did not mean we should reduplicate what the critics and reviewers were doing: I meant we should provide understanding and interpretation in the same way as we did with other important events. Treatment of the arts as important news (as distinct from reviewing and gossip) were almost nowhere to be found in the media at that time, and I wanted us to pioneer it on *This Week*. Cyril was inclined to agree with the things I said, but I got the impression he felt personally inadequate to take responsibility for it, and hung back.

At just that moment, because of *This Week*'s success, it was offered an extra fortnightly slot as an offshoot of the main programme. The executives who made the offer envisaged it as extra time in which *This Week* could develop its treatment of the sort of affairs it normally dealt with. Instead, Cyril offered it to me as a regular series in which I could apply *This Week*'s treatment to the arts. I had not, in fact, wanted the arts to be ghettoized in this way – part of my point was that they should be treated alongside everything else – but I knew this was the only chance I was likely to get. The series was launched with the title *This Week in the Arts* (in spite of being fortnightly). It was the first series that I both ran and presented on the screen. A couple of years later, when I regarded myself (mistakenly) as having left television, the BBC's best producer of arts discussions on radio, Philip French, invited me to launch a weekly series on BBC's Radio 3 applying the same approach. I did, and to underscore the identity of approach we called it *The Arts This Week*. It was so successful that it carried on after I left it, and ran uninterruptedly – through two changes of title – for decades. The approach it represented is now one that has long been taken for granted on both radio and television.

From the time when the inevitability and soonness of my death got their fangs into me I had been struggling with demons internally. Although this was a terrible experience for me, it was good for my work as a broadcaster. It shifted my sense of what was important away from the public and political towards the individual and private – the inward, the personal, the artistic – and gave my work an intensity it had not had before. Even so, I still chafed under the constraints of having to do this kind of work at all. I wanted to live a life that was directed from within – especially now, with these almost overpowering experiences and emotions going on inside me. Specifically, I felt a need to channel the high-tension current that was running through me into a novel. I did not know what novel, but I knew I needed to write one, and this meant giving myself up to thinking about it without the perpetual distractions of having to do other work. I had money enough to live on for a year or more, and I hoped to be able to write the novel in that time. If not, I was sufficiently in demand as a broadcaster to get short-term work that would see me through. I made the decision that from now on money-earning would have to be subordinated to my needs as a writer, not the other way round. I would get by financially as best I could, as I needed to and must: I would have no more contracts. I was now in the second half of my life. If ever I was going to do the sort of work that mattered most to me I had to make a start on it now, and give it my all.

I told Cyril Bennett that when my current contract came to an end I would not renew it, and that I could not give him any more fixed undertakings to be available for *This Week*. His reaction was first astonishment, then incredulity. He saw me as chucking away a successful career, and thought I was doing something crazy. He became concerned for me, worried about me, and tried to talk me out of it. He offered me higher fees, and then other inducements to stay. Each time I declined one of these offers he raised it.

This is something I experienced with other companies too. When the word went round that I was no longer attached to *This Week*, other television companies approached me with offers; and when I declined them their first response usually was to raise them. For more than a year after I left *This Week*, Cyril went on trying to persuade me to come back and improved his offer each time. The result was that when – between one and two years later, financially cleaned out, and with my novel no more than a third written – I was forced back into television, I commanded fees between two and three times as high as they had been when I left. They would not have reached anything like this level if I had stayed. One or two of my colleagues suspected me of playing a poker game to get my fees up to the very highest level they would go to, but the truth is that no such thing ever entered my mind, and it took me by surprise. In fact I had expected the opposite to happen: I thought that once I stopped appearing on television and stepped out of the rat-race my market value would fall. Indeed, I still believe that this is what would have happened over a longer period, after offers stopped coming in. At the time, though, people were unable to accept that I was turning my back on television success merely to write a novel. (*'You can't just be writing a novel – what else are you doing?'*) To them it seemed so disproportionate – eccentric, crackpot, unserious. I can count on the fingers of one hand acquaintances who were genuinely understanding and expressed approval.

5

Cutting Free

The exhilaration that swept through me when I cut loose made me feel new. It was as if I was able to take a deep breath for the first time. I could not understand why I had not done it before. To be free for as far ahead as my eye could see was indescribable. I could be myself now all the time instead of spending half of it doing what other people wanted. When, at some distant point in an unforeseeable future, I would have to turn aside to earn money, it would be precisely that, a turning aside: never again would I put my real work aside for half my life in order to do something else. This attitude led me, when the time came, to look for ways of being paid to do what I already wanted to do. And when eventually I did return to broadcasting it was as a paid way of pursuing some of my most intense interests in philosophy and the arts. Because of the nature of this break, I was to have, in effect, two broadcasting careers, of which the second had a markedly different character from the first. And it is for the second that I am now remembered.

Meanwhile there was freedom, and the gradual creation of a new way of life. I had been free before during my regular periods away from *This Week*, but then I had been tied by invisible strings. I had felt myself under obligation to watch the programme each week to keep abreast of what it was doing; and I was frequently telephoned by Cyril Bennett about forthcoming programmes – not only my own but also, because he used me as a consultant, some of the others. It was never fully possible for *This Week* to be absent from my thoughts, and I always had a sense of partial responsibility for it. Always, too, there was a rapidly approaching date when I knew that – however deeply immersed I might have become in my real work, and however well it might be going – I would have to abandon it for another six weeks. All this ceased. I really was now free.

It took a while for a working pattern to emerge that was motivated solely from within, unpressured by external demands. Once it had formed itself, it was to stay with me for the rest of my life. It was rooted not only in my passions but also in my metabolism. I would work at home in the mornings, and never consider doing anything other than work, by which I meant writing for publication. When eventually I needed to eat again (having always eaten breakfast) I would leave my desk and go out. This gave me a long break in the middle of the day, with physical movement and fresh air as well as food. While I was out I would do the things everyone needs to do, like shopping, going to the post office, the cleaners, and so on. When I got back home I would deal with that day's mail and telephoning. Then, with luck, I would get a second wind for writing, and do an hour or two from about five onwards. Then I would go out again for the evening. Having, usually, been alone all day (and content to be so) I would have a compelling need for company in the evening, and also a need to be out and about. I never, not even once in a month, spent an evening alone at home – which means, among other things, that I almost never watched television, except perhaps an early evening news bulletin before leaving home. Most evenings I went to a live performance of some kind – concerts, opera, theatre – and had supper out afterwards. Seldom was I in bed before one o'clock. My nightlife was not just a diversion and relaxation: it was an essential part of my most basic nourishment in life, indispensable to me in a way I can never properly express to others. While I was doing it, all my libido went into it. It was far from being only music and theatre, indispensable as those were to me: it embraced also my love life, and some of my closest friendships.

I never set an alarm clock, unless I were catching a plane, and never subjected myself to fixed hours. I would have found that abhorrent. I needed a lot of sleep, and would let myself sleep every morning until I woke naturally, which was never until after nine o'clock. I would then get straight out of bed into a warm bath, and lie in it clearing my mind about the writing I was going to do that morning. Usually at this stage I would be either groping for an underlying form, a shape, a meaning that would be exhibited but not stated, or else formulating some of the most elusive sentences. The bath would be followed by breakfast (orange juice, cereal and coffee) and then, still in a bathrobe, I would sit at my desk until enticed away by the first pangs of hunger. When that happened I would shave, dress, and go out. My mind was always at its clearest and sharpest in the morning, and because of that I would have considered it a waste to spend any part of the morning on anything other than writing, or occasionally the most difficult reading. Everything else could be done after lunch, including most of my reading. By dealing with each day's post on the day I received it I reduced to a minimum the amount of time and thought it required. I never had to remember to answer a letter, or pay a bill, or make a telephone call. And the mail never piled up. I made it a rule never to waste time thinking about any such thing twice. I kept my mind free of clutter, in so far as I could.

Ever since I began this way of life, people have said how self-disciplined I must be to sit at my desk every morning and write, and to deal with each day's post on the day I receive it; but the truth is that both of these activities are pure self-indulgence. I deal with the post immediately because that minimizes the amount of both time and thought it takes. All the alternatives are worse. And I write every day because I find it more deeply fulfilling than any other activity. As Noël Coward said: 'Work is far more fun than fun.' This is true for me provided the work I am doing is work of my own choosing. It is what I want to do more than I want to do anything else, and therefore there is no question of my having to force myself to do it. People who assume that it requires self-discipline must also assume, if only unconsciously, that I do not really want to do it. It requires no self-discipline at all. On the contrary, it used to require self-discipline not to do it: I had to force myself to turn away from it in order to do other things. If I go for more than a short time without writing I feel disturbed, like a habitual smoker having to live without cigarettes. For me, writing is a compelling need, a necessity. I could speculate on the reasons for this, but it would be only speculation.

I do not work *every* day. Like most people, I take days off, and sometimes longer breaks. I have always been a devotee of generous holidays: I find I get more (and better) work done in a year if I take six or eight weeks of it off than if I fill the year with work. A holiday for me needs to be abroad: if I take time off in Britain I may enjoy myself, but it does not count as a holiday. Full refreshment of spirit comes to me only from being in radically different surroundings, with everyone around me talking a foreign language. Even time off in the United States is not quite like a holiday: I feel too at home there.

The number of consecutive days on which I enjoy working is usually about ten, but whenever I want a break I take it. Then, more often than not, after a day or two I want to go back to work, so I do. At each point I am behaving spontaneously, doing what I most want to do, motivated entirely from within. Sometimes I need a change of scene, so I go somewhere else. I am given to taking unplanned breaks in not-too-distant towns or villages where I have never been before, and looking around them at leisure. I like weekends in attractive small towns, for instance cathedral towns, where there is usually a nice old hotel offering 'bargain weekend breaks'. If I carry on my basic work for too long in one place I start to feel in a rut – everything begins to seem over-familiar and stale – so I keep myself refreshed by having long periods of work in other places: writers' retreats, Oxbridge colleges, locations abroad. Whatever the work calls for, I do, and then organize the rest of my life round it: I do not, in my day-to-day life, compromise between my work's requirements and other things. However, since I never, or almost never, devote most of the hours of any given day to working, there is plenty of time for all the other things. There is no question of conflict in the evenings because I find that if I work after about eight o'clock I cannot sleep, so I never want to do that.

My body's metabolism makes me an owl, not a lark. I detest being woken artificially in the morning. Not only is it hateful at the time, the fogginess it causes never leaves my head entirely for the rest of the day, which is therefore ruined as far as good writing is concerned. Not until the following day will I be at my normal best again. Sleep is the petrol on which my life runs, and it has never been an option for me to lengthen my working day by forcing myself to get up earlier. In any case, it would never have been possible to live the nightlife that was so necessary to me without going to bed late; and if one does that, and also needs a lot of sleep, there is no alternative but to start late in the morning. A friend of mine once asked Rebecca West, who wrote some of the most disconcertingly good prose of the twentieth century, how she managed to retain all her mental vigour and clarity at the age of ninety, and she replied: 'Never let them wake you.'

When I became an MP and had to absorb Westminster's working hours into my own I found the fit an easy one. The debating chamber's minimum-of-eight-hours day began at two thirty and finished, on average, at midnight. Carrying on indefinitely after that was not a problem for me. On the other hand I did everything I could to avoid morning engagements, and declined absolutely to serve on any committee or attend any meeting that convened before eleven o'clock. This never caused problems. I did all my most difficult writing and reading at home in the mornings, and was able to do what other people called work at any other hour of the day or night – committee work, discussion meetings, decision-making, drafting, speechifying, everything involving my secretary, making telephone calls, travelling, whatever it might be. It made for a long day, but it was a highly varied and interesting one, and included the most essential thing of all, a morning of writing at home. It was during my first year as a Member of Parliament that I produced the finally published draft of my novel *The Story of All Our Lives*. Also, while I was an MP, I wrote the first edition of *The Philosophy of Schopenhauer*, and made the 15-part television series *Men of Ideas* (later called *Talking Philosophy*) and turned it into a book.

The first draft of *The Story of All Our Lives* had been my dominant preoccupation in the second half of my thirties, the years after I left television. It took me four years to write, though while I was working on it I also wrote another book called *Aspects of Wagner*, published in 1968. Even so, writing *The Story of All Our Lives* was more demanding than I had bargained for, and made a mockery of my hope when starting it that I might be able to finish it in a year. The reason for this lay not in the writing but in what the writing demanded of me, which was facing death. It was to face death, to face it and master my fear of it, and come to terms with it, that I had left television. And the only way I could make myself do that – keep myself involved in it, not let myself evade – was to write this book. What took me so long about it was coming to terms with death, in so far as I ever did. When I first published the book it was called *Facing Death*.

Many people imagine that a writer's work consists of putting the words down on paper. They think that if one can find a quicker way of doing that one will be able to write more. This view sees technology as the decisive factor: the word processor, the dictating machine, the typewriter. For my kind of writing, at least, this is entirely mistaken. For me, nearly all the labour of writing consists of finding out what the right words to put down are. I do not start out with them, I finish up with them; and then only when I am lucky. It involves digging down deep into my own feelings, imagination, thoughts, memories, and so on, and finding what is really there at those deepest levels, then puzzling it through, teasing it out, and confronting it, experiencing it to the full while at the same time evaluating it with critical emotional intelligence. Then comes the whole process of putting what I have thus arrived at into words, and this again is likely to be difficult, sometimes impossible. The whole process is one of struggle. It demands everything I have, and by the end of the longest, most exhausting day I seldom find myself with more than three hundred words. If these appear to run fluently, and are easy to read, it is because I have slaved with all the skill I can command to make them so. The notion that if something reads easily it must have been written easily is pure illusion. As Sheridan said, easy writing is hard reading. People who know me personally often say that when they read my writing they hear my voice saying the words. 'It's exactly the way you talk,' they say. If only that could be true. My writings are indeed my true voice, but they come from levels of myself that are not accessible to me directly, but only through the processes I have described. I suspect that the need to make contact with my true self is my chief motive for writing. It would be impossible for me to think straight into my printed prose, or to talk the way I write.

Before settling down as a writer I used my newfound freedom to do some things that were unconnected with writing. For six weeks I knocked alone round the Middle East, in the Lebanon, Syria, Jordan and Egypt, staying in the walled city of Jerusalem when it was still part of Jordan, and seeing many wonders, from the Sphinx to Crusader castles. Then I spent three months studying musical composition, with the composer Anthony Milner as my teacher. Only when a need to put this aside and turn to writing asserted itself did I do so.

The Story of All Our Lives embodies the inescapable need I felt in the prime of my life to confront my own death. Writing it was the only way I could compel myself to do this. It was a slow process, possible one stage at a time, and each stage difficult. Contrary to all the plans I had made, I seemed to myself to have made pitifully little progress before the prospect of my finances running out became palpable. I thought at first that I would solve my financial problem by making a few radio programmes, because radio, while being more intellectually satisfying than television, is less demanding of emotional commitment, indeed of the personality as a whole. I did a lot of broadcasting for the BBC's Radio 3 about the arts, and tried to do it at minimum sacrifice to myself, reviewing plays, operas and concerts that I would have gone to in any case, and reading books I wanted to read, by authors I wanted to meet, and with whom my programme gave me the opportunity of discussing their work. It was because of my intensity of involvement that these programmes came off as well as they did. 'You sound so *interested*, and that comes over,' was the standard comment. The snag was that radio paid only a fraction of what television paid, so I needed to do a great deal more of it to earn the same amount of money. I tried to cut down on this by making, reluctantly, a few television programmes. So – in a crab-like, sideways movement – I did, after all, return to television, though for a long time only sporadically.

Facing death imposed on me a need to come to some sort of understanding with life. Was it going, in the end, to mean nothing at all to have lived, or did life have some significance beyond itself? If it had, what could any such significance be? I never *assumed* that life had a meaning. That is wholly illegitimate, the starting point of much if not most religious belief. I just *hoped* that it did, and in that spirit I desperately searched for one. What made the search indeed desperate was the inevitability of death.

In this search I used – used up – all the resources of insight and understanding that I possessed at that time. These included such understanding as I had acquired from my years of studying philosophy. I had taken an Oxford degree in it, followed by a year of postgraduate work in Oxford, and another at Yale. Since then my knowledge of it had never ceased to expand through reflection, reading, and discussion with others. Among my contemporaries, two of my closest friends had become, while in their thirties, professors of philosophy: Ninian Smart and Bernard Williams. Among older generations the two people I regarded as the most gifted philosophers alive, Karl Popper and Bertrand Russell, had become my friends. So philosophy was a living, active part of my life. Yet it seemed radically inadequate to the task I was now trying to use it for. All it seemed good for was to help me clarify my thinking. Most professionals would have said that this was all it could do anyway, and that this was what made it valuable. But I wanted more: I wanted penetration, insight, illumination. I thought perhaps I had been too young when, as a student, I had read those so-called masterpieces. Perhaps if I reread them now, from the level that the writing of *The Story of All Our Lives* had carried me up to, I would get more out of them. I conceived a desire, which became overmastering, to reread the modern classics, at least those of them written in English. Having read nearly all of them once already, and therefore knowing what I was taking on, I calculated that I could do it in less than a year of full-time work.

It was in search of a way of being paid to do this that I had the idea of broadcasting a long series about contemporary British philosophy. At that time there was no prospect of any such series being broadcast on television, so it would have to be on radio. The intellectual level of the BBC's Radio 3 was higher then than it is now, and I had already done a good deal of broadcasting on it, including having my own series about the arts. Even so, it was without any great confidence that I put the proposal to the head of the network, P. H. Newby (who was also a novelist, the first to win the Booker Prize). To my joy he accepted it. I was launched into a new stage of life that was to develop and become essential to my future, namely producing not only books about ideas but also programmes about ideas on radio and television. The radio series was broadcast in due course, and was then published as a book called *Modern British Philosophy*. It was eventually issued as a paperback by Oxford University Press.

An unexpected side-effect of my making this series was that I was invited to become a lecturer in philosophy at Balliol College, Oxford. The college was in need of someone to fill a two-term gap between two permanent appointments, and one of the dons there thought, as a result of his contacts with me, that I would be good at teaching. For two terms I became an Oxford don, giving nine tutorials a week. To minimize the necessary toing and froing between my home in London and Oxford I arranged that all the tutorials should be held on two consecutive days, Monday and Tuesday, so I spent only one night a week at Balliol. It was many years since I had done any face-to-face teaching, so I had to start the preparation of many of my tutorials with a clean sheet – the more so in that they were on a wide range of subjects within philosophy, and by no means all of them connected with my personal interests. By the time I got home on Tuesday I was drained, and would spend Wednesday recovering. Then the work of preparing for the next week's tutorials would begin. Nine hours of teaching became almost a full-time occupation – and, I have to say, a highly rewarding one. Rarely have I absorbed so much philosophy in so short a time. One learns more from teaching than from studying.

The preparation of my programmes, and then turning them into a book, involved me in active co-operation with most of the leading philosophers in the Britain of that day. I was not only reading – and in most cases rereading – their work, I was discussing it with them personally, asking them exactly what they meant by this or that passage, pressing them for further clarifications. I was also putting to them criticisms of their work made by their colleagues, and taking issue with them about some of their replies. This built up an altogether deeper and more assured understanding of their work than I had possessed before. And I felt myself unable to escape the conclusion that, in the hands of its professional practitioners, philosophy had taken a wrong turning. This conviction was strengthened by the experience of teaching. The only philosopher who was currently producing new work in Britain that offered deep, original insights into non-linguistic first-order problems of the highest importance was Karl Popper. Others, even good ones, were doing second-order philosophy: they were writing *about* concepts and logical connections rather than using them in the search for solutions to first-order problems. They were like a skilful carpenter who has some very good tools but uses them only on one another – perpetually strengthening his hammers, sharpening his chisels, greasing his saws, re-aligning his planes: he is using his skills and his tools all the time, but never brings them to bear on what they ought to be used for.

As a result, nearly all the most exciting developments in thought that were happening at that time were happening outside philosophy. This led me to move on to two parallel tasks. One was to present a new television series, *Something To Say*, devoted to putting before the public ideas that were bringing about large-scale changes in whole fields of thought. I made about forty of these programmes, and they featured such figures as Hayek, Marcuse, Galbraith, Isaiah Berlin, and several Nobel Prize winners in the sciences, not to mention the leading intellectuals among present and former politicians. Each programme was an hour long, and consisted of discussion between only two people, with me as chairman. The other task was to write a book about the philosophy of Karl Popper, the only contemporary who I thought was publishing new ideas of fundamental significance in philosophy. It was the first book to be published about his work (there are now many, and in many languages). In the early 1970s I pursued these tasks simultaneously. The programmes went on the air in 1972-73, and the book, *Popper*, came out in 1973. I was disappointed that Thames Television was so small-minded as to refuse me permission to turn *Something To Say* into a book. It was one of several books that escaped my grasp over the years, books that I envisaged clearly, and had a desire to write or edit, but for one reason never came into existence.

Throughout the whole of my life I have been trying to understand life itself. By my late thirties the need to find significance in it was almost overwhelming. Behind this, of course, lay always the fear of death. So the search for meaning was far from being only a mental activity, and even farther from being just a philosophical one. If anything, it was rooted in animal biology – an attachment to life at any cost. It involved the whole of me, passionately: heart, head, senses, feelings, guts, everything. It was existential, not intellectual. Nevertheless I did want philosophy, as a part of this whole, to come into it: I wanted whatever sense of significance I could manage to achieve, however arrived at, to be such as would withstand critical scrutiny: I did not want it to be just an unsupported faith, a matter of assertion, unable to meet rational argument. So by my early forties I was looking desperately for an approach to philosophy which, without forfeiting its legitimacy as philosophy, would go beyond the narrow limits embraced by its current practitioners – including even Karl Popper, who agreed with me that existential questions were meaningful and fundamental, but said he had no worthwhile conjectures to offer in answer to them. In the end, to my surprise, I found in the philosophy of Schopenhauer what I was looking for. But before I did, I went through a dark night of the soul. The strange thing is that Schopenhauer was the only philosopher whose name was known to every educated person but whom I had not read. My life was changed by my discovery of him.

I wanted to immerse myself unhurriedly in Schopenhauer's thought, and get everything out of it that I could. The only way I could envisage doing this was to write a book about it. I discussed my intention with Isaiah Berlin, who had become a friend after his appearance in *Something To Say*, and was the most creatively imaginative, if not the most scholarly, of historians of ideas. At first, mistaking my motives, he said I deserved a high intellectual reputation but he did not think this was the way to acquire it. ('*Who's going to read a book about Schopenhauer?*') He tried to talk me out of the project. However, increasing my reputation had nothing to do with my motives for writing, and I was unbudgeable. When he realized this he changed tack completely, and suggested that I apply for a visiting fellowship to All Souls College, Oxford. It would be the ideal place, he said, to start work on such a book, and he would support my application. I applied, and the college took me. Afterwards I discovered that because of the *Something To Say* series, of which Isaiah had been an addicted follower, he had represented me to All Souls as the Diderot of the age, a person who was giving the most important contemporary thinkers, across the whole range of subject matter, a means of communicating their ideas to a wider public. This was a startlingly grandiose way of describing what I had been doing, but I had unquestionably been doing it, and it was because Isaiah saw it in those terms that I became a member of All Souls.

I moved into residence in September 1973. I decided that before starting the actual writing of my book I needed to reread

Kant as well as Schopenhauer, so I settled down to do that. My life could scarcely have moved farther away from what it had been only a few years before as a television reporter, rushing round the world in aeroplanes, living out of suitcases in foreign hotel rooms. In ways that some of my former colleagues did not understand (*'He's become an academic!'*) I was profoundly happy, having been brought to what I was doing by the operation of forces inside myself instead of responding to external demands. The college gave me complete freedom to use my time as I wished, and I could scarcely have enjoyed it more. The move to All Souls seemed to me the most worthwhile change in my life up to that time, because it was a change to both freedom and security. But it was to prove shorter-lived than I expected.

For several years I had been so absorbed in other things that my parliamentary ambitions had been losing their hold on me. My values had changed so much since my young socialist days that I no longer thought of the most important human problems as having political solutions. When I was asked – partly because of my frequent appearances on television current affairs programmes – to let my name go forward for consideration as a parliamentary candidate, I usually said: 'Not yet.' When I did let it go forward it never went far, because my rivals were actively organizing support, whereas I never was. I had stopped going to political meetings. The only way I was still in touch with the Labour Party, apart from through those of my friends who were active in it (several were MPs now) was by going to the annual party conferences. I found these not only interesting but fun. Over the years I had made some good friends at them who travelled there from quite distant parts of the country, and seeing them became my reason for going.

At the party conference of 1972, the year before I went to All Souls, I met a trade union official called Harry Robertson. Something about me rang a bell with him. He was much taken with the fact that I had come from a working-class background in

Hoxton and then gone to a public school and Oxford. He had received little education in spite of his obvious intelligence; and I think he saw my life as representing what he would like to have done himself. He told me I ought to be a Labour MP. I said I was going to have a try one day.

One day ... a knock came on my door at All Souls, and there in the doorway stood Harry Robertson with a piece of paper in his hand. It had taken him a long time to track me down, and he was now in a hurry. The MP for the safe Labour seat of Leyton, Patrick Gordon Walker, had announced that he was not going to stand at the next general election. Although that election was not expected for another year or more, his local party was selecting his successor straight away. In fact, nominations for the selection conference were about to close. Harry had persuaded the branch of his trade union that was affiliated to the Leyton Constituency Labour Party that I would be the right man for them to nominate, but of course my agreement was required for this, and that was what he had come to obtain. He made it clear that the constituency was not in his gift or the gift of his union. But he thought that their support would at least result in my being considered.

Obviously this was a matter that needed careful consideration from me. I could see that Harry was trying to bounce me into it – that was, I learnt later, his habitual style, his usual way of trying to bring about what he thought ought to happen – but this in itself was not a problem for me. I could sign the paper now and withdraw at any time I chose before the selection conference. Harry stressed this himself, as a way of trying to persuade me when he found me undecided. So I signed the paper, and in subsequent days sank into deep reflection about what to do.

Seventeen years earlier I had returned to England from the United States with the full-blooded intention of making a life for myself writing books and being a Member of Parliament. If the present opportunity had presented itself to me at that time I would have leapt at it, grabbed it with both hands. It would have been exactly what I wanted. But now, I realized, there was an element of confusion in my attitudes. When I was younger, in addition to wanting to be an MP, I had taken it for granted that I would become one; and because I took it for granted I had not subjected the assumption to as much critical appraisal as I ought to have done. Although I was doing less and less about it, I had carried on assuming that it was something that was bound to happen at some future time – almost by itself, so to speak. Well, now it had caught up with me. What was I to do about it?

The fact that I was happy at All Souls was far from being a problem. My visiting fellowship was for only one year anyway, and the next general election was not due until after that, so the two would fit in nice and snug. The real question that confronted me now was, did I want to be an MP? With the choice thrust into my face I really did have a decision to make. I was forty-three, which was already getting on a bit for starting a political career. If I was ever going to do it, I had to get moving. I would never get another chance like this without actively going out and seeking it – which was something I had ceased to do. The more I thought about it, the more my atavistic expectations re-asserted themselves. I had moved a long way from regarding politics as the most important thing in life, but I did not deem it necessary for a politician to take that view of it, or even desirable that he should. Most politicians did other jobs. Many were lawyers with lively practices. Many spent their mornings in the City. Many had their own businesses. Many were prolific journalists. Quite a few wrote books. Some of these categories were represented at All Souls itself, and I was used to meeting such people when they came to visit the college at weekends. I had never supposed that I would have to give up serious writing if I became an MP, and for most of my life I had expected to do both. I had long been experienced in carrying on two professions at the same time. Throughout the years when I had been a television reporter I had also been writing books. Most recently, while presenting *Something To Say*, I had written my book about the philosophy of Karl Popper. In the end, as may have been inevitable from the beginning, I decided to go after the seat at Leyton and, if successful, combine writing books with being a Member of Parliament.

I was invited to Leyton to meet the people who were nominating me. They introduced me to others, in the hope of getting their support. I found all of them pessimistic about my chances of selection. It was in process of being sewn up, they told me, by the leading local political family, whose members were, or had been, councillors, one of them mayor of the borough and chairman of the local party. These people enjoyed widespread loyalty that went back many years, and they were now getting it organized behind their favourite son. All this was true. When it came to the short-listing it was only the fact that I was known to local activists from my television appearances that got my name included on the list of six. Also on the list were the favourite son, two ex-MPs trying to get back into the House of Commons, and a couple of no-hopers. The seat was considered so safe for Labour that everyone regarded the selection conference as nominating the next MP.

When the conference took place, its atmosphere was electric – quite different from that at the selection conference I had attended in Mid-Bedfordshire. I had gone into that expecting to be selected, but I went into this one very unsure. The six of us drew lots for the order in which we made our speeches and answered questions, and after us there was secret voting. I came second on the first ballot. The favourite son came top by quite a long way, but not with an overall majority. This meant that the no-hopers were eliminated and there was a second round of voting. It turned out that the favourite son had received, on the first ballot, all, or nearly all, the votes he was going to get: most of the rest, when redistributed, came to me. It is an unglamorous truth of arithmetic that, provided you survive the first round, however low down in the order you are and however few votes you get, if you are everybody's second choice you win. My vote climbed in the third ballot to reach an overall majority, and I was elected as the candidate.

By that time Leyton was a safe seat, though it had not always been so. It has remained safe ever since. This means that when I was selected I took for granted that I would be MP for Leyton for the rest of my working life. In the normal course of events that would be at least until my late sixties, and perhaps later. So I had, so to speak, arrived; I had reached my goal. Since boyhood I had wanted to write books and be an MP, and now I was solidly positioned for both. I had embarked on the life I had always wanted, the life I had dreamt about in school classrooms.

It pleased me very much to have the prospect of the rest of the academic year in All Souls, not only because I liked being there but because it would give me time to prepare myself for my plunge into the House of Commons. I met the sitting MP, Patrick Gordon Walker (whom I already knew) and got his advice about the job, and the constituency, and also his individual views about local party activists. When he held his next MP's surgery I went with him to the constituency and sat by his side, absorbing everything he was doing. I dunned my MP friends for *dos* and *don'ts* about becoming an MP. These were all valuable, the most immediately so being Tony Crosland's: 'Don't, in the enthusiasm of your first weeks and months, create expectations which it later becomes a bore to fulfil.'

Then, suddenly, events pitchforked me head first into this future. Scarcely had I embarked on what I had expected to be a year of preparation for my new life when the prime minister, Edward Heath, called a snap general election for February 1974, more than a year before he needed to. It turned out to be a disaster for him, as well as being inconvenient for me. Parliament was dissolved and I, having attended only one of Patrick Gordon Walker's surgeries – and having been only five months at All Souls – found myself fighting a general election as the Labour Party's candidate for the safe seat of Leyton.

6

Becoming a Member of Parliament

Walking through the Members' Entrance of the House of Commons for the first time I found myself in a large cloakroom filled with racks of coat hangers, hundreds and hundreds of them, stretching away all round me at eye level like a sea in which I was swimming. Each had a little loop of red ribbon dangling from its crossbar. An attendant in black clothes of a bygone era approached me self-effacingly, peeled my overcoat smoothly off my back, and beckoned me to go with him to be shown my personal coat hanger.

'What's the red ribbon for?' I asked him.

With no change in his expression he said: 'It's to hang your sword from, sir.'

The cliché about one's first day in the House of Commons being like one's first day at a new school is true. I was shown where my locker was, and tried to remember its number. I was shown where the lavatories were. And so on. My nursemaid on this occasion was called not Jennings but Whitehead, Phillip Whitehead, who had briefly been Editor of *This Week* at the end of the sixties, and became a Labour MP in 1970. He was brimming with good advice. 'Never,' he said, 'underestimate the enmity towards you of colleagues in your own party. If your aim is to become Foreign Secretary, the man who can rob you of your life's ambition isn't going to be a Tory. When the Tories are in power there's no question of your being Foreign Secretary. The man who does you down will be the Labour MP who becomes Foreign Secretary instead of you when your party is in power. He's the man who ruins your career. And everyone here understands that.'

The sheer size of the Palace of Westminster – which contains both the House of Commons and the House of Lords – was a revelation to me. Without giving serious thought to it I had imagined it as being on the same sort of scale as, say, the largest Oxford colleges; but that is quite wrong. The multi-storey building covers eight acres, and contains sixteen miles of corridors. Several thousand people work in it: not only all the MPs and peers, with their secretaries and researchers, but the staffs of a complete telephone exchange, a whole postal sorting office, two large libraries, and one of the biggest historical archives in the country, not to mention a substantial engineering and maintenance staff, a big cleaning staff, a big security staff, and a considerable staff of messengers. There is a branch of Her Majesty's Stationery Office, and also the publishing organization that produces *Hansard* every day. When I was there, more than 200 journalists and other media people worked there – *The Times* had its own set of offices. These thousands of people need to be fed and watered, so there are restaurants, bars, tea rooms and cafeterias all over the place, with their kitchens and store rooms; and hundreds of people work in those too. The whole thing is like a small town under one roof, and is one of the most extraordinary centres of activity in the British Isles.

The parliament to which I was elected was the first in which each MP had a desk of his own. Before that many MPs had had to open their letters and dictate to their secretaries sitting on benches in lobbies and corridors. We were still a long way from each having an office, though, and some of us were given desks in strange places – a few, including me, in a cloister. In depths of the building to which the public has no access there is a Tudor cloister which survived the fire that destroyed nearly all the old building in the nineteenth century, and this was incorporated in the new Victorian palace. Eight of us were given desks there, four Labour and four Tory. My neighbour on one side was the Tory MP for Harborough, John Farr. I had spent a year and a half in Market Harborough as a child evacuee from London, and had always had a special affection for it, so John and I were on good terms from the beginning. I knew his constituency street by street (which is more than he did), but was curious to learn more about it from him, and had many questions to ask him. My neighbour on the other side was a young Labour MP called Robert Kilroy-Silk, one of the handsomest men I had ever seen. He was always beautifully dressed. I began to notice that whereas he spoke to me and our neighbours with received pronunciation, on the telephone to his constituency near Liverpool he spoke scouse. (I was in process of discovering that our leader in the House of Commons, the Prime Minister Harold Wilson, had not two accents but three, including an intermediate one for small public occasions.) Kilroy-Silk was intelligent, and I got on easily with him, but I came to feel that presenting himself was what he was really about. It seemed to me fully in keeping – years later, after he left Parliament – that he achieved nationwide celebrity as the presenter of a decades-long and almost daily television series.

Another Labour MP of my intake was Robin Cook. A ginger-bearded garden gnome, he was humorous but prickly, and bent on mischief. It was obvious from the beginning that he would be good at making trouble, and he developed into the chief scourge of the Conservative Party in the House of Commons. As a newcomer he was insecure, and I found him difficult to talk to. Once when we were travelling together on the tube we were discussing how Britain should plug in to the complicated relationship between the United States and the Soviet Union, and Robin said that in all our attitudes to the two superpowers we should keep in mind not only our own day-to-day politics but the differences between the philosophies underlying those two societies. One of them was openly materialistic, while the other, for all its faults, was dedicated to an ideal. Obviously I took it for granted that the Soviet Union, which openly proclaimed its materialism and its militant commitment to Marxism ('dialectical materialism'), was the former, and the United States the latter, so I took up Robin's point on that assumption. But we were ridiculously at cross-purposes. He had meant it the other way round. There was something comic about that conversation in which we were talking from opposite assumptions. I came to learn that there was a lot of discredited leftism in Robin. He would always defend, if apologetically, communist tyrannies, at the same time as evincing a deeply felt hostility towards the United States. His years at Westminster changed these attitudes considerably, but never totally, and as a result I always felt there was something untrustworthy about his politics. None of this was to prevent him from becoming Foreign Secretary. But he was at his best in opposition, as a destructive debater, savagely but humorously taking to pieces inept speeches by Conservative ministers.

A new MP needs to learn a lot in a short time. In his constituency, and to interviewers, he is expected to have an informed opinion on every political subject of the day, and be prepared to defend it against all comers. '*Where do you stand on nuclear weapons? On abortion? On pensions? On housing? On comprehensive schools?*' and so on *ad infinitum*. The election campaign he has just fought is a preparation for this, but when he becomes an MP the stakes are higher. His local newspaper will telephone him constantly for his views, usually on controversial and therefore tricky matters, these being the ones of greatest public interest; and of course his constituents are readers of that paper. So he is always on record, his words on paper, for the people whose votes he needs if he is to be re-elected. He has to master the complicated procedures of the House of Commons itself, and also of his national and local political party. Each day he receives a post bag from constituents with which he has to deal – I used to get between twenty and thirty letters a day, many needing more to be done about them than just a reply. He is co-opted to committees, and will want to join all-party groups with special interests that may range, as in my case, from Anglo-Swedish relations to public subsidy of the arts. All these groups and committees have their regular meetings outside the debating chamber, which in my day convened at two thirty. The chamber would call key votes at seven o'clock and, most important of all, ten o'clock – and then mount another debate after the ten o'clock vote. The average time at which it concluded its business was midnight. Alongside all this, the new MP would find himself in perpetual demand in his constituency, where he was expected to spend at least half his weekends, and to hold regular surgeries.

When people see House of Commons debates on television, and see the rows of empty benches, they often imagine that the politicians are malingering, but this is a crude misconception. MPs have so many other things to do during their afternoons – I, for instance, would spend two or three hours with my secretary and on the telephone, whatever else I had to do. They cannot give time to just sitting in the debating chamber when they themselves are not going to speak in the debate. A verbatim account of it, *Hansard*, will be delivered to them at home first thing next morning by special messenger – and, of course, a debate can be read in far less time than it takes to listen to. Except when the discussion is of compelling and immediate interest, any MP who attends a debate in which he has no intention of speaking is misusing his time.

People may say: 'Well how can an MP cast his vote responsibly at the end of a debate if he hasn't listened to the arguments?' This again is to misunderstand the way debates function. There are some 650 MPs, and it is out of the question for more than a handful of these to speak in any one debate. It is essential for ministers to speak, and at length, because they are spelling out the government's policy, explaining it at the beginning of the debate and answering criticisms of it at the end. And it is desirable that shadow ministers, official spokesmen for the opposition, should be given equal time. This leaves little space for other speakers, and such time as there is has to be fairly apportioned between the parties. The Speaker tries to call individuals with special claims – this person is known to be expert on the subject, that one has a constituency that will be specially affected by the legislation; and so on. This means that nineteen-twentieths of the MPs have no hope of being called in any given debate. Most will make only half a dozen speeches in the course of a year. But they still have their opinions, and their votes, both of which have to be taken into account. Discussion among them goes on never endingly outside the chamber. 'How are you going to vote on so-and-so? How would you answer such-and-such an objection? What does Peter/Joe/Charlie think about this one – what's he going to do, do you know? Do you think the government is handling it the right way? How highly do you estimate X? Do you think Y would do his job better?' And so on and so forth. Over coffee, tea and drinks, over lunch and dinner, among groups standing in corridors or waiting for their turn in the voting lobbies, between pairs perched on benches on quiet staircases, shop-talk goes on day in and day out. It is the way personal opinions are arrived at and become known, and the way climates of opinion form and make themselves felt. All this feeds into the voting lobbies. What is said in the debating chamber constitutes the record in *Hansard*, but what I have just described goes on unceasingly behind the scenes, and it influences the voting – and so it should.

At the constituency end of the job, as a new MP I received invaluable help from my secretary, Betty Norden. She had been secretary to Patrick Gordon Walker, so she knew the ropes not only in Westminster but in Leyton, where she was well known to the party activists. She tactfully saved me from errors in my early days. I would be dictating a letter to a constituent, telling him what I was going to do about his problem, when she would say pensively: 'Well, I see that you could deal with it like this. But I think what Patrick would have done would have been to ...' And I would only have to hear her say what Patrick would have done to realize that it was a preferable course of action. She corrected me without criticizing me. It was neat, and it taught me a lot when I needed it. For my first couple of years I dictated every letter that went out of Betty's office. (Secretaries were given offices even if their bosses were not.) Only when I was a hundred per cent certain I could deal with everything myself, no matter how small or routine, did I delegate a lot of it to Betty. I wanted to master it all myself first.

Betty remained my secretary for the whole time I was an MP, and over that period of nearly ten years she never missed a day. Her loyalty was complete, her dedication to the job total. Yet I had been reluctant to take her on. When Patrick was still an MP, and asked me if I would take her over after the election, I said No at first. I was used to the young, socially bright, modern-minded, sexually attractive secretaries in television, and Betty was none of those things. Although she did not look her age, nor admit to it, she was at least twenty years older than me (I was forty-three). Patrick persisted. She was an outstandingly good secretary, he said, and would do an excellent job for me. And if I did not give her the job, he said, she would not be able to get another at her age. There were, scandalously, no pensions for House of Commons secretaries at that time. She had never married, and she lived in central London with an older unmarried sister who had already retired. With no job and no pension she might find herself partially dependent on her sister, and that would be mortifying. I told Patrick I would have a private talk with her, and perhaps offer her a trial period of three months during which we could be on probation with one another. I did; and by the end of three months I was in no doubt of her value to me. We worked happily together until six months after I left the House of Commons, by which time she was in her mid-seventies.

During our first private talk she dragged into the conversation, out of nowhere, the fact that she was Jewish. It was so irrelevant that it was jarring. Years later, when we were close friends, I asked her why she had done it. She said that her father had dinned into her when she was a teenager that she must never get herself into a position of closeness with someone who was anti-Semitic but did not realize she was Jewish. The consequences, he told her, could be humiliating. She assumed he must have had this experience, and she followed his advice for the rest of her life: whenever she met someone she thought she was going to see a lot of she told them straight away that she was Jewish. She once, after copying all the entries from an old address book of mine into a new one, paid me what she thought was a great compliment: 'It actually is true, isn't it,' she said, 'that some of your best friends are Jews?' Jewishness, and what it means to be a Jew in British society, were among the things she and I discussed with much interest over the years.

Although I learnt a lot through being an MP, and gained a great deal from the experience, I became disillusioned with it as a way of life. So much of what MPs spent their time doing was shadow-boxing. Nearly every important decision was made by the government outside the House of Commons, and governments then manipulated the House accordingly. Opposition was hollow. Half the time the opposition agreed with what the government was doing, and knew that it would do much the same itself if it were in office, yet still tried to make capital out of criticizing, especially if the measure was an unpopular one. Characteristically, each MP behaved like a lawyer: without lying, he would put the best construction he could on the case for his own party and the worst on the case for its opponents. Intellectual insincerity, and insincerity of purpose, were all-pervading. Everyone knew this. In the debating chamber, people would pretend to misunderstand what a speaker was saying so that they could make fun of it, or attack it more sweepingly. I hated this. When I said so to my colleagues most of them laughed and said it was a trivial aspect of a game that was fun if you took it in the right spirit. That was precisely my objection: scarcely any of the things I was objecting to made a significant difference to what actually happened. Scarcely any of it mattered. It came dangerously close to being true that the only worthwhile reason to be in politics was to be an active member of a government.

This, it seemed to me, was among the chief reasons for the distorted behaviour of MPs. The most able of them were usually careerists, as well as being other and better things at the same time, and they were anxious to get on; and the only way for them to get into government was through the House of Commons. So most of what they did in the House was aimed at improving their chances of promotion by attracting attention and impressing their colleagues. This was their chief concern when making speeches and serving on committees. The reason they were so compliant to government was that they wanted to join it – or else they were trying to make a name for themselves in opposition, so as to be in the next government. The issues were often secondary – or, worse, were being used. When you heard a colleague put forward an argument, the first question in your mind was expected to be not about the validity of his argument but about his reasons for putting it forward. What motivates most utterances in politics, including government, is not an abstract concern for truth but an attempt to bring about the consequences that making the utterance will have. Understanding what these are, and why the speaker wants them, constitutes the greater part of understanding a speech.

Professional politicians take this for granted among themselves, and decode one another's words accordingly.

Consequences is the key word. It is as true of practical matters as it is of spoken ones. If MPs have a dispute about committee procedure, or voting methods, it is not because they take differing views on the objective merits of these, it is because different procedures will produce different outcomes; and it is the outcomes they are fighting over. Normally they do not say this. They couch their arguments as being for and against the merits of the various procedures, the best of those being always the one that will have the outcome they desire. Observers commonly fail to understand this, and see politicians as quibbling over technicalities and procedures.

Because I found that so little of what happened in the House mattered – and because so much of it was playacting, insincere – I came to the conclusion that a life given up to it was not for me. Occasionally it happens that an incident that is trivial in itself causes important thoughts to click into place in one's mind, and this happened to me over this. I was sitting in the debating chamber listening to an exceptionally foolish speech from a Conservative when the Labour MP sitting next to me, Renée Short – who had a gratingly strident, fishwifely voice – started screeching at him: 'Sit down, you twit ... Twit ... You're just a twit ... Stop it, you twit ... Oh, go home, twit ... Twit,' and so on. She was all the time brushing up against me while bouncing up and down on her buttocks screeching 'twit' beside my ear. (I doubt whether any of this is in *Hansard*.) While this was going on a thought came into my mind with abnormal clarity: 'I don't belong here. This is not for me. I can't function in an environment like this.' In that moment I knew I was going to create a life of my own in the House of Commons that would meet my needs.

A fundamental fact about being an MP is that you are your own master. Because you are elected to represent the people, no one else can tell you what to do. Only those who elected you can remove you. And they will not get a chance to do so until the next general election. If you yield to pressure from any source, it is up to you. No one can make you do it. This being so, I decided to fashion a way of life I wanted in the House of Commons, and defy the consequences.

My first thought was that I was not, any more, going to waste hours of every day on this sort of tomfoolery. There were any number of useful activities I could take up, more than enough to fill my time. Of the occupations thrust at me by parliamentary life, only two were of genuine importance. One was my vote on significant issues. The other was my constituency casework, the things I did for individuals and families in Leyton. For the former, I needed only to be present in the voting lobbies for votes at seven and ten o'clock, and even this did not happen every day. For the latter, I needed to set aside two or three hours most afternoons, part of the time dictating letters to my secretary, part on the telephone to ministries and other public institutions such as local government offices in Leyton. The work I did then made a real difference to the lives of individuals. It got them decently housed, or properly compensated for injury or loss, or given the pensions they were entitled to, or got their child into the school they wanted, or reunited immigrant families. Actually it was my opinion that this sort of work ought not to be done by MPs at all, but the fact is it was, and I resolved to do it to the best of my ability. House of Commons voting and constituency casework rarely took up more than four hours of any one day, sometimes less, although the need to be available for votes frequently penned me within the precincts of the House for long and unpredictable periods. I decided that from now on, whenever I was in the House, I would use its library as my chief place of work, and get on with real work of my own while I was on hand for votes. And I simply stopped 'shadow-boxing', which had become my mental term for all the pointless activities that took up most of the time of the House of Commons.

I applied a similar decision to my constituency. Because it was in London I was constantly being expected to put in appearances at social functions there, attending meetings to which I contributed no more than my presence. In fact it was often specifically my presence that was required of me – to be there, but not to intervene in what was going on. I decided to cut out nearly but not quite all of that. I kept on with my surgeries, because they were important. But apart from those I tried to go to the constituency only when my presence actually made a difference to something. There was need for flexibility here – I realized that sometimes I ought just to be at a committee meeting or a party. Overall, though, the change made an enormous difference to my life. For a start, it enabled me to have a reliable private life, especially at weekends, instead of continually having to cancel worthwhile private engagements for trivial constituency ones. In my own defence I would stress that in the constituency, as at Westminster, I skipped nothing of significance. Inevitably there were people at both ends who objected. They thought I ought to show more willingness to go through the motions and simply do what was expected of me. I did *some* of it – *some* is indeed a part of the job.

I made full use of the time I saved. In my first few months as an MP I presented a new series of half a dozen television programmes about the press called *Don't Quote Me*. It was my first television series for the BBC. At the same time *The Times*, a Conservative newspaper, decided it would be a good idea to publish a regular column by one of the new Labour MPs, and invited me to write it; so for my first two years in the House, 1974-76, I had a monthly column on *The Times*'s main features page. I worked continually at my book about the philosophy of Schopenhauer; and I rewrote my novel *The Story of All Our Lives*.

Some of my critics in the party went round complaining that I was lazy, but the truth is I have never worked harder in my life. It was simply that, unlike them, I was doing only work that had point to it. Only half my working time was given to politics.

Because I had already made a name in television I was invited to appear on it at least once a week when I was new in the House, usually for a sentence or two in one of the news or current affairs programmes. But what they wanted from me now was party hack stuff, and I always declined. Apart from my own series, I appeared on television only twice during my first two years in Parliament: to co-present, with the prime minister, the Labour Party's eve-of-poll programme for the general election of October 1974; and to stand in for a colleague who was suddenly taken ill. Eventually the producers stopped asking me. They knew I always said No.

I turned down, too, a scandalous invitation from the *Sunday Times*. Its Colour Supplement offered me a large sum of money to keep a secret diary during my first year in the House of Commons in which I would record confidential conversations among my fellow MPs, especially their back-biting and their criticisms of their own leadership and government – and then publish it all in the *Sunday Times*. When I expressed outrage at this suggestion they were uncomprehending. 'The public has a right to know,' they said. To this I made the obvious point that there was a need for confidentiality in every profession. 'You yourselves,' I said, 'carry on a rivalry with *The Observer* which causes you to plan strategies against them. What would you think of one of your number who sold your confidential conversations about this to *The Observer*?' They said this was different, because MPs were elected. Their incomprehension and their amorality were impenetrable. No television programme I had ever worked on had conducted itself like this, nor did any of the people whom I had known personally in good journalism. It was my first intimation that corruption from the tabloids was infiltrating what had previously been quality newspapers. It has since pervaded the British media altogether. Because most members of the public get their view of politics through the media, they increasingly attribute the rottenness of the media to politics itself. In fact, politics in Britain is nowhere near as corrupt as the media, though it certainly is a rough old trade.

Actually, I found that most people did not hold as low an opinion of politicians as they thought they did. In conversation they often talked as if politicians were figures of mockery, but when I became an MP I was made aware that people began treating me, no doubt unconsciously, with just that little bit more respect – even my old friends. They deferred to me just ever so slightly, asked more often for my opinion or advice, and took more notice of what I said. Acquaintances got in touch with me more often. My social invitations doubled, then trebled. Also, being an MP opened doors to me. I found that – provided I was polite – I could get into almost anything, down to such non-political places as over-booked restaurants and sold-out theatres. I could walk without notice into any public institution, from a hospital to a prison, as if I had a right to be there; and if I asked to see X, X would see me, usually immediately. Everywhere people took more notice of my complaints, and did more about them. From experience I know for a fact, whatever anyone may believe to the contrary, that being a Member of Parliament, certainly at that time, had a cachet in our society, and one that made a difference for the people who had it. Of course MPs came to like it, especially those who had no other claim to attention. I would say that the commonest professional deformation of Members of Parliament when I was in the House was self-importance.

Something that still happens to most MPs is a dramatic widening of the range of their social experience. In their constituencies they have to come to grips in specific and individual terms with social problems of every kind, and what is more do something about them. They have to visit schools, hospitals and old people's homes, and canvas from household to household in council estates – while at the same time, in central London, they are being invited to City boardroom lunches, embassy receptions, and Buckingham Palace garden parties, and rubbing shoulders with members of present and previous governments in the House of Commons. My years in television had familiarized me with most of these experiences, but nearly all new MPs are having them for the first time. The popular idea that MPs live in a Westminster hot-house in which they never get to see anybody except one another is the opposite of the truth. I can think of no other profession that brings its members into direct contact with so many contrasted people in society, unless it be that of a hospital doctor.

Being an MP taught me an immense amount about my own society, not least the realities of how it is run. The aspect of this about which I had been most ignorant was local government. This decided many of the things closest to people's lives. What were inaccurately called state schools were built and run by the local authorities, who also owned about a third of all the housing in the country. They were responsible for the roads, the lighting, the traffic. The health services, the police services and the fire services were separate but likewise organized at a local level. There can have been few of my working days on which I had no direct dealings with the London Borough of Waltham Forest.

I did everything I could to use my local influence on behalf of individual constituents while being realistic about the problems facing the authorities. The constituents were not always in the right. On one occasion I was asked to give my support to an organized protest against the closure of an old and much loved local hospital. When I looked into the matter I found that the local health authority was not able to provide up-to-date, increasingly expensive medical technology to every little local hospital, so it was following a policy of concentrating investment in carefully chosen centres. I thought they were right, and declined to support the protest. I explained why – whereupon the left of my local party, which was organizing the protest, came out in a public denunciation of me. I was unbudged by this. But when I made an ironic complaint about it to one of my left-wing fellow MPs, Jo Richardson, she said I had a lot to learn. Of course, she said, the health authority was in the right, and for that reason the hospital would be closed quite regardless of what I did. Therefore the thing for me to do was put myself at the head of the protest. It would do no harm, and the left would march in my support. The hospital would close just the same, and I would be hailed locally as the person who had led the fight to keep it open. This would increase my popularity. 'It's what I'd do,' she said. This conversation was a milestone in understanding for me. I came to see, close up, that this was the way the left operated. And I developed an inexpressible contempt for it. It makes me smile when I hear them described – or, even worse, hear them describe themselves – as the conscience of the party.

My constituency was one of three that made up the London Borough of Waltham Forest: Leyton, Chingford and Walthamstow. Their three MPs needed sometimes to co-operate, and we would also be invited together to many public events within the borough. Walthamstow's MP was a fellow Labourite, but Chingford's was the most waspish Conservative in the country, Norman Tebbit. I found him refreshingly astringent in conversation, always enjoyable to talk to. At dinners his wife Margaret, a warmer personality than he, was usually seated next to me, and I came to know her and like her. She was permanently paralyzed from the neck down by the IRA bomb that was intended to kill Margaret Thatcher in Brighton. Norman himself was seriously injured, and behaved with striking courage. Killed by the same bomb was Roberta Wakeham, another MP's wife whom I particularly liked. I knew several people who were murdered by the IRA, some of them totally innocent by any reckoning.

Being an MP brings home to you how horrible some aspects of human nature are. At one time we were facing a beef mountain created by Europe's agricultural policy. Because of the costs of storage, and the fact that beef could not be stored indefinitely anyway, we wanted to get rid of it quickly. But if it were simply unloaded on to the market this would cause prices to collapse: shopkeepers would be unable to sell their existing stocks at existing prices, and would suffer serious losses. After much discussion we decided to make the beef available either free or almost free to old age pensioners who were so poor that they were having to live on supplementary benefit. Because they did not have the purchasing power to buy beef normally our action would not affect normal demand in the shops, and we would be giving beef to the most indigent, most neglected members of society, those most likely to be suffering from undernourishment. One might have thought that no one could object to such a course of action. Yet MPs were inundated by letters of protest from their constituents. These came from old age pensioners who were not on supplementary benefit. Their common theme was 'Here am I, worked hard all my life, saved enough to scrape along now on an inadequate pension: you don't give me anything, but those layabouts down the road, who have never worked, never saved, and always lived on government handouts – after all those handouts you're now giving them free beef! What about me? I haven't eaten beef in years. I can't afford it.' Envy and resentment on this scale are universal in human nature, as are greed, pride, aggression, selfishness and a host of other deadly sins; and they are universal in politics. I learnt the hard way that in politics you cannot do anything at all, however simple or good, without creating antagonism and hostility. Every action is opposed, and passionately. Every change is fought against, indignantly. Idealists imagine that they can do things that will get everyone's approval, but experience of office always cures them of that delusion.

Even so, one sees the point of the letters. There was a logic to them. And this was another lesson I learnt: human beings usually act and react in accordance with the logic of the situation as applied to their self-interest. They might be secondarily influenced by their, or other people's, ideas of how they *ought* to behave, but if you want to predict their behaviour correctly you will give pride of place to self-interest and situational logic. Otherwise you will find yourself perpetually surprised and disappointed. This is true of politics in general. Professional politicians learn this and have to live with it, and either accept it or live in permanent revolt against it. In their discussions with one another – though not with their supporters in their constituencies – they take it as axiomatic. It explains most of the disjunction between what they say in public and what they do. It will never be possible to carry on real politics or real government as if the truths I have just uttered were not truths, but most people are reluctant to acknowledge them, and require of their leaders a certain amount of pretence.

Members of the public often expect politicians of opposing parties to behave with personal antagonism towards one another, but life is not like that at all. They are professional colleagues, understanding of one another's problems, and they talk privately with professional candour. On committees they need to exercise mutual understanding if they are to get the business done. There are many cross-party friendships, some of them warm and close. They trust one another's confidentiality, and it is rare for this to be betrayed. A memorable example of such candour from a complete stranger came to me early on. I was on the standing committee for the finance bill (the budget) and we met three times a week for eight hours each time: we convened at four in the afternoon on Mondays, Tuesdays and Thursdays and rose at midnight. Even so, we still had to have a couple of all-night sittings. During these, we would take turns as individuals to have a twenty-minute break, but so as not to affect the voting, MPs of opposite parties would go out of the room in pairs. At four o'clock in the morning I found myself going out into the corridor with one of the so-called knights of the shires, an elderly, titled Tory MP who had been in the House for decades, and whose family had represented the same constituency for generations.

'You're new here, aren't you?' he said in a friendly way.

'Yes.'

'Tell me, in all honesty, what do you think of our front bench?'

'Well,' I said, hesitating: 'To tell you the truth, I'm disappointed. I expected them to be formidable, at least, though I knew I wouldn't agree with them. But they're not. In terms of personal ability they aren't a patch on the Labour front bench.'

I expected him to leap to their defence, but instead he heaved a sigh that seemed to come from the soles of his shoes. He shook his head sadly: 'I know. I know. Nowadays we're being led by the sort of people one used to employ.'

This is typical of the way members of opposite parties talk to one another in private. Over a period of years one hears opponents say numberless things that would embarrass them if made public.

Even so, the notion that the House of Commons is like some sort of club is not valid. It is too much a place of work for that. Nobody goes there for relaxation. Usually, as soon as people feel free to get away from it, they do. It is only when they are pinned down by the need to vote that they sit around and drink, and then they do it impatiently. The atmosphere is nothing like that of a club. The only topic of conversation, never-ending and obsessive, is politics.

One characteristic that it does have in common with a club, however, is that within it all members are equal, whatever their status may be outside. You pick up a tray at the cafeteria in the tea room and find yourself standing in a queue next to the prime minister, with whom you then have tea. When you go to the members' dining room you are expected to take an empty seat at a table already occupied by members of your own party so that their conversation can remain uninhibited; and again you may find yourself lunching or dining with some of the most powerful individuals in the land while they talk shop. I once found myself at a table set for three with two prime ministers, Wilson and Callaghan, who had beckoned me to join them. They were exchanging anecdotes about their weekly private audiences with the Queen. At the end Callaghan said: 'If she weren't the Queen she'd make a good politician,' to which Wilson replied: 'She *is* a good politician.'

On another occasion I was dining with Wilson and one of his cabinet ministers, Barbara Castle, when the division bell rang in the middle of our main course, and we had to leave the table to vote. When we got back, Wilson's dinner and mine were still there but Barbara's had been taken away. She gave the waiter a noisy dressing down for removing her dinner, and then stalked off angrily to complain to someone of higher authority – at which Wilson turned to the abashed waiter and said: 'Don't let it worry you. She'd rather have the grievance than the dinner.'

I was still new when I found myself in the cafeteria queue next to Margaret Thatcher, then a not-very-highly-thought-of ex-minister in opposition. She smiled at me nicely and said: 'You're Bryan Magee, aren't you?'

'Yes.'

'Oh,' she said, her smile sweetening: 'I must tell you how *very* much I enjoyed your book on the philosophy of Karl Popper. In fact I enjoyed it so much I read it twice.' She went on talking about the book for some time, moving her tilted head from side to side in a way that bordered on the ingratiating. This whole way of talking could scarcely have been more different from the queenly demeanour she developed later as prime minister. After our first encounter we talked whenever we met. I watched her, over the years, become a different person.

I was in the unusual position of knowing quite well the then leader of the Conservative Party, Edward Heath. Four years previously I had made a one-hour television documentary about him as a musician, and this had involved working almost daily with him over several weeks. We went together to his family home in Broadstairs, where I met his father and brother, and filmed him rehearsing the local orchestra. We went to his old Oxford college, Balliol, where I filmed him playing the organ. We went together to the Edinburgh Festival. Between these occasions I was often alone with him in his flat in Albany, listening to records with him and discussing them, or watching him play the piano. I now found, to my surprise, that I knew him better than most of his colleagues in the Conservative Party, for he was an abnormally solitary man, especially for a politician.

While making that programme I had tried to find out everything I could about him as a man of feeling, so I discussed him confidentially with the people who knew him best and had known him longest. One conclusion I came to, which of course was not hinted at in the programme, was that his sexual orientation was solely towards men, and that he had become aware of this in late adolescence. At Oxford, where as President of the Union he conceived the ambition to become prime minister, he made the long-term decision not to give rein to his sexual desires, for to do so could wreck his political hopes. So he became a consciously repressed homosexual, without intimacies or a sex life, seeking his most important emotional outlet in music, his ruling passion. What was crucial for him about music was that it enabled him to experience deep and passionate emotions without personal relationships. So it became indispensable to him. Nevertheless, he had to fight against depression. Emotional deprivation made him

415

an awkward, lonely figure. He acquired fewer of the social graces which are normal in public life than anyone I have ever known. So awkward and graceless was he that one wondered how he could have become prime minister.

Music was my ruling passion too; and although there was no homosexuality in my life, repressed or otherwise, the fact that I was going to be an MP had always required me to keep my sex life very private; so I empathized with him on that score. We communicated easily. We both had a passion for Mahler, and one night we sat up into the early hours arguing about the relative merits of different recordings of the same Mahler symphony, giving one another illustrations on the record player. I felt particularly close to him then.

It made a great difference to my experience of going into Parliament that, when I did, I already knew a lot of MPs. I had interviewed most of the leading figures in all parties on television, and talked to them at conferences, or across other people's dinner tables. I had been meeting MPs of my own, younger, generation in the general social life of London. And I was surprised at how many of my new acquaintances I had known as a student at Oxford. Going into the House of Commons was like attending an Oxford Union reunion. All this meant that from the beginning I was eating and drinking with friends every day, stopping to chat with them in corridors, sharing taxis with them. True, we tended to talk about little but politics, but that interested me. Between such meetings I might spend solitary hours in the House of Commons library working on my books, or on my *Times* articles, or my television programmes; or doing homework for committee meetings, or for speeches. I felt very much at home in that library. Friends and the library became the most enjoyable features of my day-to-day life in the House of Commons.

On almost every evening when there was not an important vote I would go out with non-political friends to theatres, concerts, operas, or other people's houses. So the old life carried on alongside the new. I still managed to see all the worthwhile opera in London – throughout my years as an MP I was one of the judges for the *Evening Standard*'s annual opera award, and this ensured that I got tickets for everything. I also saw most of the plays I wanted to see. On many evenings I would slip over Westminster Bridge to a concert on the South Bank, and then come back to the House of Commons. If you were flexible, things could be fitted in. Occasionally, when it was the only way of seeing something special, I would go to a matinee; but I have never liked going to matinees, and do so only as a last resort.

Perhaps a word should be said about the implications for foreign travel of being an MP. One gets many invitations, and is treated as an important personage in other countries, with top-level meetings, five-star hotels, chauffeur-driven cars, public banquets, doors being flunkily opened on all sides. Although this has its own limitations, it does extend one's experience. In this way I visited the Soviet Union for private meetings in the Kremlin with President Podgorny and members of the Supreme Soviet. I visited Iran for private meetings with the Shah and his cabinet. I met the prime ministers and governments of Belize and Bermuda on their home ground. I also made less elevated, though still official, visits to other countries. These had something in common with my travels as a television reporter, though I was now being treated as if I were far more important than that, even on the many occasions when I accomplished less.

7

About the House

A substantial literature exists about British politics during the years when I was in the House of Commons, 1974-83: about the governments, their policies, the economy, the leading personalities, the political parties, and so on. Although I had an insider's view of it – sometimes a participant's, though never with more than a very small role – I think it would be a mistake in this book to attempt to write the history of high politics. Personal observations are more to the point. But it will clarify the story for some of my readers if I give a brief sketch of the overall political situation that forms the background.

At the same time as I entered the House, in February 1974, the Labour Party came back into power after four years of opposition. Harold Wilson replaced Edward Heath as prime minister. But he did not have an overall majority, and he called another general election in October of the same year. 1974 was the only year during my lifetime in which there were two general elections. The second did give Labour an overall majority, but of only two seats, which it soon lost. On this hyper-vulnerable basis it governed until 1979. Meanwhile Wilson resigned as prime minister in March 1976, and was replaced by Jim Callaghan. Labour lost the following general election, in 1979, and the Conservatives came back into power under Margaret Thatcher. The Conservatives were then in office for eighteen years. But I was in the House for only the first four of them: I lost my seat in the general election of

June 1983. So I was an MP for a total of nine years and four months, and sat in the House of Commons under both Labour and Conservative governments, with three prime ministers: Wilson, Callaghan and Thatcher.

Harold Wilson I despised. I saw him as shabby. What was so exceptional about him was his combination of smallness of character and high intelligence. He was indeed a remarkably clever little man, and in dealing with him you had always to keep both the littleness and the cleverness in mind. His sense of proportion was petty: he was continually doing big things for small reasons. If he unexpectedly jumped on a plane and flew to Moscow to confer with Russia's top leaders it could easily be to head off an evanescent rebellion from his left-wing backbenchers; so if you started looking for weighty explanations you would be deceiving yourself. He was obsessed by the short term. A lastingly famous phrase of his was: 'A week is a long time in politics.' Tactics absorbed him. He was narcissistic about his tactical abilities, an admirer of his own footwork: I sometimes imagined him secretly dancing for himself in front of a mirror. He did have a few principles, but not many. In the main he just wanted to be prime minister. He was like a friend on a motor trip who has little interest in the places you visit and does not really care where you go, so long as he drives the car. With rare exceptions he had equally little difficulty in adopting a policy or opposing it, as circumstances suggested. He would tell you whatever you wanted to hear, and was altogether untrustworthy. It was said of him that he could not tell you the time straight. He used these gifts, which were exceptional, with one overriding set of aims: to hold the Labour Party together and keep it in power, with himself at the head of it. When these aims came into conflict with one another he could be prodigiously Machiavellian.

An example occurred during my first two years as an MP, and concerned Britain's membership of Europe. Heath's government had taken us in, but majority opinion in the Labour Party was so passionately against this that it would have been impossible for anyone who was openly pro-European to become or remain leader of the party. Yet Wilson was privately convinced that it was essential to Britain's interests to remain in Europe. So he at once declared that the terms of our membership were unacceptable, and that before there could be any question of our remaining in Europe the terms would have to be re-negotiated. He thus appeared to be on the side of the anti-Europeans, so they went along with him. He met all further criticisms of our existing membership by saying that we were now renegotiating the terms, and we must wait and see how the new terms turned out. No one knew better than he that renegotiation was a sham, and that the new terms would be little different from the old. He pretended to think otherwise. When the new terms were arrived at he declared them to be a vast improvement. He then said there should be a referendum on whether or not we should stay in Europe under the new terms. That would mean that the government would not itself declare a preference, but would do whatever the British people decided; and he was confident that a majority would vote Yes. Then, because the government was precluded from declaring a preference, he announced that there would be a free vote among Labour MPs, thus avoiding a split in the Labour Party. The vote in the country went two to one in favour of our remaining in Europe, as did the vote in the House of Commons, though of course the Commons majority was dependent on Conservative votes. Wilson thus calculatedly brought about something that a majority of his own party passionately did *not* want, without at any time declaring himself to be in its favour, still less endangering his leadership, and without splitting the party or loosening its hold on power. It was a virtuoso performance. I watched it step by step from a ringside seat. It was done in full self-awareness – in private I heard him boast about it. He said it would win him greater credit in the eyes of history than anything else in his career. He was unperturbed by the deceptions it involved: he saw these as indispensable to the outcome, and he regarded that as essential for the country. He also knew that no one other than himself could have done it.

Perhaps because he was so devious, he saw plots and conspiracies against his leadership all round him. To counter these (nearly all of which existed only in his mind) he was endlessly playing his colleagues off against one another. He did not want any of them to shine too brightly in case they should become a threat to him, so he withheld from most of them the jobs they would have been best at. In consequence he had much less able governments than he should have had. In Denis Healey he had the ideal Foreign Secretary, in Tony Crosland the ideal Chancellor of the Exchequer: both men had wanted these jobs and prepared for them all their political lives, but they never got them. Callaghan, who did, made a poor showing at both, but would have made an ideal Leader of the House of Commons. Roy Jenkins – who could not have become party leader in that period because he was publicly at the head of the pro-European cause – was the best Home Secretary since World War Two. These people could have formed good governments. But because of Wilson's pettiness and paranoia they muddled along in the wrong jobs, and were among the worst governments Britain has had since the Second World War.

When Wilson resigned unexpectedly in March 1976 there was a flood of speculation about the reasons for it, speculation that went on for years. Article after article appeared, desperately searching for his reasons. The chief explanation offered was that he could see a major economic crisis coming and wanted to bale out before it arrived. Others insinuated that he feared that some scandal in his private life was about to break – there were even suggestions of blackmail. Years later there were those who speculated that he had become aware of the first signs of the Alzheimer's Disease into which he declined. All this was demonstrably baseless from the start – an object lesson in how large-scale speculation can flourish in disregard of evidence. In his resignation speech, which I watched him make, he said that when the Queen invited him to form a government in March 1974 he had accepted, but told her he would not personally remain at the head of it for more than two years. The two years were now up, and he was resigning. Self-evidently, nothing that happened during those two years could have been the reason for his resignation. (The true reason had to do with promises he had made to his wife, Mary; but the story of that is too detailed to go into here.)

In those days the leader of the Labour Party was elected by its MPs alone. And Wilson's successor would be elected straight into the Premiership of Great Britain. There were six candidates, four from the right of the party and two from the left. The right-wingers were Callaghan, Jenkins, Healey and Crosland, the left-wingers Michael Foot and Tony Benn. Jenkins, Healey and Crosland were friends of mine, Crosland especially so; but I knew that none of them could beat Foot. In fact I expected Crosland to come bottom of the poll. My chief concern was that the left should not gain control of the party. It was obvious that the election would spread over more than one ballot, so I decided to vote for Crosland on the first, to do what little I could to minimize his humiliation, and then, once he had been eliminated, to vote for Callaghan, the only candidate who could beat Foot. Foot duly came top of the first ballot: the order was Foot, Callaghan, Jenkins, Benn, Healey, Crosland. Jenkins, Benn and Crosland dropped out, and in subsequent voting Callaghan overtook Foot. Thus Callaghan became prime minister. He was voted for by many MPs who, like me, would have preferred Jenkins or Healey but took the view that either of those would be beaten by Foot. This view was confirmed by the voting. And our fears of a Foot leadership were validated a few years later when he became leader: the party fell apart under him, was massively rejected by the electorate, and remained in opposition for eighteen years.

When Callaghan became prime minister he was more relaxed than he had been before. On his way up he had become a byword for sharp-elbowed careerism. In the sixties, as he was later to express it himself, he ached to be prime minister. His wheeling and dealing for the succession to Harold Wilson dominated his behaviour during those years, and made him a bad colleague. Then, when the Conservatives unexpectedly came back into power in 1970, he thought his age was such that the possibility of becoming prime minister had now passed him by. This was the point at which he relaxed. Driven by ambition no longer, he acquired a mature, cheerful calm, accepting his lot in life, and being a much nicer person in consequence. The nickname 'Sunny Jim' was used. It happens often in life that a person achieves success only after he stops striving for it, and this happened to Callaghan. He did become prime minister after all, but as a warm, avuncular figure and not the ruthless political hustler of old. He is the only politician in British history to have held all four of the top offices of state: Prime Minister, Foreign Secretary, Home Secretary and Chancellor of the Exchequer. He was personally popular throughout his period as prime minister. Although he lost the 1979 general election to Margaret Thatcher, the polls at the time showed that his personal popularity was much higher than hers. The maturing of his character continued after he left office. He was to live for another quarter of a century and to become exceptionally mellow and wise, yet always still sharp. When he was in his eighties I attended a three-day international conference whose members included heads of state and foreign ministers, and which was chaired by Callaghan with untiring control throughout, a sustained quick wit and good humour that no one else in the room could have bettered. He had become, in the end, an unusually attractive person.

His Achilles heel, and he knew it, was intellectual: he did not have an especially good mind. For that reason a good education would have made a great difference to him. And he knew that too. There had been individuals in the Labour movement of genius-level natural intelligence but little education – Alan Bullock, who wrote a three-volume biography of Ernest Bevin, believed this of Bevin; and I thought it of Aneurin Bevan – but Callaghan was not one of them. Had he gone to university he would have worked hard and got a respectable degree. He was nobody's fool and he had other qualities in abundance: common sense, cunning, an eye for the main chance, application, natural authority. He was a natural politician, completely at home in a political environment. Yet he never ceased to feel prey to the fact that some of the people round him were both cleverer and better educated than he. When, as an ex-prime minister, he congratulated me on my philosophy programmes on television, the way he did so, and the expression on his face while he was talking, and above all the look in his eyes, betrayed the fact that I and the programmes made him feel inadequate. It was absurd, given his personal gifts and his success in life, but it was so. It was something he never got over.

When he became leader of the Labour Party he did everything he could to hold the party together. In pursuit of that aim he made his chief opponent – the acknowledged leader of the left, Michael Foot – his deputy. Foot was outstanding as an orator and journalist, but lacked any vestige of managerial or practical common sense. He would have been incapable of running even a government department. The right job for him, as Callaghan saw, was running the debating chamber as Leader of the House, with all the expertise of the Speaker's office being permanently fed to him.

425

Because of Foot's impracticality and the idealistic socialism of his rhetoric he acquired a reputation for saintliness that was undeserved. I had been aware of this for many years, but it was brought home to me with peculiar nastiness on one issue. The government introduced a trade union bill that would have meant, as one of its side-effects, that only members of the National Union of Journalists could write regularly for newspapers. A dozen or fifteen Labour backbenchers were outraged by this destruction of a basic freedom of expression, and we went privately to Michael Foot, as Leader of the House, to tell him that in no circumstances would we vote for it. The government's majority was so small that without our votes the bill would not go through. Foot did everything he could to persuade us, but in vain, and the meeting ended with his asking us to come and see him again in a few weeks' time. We did – and then again – and then again. For months, while the bill was progressing through its various stages, we carried on our private meetings with Foot. At these he used every strong-arm tactic known to politicians to pressurize us into voting for the bill. He showed not the slightest concern for *our* concerns, and was unbudged by our rational arguments, which he made no attempt to answer. Over all those months he did not shift one inch. All he cared about was pressurizing us to vote; and some of the methods he used were bullying and contemptible. When, finally, we were up against the deadline, and he had to face the fact that we were not going to vote for the bill in its existing form, he caved in completely, and got the government to change the bill in accordance with our demands. But he did this only in response to *force majeure*, not in response to either principle or rational argument, and still less out of any concern (not even any *show* of concern) for freedom of the press. It became clear through his ever-changing way of dealing with us that he ended up hating us. He felt we had humiliated him. He had been a journalist all his life, a journalist by profession, editor of the *Evening Standard* and

Tribune, and had posed doughtily as the champion of press freedom. But it was only words. When it came to deeds, to the freedom itself, he was without concern for it, and in this case allowed it to survive only because he was forced to against his will, against his fierce and long-sustained opposition. Everything that was apparently good about him – his socialism, his idealism, his public personality – had its existence only in words. Behind the words there was nothing, or rather something worse than nothing.

The government of which Foot and Callaghan were the two leading figures was abject in its attitude to the trade unions. In many areas their idea of making policy was to find out what the unions wanted and give it to them. The leader of one of the country's most powerful unions confided to me that he and his fellow union leaders were disoriented by this. What trade unions essentially were, he said, was bargaining organizations; and what he and his fellows spent their lives doing was negotiating. Always and invariably, they started by asking for more than they expected to get. This gave them the leeway to make concessions during negotiations and, while appearing to compromise, still come out at the end with what they wanted. But this government gave them everything they asked for straight away. They did not expect it, and they found it bewildering. In their hearts they disapproved of it: it seemed to them weak and irresponsible. They despised it, and considered that no self-respecting government should behave like that. They themselves, if in government, would certainly not have done so.

It was during the years of the Callaghan premiership, 1976-79, that the bankruptcy of the Labour Party's traditional policies – the impossibility, even in theory, of their solving the country's problems – became most painfully evident. The old Labour movement was now at the end of the road. Successive governments had implemented its traditional policies, and they had not worked. Britain had been under Labour governments for

427

all but three and a half of the previous dozen years or more, and it was now the sick man of Europe. There were not even any new ideas. The left of the party cried out for bigger doses of socialism, but the right saw, correctly, that this would make things even worse. The trouble was, the right had no notion what to do instead. Continued national decline seemed inevitable. All a Labour government could do was ensure that the lower standards brought about by decline would not be forced on those who were already the least well off. The management of national decline on the principles of fairness became, in practice, its programme.

By chance, at the time I am writing these pages, I happen to be reading a book called *The Strange Death of Tory England* by Geoffrey Wheatcroft, in which I find the following sentence: 'Scarcely any government from the 1950s to the 1980s could be accounted a complete success by any measure, but the Labour government of 1974–9 was in a class of its own, with few positive achievements to its credit except a grim struggle to survive.' This is true. And those years made up half of my experience of being a Member of Parliament – and, what is more, the first half, when the experience was new. I cannot pretend that my ideas about what to do were superior to everyone else's. I had come to see that democratic socialism either did not work or was unachievable, depending on which way you looked at it. In either case it was not an option. Many if not most of the leading figures of the Labour Party had come to that conclusion too; and I, like them, found myself without a compass-bearing. I belonged emphatically to the liberal, anti-Marxist tradition within the Labour Party, and in those rudderless times I banded together with like-minded MPs to form what we called the Manifesto Group. The point of our name was that the Labour Party in the House of Commons, now obviously threatened with fragmentation, could still remain united on the basis of the manifesto on which every one of us had been elected, but would fall apart (as it was to do) if the left imposed other, controversial and unpopular, policies on the party. We could unite *only* round the manifesto, and should therefore do so. A sub-committee of the Manifesto Group, which did not include me, held a number of meetings, and drew up a thirty-page document putting forward a diagnosis of, and cure for, the nation's ills. Everything in this document was compatible with our election manifesto, and we hoped that all Labour MPs would support it. The penultimate draft, the product of many different hands, was sprawling, lumpy and uneven. So they asked me if I would pull it into shape and sub-edit it into consistent prose. I did that, and it was published with the title (not mine) *What We Must Do*. What struck me while I was working on it was that its diagnosis was good – excellent in fact – while its cure was inadequate, in fact pathetic, manifestly *not* a cure for the ills spelt out in the diagnosis, just a mixture of tinkering and pious hopes.

A press conference was held in the House of Commons to launch the document. When people came in and took their places, the members of the sub-committee sat on the platform while I took a seat in the front row. At the last moment before the proceedings began, the chairman, Giles Radice, leant forward and asked me to join those up on the platform. In a hurried exchange I said I did not want to, since I had had nothing to do with deciding the content of the document; but he said there might be questions about wording. There was no time for an argument, and this was not the place to have a public one – and in any case I saw his point – so I went up on the platform. The first journalist to speak – after Giles's lengthy introduction, which consisted of a good analysis of the nation's ills – said that what they really wanted to know was what we thought the government ought to *do*. Please, he said, don't keep going on about your analysis of what's wrong. It's very good, and a lot of other people will agree with it. What matters is what's to be *done* about it. After all, you yourselves have called the document *What We Must Do*.'

There were beefy murmurs of approval from other journalists present. To my incredulity and terror, Giles then said: 'I think the person who can explain that best to you is Bryan Magee.' I immediately tried to pass up the honour. 'But,' I said, addressing both him and the audience simultaneously, 'I'm the only person on this platform who had nothing to do with deciding what the document should contain. I think it would be much better if one of the others explained.'

'But you wrote the final draft,' said Giles, also in a public voice.

Immediately a buzz went round among the journalists. *The document was written by Bryan Magee.* They scribbled hastily on their notepads, then leaned eagerly forward to see what I had to say.

I was trapped. I could not sabotage the document at its own press conference. But then, if I was not willing to support it in public, why was I sitting on the platform? For the only time in my life I spoke like the kind of politician I despise. I flannelled. I tried to present proposals which I myself saw as inadequate, as if they would meet the country's needs. I felt deeply ashamed, actually, even while I was talking. In the hope of not sounding as hollow as I felt I made a conscious effort to speak as effectively and persuasively as I knew how, so I pulled out all the stops. Afterwards the MPs complimented me with obvious sincerity on how well I had answered. But the best one of the journalists went away and wrote about the proposals in the same terms as I myself saw them. In other words, he was aware of the vacuity of what I was saying, and contemptuous of it. It embarrassed me deeply that he should think I believed it. But I could scarcely tell him or anyone else that I did not believe a word I had said. That whole incident has haunted me ever since, like the memory of a nightmare.

In 1979 the Callaghan government collapsed, dragged down by the failure of its policies. Into power came Margaret Thatcher at the head of a radical Conservative government. They saw socialism as the problem, not as the solution. Their prescription, in one sentence, was to free the economy as much as possible, putting an end to restrictive practices in the City, the professions, management and the trade unions. On the economic front it worked magnificently, and carried the country up to unprecedented levels of prosperity. An old-style Labour government would never have done it. It was a practical demonstration of the fact, beginning to be realized by the left not only in Britain but throughout the world, that the traditional economic prescriptions of socialism were worse than useless. However, in other areas of public policy – welfare, the National Health Service, education, the arts – a damaging price was paid for this economic success. The public services were starved to help finance economic growth. And the serious deficiencies they developed in consequence were to become the leading problems facing Britain in its domestic politics. The eventual renewal of the Labour Party was to take the form of embracing the economic transformation of society brought about by Margaret Thatcher while seeking solutions to the social problems which she had made so much worse. This required the Labour Party's abandonment of socialism, and also of the entrenched interests of the trade unions. There have remained some irreconcilable socialists who saw these things as betrayals of everything they had always believed in, but there were never again enough such people to play a positive role in British politics.

When Margaret Thatcher came to power she announced: 'We're going to *kill* socialism.' And I thought: 'You stupid woman, how can you possibly kill socialism?' But she did – or rather she killed the misconception that socialism was still alive, and spearheaded the public's abandonment of the socialist illusion. In countries all over the world, from the Soviet Union to Chile, she was revered as the stateswoman who took the lead in that essential and historic act of truth-facing. In global terms, as well as inside

Britain, she is without question the most important British politician since Winston Churchill. But there is a disparity between this fact and the woman herself. She was not a big person, and in some ways was a small one. Her life story gives an impression of bigness. She took a degree in chemistry at Oxford, and worked as an industrial scientist. Then she qualified as a lawyer. Then she became a Member of Parliament, and rose to become Britain's first woman prime minister. She did all this while being a wife and mother, bringing up two children. One looks at it all on paper and thinks: 'Good God, here was an amazingly all-round human being, a Renaissance woman.' But when you got to know the woman herself you found her limited, narrow, even blinkered.

Part of the explanation is that she brought a ferocity of concentration to bear on everything she did. It was actually a kind of tunnel vision, but it enabled her to achieve most of her aims successfully. In politics she had one big, simple idea and its time had come, and she was one hundred per cent certain of its rightness. This last element, her iron-clad sense of being right, combined with her aggressive energy to make her an irresistible force. A world in the throes of disillusionment with left-wing politics was crying out for an alternative, and she had it. Then came the most important fact of all: at the economic level, which was regarded universally as the most important level, her politics worked, unlike the socialist approach it had superseded. And nothing succeeds like success.

Although her belief in her policies was unshakable, she did not always feel secure personally. She was a woman in a man's world, and was susceptible to good-looking men, especially if they were tall, well dressed and smooth. She came from comparatively humble origins in a party that was class-conscious. She had, and knew she had, what academics call a second-class mind, whereas some of the politicians closest to her had first-class minds – for instance, in the early days of her leadership, Keith Joseph, and later

Geoffrey Howe and Nigel Lawson. For quite a time she was unsure of herself. It was only slowly that she came to terms with her possession of supreme power, and then with becoming a world figure. An element of give-away insecurity still showed after this in the way she started trying to bully her senior colleagues, humiliating them in front of other people, while at the same time being always kind to underlings. Like an overbearing mother, provided she was the boss there was nothing she would not do for those in her care. Her husband's nickname for her was 'The Boss'. She was not – to use words in their most simple sense – a nice person. But the country needed her, and she was its salvation. Not only would no Labour government have done what she did, no Conservative government under anyone else who was available would have done it either.

In retirement she shrivelled, and became obviously a small person, knotted up and insubstantial, white-faced and tense – with attitudes to match. Looking at her then, and talking to her, it felt impossible that she had been a world figure, and had achieved what she had. Of personal greatness there was no hint. But then, there never had been.

The knock-out blow to the preceding Labour government had been delivered not by its socialist left but by the trade unions. For this reason, when Margaret Thatcher set about removing the irresponsible powers of the trade unions she had the silent support of many in the Labour Party who thought a Labour government ought to have done that itself. Officially, though, the party – still financially dependent on the unions – felt that it had no alternative but to oppose her legislation in the House of Commons, especially since it was going to pass anyway. When I read the first of Thatcher's anti-union bills I could find scarcely a word in it that I disagreed with. In fact I was surprised by its mildness. Obviously she was being cautious, at least to begin with. I went along to my Chief Whip, Michael Cox, and told him I was not going to vote against the bill. There was no need, I said, for me to vote *for* it: it would go through without me, and in those circumstances I did not care to be the only Labour MP in the Conservative lobby. But I would not attempt to conceal my lack of support for the Labour Party's official line: I would attend the debate, and be publicly seen not to vote.

He invited me to sit on the comfortable sofa in his office, and sat down cosily beside me. He was very, very sorry to hear this, he said, because the leading figures in the party had singled me out for ministerial office when they returned to power; but of course that would not be possible if I publicly refused to support the party's policy. I was unbudged. He then put it to me that since most of the party's bills were paid by the trade unions it owed the unions some support in return. That left me unbudged too. As a third resort he tried to argue that the political merits of the case justified opposition to the bill. We went on for some time about this, but he found himself unable to produce convincing replies to my counter-arguments. After a long time he changed tactics again, and began to insinuate threats. The left were angrily opposed to this bill, he said, and were up in arms about it, making this the spearhead of their onslaught on Margaret Thatcher. He knew that the left in my constituency had given me a lot of trouble in the past, and had tried to deselect me as their MP: it would be possible, he said, for them to be given fresh encouragement, and to renew their endeavours, not on left wing grounds this time but on disloyalty grounds, for which they could expect to receive support from outside their own ranks, including all the trade union delegates to the local party. I told him he was too late. I had fought and won the battle against attempts to unseat me, and had settled the issue. Although some people would go on making trouble for me, they would not be able to get rid of me now.

We argued for over an hour. Most of the arguments he used I had heard already from the lips of Michael Foot on an earlier occasion of my withdrawal of support from the party's leadership over a trade union issue. And as with Michael Foot, so now with Michael Cox: after he started to make threats, the feeling in the air became horrid. I left him no alternative but to accept that nothing was going to make me vote against the bill. He signalled this acceptance by falling suddenly silent, then relapsing back into the deep sofa with a sigh like a punctured tyre. He put a hand on my thigh. 'Entirely between ourselves,' he said in a confidential, peace-making voice, 'I agree with you.' He subsequently became Lord Cox.

Although most of the Labour leadership privately approved of Thatcher's anti-union legislation, it was a long time before they woke up to the fact that it was no more than part of a wider programme for the deregulation of the economy as a whole, and that similar treatment was being meted out to business management, the Stock Exchange, the City of London, and most of the professions. As for the left, all they ever saw in Thatcherism was a right-wing attack on the working class and on socialist values, everything they themselves held dear, when in fact it was not a class thing at all. So the Labour Party as a whole never understood Thatcherism, never grasped the real point of it. And since the party was now in opposition, this enabled the left within the party to take over the party, a process which had been building up through the second half of the seventies. The decisive election for Labour's leadership came when Jim Callaghan retired in 1980.

For what occurred then, a failure of understanding on the part of Roy Jenkins was partly to blame. Roy had responded to his previous defeat for the leadership by leaving the House of Commons and going off to Brussels to become President of the European Commission. He did this because he thought that coming third in the leadership election – not even runner-up, he thought – meant he had no prospect of being elected leader of the party, when in fact it meant that he was now the crown prince and would succeed Callaghan (who was obviously not going to stay long). Roy had been the most successful right-wing candidate after Callaghan, so with Callaghan gone he would have inherited the vote of the right-wing majority (including mine). The referendum of 1975 having settled our membership of Europe, the passage of time had relegated the divisiveness of that issue to the past, and rendered Roy electable. In the discussions that went on among the Labour MPs about who we should vote for, one left-winger after another lamented to me the fact that Roy was not available. Because they knew Michael Foot well they knew him to be without leadership qualities, and they feared he might not be able to hold the party together. With Europe no longer an issue, they respected Roy for the social revolution he had brought about during the sixties, when he had been Home Secretary, and for his personal mastery of the House of Commons: he would, they thought, be the best leader for the party in existing circumstances. But he was no longer in the House. Of the four right-wing candidates last time, only one was now in the House, Denis Healey. (Crosland had died of a stroke in 1977, when he was Foreign Secretary.) Few on the left felt able to vote for Healey. He had been the first Chancellor of the Exchequer in any party to introduce monetarist policies, and the left saw these as a betrayal of socialism, the precursor of Thatcherism. In addition, he had been personally abusive to left-wing MPs who withheld their support from him at a time when he was desperate – I myself saw him shout 'You fuckers! You fuckers! You fuckers!' into the faces of a group of them in the debating chamber during a division. (Not, one might have thought, a way to win their support.) He had also incurred the enmity of the unions by insisting on real sacrifices from them. In ways that were to his credit he had been a precursor of the best aspects of Thatcherism. But it caused him to be hated both by the left and by the trade unions.

I know for a fact, from my own immersion in that leadership election and my knowledge of the way many MPs voted, that if Roy Jenkins had been a candidate he would have won. If this had happened, the Labour Party would not have split as it soon did; people like me would have remained in it; and the Social Democratic Party would not have come into existence. It is impossible to know how British politics would have developed then, but history would certainly have been different. As it was, Healey, for whom I voted, lost to Foot by only a dozen votes. This means, of course, that if only seven MPs had voted the other way he would have won. Some of the hard-nosed right-wing MPs, such as Neville Sandelson, had already decided that they wanted to break away from an increasingly left-dominated Labour Party, and claimed afterwards to have voted for Foot to precipitate a split. If they really did, it was culpable.

So the Labour Party did split, and the Social Democratic Party came into existence, under the leadership of Roy Jenkins. I had been publicly opposed to Foot's leadership, but for a year I went on hoping that sanity would be restored in the Labour Party, and did not immediately join the new party. I also knew that if I did I would lose my parliamentary seat. Leyton was such a safe Labour constituency that I used to say, when I was its MP, that if a chimpanzee stood as Labour candidate the chimpanzee would be elected. To me the decision to leave the Labour Party always presented itself as a decision to leave the House of Commons. When finally I took it I did so in that full knowledge. My departure from the Labour Party came at the beginning of 1982.

It is important for me to say that I left the Labour Party not in order to join the Social Democrats but because I could not go on any longer in the Labour Party. I was not enthusiastic about the new party, and did not join it immediately on leaving the Labour Party. For something like three months I was an independent MP; and, being free to call myself whatever I liked, I called myself

Independent Labour. During that period I considered all the options open to me except that of joining the Conservative Party: I considered resigning from the House of Commons, or remaining an Independent until the next general election, or joining the Social Democrats, or joining the Liberals. Two things, in the end, decided me to join the Social Democrats. First, I found being an Independent MP ineffectual. I was excluded from all the party networks of information, which meant that after a short time I had only an incomplete idea what was going on in the House of Commons. Finding out was time-consuming and only partially successful. I was like an isolated atom. There was almost nothing of significance that I could influence. Politics is a group activity, and I was made increasingly aware of the necessity of allying myself with others. At that point my second reason for joining the Social Democrats kicked in: some of my closest friends among MPs had joined them, while friends outside the House were increasingly doing so. If I wanted a political home, this was the one in which I would feel most at home.

When I joined, Roy Jenkins as leader asked me to be the party's front bench spokesman on Education. I immediately saw this as a shadow-boxing non-job, and one that would be all-consuming of my time: I would have to keep abreast of all developments in education, and establish myself as a public figure in the field, go to conferences, write articles for newspapers, be interviewed on television and radio, make speeches, and produce a policy for the party. I told Roy that this would entail the sacrifice of all my private working time, which was too valuable, and too productive, for me to give it up in exchange for work that was going to make no actual difference to anything. He said that this had been exactly his attitude during the long years of Labour opposition 1951-64, when he had been what he called a semi-detached MP. He had half-expected me, he said, to respond in that way. But he thought he ought to ask me.

I never formed an emotional attachment to the Social Democratic Party. When I lost my seat the following year, 1983, I quietly let my membership lapse.

There is a wry postscript to the story of the now-defunct Social Democratic Party. When the left seized control of the Labour Party they reversed its policies in three huge areas in particular, and it was over these three, more than any others, that the Social Democrats broke away. The left demanded large-scale further nationalization of private industry, unilateral nuclear disarmament by the West, and Britain's withdrawal from Europe. The former policies of the Labour Party had been the opposites to these. There would now be no question of Labour winning a general election until at least the first two had been turned back to what they had been. This meant, inevitably, that when Labour returned to government, in 1997, it did so on the policies of the Social Democrats. At the level of policy, therefore, the Social Democrats won, in the long run, in getting theirs accepted. But they did so at the cost of their personal careers in politics. I myself have never regretted this, but that is because I had other things to do. Some of my most gifted friends, on the other hand, experienced the loss of the only way of life they really wanted, and they lost it because they clung to what they believed to be right. In politics it does not do to be right too soon. More often than in any other profession, what happens to a person in politics may be decided by factors unconnected with his own abilities.

The eighteen years of Conservative government, 1979-97, coincided with the peak years of my professional life. If I had chosen to remain in the Labour Party, and therefore in the House of Commons, I could never have had much of a ministerial career, because I would have been on the opposition benches throughout those eighteen years, and would have been sixty-seven years old when they came to an end. This is the sort of thing that happened to a whole generation of talented left-of-centre people, many of whom I know. In politics they are a lost generation, and they are my own generation. They were not responsible for what happened to them – indeed, they fought to prevent it from happening – but their legitimate hopes for their own careers came to nothing. Some would have made good cabinet ministers; but they had to accept less interesting, less challenging lives.

I would not un-wish the period I spent in the House. It was an enormous, many-sided experience, and taught me a great deal. I learnt, from close up, how the country is actually governed, not only nationally but locally, and I was a small cog in the process. I got to know many people, sections of society, and institutions that I would never have known otherwise. As in all genuine learning, I was brought up against the difference between reality and expectation – how different society is from the way we usually think of it; and how different, too, politics and government are. Now that I am once more dependent for my knowledge of these things on newspapers and broadcasting I know how to decode the media. And I see with dismay how seriously they mislead people who do not have independent experience.

The lessons in practicality were great. But the experiences also changed my political philosophy. I saw how, in one case after another when the government intervened in problems of business and industry, always with good intentions, it made matters worse. The government is not fitted to run the economy. The entrepreneurial function is the motor of economic development, and can never be carried out successfully by bureaucrats. I came to realize that it was this last fact more than any other that had brought about the failure of socialist and communist economies. Only a successful economy can produce enough wealth to pay for the social policies I believe in for health, education, the arts, welfare, and the rest. And a successful economy can be based only on acknowledgement and acceptance of market forces, restrained and civilized in various ways but not denied or repressed, still less repudiated. What is needed, therefore, is a way of bringing the permissive and supportive social policies traditionally associated with the left into harness with the market economics traditionally associated with the right. Pursuit of the former without the latter has always led to bankruptcy and authoritarianism: pursuit of the latter without the former has produced affluent democracies that are marred by large-scale and avoidable social evils.

I was, of course, far from being the only person who passed through this learning process. All over the world, disillusionment was setting in with socialist economics. Only five years after I ceased to be an MP they were finally abandoned in the Soviet Union and the communist countries of Eastern Europe. A veteran and distinguished Austrian Social Democrat, Friedl Scheu, once said to me in Vienna: 'Between the wars we all thought that the difference between us and the communists concerned only means, not ends. Both of us wanted a socialist society, but the communists thought it would have to be achieved by violence, whereas we Social Democrats believed it could be achieved by peaceful means. What never occurred to either of us was that, regardless of how it was achieved, it wouldn't work anyway, and was undesirable. Our argument about method, which we supposed was the only issue, was superfluous. Socialism was undesirable, no matter how it was achieved.'

Such disillusionment was a personal upheaval of tragic dimensions for many individuals who had devoted their lives to the socialist cause. Some – understandably but mistakenly – tried to salvage as much as they could from the wreckage of their former beliefs, but this meant that, being desperately in need of orientation, they went on clinging to secondary socialist illusions after having abandoned the primary ones. A more fruitful response would have been to meet the challenge head-on and start thinking afresh, from the very bottom up, liberated from the erroneous suppositions of former days. The most common example of the mistake was to hang on to socialist assumptions about equality. These, I am sure, are mistaken, a hindrance, and an unnecessary one.

This was the biggest single thing I learnt from my constituents in Leyton, who taught me so much else besides. In the first public speech I made there, in the general election campaign of February 1974, to a packed audience in a large hall I demonstrated how the Heath government that I was fighting against had made the rich richer and the poor poorer in each one of its successive budgets. In the questions that followed, the main theme of the questions was: 'That's all very well about the rich getting richer, but what we want to know is, if we elect you, what are you going to do for *us*?' Over the following years I became familiar with the fact they did not mind other sections of society being a lot better off than they were. What they wanted was properly paid jobs for themselves, decent housing conditions for their own families, acceptable schools for their own children, adequate pensions for their own elderly parents, effective health care for all their family when they were ill, and so on; and they were angry if they were denied these things. However, if they had them, they did not really care what other people had. To mind that would have been envy, and they were free of that, for the most part. Equality, which is such a shibboleth among middle-class socialists, seemed to them an irrelevance. If one quizzed them about it directly, as I did, they tended to say that they did not actually like the idea of a society in which people were all in the same circumstances. They would rather have one in which there were different lifestyles, including those of stars and celebrities, and some people living colourful lives; most important of all a society in which it was possible for an individual to rise by ability or hard work, or good luck. That was both fairer and more interesting, they thought; and they enjoyed reading about it in the newspapers, and seeing it on television. Without those things the world would be a dull place.

Often they had aspirations for their children, and wanted them to rise – in which case, again, they considered it of prime importance that rising should be possible; and they were opposed to the creation of impediments to it. Opportunity was the thing, they thought, not equality – which was so often appealed to in order to deny people opportunity. If they had resentments it was not against social classes outside their experience, not against individuals they never met, it was against those within their world who appeared to them scroungers or layabouts, or against immigrants coming in from outside and taking their jobs or jumping the housing queue. They were not particularly class conscious. I had been familiar with this latter phenomenon as a small child. I lived my first dozen years among working-class people and scarcely heard them mention social class: I do not think I ever heard my parents mention it. Now, as MP for a working-class constituency, I was encountering the same thing again. During the years in between, I had become used to hearing middle-class people refer to class constantly, and mistakenly take it for granted that their class consciousness was shared by everyone.

I concluded that my constituents were right. The sort of equality that is valuable is the sort associated with the United States, not the sort associated with socialist societies. There has to be a rule of law, and all individuals must be equal before the law. The government itself must be subject to the law. In social life, the rights of each individual must be respected, and the doors of opportunity must be open to everybody. But this very openness and freedom is bound to produce a variety of disparate outcomes, and these are to be not only accepted but respected, so long as the openness and freedom remain. The great defect of the socialist conception of equality is that it can be achieved – and, once achieved, maintained – only if enforced; and therefore it runs directly counter to openness and freedom, and hence to opportunity. This is another reason, in addition to the requirements of planning, why in the real world socialism has been associated extensively with authoritarianism.

All my adult life I have reflected and written about politics, and I published two or three books of political ideas before becoming an MP. But being a professional politician for nearly ten years greatly enriched the substance of my thoughts, and forced me to change some of them in the light of experience. It also compelled me to relate them more insistently, and more rigorously, to reality. In doing so it provided more solidity to my outlook, and improved my practical judgement. But I fear it also made me impatiently dismissive, as perhaps I ought not to be, of some of the ways of thinking I was guilty of once myself: people who talk like that lack knowledge and experience – but then so did I.

When I am asked if I achieved anything as an MP, anything that would not have happened without me, I mention first and foremost the release from prison of my constituent David Cooper after he had been there for more than ten years (with the prospect of another ten) for a murder which he almost certainly did not commit. All the achievements I value most were in constituency casework, and all of them changed somebody's life, but this one was far and away the most worthwhile; and also, by a long way, the most difficult.

The story of the crime itself, which would make a good thriller, is this. Four men set out to rob a post office, the robbery goes wrong, the postmaster is shot dead, and the criminals scatter. Police pick up one of them. Unknown to the police, he is the one who fired the lethal shot. He knows that if the police catch any of the others they will reveal this in order to exculpate themselves. So he offers to turn Queen's evidence, in return for immunity, and then names as his accomplices three people who were not there. These are professional criminals, well known to him and to the police, men whom the police want to see behind bars in any event.

So, together, the murderer and the police frame the three men, the police believing them to be guilty. (Some of my readers may not realize that it was not uncommon for police to frame the evidence in a trial against people they believed to be guilty. Naturally, they sometimes made mistakes.) A high-profile trial is held, to great public attention, and the three men are found guilty and sent to prison for life. Some of the reward money offered by the post office is then paid to the murderer, and some to the police chief who supervised the framing. The latter is himself sent to prison a few years later for corruption in another case, and finds himself as a fellow-prisoner with convicts he has framed. At this point the real murderer disappears.

That is the story. But in real life it came out in small pieces, and in higgledy-piggledy order, partly backwards, over many years, and oh so slowly, uncertainly. For most of that time I was in the position of not knowing what had happened. It was like putting together the pieces of an almost intractable jigsaw puzzle. At the original trial the judge said that this was a particularly horrible murder and recommended that the three men be held in prison for not less than twenty years. This has to mean that if we had still had the death penalty (which had only recently been abolished) they would have been hanged. In that case, that would have put an end to the matter, and the true story would never have come out. I would not have struggled for six years, as I did, to clear the name of a dead stranger.

For years I badgered Home Office ministers, had long sessions with them in their offices, wrote them long and closely reasoned letters. In response to this the case became the first in British legal history to be referred back twice by the Home Secretary to the Court of Appeal. I persuaded people in television to make programmes about it. I wrote newspaper articles, and persuaded others to write them. One of my *Times* pieces prompted the *Daily Mail* to mount a national campaign to get the three men freed, and the paper put its chief crime reporter on to the case full-time for three months. I never let up – and never would have let up. I was determined to keep the case before people's minds. Two of the things I did turned out to be decisive. I secured the interest of the most respected legal mind in the country, Lord Devlin, a former judge now in retirement; and he lectured and wrote about the case. And through my literary agent I got Ludovic Kennedy, the country's best known author of books about miscarriages of justice, to edit a book about it, to which Devlin and I contributed. This book, *Wicked Beyond Belief*, was published on 26 June 1980 – and three weeks later, on 18 July, my constituent David Cooper was released from prison.

The story in full, fascinating though it is, has too many twists and turns for me to re-tell it here. Readers who would like to see it should look at the Kennedy book. In the summary I have given, I have omitted major elements and characters – for instance the two other accused – and not even attempted to answer some of the questions that may have arisen in my readers' minds. In the section I wrote for the Kennedy volume I downplayed my own role. When I was writing it, Cooper was still in prison, and I knew it would leave a nasty taste in the reader's mouth if I seemed to be claiming credit – 'first I did this, then I did that' – while the brute fact was that my constituent was still in prison despite my efforts. I would look as if I were claiming credit for not achieving much. At that time I was painfully aware not only that I had not yet succeeded but that I did not know if I ever would; so I leant over backwards not to claim too much for myself. I wrote as if I had played only a secondary role – to the point, I now realize, of giving a wrong impression. The truth is that for many years it was I who kept the case alive when it would otherwise have died; and over that long period I got, one by one, each of the other people involved who together were to produce the successful outcome. Without Devlin we would not have succeeded. Without Kennedy we would probably not have succeeded. But without me none of it would have happened. So I hope I will be forgiven for claiming, now, if only for the record, a little of the credit.

8

My Forties

If I had to choose one of the decades of my life to live over again it would be my forties. This fact would have astounded me on my fortieth birthday. I woke up on that morning already depressed that I was forty. No longer a young man, my hair grey at the temples, I had now embarked on middle age, with nothing to look forward to after that but old age, if I should be lucky enough to get so far. No matter how much longer I lived, from now on the path could only run downhill.

But things looked even worse than that. At the beginning of my forties I was in a state of what could be called existential despair. All my life I had been trying to understand life, and I was now beginning to lose hope of ever doing so. I had studied the writings of nearly all the great philosophers, and although they taught me an extraordinary amount they did not dispose of the ultimate questions. These had continued, century in and century out, to be raised without being settled. I had explored religious thought too, but I found it – more so than philosophy – inadequate, because going less deep, though containing some good insights. I had feasted on the greatest of music, and seen the greatest plays and operas; and these perpetually brought transcendental reality into my life, yet they left me always grasping after something un-understandable, something unattainable. They left me with no room for doubt that there were important, perhaps all-important, realities outside the limitations of my understanding.

But because they were beyond my understanding I had no idea what they could be. The conviction deepened that there was no way in which, from inside this life, life could be understood. And the fear intensified that there might be no significance to it at all – that our existence might be a by-product, without any meaning, of accidental features of unknowable processes. All this was given the sharpest possible edge by death. It seemed I was going to be snuffed out, annihilated, obliterated, reduced to nothing, without ever having understood what it was about.

The prospect caused me despair and terror. I found it uncomeable-to-terms-with. Yet within a few years of being in this state I was living an exhilarated and fulfilled life. There were many reasons for this, but two were pre-eminent. They could be summed up by two words: philosophy and sex.

By the time I reached forty there was only one philosopher who was known by name to every educated person and yet whose works I had not read, and that was Schopenhauer. I read him belatedly. I can only say that he changed my life. His works teem with errors, some of them on a big scale; but so also do the writings of every other great philosopher, from Plato to Kant and beyond. Any competent philosophy student today can write essays exposing their faults. Yet, as Voltaire said: 'It is the privilege of true genius, and especially of the genius who opens up a new path, to make great mistakes with impunity.' What makes a philosophy matter is not being right about everything (none is: all the greatest philosophies are false theories) but how close it gets to the bone of truth about some things of the deepest consequence. Starting from the achievements of his mentor Kant, Schopenhauer writes with the deepest insight about the profoundest of all questions for human beings, namely how human experience itself is to be understood. What is it to be human? Why does our experience take the forms it does? What is the inner nature of this world in which we find ourselves? How do we relate to it? What limits are there on our ability to understand it – and why are they limits? These questions are answered by Schopenhauer with a profundity of insight that has never been surpassed. They are not evaluative or normative questions: they are about the way things are, the way reality is. He has a lot to say about other questions too – which things are good and bad, and how we ought to live. But that is not where his supreme value lies: it lies in his overall framework of descriptive metaphysics, his proffered explanation of how things actually are. In this I believe he and Kant have lifted the veil higher than anyone else. When I discovered his work it swept my understanding out to new frontiers, and in doing this it excited me in a way I have not been excited before or since. I studied his work for many years, together with that of the writers who had most influenced him, plus the creative people he most influenced. I knew that for me the only way to acquire a proper grasp of it all was to write a book about it, so I did. I worked continuously at this for ten years, intellectually the most nourishing years of my life. The book, *The Philosophy of Schopenhauer*, was published in 1983 by Oxford University Press. In 1997 they brought out a revised and enlarged edition, which is now the only one I would wish anybody to read: the second edition is the book as I ought to have published it in the first place. (Hume once remarked that a common mistake of authors, including himself, was to publish what they ought to regard as the penultimate draft of a book.)

During my second year in the House of Commons I was asked by the BBC to make a fifteen-part series of television programmes about contemporary philosophy. At first I was dubious about the possibility of bringing this off, and also dubious about my ability to manage such a huge addition to my work-load. But I took the plunge. It took me two and a half years to make the series, because each one of the programmes required several weeks of preparation. It then took me another six months to turn the series into a book. Throughout that period I was not only marinading in the work of many of the best contemporary philosophers, I also had ample opportunities of discussing their work with them personally, and in private. Some became friends. It is hard to indicate how much I learnt from this: among so much else it gave me an authoritative knowledge of their intentions – what they had been trying to do, and what they believed themselves to have done – and I also heard their privately expressed evaluations of one another. This was in addition to acquiring an understanding, which they themselves endorsed as accurate, of their work. I was now pressing against the outer limits of my own capacity for work; but I was finding it nourishing beyond expectation. It also brought me public rewards. When the series was shown, it turned out to be the biggest personal success I had ever had on television up to that time. The Royal Television Society awarded me its silver medal. More than thirty years later the book, now called *Talking Philosophy*, is still in print with Oxford University Press, is still widely read, and has been translated into many languages.

While I was feasting on this work I was also, to a degree I had never done before, living a satisfying sex life. This is not a subject I have ever discussed much, but if I am to tell the true story of my life I cannot ignore it. To find a satisfactory place to start I have to go back a long way.

I have been a divorcee for over half a century, during which time, inevitably, I have had a number of relationships with women. Some of these lasted for many years, some were flings, others lasted for durations in between – several months, a year, two years, three. I was never promiscuous. Until I was forty I had almost only ever had one relationship at a time. I had a powerful need not just for sex but for the affection of women. (If it needs to be made explicit, I am an ordinary heterosexual without any kinks, and without any homosexual leanings that I know of.)

During the first years of my separation from my wife, Ingrid, scalded by the experience, I was terrified of getting involved again, though I still needed sex. This resulted in a sequence of thin, evanescent affairs which were nearly always brought to an end by the woman because of my unwillingness to get more deeply involved. When Robin Schur broke up with her husband Val I did get involved, and she with me, but she refused to marry me. She did not believe we would be able to live together happily. In retrospect I think she was right. But she has held a special place in my affections all my life, and I have never lost the feeling of closeness to her.

In my early thirties I started to relax from my post-Ingrid angst and become more hedonistically involved. Sometimes, because of the social life that went with my work in television, it was with actresses whose attitude was the same as mine. These relationships could be enjoyed without any demand on either side for commitment. In connection with one of them there is a story to tell that would have made a good fictional short story.

I met an actress casually at a party, and discovered that we lived in neighbouring streets. There was no particular attraction between us, but out of neighbourliness she dropped in for a drink a couple of weeks later. While she was there a male friend called, and found the two of us drinking side by side on the sofa. I did not see either of them again for three or four months, but then she dropped in again, and while she was there the same man called and found the two of us in exactly the same position as he had left us in months before. She and I scarcely knew one another, but he assumed quite naturally that she was either living with me or was my girlfriend. He had actually come to invite me to a house party that was being given by his sister in Kent, so he said to the girl: 'And of course you would be welcome too.' I could scarcely say: 'No, don't invite her,' and was wondering how to deal with the situation when she looked at me and said: 'I could drive you there.' It was obvious to both of us that the man had mistaken us for a couple; but since in those days unmarried couples were automatically given separate rooms when they were guests, it did not occur to us to anticipate any problem at the other end. However, when the day came and we arrived at the house in Kent, we found it overflowing with guests. Our hostess came out to greet us as we got out of the car, and said: 'Every square inch of room in the house is taken. I've practically got people sleeping in the baths. I hope you won't object, but I've put you in the same bed. It's the only way of coping, and the truth is, I know you prefer it anyway. Come along,' – and, giving us no time to reply, she led us to our bedroom.

In what was the typically English way of behaving in those days, neither of us wanted to say anything that might embarrass our hostess, so we carried our luggage to the bedroom as if we, too, took it for granted that we were a couple. When she left us standing beside the bed we looked at one another and burst out laughing.

It was an enjoyable party, but the girl and I avoided one another – we left the awkwardness of our situation to be dealt with when we were alone. In particular we avoided dancing together. But when the party broke up we maintained appearances by heading upstairs together. It was now two or three o'clock. We undressed with our backs to one another, put on the pyjamas we had both brought, used the bathroom separately, got into bed, and switched out the light. Then, having barely communicated throughout the evening, we started gossiping about the party. We discussed the other guests. She questioned me about our hosts. We lay on our backs in the darkness chattering animatedly. We could hardly help being conscious of the sexual possibilities of the situation, but circumstances had dumped her into bed beside me without the slightest indication from her that she wanted it, and there was still no such indication. I was determined not to put pressure on her. So we just talked, for literally hours – we had both drunk a great deal – before we fell asleep. So it was getting on for noon when we woke up. When we emerged from our bedroom we found that the other guests had been up a long time, and were developing a running joke about what the two of us were up to. We entered to applause, followed by chuckles and innuendos. We could scarcely blow our own cover at this stage – it would have covered our hostess with confusion – so we let ourselves respond sheepishly, as if the teasing were justified. When our hostess finally saw us off in front of the house, it was with a complicit smile and an assurance that we must have had an especially enjoyable time, for which we had her to thank.

On the drive back to London we laughed about it delightedly all the way. When we drew up outside my flat I asked her to come in for a drink. As soon as we entered my front door, in response to a common but unspoken and immediate impulse, we went straight to bed together and made love. Something partly conscious but also partly unconscious had been held in check by both of us; and now came the release of all that pent-upness.

Our relationship lasted only a few weeks. There had never been a lot of warm sexual feeling between us, and after our first lovemaking, which was fairly fierce, the temperature cooled and we drifted apart. But among the guests who had been at the party we retained for a year or two the reputation of being insatiable lovers.

I went through a period in which I had a predilection for actresses. It was usual for them to combine physical attractiveness, and social ease, with inner insecurity, and this made them needy, intense lovers. I shared some of these characteristics myself, so I was on the same wavelength. But I moved in other circles too, and acquired other sorts of girlfriend. The most insubstantial were the political or Sloaney ones. The closest and longest lasting are not possible to pigeon-hole.

Only two or three of these relationships were with writers. One was Penelope Mortimer, author of *The Pumpkin Eater*. At that time

I did not know her husband John: their sex lives only occasionally coincided. She was saturninely beautiful, and I found her addictively attractive. She had an unusual degree of perception of what was going on inside other people, and yet scarcely any at all of what was going on inside herself. Her internal view of things was, for the most part, a solipsistic fantasy. This dislocation enabled her to behave impossibly with other people while at the same time understanding how they felt – two things that seldom go together. This prevented her from sustaining relationships, and eventually she decided she could do without them altogether. She ended up living alone for many years, during which time she was less discontented than she had ever been.

Another writer with whom I had a relationship was Anthony Storr's first wife, called (like his second) Catherine. It came about after he had left her. I had for some time been a family friend of the Storrs – Anthony, Catherine and their three daughters – and a frequent visitor, feeling quite *en famille* at their home in Hampstead. Suddenly, out of the blue, Anthony left them, and went to live by himself in Islington. They were devastated. Catherine said to me that it would have been easier for them if he had left for someone else, gone off with another woman, but this way showed he simply could not bear living with *them*. The three girls were similarly bereft. This wholesale rejection stunned them. Catherine was inconsolable at first, and wept repeatedly on my shoulder. It came naturally to me to put my arms round her at such times and murmur words of comfort. She turned to me increasingly often, and – I do not actually know quite how it happened – we ended up in bed together. It was not a situation I felt comfortable with. But it went on for some months. Not long afterwards she – who as well as being a novelist was a doctor and a psychiatrist – wrote a review of my book *One in Twenty* for the *Times Literary Supplement* (which in those days printed only anonymous reviews). In it she said how rare and refreshing it was for a book on homosexuality to be written by an author with no personal axe to grind. An alert reader might have wondered how the reviewer could possibly have known that.

The girlfriend I had for longest during my thirties was Philippa Copley-Smith, who was with me for two or three years. She worked as a secretary on *The Economist*. I had known her at Oxford, where we overlapped as undergraduates and she was the girlfriend of a student I knew. She was a curvaceous, peaches-and-cream blonde, famously attractive, but it had never occurred to me in those early days to think of her as a possible partner for me. It was to be another dozen years or more, when we were both well into our thirties, before the two of us got together. We had a lot of important past in common, and many friends. By that time she had become used to being spoilt by her boyfriends, and she behaved with them in a prima-donna-ish way, but I simply refused to have any of that. I was afraid of losing her because of this, but instead she became devoted. Her love-making was selflessly loving. Of all my long-past girlfriends she is the one I find myself thinking about most often now, and with the most heart-catching nostalgia.

Philippa died of cancer before her thirties were out. The disease was diagnosed at a time when her relationship with me was disintegrating, and her last months were unhappy beyond normal endurance. She knew she was dying, and was at the same time still in love with me and in the grip of our dying love affair. As for me, I was trapped in an impossible situation, but my plight was as nothing compared to hers. I was appallingly distressed by her situation, but about the central facts of it there was nothing I could alter. To this day I quite often think – only for a split second, before the absurdity of it hits home – that I see her, on the other side of a crowded room, or in the distance. There is no other long-lost love, or friend, with whom this happens.

Between Philippa and the onset of my forties I had only one relationship, and that was with a married woman who was still living with her husband. She was fifteen years younger than me, and had woken up inside a non-functioning marriage which, indeed, was soon to break up altogether. My relationship with Philippa had been a deeply sensual one, and this now carried on into the new relationship. I was now finding sex profoundly fulfilling. Yet I was still not able to commit myself to a life shared with a woman in other ways. It was as if the sexual relationship had its being separately from the rest of my life. My new girlfriend found this doubly isolating, accompanying as it did a failed marriage. Because of it, after several months, she brought it to an end, and left her husband at the same time.

As a young divorcee I had realized from the beginning that it was not only morally imperative but in everyone's self-interest, including mine, for me not to be a wrecker of marriage, a destructive force in the lives of my friends. I never made any hint of an overture to the wife or partner of someone I knew, not even when we were larking about. I did not want to risk destroying anyone's happiness. At any given time there were bound to be one or two already attached women in my circle to whom I was attracted, perhaps strongly, but I never showed it, nor did I ever do anything about it. When the relationship I have just been writing about ended there were two such people. One was the wife of an old but not especially close friend. I found her so discombobulatingly attractive that I could scarcely control my tongue when I was with her, and sometimes fell over my words when I talked to her. I kept dreaming about her. We are going to call her Isobel. The other was Maria Rossman, the partner of Michael Meyer, of whom more later. In the year I became forty I went to a party at which both of them were guests. It was to be the most consequential party of my life.

On a Sunday evening, when it would otherwise have been closed, a smart-ish night club was hired by a friend of mine for a private party which went with a swing. Late in the evening, feeling about Isobel as I did, I asked her to dance. By this time most of the couples were wrapped around one another, but I held Isobel at a respectable distance. However, the dance floor was almost impenetrably dark, and as we shuffled around it, hidden from view by crowded couples as well as darkness, I became aware that she was easing her body into mine. In particular she was easing her pubic area into mine – and then making tiny movements. These movements gave me an erection – whereupon she pressed herself hard against it. At the same time, with the hand that was behind my shoulders, she stroked the back of my neck. We were almost as close to making love as two people with their clothes on could be. I embraced her as passionately as circumstances permitted. By the end of the dance our blazing cheeks were crushed against one another. When the dancers began to disentangle themselves she murmured into my ear in ironic tones: 'I'd better be going back to my husband.'

She slid away from me in the darkness, and I reeled off the dance floor alone. I was in a welter of violent and contradictory emotions. There were no two ways about what was happening: she was offering herself to me. And for some time I had been almost uncontrollably attracted to her. And I was now unattached. What about my so-called principles? What about my determination not to get involved with a friend's wife? My insides were in turmoil. There was a sudden craving for a strong drink, and I headed for the bar.

On the way I bumped into Maria Rossman. Not having hitherto noticed her at the party I was surprised to see her there. Aroused as I was, and having always found her unusually attractive, I asked her to dance.

'I'm just leaving,' she said, not in the friendliest of tones.

In that case I could see she must be heading for the exit alone. I said: 'Is Michael here?'

She put on a resentful expression. 'Didn't you know? He and I have broken up.'

'Really?'

'Yes.'

'Permanently?'

'Yes.'

'Can you be sure it's permanent?'

'Yes.'

'Is he here?'

'No.'

'Are you here by yourself?'

'Yes.'

'Have you been here all evening?'

'Yes.'

At this point she precipitately gave me an automatic-pilot goodbye kiss and left. (In those days, among my friends in London, the two sexes always kissed on meeting and parting.)

More turmoil. Maria was free.

I could see a way out of my dilemma. I knew I was incapable of living for long without a sexual relationship, but if I could establish one with Maria – with whom I had always wanted one – I could stop myself from getting involved with Isobel. Otherwise I knew I was lost, for even when I had had a happy relationship with someone else I had found Isobel almost irresistible.

I telephoned Maria the next day.

I suspect that readers will have guessed already what happened. I did indeed form a relationship with Maria, which lasted, with two gaps, for eleven years, and was the longest in her life (and the longest open relationship in mine). But at the same time, during those immediately early days, Isobel invited me first to one thing and then another, and I always accepted, and became involved with her too – and that turned out to be for a lot longer than with Maria. Suddenly, in my forties, I was passionately involved with two women.

This was the bedrock on which my profound happiness in ensuing years was built. Everything else took its place on top of that: my many-sided life as a Member of Parliament, my music-loving and theatre-going, my television work, my London social life, my travels abroad, my saturation in the philosophy of Schopenhauer. My health was good, and my energy seemed inexhaustible. There was nothing in life that I wanted and was not having. I felt I was living to the full, living to the uttermost.

Once, early on in this wonderful period of my life, Isobel spent an afternoon in bed with me on a day when I was due to meet Maria in the evening. I was alarmed at the prospect, not just because I feared that the bed might smell of Isobel but because Maria would think there was something wrong if I did not make love to her, and I was afraid I might not be able to. However, when night came I was so aroused with Maria that she remarked on it, happily. From then on I never had any fears about making love to both on the same day. It did not happen all that often, but when it did I was always more deeply aroused the second time than the first, no matter which way round they came. I made the surprising discovery – surprising for me at least – that the most deeply arousing of all aphrodisiacs is sexual intercourse itself.

Each of the women knew there was someone else, but did not know who it was. And I never talked to one about the other. Isobel said she considered it inevitable that there should be someone else: she herself was married, after all. Also, she could never be seen alone with me in public, and she knew that with all my theatre and party going I was bound to go out with women. She said once – and I was humbled – 'I don't care who else you make love to so long as you don't stop making love to me.' She claimed, though I never knew whether to believe it fully, that it was her relationship

461

with me that enabled her to stay with her husband, and hold her family together. She had children whom I would not have been able to bring up in the way they were accustomed to, so it is possible that the course we were following was the best for all concerned. I later acquired reason to believe that her husband was involved with someone else anyway, though when I said this to her she refused to believe it.

Now, as I sit here writing these words, it is more than forty years since my relationship with Isobel began. Over those years we have managed to meet abroad, and in other parts of Britain, as well as (perpetually) in London; but as far as we know there is no one else in the world who realizes what the relationship between us is. It has illumined my life. It means more to me than I would ever be able to put into words. To have enjoyed both it and freedom at the same time has been an unbelievable blessing.

Maria, at first, was unaccepting of the fact that I had another girlfriend. She said she was in love with me and wanted to marry me. But in those circumstances the last thing I wanted was marriage. The existing situation suited me to perfection. But it could go on only if I lived alone. Isobel was living with her husband and children, and Maria lived with her daughter Nora in a flat that she had been set up in by Nora's father, Michael Meyer. The role of Michael in this story is one to which I must now turn.

Michael and I had known each other years before, through our common association with Sweden. He was well known in that country: from the time I first went there I met people who asked me if I knew him. Having translated Ibsen's plays from Norwegian into English, and written what established itself as the standard biography of Ibsen, he went on to do the same for the most famous of Sweden's writers, Strindberg. Michael's family were timber merchants who carried on a large-scale business with Scandinavia and kept a flat in Stockholm. (The whole family background, Jewish, is of unusual interest – for instance Michael's grandfather owned Lords cricket ground – and Michael has told the story sparklingly in his autobiography *Not Prince Hamlet*.) He was rich by inheritance without having to be involved in the family firm. It was his brother Peter, a brilliant translator of classic French farces, who became chief executive. Michael never wanted to marry, but in middle age he began to feel a desire for an heir. Maria, a lot younger than him, had recently become his girlfriend, so he suggested to her that they have a child. He promised to go on supporting both her and the child whatever might happen to their relationship. She wanted a child, so she agreed. Their daughter, Nora, was named after the heroine of Ibsen's play *A Doll's House*. Michael doted on Nora; but after her birth his interest in Maria dwindled. She told me years later that she had said to him during that period that she was attracted by me, and it became a running joke between the two of them that she was 'in love' with me; but no such realization had ever entered my head. She also told me that when she bumped in to me at the party at which our relationship was triggered, the reason she was leaving was that I had been ignoring her all evening.

Maria was twelve years younger than me, so at that time, when I was forty, she was twenty-eight. She had a Swedish passport, and everyone, including me, thought of her as Swedish. In fact she was Estonian. She was born in Nazi Germany in the depths of the Second World War to Estonian parents in a refugee camp. Her parents (if she is to be believed), acted as stool pigeons for the Nazis among the refugees. When the Russian army swamped them all at the end of the war her parents fled for their lives to Sweden with their children, of whom Maria was the youngest, and still very small. So she grew up in Sweden, in a family that spoke Estonian at home, and she was bilingual in Estonian and Swedish. By the time I knew her she also spoke excellent German, French and English, her English having only the slightest trace of a Swedish accent. To look at, she was classically Swedish: tall and well built, with long shanks and blonde hair, very striking. She strode rather than walked: I was always conscious of her thighs, though that may have been partly due to unconscious sexual communication on her part. In practice, her life had organized itself round sex. She was more dedicatedly desirous of sexual intercourse than any other woman I have ever known, but she attached herself exclusively, and with great intensity, to one man at a time. She had had a baby at the age of sixteen, and given the child up. Although she had no money of her own, she had never had a job. She regarded the very thought of a job with contempt, as something beneath her. She was a painter, and she thought of herself as an impecunious artist who managed to rub along in one way or another in a bohemian sort of way. In fact she had always been kept by men. Throughout the years I was with her she was kept by Michael.

A couple of nights a week she would hire an overnight baby-sitter and go out with me, usually to a theatre, concert or opera. We would have supper out somewhere afterwards, and then go back to my flat for the night. On other evenings she would be with Nora. Michael visited them frequently. Although he and I got on well, neither of us felt it appropriate that I should be around during the time he spent with his daughter, so I was seldom there. This pattern of life had unintended side-effects. Because I was rarely at Maria's flat I seldom met her other friends; and because I saw my own friends on evenings when I was not with Maria, my friends seldom met her. Years after my relationship with her had begun I still had good friends who had never met her. I went to the theatre a great deal with other women, and naturally invited most often the ones I liked best or found most attractive, yet I never made overtures to them, and they were sometimes surprised, even puzzled. I did, over the years, have one or two flings, but they were very short, for the simple reason that I found it impossible to handle three women at the same time. The only third relationship that acquired any longevity did so because it was located in

Denmark. At least once a year I visited my daughter Gunnela in southern Sweden, and this involved flying to Copenhagen and then taking a ferry across the sound. A chance sequence of events resulted in my acquiring a girlfriend in Copenhagen, so I took to staying with her for a few days on the way to Sweden and then again on the way back. Occasionally she would fly to London and stay with me in my flat. Although she was never there for more than a week at a time, I found the juggling involved disconcerting. My feelings for her were true and tender, and our relationship carried on for several years. We are still friends.

In the account of events that I have just given, I find I have telescoped time for the sake of clarity and brevity. In the first couple of years when I was with Maria and Isobel, Maria, who was exclusively faithful to me, chafed under the fact that I was not exclusively faithful to her. Nothing would have induced me voluntarily to give up either her or Isobel: I needed both. That it was possible to have both, and without deception, was proved by the fact that I did, and I simply wanted that situation to continue. Isobel had no objection to it. But at first it was not to be. After a couple of years, Maria went off in dudgeon, and married a man who had been importuning her to marry him. I was left with Isobel alone for a couple of years.

In some ways these were her and my happiest years together, because my most powerful emotions were all concentrated on her. It was my period first at All Souls, then as a new Member of Parliament, so there was a lot else going on in my life; but although Isobel was a woman of character she was always supportive of me, and was never demanding. Our relationship had to be sealed off, kept apart from everything else. Often at the end of a morning she would arrive at my flat with a basket, and we would have a picnic lunch on the sofa, then go to bed and make love. Afterwards I would lie beside her feeling a kind of radiant joy towards her, and only the faintest touch of guilt or satisfaction about the Prime

Minister's Question Time I was missing. As between attending the House of Commons for a pointless charade or being in bed with Isobel I never had the slightest doubt which was the more worthwhile.

One day, when this monogamous relationship with Isobel had been going on for a couple of years, and I was in my flat alone, there was a ring at my front door bell, and there stood Maria. For a moment we just stood looking at one another. The situation was self-evident.

She said: 'It's no good. I've never not been in love with you. I want to come back.'

I did not say a word, but just stood aside to let her in. She walked straight past me into the bedroom, and without another word we made love for the first time in two years.

During that interim Maria had not only married but had had another daughter, Tiu (an Estonian name). In the same way as she had come to me first of all with baby Nora, now she came back to me with baby Tiu. The three of them proceeded to live happily together, and her life with me went on exactly as before. My relationship with her and Isobel was now one of unalloyed happiness. There was a new depth between me and Maria, who accepted the situation now – as had, from the beginning, Isobel. Our appetite for one another, sharpened by separation, grew. To lovemaking she brought a devotion of heart and soul, as if our sex were what she lived for. Something developed between us that eludes expression. When we made love I would lose all ordinary consciousness. We became ecstatic, both of us. She spoke for me when she said once: 'After we've been making love for half an hour I no longer know what's happening. I don't know what's going on any more. I'm fucked out of my mind. It's the same in the morning. When I leave here after breakfast I stagger across Hyde Park half not knowing where I am, or who I am. I'm completely fucked out of my mind.'

For both of us it was unlike anything else, and we formed what I can only describe as a shared addiction to it. I used to think: 'There's no possible way this can get better. I can make love to her in any way I want to, whenever I want to, as often as I want to, and none of it could be better than it is. There isn't anything that could possibly be "more", except just to go on doing it.'

I wanted this to go on for the rest of my life. In fact it went on only for the rest of my forties. Ever since I was a teenager, sex had had a central place in my life, but at no other time had it, or has it since, been so nourishing as it was during those years. Nowadays we delude ourselves that we are completely liberated in writing about such things, but in fact there is no way words can express them. The fulfillingness of the relationships I had with Maria and Isobel was something that could be lived but not communicated. It was, quite simply, the most important thing. It remained so through the bulk of my period as an MP, which saw the demise of Old Labour and the advent to power of Margaret Thatcher. It was so throughout the making of the fifteen-part television series that brought my reputation in broadcasting to its highest point. It was so throughout my foreign travels, which were numerous. It was of co-equal importance with my saturation in the philosophy of Schopenhauer – and these two were interconnected: one was the orgastic incarnation of something of which the other was an abstract realization. Only music was a presence of the same magnitude and importance. It was the completest life I could conceive of.

Because of Isobel's marital situation, and especially her attachment to her children, I had always had a vague apprehension that some day she might end our relationship; whereas Maria was so emotionally dependent on what we had between us that I believed she would always be passionately devoted to me. In fact I got it the wrong way round. Isobel never wholly left me (though she did drift away once or twice) whereas Maria did leave me –

first for a short time after she had been with me again for ten years; then, the following year, for good.

I was bereft. The fact that she had already left me once, long ago, ought to have taught me that it could happen again, but I failed to learn the lesson. I was incredulous when it happened, and I doubt whether I have ever wholly got over it, or ever quite come to terms with it. I reacted as to an amputation. The truth is, I think, that she had begun to fall out of love with me and then, because of that, to resent once more the fact that she was not my all-in-all, which in her heart she had always wanted to be. She started chafing about it again. It came to a head when I talked about taking a holiday alone. All my life I have had a need to go away by myself at times. It usually involves travelling abroad, in those years often to wander around a corner of the Mediterranean, or visit a new city I wanted to explore, or go to a music festival. This time I planned to spend the month of August (1980) exploring Switzerland, where I had never been, with a run-around ticket on those faultless railways. Maria wanted to come with me, but I said I wanted to go alone. Her general resentment at my not wanting to be with her all the time focused itself on this single issue, and she started threatening to leave me if I went without her: 'If you go, don't expect me to be here when you come back.'

I knew that if I gave way to her over this she would try to force the same issue over other things, so I would have to confront it sooner or later. I declined to change my plans. We spent the weekend before I went as guests in the country cottage of a couple who were two of my oldest, most trusted friends. On our first evening Maria announced that she was going to bed ahead of me, and did. After she had gone, our hosts asked me if anything was wrong, and I explained the situation. 'The most frightening thing,' I said, 'is that if she left me while I was here in England I'd know within forty-eight hours, and I'd be able to take instant action to get her back. But if she leaves me when I'm abroad I shan't even know she's done it till I return to England, and that could be three or four weeks later – by which time she might be dug in with somebody else.'

After pouring my heart out I went upstairs to Maria, and we made love as passionately as we had ever done – which seemed to assuage some of my fears. A day or two later I left England. What in fact happened, though I did not know any of this until much later, was that as soon as my back was turned our host, unknown to his wife, got in touch with Maria and arranged to meet her. Playing on her resentments as I had confided them to him, he seduced her – getting her to feel, as she told me later, that this was a way to get back at me for going off without her. They plunged into an affair, which by the time I returned to England was at the height of its honeymoon period. They intended that neither I nor the wife should ever know – Maria was going to refuse to communicate with me. However, by a coincidence so unlikely that it would take a long time to explain – a double coincidence (it would make a very implausible short story) – I found out almost as soon as I got back. The enormity of this betrayal by one of my closest friends, using the intimate confidences I had entrusted him with, enraged me so violently that I would have attacked him physically if I had met him during the first forty-eight hours, and might have done him a serious injury. But I simmered down, and began to think how I could get Maria back. She refused to meet me or talk to me. This left only one way I could see of ending the affair: I told the wife. Almighty rows exploded, but they trailed off, as I had calculated they would, and it all ended with the man staying with his wife and Maria coming back to me. I was scrupulous in doing this with maximum damage-limitation for the man: I could have disclosed a great deal more about him than I did, but I uncovered only as much as I needed to get Maria back.

In literally the middle of all this I was dispatched on a parliamentary delegation to Central America. It was a two-man delegation that at any other time would have been of unusual interest. The British colony that had formerly been British Honduras, and was now Belize, had become self-governing internally but was still dependent on Britain for its defence. This mattered, because its much more powerful neighbour, Guatemala, was asserting an active claim to it that went back to the nineteenth century. Belize was a small territory with a population of fewer than 200,000 people. Its biggest town, Belize City (built on stilts over a swamp) had fewer than 40,000 inhabitants; and the other towns were tiny. If the British were to withdraw, there would be nothing to prevent Guatemala from taking over. So the Belizean people were terrified of us going. However, the political class in Britain was frightened of getting into conflict with Guatemala of the kind we subsequently did get into with Argentina over the Falkland Islands. So the Belizeans were warned that they would have to prepare themselves for independence. Some of them went on clinging to the hope that a change of government in Britain would lead to a change in this policy, but in fact the two main political parties in Britain were agreed about it. So I and a Conservative MP were delegated to go to Belize and impress on the Government, and everyone else there, that whichever of our two parties was in power, Belize would still have to be independent.

Our arrival was momentous news. Everywhere we went, masses of people turned out to impress on us their hostility to independence – Guatemala was at that time a vicious military dictatorship. In one of the little towns, what looked like the entire population poured out to greet us carrying huge banners which read NO INDEPENDENCE. It was, I could not help thinking, like something out of an early Evelyn Waugh novel.

Our report when we got home contributed to a deal whereby Belize accepted independence, and became a full member of the Commonwealth, while at the same time requesting military advice from Britain in training an army of its own. This would be a cover for British troops to remain there, ostensibly to train Belizeans, but really so that any Guatemalan invaders would immediately find themselves confronting British troops. It was a high-risk strategy for Britain to follow, but it worked, and newly independent Belize was left unmolested.

A couple of things incidental to this trip are worth recalling. On the way out we visited another self-governing British colony, Bermuda, to give the people there the opposite assurance, namely that there would be no question of their having to become independent. So closely tied was their economy to that of the United States that they simply used American currency, and were happy with that, but they wanted to preserve political independence of the United States. We promised them that they could remain a British colony for as long as they wanted. Not only was no one threatening them, there was a US naval base on the island, so anyone attacking Bermuda would find himself engaging the Americans. This made us feel that our commitment carried with it no risk for us.

When we flew from Bermuda to Belize we changed planes in Miami, and on my arrival in Belize I found that my luggage had been impounded in Miami. Someone – it could have been an act of political malice – had mendaciously informed the authorities that I was carrying drugs. They took the contents of my luggage completely apart – took the heels off my shoes, squeezed all the toothpaste out of the tube, and so on. With its contents in this condition, my luggage arrived in Belize just as I was about to leave there for home. During the interim I had been dressed by the Brigadier in command of our forces. By the sheerest luck he took the same size in clothes as I did, so for the whole of my time in Belize I wore his civilian clothes.

Throughout my period in Bermuda and Belize I had, of course, to carry out my job in a professional manner while coping inwardly with the upheavals of my private life. I managed it, as British people are known for doing, but the heat and stress going on inside me were blistering. Rarely have I been under such strain. All the time I was away from Britain a searingly painful, ever-changing situation was working itself out back home; and it was still a little while after I returned before Maria came back to me. It was soon evident, though, that something between us had died. We both did our best, but it was not the same. Our mortally wounded relationship staggered, stumbled, halted, started up again, then fell dead. In one giant blow I had lost a whole family among my closest friends and also the woman with whom I had shared the most profoundly significant sexual relationship of my life.

Maria was now thirty-nine. She was to live only another ten years before dying of a heart attack, an especial tragedy for a woman of her age. During those years she married again, separated again, and then became the official mistress of a high-profile figure in Swedish diplomatic life, a prominent hostess on the international circuit. She had no more children. (I have to this day never met the child she had at sixteen, a boy called Joachim, though after she broke with me she made an unsuccessful attempt to re-establish a relationship with him.) Not long before she died she told her daughter Tiu that of all her relationships with men the one that had meant most to her was the one with me. In a fundamental respect I could say the same about her.

I suffered permanently from the loss of Maria, but inevitably I got involved in other relationships. I still had my long-established, secure and happy relationship with Isobel, which continued undisturbed by those other affairs. About some of them there are good stories to tell; but the women are now with other men, so the stories have to remain untold. At one point I came close to marrying, or at least to the brink of selling my flat in order to live with someone – at which moment she panicked and cried off. I have lived alone ever since. In my fifties I had an Australian girlfriend of whom I was especially fond. In my sixties I fell, for the first time, in love in the way that writers of popular songs describe: the image of the woman filled my head night and day, to the exclusion of all else, every second that my mind did not have to be specifically occupied with something else. After thinking about her all day I would get into bed at night thinking about her, dream about her, and wake up the next morning thinking about her. It was the only time I have ever had this experience. In a way it was quite pleasurable, but I did begin to feel that it was cutting me off from everything else. It carried on like this for about a year.

It is a melancholy fact that more than half the women who have been closest to me are now dead: my first big love, Caroline; my wife, Ingrid; Philippa; Maria. Isobel is still here, thank God – and so is Robin, who for most of my life I thought of as the woman I wished I had married. I believe I am still loved. But in my eighties I no longer expect to form new relationships of this kind.

If that is so, I can look back now and view this aspect of my life as a whole. It has been foundational. During those early periods when I was sometimes without a sexual partner I was obsessed by the need for one; and when there has been sex in my life it has been at the centre of everything. Sex is inexplicable, un-understandable. As the means whereby life itself comes into existence it is miraculous. The roots of the being of each one of us reach down into it to unfathomable depths. I am surprised that the great philosophers have not given it some of their profoundest reflections, but the fact is they have not – except for Schopenhauer, a lone voice in this as in so much else. I feel the same incredulous and astonished gratitude for it as I do for music. Even by itself, it makes life worth having lived.

9

Becoming a Full-Time Author

1982 was a milestone year for me. In January I finished the book on Schopenhauer I had been working on for ten years, and it was accepted by Oxford University Press. I left the Labour Party after twenty-seven years as an active member of it, knowing this would also mean leaving the House of Commons at the next general election. Maria broke with me for good, having been with me for most of eleven years.

During the long parliamentary summer recess I went to Australia for the first time, a visit of nearly three months, at the invitation of the philosophy department of the University of Sydney. The chief thing this visit cost me was my relationship with a woman back home who had been solacing me for Maria's loss. At first she sent me hotly passionate letters every day, then no letters at all for a while, and finally one starting 'Dear Bryan'. Left alone by me on the other side of the globe, she had become involved with someone else. Fortunately, Australia turned out to offer compensations. I loved it, and have remained an Ozophile for the rest of my life.

When I returned to England I knew that the next general election could not be far away. Not altogether consciously, I was already loosening my ties with the House of Commons, and orienting myself to a life outside it. When the transition came, in June 1983, I was surprised by how easy it was.

The day after the general election – having been up all night watching the results, and been interviewed on television at three or four o'clock in the morning, and having lost my seat – I was elected President of the Critics' Circle of Great Britain. This consisted of six self-governing sections – Drama, Music, Dance, Film, one section for Art and Architecture, and one for Television and Radio. I had for many years belonged to the Drama and Music sections. The following month my book on the philosophy of Schopenhauer was published. At the same time the BBC invited me to present a weekly series of television discussion programmes, on Sunday afternoons, to be called *Thinking Aloud*. I did that, and the series carried over into a second year. During this period there was also a carry-over in my love life from the time I had been in Australia. Altogether, then, I felt I was still living actively on all fronts, and with a new freedom. My friends began to say I looked younger. To my own surprise I did not miss being in the House of Commons.

Even so, connected with my leaving the House, a change had occurred in my view of myself. Since I was a schoolboy I had thought my true self was a writer of books and a politician. It seems to me today that I ought to have examined that thought critically when I reached maturity, but I did not: I just carried on with it. Even when I became a television reporter and got to know many of the ablest MPs at close quarters, and found the experience a disillusioning one, it still did not cause me to question my expectation of becoming one of them. Only when I found myself in the House of Commons did I realize that this was not the place for me, and not a life I wanted. Perhaps my self-development required me to grow in that direction up to that point. This could be so: I learnt an enormous amount from doing it, and have never regretted it. It is part of the me that I am. But I had nevertheless come to realize that being *now* a politician was not for me, and I did not want even to continue being active in politics. I had done with it. At the end of 1983, without making any public statement about it, I slid quietly out of the Social Democratic Party by simply not renewing my subscription. I have not belonged to any political party since.

So I was no longer, in my own mind, a politician and a writer. I was a writer. And for myself I had always thought of writing as writing books. I learnt early on from experience that I did not enjoy writing articles. They are irritatingly short-breathed, stop-and-go, unsatisfying, frustrating. I was a natural broadcaster, and derived pleasure from earning my living on television and radio, but I was not a natural journalist, and I began to avoid writing articles. Never have I done it for a living, and for decades now I have turned down almost every request I receive to review a book or write an article.

But of course the age-old financial problem of being a writer of books returned. I no longer had a parliamentary salary, so I needed to do something else to earn a living. Because of my previous experience, television offered itself to me automatically – and I accepted it automatically. But the reason why my broadcasts had possessed whatever quality they had was that I put so much work into them: I prepared each one obsessionally. If I were running a whole series, it squeezed the time I had for everything else. I was now, once more, back in that dilemma.

I had completed three books while I was in the House of Commons. I had written the final draft of *The Story of All Our Lives*, the whole of *Men of Ideas* (today republished as *Talking Philosophy*), and the whole first edition of *The Philosophy of Schopenhauer*. *The Story of All Our Lives* had pushed my emotional understanding of life to what at that time were its limits; and the Schopenhauer book had come near to doing the same with my intellectual understanding. In that sense the two books were complementary. *Men of Ideas* had brought me up to speed on what contemporary philosophers were doing. I now wanted to make further advances.

My own reflections, and all my studies in philosophy, had led me to the conclusion that our human ability to grasp reality is radically limited. The philosophers whom I regard as having taught us most about what our limits are, and why they are limits, are Kant and Schopenhauer. In their attempts to identify these limits they each made wonderful advances in our understanding of them – our understanding of our own powers of understanding. Throughout my forties I was learning from Schopenhauer, and advancing with seven-league boots. However, I was not convinced that the limits of human understanding are as constrained as he believed – and he was the more liberal of the two philosophers in this respect. That such limits exist is a fact, and we need to face it and live with it if our attempts to understand our situation are to have any chance of approximating to the truth. But I think there may be un-annexed territories that can be brought within the bounds of what we can understand.

I had spent my time in Australia trying to find out where these territories might lie. My attempts came to nothing. I went on to reflect that if I could not find a way forward by myself it might be a good idea to seek more help from the greatest of the philosophers. From the position I had now reached, I might be able to learn new things from some of those I had already read, and be stimulated by them to new thoughts. I decided to follow, in an enlarged form, an option I had taken once before. The radio series that was published as *Modern British Philosophy* had enabled me to reread and reconsider, after something approaching twenty years, the philosophy I had studied as a student. My two subsequent television series, *Something To Say* and *Men of Ideas*, had enabled me to saturate myself in the most interesting of contemporary thinking across a much wider spectrum, but including contemporary philosophy. Now that I found myself pressing against the limits of understanding *as such*, of 'understanding' itself, I wanted to try to rethink my way, if I could, through Western philosophy, starting with the Ancient Greeks – to reread in chronological order the greatest of the philosophers from Plato to Wittgenstein. My hope was that doing this would give me continual prompting and stimulation, and lead me to think of some possible way, or possible ways, forward. I knew it would constitute two or three years' work; but if, as before, I could make a broadcast series out of it, I could be paid for doing it, and survive.

After *Men of Ideas* the BBC had left me an open invitation to make a television history of Western philosophy. I had left it lying on the table for several years, even allowing myself to get involved with *Thinking Aloud* instead. Now I picked up this long-standing invitation. Like *Men of Ideas*, it was for a series of fifteen 45-minute programmes which would then be turned into a book that the BBC would publish. At first I imagined I could combine my earliest preparations for it with continuing work on *Thinking Aloud*. But when I found myself having to spend a Christmas Day morning studying Aristotle's *Metaphysics* I knew I had bitten off more than I could chew. I asked to be released from *Thinking Aloud*. The result, eventually, was *The Great Philosophers*, both the television series and the book. I learned an indescribable amount from doing this. By immersing myself once more in the supreme classics of Western philosophy, in a systematic and disciplined way, and then discussing each of them at leisure, in private, with an esteemed specialist, I deepened my understanding of them incomparably, and secured a tighter intellectual grip on all of them. Yet at the end of it all, as at the beginning, I could not see how to make a significant forward move from them. Although I had solidified and strengthened my understanding of *them*, I had still not advanced beyond them. I valued highly what I had done, but it was not what I had hoped for. The television series and the book were, each of them, my most successful to date: the programmes were screened at a peak viewing hour every week for nearly four months, and during the same period the book was in the best-seller list.

Perhaps, I thought, until I can achieve some kind of intellectual breakthrough, writing a novel is the only way to carry on the sort of exploration I feel a need for: something freely created, allowed to find its own way up from my unconscious, my intuitions. It was many years since I had finished my previous one, and I had done a lot of living since then: perhaps unconscious feelings and perceptions had developed to a point where they would be able to carry me forward.

Fundamental to my development, and to my happiness, had been my sex life, so the new worlds this had opened up would have to come into the novel. But I did not want a novel that was only about sex. I wanted to write about that truthfully, as it is, but also about its organic relationship with the rest of life, including public life. I wanted to write about political affairs on an international scale, in a way that integrated the private lives of some of the individuals involved, including their sex lives. To make it unsurprising that my two main characters should find themselves in flesh-and-blood closeness to global high politics I made one of them a television reporter and the other a Member of Parliament. Having myself been both, I felt I could provide true-to-life depictions of those two worlds, depictions from inside. Communist governments were still at that time in power all over Eastern Europe and Russia, so I worked out a realistic plot involving personal contacts and betrayals at the highest level between individual members of the British and Russian governments, including a hair-raising risk of world nuclear catastrophe. I was helped in making my details of place and atmosphere authentic by having been one of a parliamentary delegation to the Soviet Union that had held talks on defence and trade deep inside the Kremlin, with members of the Supreme Soviet, and had also had a long meeting in his office with President

Podgorny. Because my canvas was large I felt the novel had to be big, but I was comfortable with that – *The Story of All Our Lives* had taken several years to write, so I already had practical experience of such a project.

After I had been working on this book for a couple of years, and was a third of the way through it, something happened which I, like everyone else, had failed to anticipate. Communist Europe imploded. Bloodlessly, and with breathtaking suddenness, one after another, its governments fell, including that of the Soviet Union. The way this happened was unprecedented in history. Tyrannies have often been overthrown by violence from within, or by invaders from without; great empires have relapsed into internecine fighting, or been defeated by other empires; over long periods of time tyrannies and oligarchies have evolved peacefully into democracies, as in Britain; but nothing like this had ever happened. A gigantic, evil empire fell suddenly to bits, without loss of life, simply because of its failure to work. Even its own privileged ruling class had ceased to believe in it – they knew better than anyone else what a failure it was. It fell to nothing, like a house of cards. This was a marvellous, wonderful thing. But with it collapsed the projected plot of my novel.

I could no longer keep the novel's setting in the present without turning it into a fantasy, an as-if novel, counter-factual, which was contrary to my whole intention. On the other hand, if I moved the action back in time to a now-defunct Cold War, the plot would be denied suspense, because the reader would know from the beginning how things turned out, and would know that they transpired differently from the risks and dangers assumed in my plot – which would now come across feebly, for that reason. The relentless realism and detailed accuracy with which I had worked the plot through to the end was now a crippling handicap. I did not know what to do. My attempt to write fiction was as frustrated at this juncture as my wish to write philosophy. I believed in the value of what I had written to that point – I thought the manuscript contained some of my best writing – but I still had only the first third of a novel. There was no alternative but to put it aside until I could see how to carry it on. I never found that out.

Frustrated, then, along the lines of both philosophy and fiction, I was wondering what to write. I felt, as always, a need to work on a book of some sort. This had always been, for me, an indispensable way of clarifying and ingesting my own perceptions, my understanding of things. That sort of work, even if it goes on only in the background, provides my life with a continuity and coherence that I otherwise miss, and whose absence disturbs me. For me there is an element of compulsion about writing. At that time, as always, I was carrying on work of another kind for a living. I was making a long series of one-hour programmes for BBC Radio 3 called *What's the Big Idea?* In these I would pick out some influential concept such as socialism, or leisure, or the family, and examine the state it was currently in, getting people with fresh ideas to discuss it. I derived, as always, pleasure and reward from this, and it kept the wolf from the door. But as a writer I was stuck.

Then I found myself following a new line of thought. Since what I was always trying to do, at bottom, was understand life itself – and therefore, inevitably (though it was far from being the whole point, or even the main point), my own life, my experience – why not try my hand at autobiography? I considered this idea, and came to the conclusion that simply to give a narrative account of my personal life would not have sufficient interest. Something outside me needed to be the chief focus. So I decided to write not directly about myself but about the things that have been of greatest importance to me, such as music, theatre, philosophy, politics, travel, sex, friendship, and perhaps places. I would do it in an overtly autobiographical way, so a narrative of my life would unfold in the process. I was thinking now of a series of short books whose titles or subtitles might be: *Music In My Life, Theatre*

In My Life, *Politics In My Life*, and so on. Since my ruling passion was music, I began with music.

I had not got far before I realized that the book was turning into something jejune. Stretching ahead of me, as I got deeper into it, were accounts of performances I had attended, usually hearing works for the first time. Why should anyone be interested in knowing in what circumstances I first heard Schubert's Unfinished Symphony – or what, as a child, I thought of it? Worse: who would want to read a whole volume of such accounts? It was not, I decided, a book worth writing, so I stopped writing it.

Theatre, I realized, would be open to the same objection. So would any art. My thoughts moved to philosophy. That was different. One of the first things to strike me when I started thinking about it autobiographically was that someone like myself, with a lifelong passion for philosophy, who has taught it at Oxford, does not come to it in the way it is presented in introductory books. He does not start by reading the pre-Socratic philosophers of Ancient Greece, and then learn about Socrates, and then Plato, and then Aristotle, and so on, moving slowly forwards chronologically through two thousand years of philosophy's history, in the way I myself had structured *The Great Philosophers*. His experience is not a bit like that. He comes to philosophy higgledy-piggledy, in piecemeal order. If he studies it at a university he is likely to start on something contemporary, or perhaps with a book like Bertrand Russell's *The Problems of Philosophy*, or with Descartes. Other philosophers, and other periods, will then come in as the accidents of syllabuses and examinations decree. It will almost certainly not be chronological. He is unlikely ever to study the pre-Socratics, or medieval philosophy. There will be several other of the so-called great philosophers he never studies. It occurred to me that if I set out to introduce people to philosophy in the way professional philosophers actually *are* introduced to it, the way I myself was introduced to it, it would result in a book quite different from any of the introductions to philosophy that had so far been written. My book would be autobiographical, yes, but only as a means: its point would be to tell the reader not about me but about philosophy and its history. That, I thought, would be a book worth writing. So I wrote it. By the time I submitted it to a publisher I had abandoned the idea of a series of similarly autobiographical works, each about one of my loves, so I called it not *Philosophy In My Life* but *My Introduction To Philosophy*. The publishers said that there were numberless books called an Introduction to something, and this made it a platitudinous title despite its double meaning. They suggested *Confessions of a Philosopher*, which was still personal but racier, and I enjoyed the sound of that, so the book came out under that title.

I knew before I embarked on it that even to come off as an introductory sketch of Western philosophy it would need to be on a large scale, and would take a long time to write. I found myself slightly daunted at the prospect. The fact that it was not the by-product of a broadcast series meant it would all be solitary work from the beginning. The shortest time I would be able to write it in was two years. *Men of Ideas* and *The Great Philosophers* had each taken me three years, for much of which time I had been working with other people. *The Philosophy of Schopenhauer* had taken ten years, but throughout that period I had been in either All Souls or the House of Commons. (One Fellow of All Souls said I had turned my membership of the House of Commons into a Senior Research Fellowship.) The last big book I had produced in solitude was *The Story of All Our Lives*, and I had found the solitude oppressive. So I felt myself dreading slightly the prospect of sitting alone in my flat for two years or more working on *Confessions of a Philosopher*. I was determined to do it, but felt apprehensive.

I said this to Isaiah Berlin when, at one of our regular lunches, he asked me what I was going to do next. His response was: 'Why don't you solve the problem by writing the book somewhere where you'll have congenial company on tap, but can work as much as you want to, like an Oxford college?'

The thought had never occurred to me. I said: 'No college would take me for something like this. The book will be academically respectable but it won't be an academic book. Anyway, a college would have me only if I gave them something in return, such as teaching. And I don't want to teach. I'm already making radio programmes to earn a living. I don't want to teach on top of that. I want to give maximum working time to the book.'

'I understand that,' he said. 'But a place like Wolfson will take you on that basis.' He was referring to the college at Oxford of which he had been the founding president a quarter of a century before. 'They won't pay you anything, of course. In fact you'll have to pay for your own board and lodging. But if you're earning money from the BBC you'll be able to do that. You'll find living there a lot cheaper than in London. And I think you'll like it.'

Just as, in 1972, it had been Isaiah who suggested that I go to All Souls, and put me up for it, so now, in 1990, it was he who suggested that I go to Wolfson, and put me up for that.

Wolfson College had been founded to meet a new need at Oxford. As the balance of the university shifted towards research, more senior members of it were working on subjects that were not taught to undergraduates. Whole teams of people were doing cutting-edge medical research in the university's hospital. Others were specializing in arcane languages of the ancient world. At any given moment archaeologists would be digging in the Middle East, and a constitutional lawyer might be seconded to Brussels, while an applied economist might be in Tokyo working with a Japanese bank. The undergraduate colleges were not keen on adding such people to their regular strength, because although they added to overhead costs they gave nothing back by way of teaching, and were often not available for administrative duties either. As a result, growing numbers of them had no home in the university, in spite of the fact that they held university posts. The idea grew of creating a college for them. In the 1960s Isaiah played the decisive role by raising the money (half of it from Isaac Wolfson), choosing the architects, getting the college built, and becoming its first president. By rights it ought to be called Berlin College. In numbers it is as big as any college in Oxford. Roughly half its members either hold senior posts in the university or are senior figures on visits to Oxford from universities abroad; the other half are doctoral students, also from all over the world. There are no undergraduates. Sceptics thought this mix would not work. They thought that because everyone would be working on something different, and the college itself have no teaching function, there would be nothing to hold it together, and it would never be a genuine community in the way other colleges were. Events proved them wrong. Wolfson works. It is a lively community, different in kind from others in Oxford. It will probably be Isaiah's most enduring achievement.

Anyone put up for Wolfson by Isaiah Berlin was not likely to be turned down, and I was duly elected as a Visiting Scholar to work there on writing a book, paying my own way. I took up residence in the summer of 1991 (being then sixty-one). The college's attractive buildings are on the banks of the River Cherwell in North Oxford, the city's chief residential suburb – only that far out of the centre could a new site be found big enough for a college. However, its distance from the centre is its only serious drawback, and I quickly grew to love it. It has played an important part in my life ever since. Going to it was to be a turning point that led eventually to my moving from London to Oxford nine years later.

But at first I had no thought of moving my home. I kept my flat in London and rented a bed-sitting room in Wolfson. For my second year I moved into a penthouse flat on the college's roof, and stayed there for two years. I would go to London every week or so, and spend a couple of days in my home dealing with the pile of mail that had accumulated, see friends, go to live performances. I saw the theatre I most wanted to see, which meant missing the goodish run-of-the-mill stuff that I had always enjoyed as well, and which had actually provided most of my diet. It was the thing I missed most about not being full-time in London – the theatre and, even more, the concerts. Even so, the fact that I did not attempt to work when I was at home made these visits pure relaxation, and I developed a strong taste for a two-ended life on a London-Oxford axis.

Oxford was an ideal place to work. Isaiah had been right about the emotional and psychological support that working in one of its colleges provided. I achieved significantly more in any given period than I would have done in London, and I enjoyed it more. I sat there on Wolfson's roof in my penthouse flat, looking out over the countryside from my desk, or straight down at the marina below with its punts and swans, and felt that there was nowhere else I would rather be, and nothing else I would rather be doing. I worked every morning until lunchtime, then drifted over to the dining hall for lunch with colleagues who were becoming friends. After that I would go to the Common Room for coffee and chat, and the newspapers. After that my day was unstructured: I would deal with correspondence and the telephone, read books (either in my flat or in the college library), go to shops, the post office and so on, doing all the things everyone has to do – and then perhaps get a second wind for writing in the late afternoon. In the evenings I always went out, either to be with friends or to a theatre, concert or cinema. In addition to Isaiah I had other old friends in Oxford whom I was now able to see more of. Bernard Williams had moved there, as had Anthony Storr, who used to say it must be one of the best places to live in the whole world, and certainly the best in Britain outside London. Because I had spent five years as a student in Oxford I had more friends there, and knew it better, than anywhere except London. When it came to the arts and public entertainment there were two commercial theatres: The Playhouse for most plays, and the New Theatre for large-scale shows such as musicals, touring opera companies and visiting pop stars. Both took in West End productions on their way to or from London; and in those days the New Theatre staged at least six operas a year from the Welsh National Opera and the Glyndebourne Touring Company. For so small a town, Oxford was, and is, exceptionally rich in theatre. The worst gap in its life is the absence of orchestral music of a fully professional standard, and of a place for it to be performed.

However, for the most part I settled in happily. And alongside *Confessions of a Philosopher* I started work on a book of a different kind.

I had never been able to see that our ability to understand life, the human condition, could *not* be limited by the apparatus we have for understanding it. It must be. It was for this reason that I had always taken a special interest in those philosophers whose chief concern was to explore the limits of what is intelligible to us. Our aim, I thought, should be to maximize what we understand without going over the tipping-point into nonsense by trying to go beyond whatever the limits of conceptualization are, forming beliefs about what is in fact unconceptualizable – beliefs which would then corrupt our other ideas. Religion does this. However, although we shall never be able to conceptualize the unconceptualizable, there is a way in which we can deepen our understanding of what *sort* of difference the difference between understandable reality and un-understandable reality is. One of our chief ways of apprehending the world, if not the chief way, is sight – a larger area of the human brain is given over to it than to language, and there can be no doubt that our visual experience plays a fundamental role in forming the conception we have of the world. Yet there are people who have never had visual experience, and in whose apprehension of the world it can therefore play no part – people born blind have never had experiences to which visual concepts refer. So not only do they not know what anything looks like, they cannot really understand what it means to say of anything that it looks like something. They do not know what a visual appearance *is* – although, of course, they know from the rest of us that there are such things; and from the way we talk about them they learn a lot about what we can do with them. Even so, the entire world of seeing which the rest of us live in, all around us and up against us, and directly touching us – unproblematic for most of the time – is unconceptualizable to them. Yet for most of us it is the dominant mode of conscious awareness. As the philosopher Fichte said: 'I am a living seeing.' What difference, then, does *this* difference make to the understanding of reality that blind people have? If we could get at an answer to that question it would tell us something fundamental about the effect which the limitations of our human apparatus, human limitations *as such* – the limitations which we all share – have on our ability to understand reality.

I had had this thought for many years. I started to do something about it before I went into the House of Commons. It seemed to me then that the most promising way to pursue it would be to find a blind person whose education and training had given him a mastery of conceptual analysis, and then work patiently with him in digging down into the differences between his basic concepts and mine – for instance the significance of such concepts as 'space' and 'a person', which I thought must be very different in our two cases. I found the man I was looking for at All Souls College, Oxford. He was Rupert Cross. Although he was Professor of English Law he had taken a serious interest in philosophy, and was genuinely knowledgeable about it. I put to him a research programme for the two of us to work on. He was excited by it, and we had discussions that remain among the most enlightening and fruitful I have ever had with anybody. We agreed that when he had finished the project on which he was currently working we would try to write a book together.

Alas, he died not long after. By that time I was no longer at All Souls but in the House of Commons, too hard-pressed from day to day to take on immediately what appeared to be the almost impossible task of finding a successor to Rupert. However, a dozen years later, having left the House, and having finished my book on Schopenhauer, I brought the project back to the forefront of my mind. Enquiries led me to Martin Milligan, head of the philosophy department at Leeds University, who had been blind since babyhood. He did not find the project as exciting as Rupert had, but he was sufficiently intrigued to pursue it. Because we lived so far apart we decided to write the book in the form of an exchange of letters. These were genuine letters, but much longer than usual, and written with unusual care. I would send one to Martin and then, during the following weeks or months of waiting for a reply, I would get down to work on *Confessions of a Philosopher*.

Alas, Martin also died unexpectedly, of cancer. But although we did not complete the book as we had intended it, we had written enough to make a worthwhile volume. Oxford University Press published it in 1995 under the title *On Blindness*. It came out as a paperback a couple of years later with the title, *Sight Unseen*.

Wolfson College had taken me in for two years, and then given me an extra year. But because I was working on two books simultaneously I had still not finished either of them when my period of three years ended in 1994. At this point I had to return full-time to London. But while at Wolfson I had taken a life-changing decision as far as maintaining myself financially was concerned. When my radio series *What's The Big Idea?* came to an end in 1992 I decided not to take any more paid employment. I would live on my savings until I became eligible for the state pension in 1995. Having been self-employed all my life I would have little contributory pension – a mere £4,000 a year from the House of Commons – but I knew that after the age of sixty-five I would at least be able to eat without having to earn money. So I was now prepared to use up all my savings. I would need to be parsimonious with them to make them last long enough, but there could never be a better use to put them to. If I was willing to be poor in order to write, and I certainly was, I had no need ever again to do any other kind of work.

I cannot express how liberating this was. Since my mid-twenties my life had been half-dominated by the need to earn a living at some kind of work that I would not have done otherwise. Naturally, I tried to find work that I enjoyed, but this did not diminish (if anything it increased) the extent to which it encroached on what I really wanted to do. I had always resented having to live like this, most of all because of the handicap it imposed on my real work. Now, for the first time, at the age of sixty-two, I was free of it. Starting then, I was a full-time author. This is the explanation of the otherwise odd-looking fact that more than half my best books have been published since I became an old-age pensioner: *On Blindness* (1995); *Confessions of a Philosopher* (1997); the final, complete edition of *The Philosophy of Schopenhauer* (1997); *The Story of Philosophy* (1998); *Wagner and Philosophy* (2000); *Clouds of Glory* (2003); *Growing Up In A War* (2007); *Ultimate Questions* (2016) and now this book. Luckily for me, they have been well enough received for me not to experience the penury I had been preparing myself for – at least, not yet. There may be time for it, though, if I live long enough and my books go out of print.

When I returned permanently to London I found that three years of living primarily in Oxford had changed my feelings about London. Oxford had been so much more conducive to writing. And so much easier to live in. If I arranged to meet a friend in the

West End of London, getting there and back took an hour, most of it on a crowded tube-train, or on a bus in which I had to stand but did not have enough head-room to stand upright. If the friend lived in Hampstead it would be nearer two hours. Sometimes I was strap-hanging in crowded tube trains at midnight. And in those days these services were continually breaking down, quite often shutting down altogether. I was made newly aware how bad they had become. They were overloaded. This turned too much of life into a struggle with the environment. My age, of course, had something to do with this feeling: whereas, at thirty-four, strap-hanging in a crowded tube train was something I barely noticed, at sixty-four I found it tiring, especially in the early hours of the morning. London's systems had become badly run down by the mid-nineties. They had, in fact, become a public scandal, of which there was a great deal of discussion in the media. I knew people much younger than myself who were talking of leaving London because of it. I began to think nostalgically of spending more time in Oxford.

I applied for visiting research fellowships to Oxford colleges. (Oxford University is a federation of independent colleges, thirty-nine at a present count.) As a result, I spent the summer of 1995 in New College, the winter of 1998 in Merton College, and the summer of 2000 in St Catherine's College. In each of these, unlike Wolfson, board and lodging were given to me free – though, just as in Wolfson, I received no pay, and had no duties other than to be there and get on with my work. It was then that I wrote *Wagner and Philosophy*. My situation was a writer's dream. It contributed not only to my productivity during those years but also to my personal happiness. I began to think that, on balance, I would rather live in Oxford and go to London on frequent visits than live in London and spend long periods in Oxford. While staying in St Catherine's in 2000 I started to look for a flat in Oxford, and found one. I bought it, and moved there in the late summer of that year.

When I sold my London flat to pay for the flat in Oxford I found that its value had multiplied more than thirty times during the twenty-seven years I had owned it. (For my first thirteen or fourteen years there I had rented it.) I bought it in 1973 for £9,700, and sold it in 2000 for £310,000. Ignorantly, I supposed that with such a sum I would be able to buy a handsome flat in Oxford and still have plenty of money left; but by the time I had paid all the costs involved in moving I had £1,000 left. But I was pleased with the new flat. It was in a street near Wolfson, which had elected me to long-term membership of its Common Room. From that time onwards I used Wolfson as a life-support system, including having lunch there most days. Merton and St Catherine's had given me long-term membership of their Senior Common Rooms as well; and I had similar rights in Balliol, as a result of having taught there. Keble, where I had been a student, had made me an honorary fellow. So altogether I could use the facilities of five colleges. It made a world of difference to living in Oxford.

Not until my sixties had I ever thought I would leave London. I was, and in some ways still am, a Londoner to the marrow of my bones. There were things about London that I missed enormously, above all the frequency with which I saw some of my oldest friends, and the almost nightly visits to live performances of a high standard. These were a piercing loss, and I have never fully come to terms with it. Even so, it is outweighed by the advantages that living in Oxford has for my work. Also, I had lifelong friends in Oxford, whom I had previously not seen enough of, and could see now whenever I wanted to. Because of those things I never unwished the move. The ideal solution for me would have been to have residences in both London and Oxford. I have known several people who do – Isaiah Berlin, for instance, who lived in what a taxi driver described to me once as the most beautiful house in Oxford, and also had a flat in Piccadilly. Some such arrangement would be mine if I were to come into a fortune. As things are, when I stay in London I stay in a club. For me to grumble about this would sound to many of my readers like a rich man complaining about how much income tax he has to pay. But the truth remains that I would dearly love to have a home of my own in the heart of London, as well as having a home in Oxford.

It is common for authors to say that, because writing books is their main activity, the chief way to learn about their lives is to read their books. Balzac, for instance, said: 'The great events in my life are my works.' Part of the point they are making is that they have organized the rest of their lives round their writing – Bernard Shaw once said he was little more than a writing machine, and so did P. G. Wodehouse. They put the best of themselves into their work, and there is not all that much of a story apart from that. Writers *as writers* do not live interesting lives: they sit alone in a room for several hours of every day. Karl Popper, about whose work I have written a book, had no other life but this for his last half-century – he just produced his work. Even as a boy I was fascinated by the disparity between the overflowing worlds of superabundant life that are Shakespeare's plays and what must have been the playwright's daily life in London lodgings and streets. I have similar thoughts about myself now when I cast my mind back over the last fifteen or twenty years: my life has been chiefly my books. My friends in London tend to think of me, not surprisingly, as having retired to Oxford, but in fact I have worked hard throughout this time, writing. And at last I have been able to devote myself to it fully. I feel the fulfilment. But the fulfilment is in the books. Outside them, there is not much to tell.

Let me tell it now. Alongside writing, I have continued to bang my head against the brick wall of the unintelligibility of our existence. I have continued to be sustained by music, philosophy and my friends. I have missed London. I have done some enjoyable travelling, mainly three long stays in New Zealand, more shorter ones in the United States, and annual visits to Sweden.

Throughout this time I have written almost every day when I have been at home or in New Zealand. I have been happy living in Oxford, but if I were to say much more about it than that this book would trail off into anti-climax.

So I reach the end of my autobiography. I am enjoying life, and would be happy for it to go on for ever as it is now. But, in the nature of life, it cannot do that. Two of the most disconcerting things about being my age are, first, that one cannot have much longer to live, and second, one has no idea how short the remaining time will be. Death may wait for me until I am in my nineties, but it is likelier to come sooner.

What will happen when I die? What will become of me? Shall I participate in some other form of existence, or shall I cease to exist altogether? This ignorance – about nothing less than becoming nothing – is an astounding situation to be in. But nothing is also what I can do about it. Some people, out of terror in the face of death, commit suicide. Others clutch at the straws of religion. Both actions seem to me forms of evasion.

If it could be revealed to me for certain that life is meaningless, and that my lot when I die will be timeless oblivion, and I were then asked: 'Knowing these things, would you, if given the choice, still choose to have been born?', my answer would be 'Yes!' I have loved living. Even if the worst-case scenario is the true one, what I have had has been infinitely better than nothing. In spite of what has been wrong with my life, and in spite of what has been wrong with me, I am inexpressibly grateful to have lived. It is terrible and terrifying to have to die, but even the prospect of eternal annihilation is a price worth paying for being alive.

Printed in Great Britain
by Amazon

80608694R00287